BUDDHISM
FOR BEGINNERS

*How to Go from Beginner to Monk
and Master Your Mind*

Table of Contents

INTRODUCTION

I want to thank you and congratulate you for reading my book, "Buddhism for Beginners - How to Go from Beginner to Monk and Master Your Mind."

This book contains proven steps and strategies on how to become a true Buddhist through your thoughts and through your actions.

The common idea which most people possess is that Buddhism is an ancient religion, belonging to antique temples, mystics, history woven with fiction, and the ways of the old. True enough, Buddhism is a religion and it's around 2,500 years old. But more importantly, Buddhism is a way of life. And from where you are at the moment, Buddhism is a spiritual journey. The goal of this book is to light your path. Through this book, you will learn what Buddhism is truly about, who Buddha really was, and what his teachings were. This book also hopes to shed light on the common misconceptions surrounding Buddhism.

That said, the most distinctive feature of this book is that it will help you see how the teachings from thousands of years ago apply to the world we live in today. These pages contain everything that a beginner in Buddhism should know, from the basic beliefs of Buddhism to the concepts of Reincarnation and Karma to the Roots of Evil. You'll find that the explanations of the principles and beliefs are presented in simple, easy-to-understand terms. That's because, in Buddhism, practice is just as important as philosophy. Get a vivid glimpse of a day in the life of a Buddhist. More importantly, learn how you can apply the teachings of Buddha in your daily life.

It doesn't take a degree in sociology or a high level of acuity to realize that modern society has long strayed from the path of spirituality and inner harmony. From as early as we can talk and comprehend the world, we are taught the importance of material success, possessions, and money. Not to say that this is inherently a terrible thing, but it does lead to greed and excessive materialism in quite a few folks if left unchecked. What's more, many people find that the so-called rat race causes them to feel a lot of stress and anxiety, ultimately leaving them bitter and miserable. These are only some of the spiritual and emotional ailments associated with the way we live today.

Although materialism may have become more rampant and ingrained into the lives of more people now than ever before, it's still hardly a new phenomenon. People have been losing their way to greed and conceit for thousands of years, including the time when the Buddha devised his philosophy. The philosophy and teachings of Buddhism focus exactly on these problems, which is why it's unsurprising that the religion maintains popularity and is, in fact, becoming ever more popular in some places.

Buddhism is a majority religion in seven countries today, with that percentage being over 90% in Thailand and Cambodia. Being the most populous country, however, China is home to the largest Buddhist population at around 244 million adherents, accounting for north of 18% of China's total population. All told, there are over 500 million folks worldwide who look to Buddhism as their path towards peace, higher awareness, and spiritual fulfillment. Unlike a few other major religions in the world, Buddhism is not an exclusive club that requires you to pass a string of rigorous rituals and sermons in order to become a layperson practitioner. Your background will be an even lesser issue, and you will find that the Buddhist path is quite accessible to you too.

Throughout your journey to enlightenment, treat this book as your faithful companion, the torch to give light when the path is shadowy when the wisdom of the Buddha is hard to understand and even more difficult to follow.

Meditation plays a vital role in Buddhism. Your thoughts possess unlimited power to shape the world. Learn how to master your mind, to understand the universe, and to use your thoughts to ease suffering and to achieve ultimate peace and happiness.

Thanks again for reading this book, I hope you enjoy it!

CHAPTER 1

THE WORLD OF BUDDHISM

Buddhism Demystified: What Is Buddhism?

Buddhism is a religion, a philosophy, and a lifestyle. The name comes from the word "budhi" which translates to "to awaken." It was 2,500 years ago when the Buddha, known then as Siddhartha Gautama, experienced the awakening himself and thus founded Buddhism. As mentioned in the introduction, Buddhism is more than just a religion. In order to be a practicing Buddhist, you must:

- Lead a moral existence

- Develop awareness and practice mindfulness in your everyday thoughts and deeds

- Practice the virtues of wisdom and understanding

Much like Hinduism, Buddhism is also rooted in the Indian subcontinent or, more precisely, Ancient India. The two faiths thus have much in common with regard to teachings, history, and core principles. Both Buddhism and Hinduism, like other Indian religions, can also be considered as dharmas.

Dharma is the doctrine and cornerstone of the philosophy of these religions, and, in the practical sense, it encompasses ethics, rituals, obligations, code of conduct, and essentially anything else that comes into the life of a devout follower. The Sanskrit word "dharma" has proven difficult to translate directly, but its meaning is quite concise in Buddhism. Dharma denotes "cosmic law and order," and this is one of the most common translations of the word. The same term is also ascribed to all that which the Buddha has taught to his followers – the

3

Buddhist dharma. Therefore, it's not uncommon for "dharma" and "the Buddha's teaching" to be used interchangeably.

What's also interesting is that various Hindu scriptures and teachings have spoken of the Buddha and acknowledged his existence and life's work. Depending on the different Hindu traditions, the Buddha was more than just mentioned in passing. In fact, while followers of some traditions believe the Buddha to have simply been a holy man, others actually view him as one of Lord Vishnu's earthly incarnations, which would make him divine. However, as we proceed, you will find that this is the diametric opposite of the way that Buddhists perceive the Buddha because they tie no concept of divinity to the Buddha.

The greatest area of overlap between the beliefs of Hindus and Buddhists are perhaps the concepts of karma and rebirth. We will go into more detail on these later on, but the beliefs are very similar between the two religions, with some key differences.

These are just some of the major similarities though, and the two major religions overlap even further in many other beliefs that are important to their philosophy. Meditation, for instance, is a crucial practice that Buddhists put great emphasis on and the same holds true for Hinduism. This illustrates that the focus of both of the religions is primarily on the believer's inner state and the way he or she relates to the outside world. In that regard, both Hinduism and Buddhism also promote the virtue of detachment from all earthly things in a material as well as a mental sense.

Unlike Hinduism, however, Buddhism does not delve too deeply into the ceremonial or ritual practices that can be found in most major religions. This might seem counter-intuitive at first if you ascribe ritualistic connotations to meditation. That would be a very wrong way of looking at it because meditation has virtually nothing to do with rituals. As you will learn later on, meditation is a Buddhist's life's work in a sense and it's a rather personal matter. A devout Buddhist works on his meditation and strives to perfect it from one day to the next, and you will see why as you read more.

All in all, Buddhism can be viewed as a unique philosophy that branched out of old Hindu traditions. Siddhartha Gautama himself came from a Hindu family before he ever embarked upon his journey. He spread these new, reformed ideas throughout India at first, but the

Buddhist religion later dwindled in India towards the middle ages. Luckily, by that time, the religion had spread through a significant portion of Asia, where it has remained popular and maintained a foothold despite its decline in the homeland.

The spread of Buddhist teachings was only gradual at first though. But a great wind that would push the religion to new heights came when Buddhists received open support from Ashoka, the emperor who held reign over the largest part of the Indian subcontinent in the 3rd century BCE, as sovereign of the Maurya Empire. Ashoka was a great admirer of the Buddhist approach to spirituality and he supported the faith with great enthusiasm. This is evident by inscriptions and carvings left behind him, which told of his support and the subsequent spread of Buddhism. This support continued through those who descended from Ashoka, and the extensive empire ultimately managed to successfully spread the Buddhist truth far and wide, beyond its borders to the north. These efforts were also what facilitated Buddhism's spread into Sri Lanka, where the Theravada tradition maintains a firm foothold today. Buddhism was also spreading westward over the subsequent centuries, and it may have gone much further had its spread not been halted in Persia in the 3rd century CE.

Looking at things from a certain angle, it could also be said that Buddhism came about as a product of its zeitgeist. This was a time when more and more intellectuals of varying levels of prominence began questioning the traditional Vedic teachings and philosophies throughout Ancient India, giving way to many new ideas, one of which was certainly the philosophy of Siddhartha Gautama. This was also the era that gave birth to Jainism, which is another Indian religion often compared to Buddhism. We'll look deeper into that comparison a bit later.

This all begs the question of whether Buddhism was a sort of rebellion or revolt against established Hindu dogma. From a certain perspective, it could be viewed as such, but Buddhism being a reform and a breath of fresh air is perhaps more accurate, evident by the support and popularity that the religion gained over time. This lack of major initial conflict may have also been due to the Buddha's clear acknowledgment of a great portion of Vedic and Hindu philosophies, as you have read above. Nonetheless, apart from these similarities, there's no denying that the two religions are separate and that their teachings traverse different paths.

One of the greatest differences between Hinduism and Buddhism is the fact that Hinduism is a clearly theistic religion where numerous gods are worshipped, while Buddhism is mostly atheistic.

To become Buddhist is to understand the world, to appreciate its beauty, and to comprehend its injustices. To become Buddhist is to develop respect for the world and for all that dwells in it, and to recognize the interconnection between all living beings. Buddhism will help you see the purpose to life. When you follow Buddhism's code of practice, it will inevitably lead you to a genuinely happy, meaningful, and fulfilled existence.

The reason why Buddhism has continued to thrive throughout the centuries is that the ancient teachings of the Buddha continue to provide generation after generation with simple answers which address the very root of their problems. Whether the problem is physical illness, emotional emptiness, spiritual starvation, psychological issues, or social conflict, Buddhism holds the solution for them all.

As history shows, clinging to religion has helped various groups of people to cope with the difficulties they experienced in this world. Buddhism has done the same and has never stopped to do so. Its philosophies have never ceased to remain relevant. That's because Buddhism recognizes that the root of human suffering throughout history is always the same. Therefore, the solution, too, is constant. In other words, the teachings of the Buddha remain applicable even to contemporary societies. In a modern world plagued with materialism, there is a greater need to learn and to live out the philosophies of Buddhism.

What makes Buddhism different from other religions?

Unlike most major religions, Buddhism does not focus on worshipping an omnipresent, omniscient, and omnipotent supernatural being. Even though some Buddhists revere gods and celestial Buddhas, the religion itself is not centered on one "Supreme Being" which is the embodiment of "all that is good." Furthermore, it does not recognize the existence of a superlative evil which is the personification of "all that is bad." And more importantly, Buddhism is not predominantly a system of belief. Though Buddhists are taught certain doctrines, students of Buddhism are urged to avoid following in blind faith.

This emphasis on the way one lives as opposed to adopting strictly defined beliefs will become even clearer later on in this book. Buddhism is practical to the point of making numerous scholars and theologians not even recognize it as an organized, mainstream religion. There are so many different traditions and schools of thought that it is sometimes really difficult to lump them all into this one, all-encompassing religion. Apart from just the official sects and denominations, the openness to interpretation and personalized adoption by new adherents adds even more to Buddhism's versatility and diversity. Above all, Buddhism itself puts great faith into the individual and supports their natural inclination to think and question matters independently. On the other hand, it could be argued that some other religions go the opposite, dogmatic route, where they strive to hardcode beliefs into the followers and do most of their thinking for them.

Buddhism recognizes that human beings possess the capacity to distinguish between good and evil. Simply put, Buddhism promotes the use of human intelligence as well as your freedom to choose. You are encouraged to possess an open mind and an open heart. However, you are also encouraged to employ skepticism when it is necessary. The Dalai Lama of Tibet couldn't have said it better: If the teachings suit you, then incorporate them into your life using the best of your capabilities. If, however, the teachings don't suit you, then just leave them be.

The Buddha himself told his followers not to embrace everything he says merely because he said it. He advised them to test his teachings as though examining the authenticity of gold. If, after a thorough examination, his teachings proved to be true, then the followers may put them to practice.

This lack of aggressive indoctrination is why many argue that Buddhism is a scientific religion if you will. The Three Marks of Existence, which form the core of the Buddhist way of perceiving the world, are subject to the scientific method and analysis. One can look into the concepts of *impermanence, no-self,* and even *suffering,* and observe that they are indeed based in reality and are very difficult to disprove. Unlike the assertions made by some of the other major religions, these claims are not hard to disprove because they are an unfalsifiable hypothesis. Rather, their sturdiness and plausibility stem from the fact that they are a result of a thorough analysis of the real world.

It has long been a powerful talking point of critics of religion that major, monotheistic faiths make use of unfalsifiable hypotheses in order to solidify their claims for the existence of God. What this means is making a proposition that cannot be disproven through logic or any scientific method by giving your claim supernatural attributes that prevent it from being observed in nature. This is quite clear in Abrahamic religions, where God is described as impossible to hear, see, or feel, making it impossible to debunk His existence. Buddhism doesn't make use of this concept. Everything that Buddhist teachings assert about the circumstances of our reality is based on that reality, and anything that goes beyond that can and should be taken with a grain of salt. There is no punishment in Buddhism for not believing in other realms and similar propositions to the letter.

You can see now the appeal of Buddhism as a religion. It doesn't command. It doesn't demand. Buddhism doesn't provide you with the illusion that you were born free and then enslave you with rules that are set in stone. It does not tell you that you are a creature of intelligence and then confuse you by setting limits on what you can do. More importantly, it does not tell you that you are loved and yet frighten you with ideas of eternal damnation.

Instead, Buddhism encourages you to become the best version of yourself, to utilize your inborn capacities as a human being, and to maximize these potentials to create a better world than the one you have found.

What's also important is that Buddhism doesn't seek to deliver you from the suffering of this life by means of fear and by barring you from temptation and possible sources of corruption through strict rules and notions of sin. Buddhist teachings don't teach their layperson followers that acquiring luxuries, pleasure, or enjoying life in other ways is an inherently terrible thing. Rather, Buddhists are taught how not to attach themselves to transient possessions and sensory pleasures so that their happiness and fulfillment doesn't depend solely on these things. A Buddhist can thus acquire material gains, but he will know better than to equate these gains with existential fulfillment. Therefore, if these things are lost, this will create no void or a deep sense of loss in a person. No matter what we do and have in life, we should look within ourselves if we value spiritual growth and true satisfaction – this is the core message of the wisdom.

Like other religions, Buddhism strives to help you find the answers to deeper questions in life such as "Who am I?" and "How can I be happy?" But the wonderful thing about Buddhism is that it doesn't just ask you to do this and that, take the Buddha's word for it and then leave you to try to make sense of it all. Instead, Buddhism invites you to *personally experience* the nature of reality for yourself.

Once you are *awakened* or *enlightened*, you will be able to experience your internal reality as well as your external reality. That internal reality is that part of you which remains constant and untouched by the external world. Think of it as your anchor which will keep you steady despite the chaos of the world around you. Think of it as the lotus which will remain untainted even as you float along a polluted pond.

Much of the Buddhist aspiration revolves around mastering this internal reality, fortifying it, and cutting all external strings that might be attached to it. The world is inherently chaotic, unstable and can change on a whim, which is why a Buddhist turns inward and strives to become independent of it. It is the most pristine form of freedom – remaining the same and retaining spiritual as well as emotional stability even if everything around you is crumbling.

The ultimate goal of Buddhism is to enable you to experience *the awakening* in the very same way as the Buddha had.

If Buddhists don't worship a Supreme being, who was Buddha, then?

To get straight to the point, Buddha was a man who lived in the 5th century BCE. He was born as a man, he lived as a man, and then like all mortal men, he passed away. Nevertheless, he was immortalized in the memory of his disciples because of the extraordinary life that he had lived.

He was born into the royal family of the Shakya clan in what is known today as Nepal. Despite the fact that he was able to experience all the sensual delights that the world had to offer, Prince Siddhartha, as he was then called, had deep compassion for his suffering brethren. Even when surrounded with luxuries, he understood the universality of sorrow. At age 29, he abandoned his wealth and all worldly pleasures. At the prime of his life, he chose to lead an austere existence. He wore a simple yellow garment and, without a penny to his name, roamed the world in a quest for Peace, Truth, and Freedom from Suffering.

For six years straight, he prayed and performed self-mortification. He tormented his body in an attempt to nourish the soul. He did this until he reached the point of emaciation. It was then that he realized that the severities which he practiced were useless. Through his personal experience, he was able to ascertain that self-mortification only served to weaken the body and consequently, exhaust the spirit. He then used this experience to form an independent path. This is when he found the Majjhima Patipada, also known as the Middle Path.

This was where Buddhist philosophy sharply diverged from that of another new religion that came up through similar circumstances and methods, which is Jainism. This is also an ancient Indian religion that persists to this day and is often compared to Buddhism due to the many similarities and overlaps in the teachings they preach. Unlike Buddhism, however, Jainism does espouse the virtues of asceticism through fasting and various other forms of penance. Jains also retain a belief in the soul, which they believe is found in every living creature on Earth.

That different view on asceticism is usually one of the most relevant factors for newcomers to these religions, as Jainism can be significantly harder for some individuals to get into because of it. As such, Buddhism is usually much more accessible and easier to introduce into a regular, contemporary life, giving it a significant advantage in the western hemisphere.

Apart from those and a couple of other important differences, both of these religions have their roots in previous Vedic wisdom and are atheistic. And much like Buddhism, Jainism sought to reform the faith and introduce new philosophy to the followers. Both of these religions also make mention of a few similar principles and ideas, such as reincarnation, karma, and other key beliefs. However, despite the common origins and all the common ground, Buddhism received much more official support than Jainism, which was probably the primary factor that allowed Buddhist teachings to spread much further. It's also interesting that just like the Buddha, Mahavir, who was one of the key figures in Jainism's creation, was also of noble birth. Both these men chose to forgo their previous lives of abundance in order to pursue a higher purpose, but the Buddha had plenty of different ideas that took his story on an undoubtedly different path.

Enlightenment came to him as he was meditating under the Bodhi tree.

It was at this moment that he awakened to Buddhahood. From then on, he became known as Shakyamuni Buddha or "the awakened wise man of the Shakya clan." He did this all on his own, as a man with no supernatural powers.

For the next 45 years of his existence, the Buddha dedicated his life to preaching all over the North Indian subcontinent. He taught whoever that was interested in living a life free from suffering.

He was 80 years old when he died. The Buddha was mortal and yet he was godlike in every respect. However, despite the fact that he had plenty of followers who revered him, he was never so arrogant as to refer to himself as a divine being.

The bottom line is that the Buddha was human, much like you and me. And like him, we, too, can achieve awakening. *Like him, we, too, can become Buddhas.* As a Bodhisatta (an aspiring Buddha), you, too, can follow that path which the Buddha has led and in so doing, find Truth, Peace, and Freedom from Suffering. The Buddha pointed out that we shall find salvation only by relying on ourselves, on our own capabilities, and on our own efforts. Simply put, *you are your own savior.*

A significant portion of the Buddha's journey, tribulations, and spiritual growth was really a story of trial and error. This was a man who exercised his thoughts constantly while trying to fine-tune his philosophy before teaching others. His arrival at the Middle Way being the right course was a result of that trial and error and Siddhartha's ability to be self-critical and think for himself. As you can see, the Buddhist affinity for critical thinking and their encouragement of skepticism is a direct reflection of the way that the Buddha himself traversed our troubled world and, as such, he led by example.

Common Misconceptions about Buddhism

- **Buddhism is not about living in extremes.**

When you look at the portrayal of the Buddha in art galleries or in pop culture, you'll see a stark, cold, lifeless effigy with an emotionless though serene countenance. It sucks the fun out of wanting to be a Buddha, doesn't it?

But as Siddhartha Gautama found out 2,500 years ago, self-deprivation is not the path towards enlightenment. Take a look at the face of the

14th Dalai Lama. He's always smiling, brimming with energy, and radiating with the beauty of life. This is the true face of Buddhism. Buddhists are encouraged to laugh, to love, and to enjoy life. The whole purpose of the awakening is not just to end suffering but also to achieve indescribable joy.

The joy to be found in monastic Buddhism is not in the strictness of routine but in the awareness, the wisdom, and the purity that a simple life brings. Devoid of the distractions of postmodern existence, spiritual awareness arrives more quickly and more clearly.

Apart from the stability and purity of this minimalistic lifestyle, another crucial source of contentment and joy for Buddhist monks and other members of the community is that very community. The camaraderie that is emphasized in Buddhist monastic life is a rarity on par with the most tight-knit groups and organizations out there. To be a Buddhist monk is to be accepted into a welcoming club of similar, spiritually-minded people who help each other and live not only to reach awakening but to spread the wisdom of Buddhist teachings to others.

While it's true that Buddhist monks live a strict lifestyle, it's crucial to understand that this is not deprivation – it is renunciation. Of course, these are two very different circumstances, and nobody forced the devout monks to give up their possessions and leave home. This is a path that they chose willingly, and after they have adopted the monastic Buddhist life, renouncing materialism and sensory pleasure starts to come easy.

Keep in mind, however, that there is a lot of difference between layperson practitioners of Buddhism and monks, who are subject to additional precepts as well as rules of their particular monastery. A great many of us would love to continue living a normal, modern life, but with reduced stress and anxiety brought on by the rat race. This is exactly what an independent follower of Buddhism can achieve by following a moderate path, with all the core principles still intact.

Still, just because laypersons don't take up the robes and move into a monastery doesn't mean that they can't be part of a particular community in certain ways. Depending on the luck of where you live, it's possible to find not just monasteries but other Buddhist organizations and institutions that allow layperson practitioners to contribute and engage with their community in many ways. Whether it's meditation lessons, volunteering or classes, there are many ways that a Buddhist can contribute to the cause before heading back home for the day.

What about those monks who burned themselves to death?

Self-immolation is known as putting an end to one's life as a form of sacrifice. Perhaps you have seen circulating videos of Buddhist monks burning themselves to death while retaining meditative postures. To some, this shows self-transcendence. But in truth, not all Buddhists agree with this kind of sacrifice.

Contrary to what the media might have you believe, Buddhists do not possess this morbid fixation on suffering and death. Suicide is generally not recommended in Buddhism. It may be performed but only if a good reason exists (e.g. if you truly believe that your death will save someone else's life). Whether the reason is good enough or not, it all depends entirely on you.

In general, though, the Buddhist view on suicide is a lot like many other views in this religion in that it has many layers and is hardly dogmatic. The question of suicide is of particular interest considering the emphasis that Buddhism puts on suffering being an integral part of life, as will become even clearer to you later on. In fact, the matter of suicide is one of the first things that many newcomers wonder about when they start learning what Buddhist philosophy is all about. If so much of our lives consists of suffering, and many people choose suicide as a way to alleviate that hardship, then one has to wonder what Buddhism really has to say about it.

While Buddhist traditions, in general, don't prescribe any kind of damnation for those who commit suicide, they do have a negative attitude toward it for the most part, with some sects more stern in their opposition to the concept than others. The Theravada tradition is particularly opposed to the deed, especially when it comes to ordained persons. In fact, for Buddhist monks in this tradition, it is explicitly forbidden not just to commit suicide themselves but also to speak of it with any positive connotation whatsoever. Lamenting how painful and harsh life is and how suicide might provide an exit from one's tribulations or even get the individual reborn into a better life or realm is a major offense for these Buddhists. Propagating these ideas to anybody, and especially newcomers and laypersons, can thus get a monk fully expelled from his community.

Therefore, suicide is generally viewed as the destruction of life, which, of course, is a major transgression against the core Buddhist precepts. Exceptions to the rule have been documented in the past, and they usually involved individuals who endured immense physical trauma and agony. The few suicides that have thus been sanctioned also involved individuals who were said to have already transcended all earthly desires, including those of life itself. These Buddhists were considered to have reached a certain level of enlightenment, which excused their decisions as euthanasia rather than suicide by traditional definitions.

Far more controversial is the aforementioned suicide as a form of sacrifice in the interest of others, where self-immolation usually came into play. These incidents usually spark much discussion and debate throughout Buddhist circles everywhere in the world, and some of them have become very famous in their time.

Perhaps the most prominent and publicized case of Buddhist self-immolation is that of a Vietnamese monk by the name of Thich Quang Duc, in 1963. Even if you don't know the details of the story, the chances are good that you have seen the famed photo taken by Malcolm Browne, of a man burning alive in the street while calmly maintaining his seated position. The deed was immortalized through this photograph and has since become an important cultural prop.

So what led this man to do the unthinkable and, better yet, endure what must have been a horrifying pain with such stoicism? It was indeed his religious convictions and protest that led Thich Quang Duc down this path. At that time, South Vietnam was led by a Catholic president who used all his power to elevate and expand the country's Catholic population, while often trampling all over the rights of the Buddhist majority. Buddhists were discriminated against to the point where even their right to properly celebrate the Buddha's birthday was impeded upon. Meanwhile, Catholics were favored in the workplace, in religious freedom, and in all other facets of society. All of this quickly galvanized much disdain and eventually culminated in massive protests, which saw violence used to suppress the Buddhists.

At this point, Thich Quang Duc decided that drastic measures were necessary in order to get the government's attention and preserve the rights of his people. He wasn't the only one either, as he formed a suicide pact with one of his peer in North Vietnam, where Buddhists were faced with many of the same problems. Although some doctrines of Buddhism in the world would have condemned such an act, Thich Quang's decision met much support and encouragement among his direct peers and other activists.

Needless to say, after the fateful act on June 10, 1963, the message echoed all over the world. The US Government was forced to leverage its influence against the South Vietnamese authorities by threatening to cease all support of the regime if an agreement was not reached. Soon thereafter, the South Vietnamese president met the Buddhist demands and signed an agreement with the protestors.

Vietnamese monk and teacher Thich Nhat Hanh were reported to have said to Martin Luther King, Jr. that burning oneself is a way of proving that what one is saying is of the highest importance. Again, not all Buddhists agree with this. As mentioned earlier, if the teaching suits you, follow it. If it doesn't, leave it alone.

The bottom line is that those monks burned themselves not because they wished to embrace death more than life. They did so because, in their hearts, they believed that their sacrifice would create a positive difference in the world. And surely enough, self-immolation brought about significant change in this case and ensured a cessation of the South Vietnamese oppressive measures against the Buddhists. How much suffering and pain was thus alleviated from the many people who found themselves oppressed is a thing of history, and the political change that Thich Quang Duc managed to effect is documented. Whether or not this was a worthy sacrifice that transcended the core Buddhist precepts in an acceptable way is up to the beholder to decide.

- **Buddhism is not strictly for Asians.**

Buddhism is not exclusive to a single race, country, or group of people. Over the centuries, a great portion of the Western population has benefitted from the teachings of the Buddha.

Celebrities practicing Buddhism include Angelina Jolie, Brad Pitt, Orlando Bloom, Sting, Naomi Watts, Keanu Reeves, Tiger Woods, Richard Gere, and more.

As a matter of fact, Buddhism is on the rise nowadays in many countries. Cultural perception of the religion in different parts of the world is definitely an important factor in this regard. If you were living in an East or Southeast Asia, you'd find that being a committed Buddhist is a thing of tradition and heritage, making it a rather conservative way of life. In most Western countries, though, that is not the case, especially in America. Buddhism has a shroud of exoticism and mystery around it, as it comes from foreign parts in the Far East. This makes the philosophy very attractive to young, progressive people who are open to new ideas and experiences, thus greatly helping Buddhism spread. Apart from this aesthetic appeal, if you will, the actual substance of Buddhist teachings is certainly what makes it attractive as well. This is a religion with a philosophy that is very easy to relate to anywhere in the world, maybe even more so in the West than in developing countries.

It's also interesting how the Buddhist philosophy relates to the changes that swept across the Western world in the last few centuries. Namely, Europe and subsequently America have come a long way since the times of dogmatic thought, giving rise to the scientific method and more open ways of thinking about the world. Such changes allowed for skepticism to flourish, which, initially, may seem like it leaves little room for traditional religious practice. And that may be rather true as far as Abrahamic religions are concerned, but Buddhism is much less vulnerable to the effects of cold rationality and the scrutinizing eye of science.

As you have learned, in general, Buddhist traditions put great emphasis on skepticism and rationality, landing this religion in a rather, unique place. Not only do the revolutions in the way that first-world people think allow for Buddhist practice but they actually open a door for it. In a world where thinking has evolved to the point where many are simply not satisfied by traditional, dogmatic faiths that make very optimistic and grandiose claims, Buddhism fits right in. Many people still need to tend to their spiritual needs, but their scientific thinking makes it difficult to fully commit to their inherent religions, and so they seek answers elsewhere. Buddhism doesn't make supernatural claims about the divine nature of things. Instead, it strives to provide earthly answers to earthly questions that concern us all.

This lack of conflict is just part of what makes Buddhism suitable for people outside of Asia, though. It takes but a few glances for one to clearly see that in most Western societies, rich, poor and regular folks alike often suffer in a lot of different ways, many of which concern inner turmoil not necessarily caused by something on the outside. This can be a feeling that something is lacking in life or that life itself is pointless. Whatever it is, many of us have certainly been there and it seems to be a mark of the age we live in.

Suffering is universal. People all over the globe suffer from pain, sorrow, emptiness, destructive behavior, and unhealthy thoughts and emotions. The wisdom of the Buddha and the experience of the awakening are open to everyone and anyone who wishes to benefit from it. Likewise, the teachings of Buddhism are applicable to the life of any person who desires to achieve lifelong happiness, mindfulness, wisdom, compassion, and peace of mind.

Buddhism might thus provide the exact answers we need while not asking us to indulge in beliefs that conflict with our scientific perception of reality. All of this serves to perfectly illustrate just how versatile and accessible Buddha's teachings really are, and it's easy to see why interest in Buddhism is constantly growing and that the religion is bound by nothing, least of all by its geographical origins.

- **Buddhism is not about idol worship.**

When you enter a Buddhist temple, you'll see numerous statues, incense being burned, flowers being offered, and monks prostrating themselves in front of the altar. Even so, Buddhists do not worship Buddhas in the same way as followers of other faiths worship their gods. Prostration in Buddhism is performed as a conscientious deed as opposed to being a mindless ritualistic act.

Worshiping and idolization, as we know these things in a few other major religions, would be somewhat contradictory to some of Buddhism's core principles. Whereas Islam, Christianity, and the like worship Gods that are perceived as eternal, omnipresent, omnipotent, and unchanging, Buddhism perceives everything in this universe, except Nirvana, to be impermanent and essentially meaningless, as you will learn in detail later on. Therefore, it could be more accurate to simply consider Buddhism as a form of utmost dedication and devotion to the truth, as opposed to an idol or divine ruler and creator.

More so than worshipped, the Buddha himself is simply respected and admired for his achievements. You can think of Buddhism as a large club of devout followers dedicated to carrying on the torch and preserving what they believe to have been the most enlightened way of comprehending the world and life itself. The Buddha set an example that is followed voluntarily, but much more important than the man himself is each individual journey that those who seek awakening will travel. The whole of Buddhist commitment is a very earthly attitude toward an earthly achievement attributed to a man who was born and has died like everyone else. What sets the Buddha apart is the manner in which he lived that entirely natural life and passed on knowledge to those who cared to listen, and that is what Buddhism is all about.

Bowing

Buddhist monks tend to bow a great deal. As a Westerner, who was raised to "bow down to no one," this practice may be difficult to embrace. However, bowing serves as a way of conveying that you willingly give up your self-centered pre-occupation.

There are times when Buddhist monks are required to bow (e.g. when facing the altar). However, Buddhists monks don't always bow because they *have* to. Often, they do this because they *want* to. It is the best way to express their gratitude, their respect, and their acknowledgment to their teachers, to the Buddhas, and even to their robes. When monks and nuns and laypersons bow to each other as a sign of respect, this helps create an atmosphere of love and harmony. So open your mind and rid yourself of Western prejudices. Understand that when you bow to show your respect to others, you are, in a way, respecting yourself.

The idea of giving respect as a means of respecting yourself at the same time shouldn't appear too radical, no matter where you were raised. Being respectful and well-mannered is a sign of discipline, which is the mark of an individual with high self-esteem and stable disposition. This is essentially a universal concept everyone is familiar with. However, respect in Buddhism also comes from somewhere even deeper – an understanding that we are all carried by the same great wind and that we are all part of the same whole. Buddhists are also respectful because it is a natural byproduct of their path, which, as you will learn, later on, leads one to do away with conceit, arrogance and an overinflated sense of self-worth.

Furthermore, the act of bowing in Buddhism reveals the strong influence of Asian culture in the religion. For instance, in Southeast Asia, one way of showing your respect is to hold your hands together as though in prayer and then raise them to your slightly lowered forehead. A full bow is done by assuming a kneeling position while sitting on your buttocks. Next, you place your palms flat on the floor, 4 inches apart from each other. Then, you bend to touch your forehead to the floor.

A half bow is usually performed in Japanese Zen. This is done by keeping your hands together, as though in prayer, and placing them in front of your chest. Then, you bend your body from the waist. A full bow is performed by assuming a kneeling position while sitting on your buttocks. Then, you hold your palms skyward.

Do note that there are many different types of bowing throughout Asia and that it has been quite an important part of the culture in some countries for centuries. The bow is deeply ingrained into Japanese customs, for example, and it may not entirely be based on Buddhism. It is indeed generally believed that the Japanese bow was first introduced between the 6th and 8th centuries when Buddhism gained traction, but the custom has gone much further than religion in the meantime. Japan is one of the countries where bowing is done by virtually everyone in many different situations as a form of greeting, expressing gratitude, congratulations and giving an apology, among other things. It's a way of showing humility and openness, as well as expressing a range of emotions in a variety of situations.

Back in medieval Japan, when the custom started, bowing was also meant as a way of showing peaceful intent and willingly making oneself vulnerable, thus showing that there is no ill will. When observed from this angle, bowing is a very natural and simple way of using body language to communicate, just like animals do.

- **Buddhists don't think that everything is an illusion.**

What the teachers actually mean to say is: Everything is *like* an illusion.

One of the goals of Buddhism is to teach people to see past the world of appearances and to let go of insubstantial dreams. Such worldly illusions are one of the primary causes of human suffering.

People tend to erroneously interpret this teaching as "nothing in this world really exists." This kind of thinking is potentially dangerous and can steer an aspiring Buddhist such as yourself towards the wrong path.

If nothing in this world is real, then nothing matters. But the world *is* real. And we do live in a universe that is ruled by the law of cause and effect. However, everything is *not always as they seem*. The physical world as you see it may be made up of separate entities. You look down at your body and see an autonomous being. You look at your pet and see a separate being. You look at a rock and see a solid object. And each of you appears to be detached from each other.

However, in reality, everything is connected with each other through an intricate web. Thus, every word that you say, every deed you perform, and every thought that forms in your mind will inevitably affect the world. As an aspiring Buddhist, you are urged to recognize this interconnectedness so that it may guide you in your way of life.

Certainly, Buddhism may come across as quite nihilistic at times to an untrained eye, but you will find that it is everything but. Firstly, Buddhist teachings do espouse the meaninglessness and impermanence of everything in life and decry attachment as one of the main causes of suffering. However, the flip side is that concepts such as karma, realms of existence, and many other things that you will soon read about, go a long way towards encouraging highly moral behavior and considerate conduct. On the other hand, nihilism generally extends its philosophy of futility to morality as well, which has led many people to criticize it as dangerous.

Furthermore, extreme forms of nihilism not only explain that we have no real knowledge of the universe but they also dismiss any possibility of us acquiring the knowledge that we lack. Quite contrarily, Buddhism is all about garnering copious amounts of knowledge and always striving to improve. Therefore, as you can see, there is no shortage of ethics in the Buddha's philosophy.

Buddhism has still been accused or at least contemplated as being a nihilistic philosophy in quite a few instances, sometimes rather prominently. As you may or may not know, Friedrich Nietzsche was one of the more prominent minds that viewed Buddhism as nihilistic, at least for a time. The Buddhist views on the impermanent nature of things in this life appealed to the philosopher, and it remains a point of some contention just how much the religion may have influenced his philosophy. Nonetheless, Nietzsche ultimately didn't see eye to eye with the Buddhist worldview and his personal philosophy went a rather different route. It is definitely fair to say that despite all their emphasis on impermanence and suffering, the Buddha's teachings are considerably more optimistic when it comes to perceiving the human position in this universe.

Furthermore, Buddhism is not to be confused with solipsism. Solipsism is another philosophical view that comes up when matters of reality and illusion are discussed. As you may or may not know, in the simplest terms, solipsism purports that nothing in this reality is actually real except for our own minds. In other words, we cannot be absolutely certain that the outside world exists in the way we believe it does or at all, but each of us can be sure that his or her mind exists. Although all is believed to be transient and impermanent, Buddhism certainly acknowledges the material world as real and is, therefore, not very solipsistic. In Buddhism, the argued illusion of mankind is that anything in this life except Nirvana can be permanent, regardless of how real it is.

In fact, the solipsistic view of the world clearly puts great emphasis on one's self, thus often leading to preoccupation with the idea. This goes very much against the teachings of Buddha as he taught that there really is no such thing as a self and that clinging to these ideas is one of the reasons we suffer, as you will learn in greater detail as we proceed.

- **Being Buddhist doesn't mean that you can't get angry.**

Often, Buddhists use meditation as a means to overcome negative emotions such as anger. For this reasons, Buddhists are often pictured as placid individuals who are able to remain calm and collected even during the worst of times. However, becoming a Buddhist monk doesn't mean that you can instantaneously get rid of negative thoughts or habits. Let's get real. Monks are human beings, too. And so was the Buddha, for that matter. That said, as an aspiring Buddhist, one of your goals is to allow your actions to be guided by the power of love. This means showing kindness even to your enemies. This means seeing the wisdom behind every adversity.

This, however, doesn't mean that you should allow other people to walk all over you. To be Buddhist is not about *ignoring* the wrong deed but to *actively* do what you can to change or stop the other person's bad behavior. You do this in a non-violent way and as guided by the spirit of compassion. Simply put, whatever action you take, it should be constructive rather than destructive.

Buddhism teaches that anger and other similar emotions merely layers of human suffering. And the only time when our suffering truly ends is when or if we manage to reach Nirvana. Up to that point, it's all about minimizing the symptoms of our affliction. Therefore, even the most devout Buddhist can slip at times and give into negative emotions, but this is a rare occurrence as Buddhist doctrines teach volumes of valuable wisdom that helps one remain in control.

CHAPTER 2

A JOURNEY TOWARDS ENLIGHTENMENT

What are the basics beliefs of Buddhism?

Siddhartha spent some time exploring the world to limited lengths before finally deciding to embark upon his famed journey. This sheltered young man knew very little of how the real world functioned outside of his comfortable and opulent life. In fact, many of life's aspects, which were completely normal to the common man, were very peculiar and sometimes even shocking to the young Buddha. During his early ventures into the unknown, he was faced with death, poverty, disease and the misery of old age, but he also observed ways in which various people dealt with these tribulations.

Being a young man of noble birth, Siddhartha Gautama was usually accompanied by a guide or servant whenever he would venture out into the unknown, and he asked them many questions about what he would encounter out there. At some point, young Siddhartha came across a man who had devoted himself to asceticism. It was explained to the Buddha that this was a path one chose in the hopes of transcending many of life's hindrances, such as need, suffering, and fear of death itself. This intrigued Siddhartha a great deal and it would play a major part in his early steps toward enlightenment. Still, Siddhartha pondered and contemplated the world for some time before moving on, and answers gradually began coming to him.

While resting under the shade of a tree, the Buddha marveled at the beauty of the countryside. Yet, underneath all this beauty, he saw unhappiness. He recognized it in the way the farmer beat his ox, in the way the trees shed their leaves so that new ones may grow, and in the

23

way a bird fed on a worm, and so on. To himself, he asked: "Why must one creature suffer so that the other may prosper? Why must one living being die in order for another to survive?" During the period of his awakening, the Buddha found the answers to these questions.

The Three Universal Truths

- **Nothing in this universe is ever lost.**

Matter transforms into energy. Likewise, energy transforms into matter. Corporeal bodies turn to dust. Solar systems crumble and become cosmic rays. The old dies so that it may give way to the new.

Each living being is interconnected. Each living being is equal. But more than that, each living being is *the same*. To destroy something from nature is to destroy oneself. To harm another is to harm oneself. It is for this reason why Buddhists neither hurt nor kill animals.

As we proceed, you will find that destruction of life is one of the gravest transgressions one can commit against Buddhist morality. Nobody has the right to put an end to another living being before that creature's time has come naturally. The only thing that should dictate when living creatures leave this life and move on to the next is the great cycle of rebirth, as you will learn a little later on. Although all is impermanent, nothing is ever really lost because of that very cycle of rebirth, wherein beings simply move on to another life in a different realm.

- **Everything is subject to change.**

The world and everything in it are constantly changing. Life is a river that goes on and on. Sometimes, it flows slowly. Sometimes, it flows with a fury. In some places, it flows smoothly. But there are areas too that are stony.

What was regarded as reality hundreds of years ago may be false today. What was true yesterday may not be true today. Once, we were convinced that the world was flat. Once, no one ever dreamed of the possibility of flight. Life and our ideas about it change ever so constantly.

Nothing in life is impervious to this inherent chaos of the universe, no matter how firm and permanent it may seem at first. Unfortunately, that includes all of your feelings, circumstances, and pleasant moments as well. Not coming to terms with this fact leaves us vulnerable to desperation, an immense feeling of loss, instability, and sometimes outright emotional catastrophe. Whenever we expect something to last forever and never change, we are setting ourselves on a course to major disappointment. That is clinging to frail straws, and you will soon learn how this attachment is one of the cornerstones of our misery according to Buddhist teachings.

- **Everything is influenced by cause and effect.**

The reason for the constant change mentioned above is the law of cause and effect. During his awakening under the Bodhi tree, the Buddha's previous lives unraveled before his eyes and so he was able to see the pattern of cause and effect.

As legend has it, this was when the Buddha reached enlightenment after forty-nine days of meditation. He gained deeper, higher-level insight into the concept of karma and how it had brought him and everyone else into the suffering or joy of their present lives. Through the understanding of how karma works, the cycle of suffering, death, and rebirth also became apparent to him. It's also told that the Buddha thus achieved a firm grasp of the Four Noble Truths and that he had gained absolute confidence that the Middle Way was the path towards liberation from the cycle. As he reached Nirvana, he was able to fully fathom the universal order of things, as well as the human condition.

In this universe, one gets what he deserves. One reaps the fruit of the seed which he had sown. Who you are now is the product of your thoughts. Through your thoughts, emotions, and actions, you have the power to achieve the kind of life that you desire. Therefore, if you want good things to come to you, you must bear positive thoughts and emotions. If you wish to receive kindness, then you yourself must show kindness.

However, it's important to understand that although we often use the word "deserve" in these contexts, as is in our impulsive nature, that's not necessarily reflective of the Buddhist view. Cause and effect truly means exactly that, and the karmic consequences one endures, whether they are positive or negative, are as sure and natural in Buddhism as gravity is in science. The Buddhist views of cause and effect are thus more reminiscent of the laws of physics than of abstract human notions of justice and payback. There is little room for emotion and especially gloating here. A Buddhist believes that this is the natural order of things and that the karmic principle just *is*. Still, although it's a simple enough concept in essence, there is much more to karma that meets the untrained eye.

Karma and why you've been looking at it the Wrong Way

Contrary to what most people might think, the Law of Karma is not something to fear. It is not a theory made up to frighten people into obedience. It is but a simple fact of the universe. It exists and operates just as the law of gravity does. As a Buddhist, you are urged not to regard karma as a form of punishment for evil deeds. Instead, you are to look upon it as an opportunity to build a brighter future, rather like a simple formula for a blissful existence.

Although karma has certainly found its place in modern popular culture throughout the world, the concept predates Buddhism itself. In fact, the Law of Karma can even be traced back to a time before Hinduism was shaped into the religion we know today. This timeframe is put into greater perspective when you consider the fact that Hinduism is widely regarded as the oldest religion in the world. The first mentions of karma are found in the ancient Vedic religion, the rather different predecessor of Hinduism. As part of these early Vedic teachings, karma referred to a commitment to good deeds as a means of attaining entrance into heaven. Alternatively, those with insufficient good deeds under their belt were to go to the underworld after they die. In essence, the early Vedic concept of karma has more in common with Christianity than Buddhism, as you can see.

The word karma literally translates to "action." But most people tend to mistakenly regard it as "fate." You might've heard someone say: "My life sucks because this is my karma." When you look at it this way, you make karma seem unpredictable, vague, and unchangeable.

On the contrary, karma is dynamic, foreseeable, and clear as crystal. You are aware that every day, each action you make, be it positive or negative, will inevitably find its way back to you. If you plant a cabbage, you don't expect a carrot to grow back, do you? Even now, you *know* what's going to happen in the future. You *know* what seed you've sown and as such, you know what fruit you shall be reaping. But more importantly, you have the power to control your karma. Your karma is constantly changing. Each waking moment, each opportunity to act

26

provides you with a fresh chance to turn karmic results to your favor. So if you think that your job is to sit there and passively accept what the universe gives you, think again. We were all born to be the masters of our destinies. It is up to you to create the kind of life that you want.

As mentioned, karma is not a system of punishment or reward (e.g. If you tell a lie, you'll be born a cripple in your next life. If you help a neighbor in need, you'll be rewarded with riches). The universe isn't judgmental or shallow like that.

Also, more important than your actions are your *intentions*. So if you accidentally step on a bug, relax. You won't be born as an insect in your next life. However, if you squash the bug on purpose, especially out of anger or malevolence, expect appropriate karmic consequences to be executed.

According to Buddhist teachings, there are three ways for our intention, referred to as "cetana" in Sanskrit, to manifest itself as karma, and that is through body, speech, or thoughts. The physical, verbal, or mental forms of action are not themselves morally judged as good or evil. Rather, the intention that has brought these manifestations about is the root and is to be judged as such; good, evil, or neutral. Therefore, it quickly becomes apparent that Buddhism puts the greatest emphasis on the mental process of a person. Whatever their form may be, the good and bad actions are divided into "good, skillful deeds" and "bad, unskillful deeds." These actions will leave a lasting imprint on the mind, and these imprints are most commonly referred to as "seeds" in Buddhist teachings. These so-called seeds are often carried over into other lives while they ripen and eventually sprout into "karmaphala," which translates to "fruit of action," denoting consequences.

It's important to understand that, since great significance is attributed to the intent and mental process behind our moral or immoral deeds, no physical action is necessary for one to garner karma. Even if you were to sit out your entire life in a locked room, the thoughts that emerge in your mind would still sow karmic seeds. Harboring resentment, immense lust, and greed, or wishing harm unto others will certainly accumulate bad karma, whether you act on your impulses or not. On the other hand, if your heart is filled with love and compassion, good karma will be achieved, albeit to a lesser extent, even without directly helping others and engaging in charity.

27

There are a couple of interesting variations among the different Buddhist traditions when it comes to this concept too. For instance, some traditions believe that one's manner of death also reflects on the karmaphala. This doesn't concern the cause of death, though, but the actions taken and thoughts formulated by one in their final moments.

Still, the best way to attain good karma, of course, is through actions, many of which are easy to adopt and conduct for most regular people. In your day-to-day life, you should always seize the opportunity to commit small acts of kindness at every turn. You can always help an elderly person cross a busy road, do someone a favor, or give another driver way in traffic. The opportunities to show kindness and compassion in these ways are abundant, and all of them will help you acquire merit and improve your karmic prospects.

In various Buddhist traditions, a particularly effective way of gaining good karma is helping and saving animals. Because Buddhism ascribes such value to living creatures and includes animals in that philosophy, helping creatures of all shapes and sizes is always encouraged. Stopping your car for a kitten or a duck to cross the road is certainly positive, but rescuing animals that are trapped, wounded, or saving those that are headed to slaughter for food are deeds that are very impactful toward your good karma. People who make it their life's calling to help and care for animals are thus held in a rather high regard in Buddhism and are on a very good karmic path. Make no mistake, however, no matter how many animals you save, that won't make up for terrible deeds in other areas of your life and interactions.

You should also always remember the important role that intent and mindset play in karma. The amount of good karma that you can acquire even from the most wonderful deeds can be lessened if your intentions are not honest, pure, and hearty.

There are other, smaller practices that Buddhists take up in order to further improve their karma. Depending on the particular tradition or teaching in question, certain mantras, chants, and recitals can be done on a regular basis as an addition to one's everyday karmic work. Reciting the names of the thirty-five Buddhas or chanting mantras such as the "Om Mani Padme Hum" are just some of the regular exercises that many devout Buddhists incorporate into their daily lives. On top of that, another key aspect of working on one's karma is meditation, which is a very important part of Buddhist life.

All in all, karma is a core belief of Buddhism and it is what keeps the "samsara" cycle of rebirth moving ever forward. It is the fuel of this great wheel if you will, and it has no divine properties at all in most Buddhist traditions. The Buddha was granted incredible insight into his own karma in his moment of awakening because he is believed to have observed all his previous lives, but this is unnecessary information for an aspiring Buddhist, as there is no way to do wrong as long as one focuses on attaining only good karma.

The rule is simple: Act with hate, and you'll attract negative things. Act with love, and you'll attract positive things.

What if you do something truly terrible, like kill someone?

When you brutally murder someone, expect to experience the consequences in this life or in the next. In this life, you may know immense sorrow. Or in your next life, you may be birthed into a world of extreme suffering. If you do nothing to cleanse your karma through positive acts, the heavier the consequences grow.

Furthermore, your state of mind when performing the terrible act makes all the difference in the immensity of the karma that you collect. For instance, if you kill out of self-defense, the karmic consequences may be lighter. But if you kill out of envy, anger, or for the sheer delight of it, then the consequences are naturally heavier.

The accidental killing of humans and other creatures can also bear varying levels of karmic consequence. Not all accidents are the same, and some might be your fault more than others. Buddhism puts great emphasis on mindfulness and wisdom, and carelessness and ignorance are thus very much frowned upon. Accidents arising from careless and irresponsible conduct, although they are inherently incidental, can still acquire a great deal of bad karma for the transgressor. One should thus always strive to be mindful of others and of his or her own actions and bring the possibility of accidental harm down to a minimum. Some things are indeed outside of our control, and bad things can happen no matter how hard we try to avoid them, but your karma will be much less corrupted if you did try. If the worst does arise and we are truly blameless, then future good deeds are more than enough to redeem ourselves.

This idea of balancing one's karma points to how these Buddhist teachings work provide valuable motivation for a follower to strive for redemption right away, and with meaningful action. Repentance, if earnest and pure, has its own positive reflection on one's karma, but it is still up to the transgressor to take concrete steps and build on that as they move forward. Furthermore, an interesting concept found in certain teachings, such as the Theravada tradition, is the transfer of merit. These teachings state that a Buddhist can acquire merit or good karma from other people, whether they are strangers or close associates and relatives, through the exchange of services or goods. Alternatively, it's also possible to willingly transfer your own merit unto others.

So if I see people suffering in this lifetime, does that mean they did something in their past lives to deserve it?

When someone is suffering in this lifetime, treat him as you are supposed to: with compassion. Find a glimmer of happiness and hope in knowing that even as they are suffering, at least they are being given the chance to cleanse their karma. This way, they will be able to enjoy a better life when they are reborn.

One should help others acquire good karma whenever possible, and with pure intentions at heart. This form of mutually beneficial action is greatly encouraged in most traditions. A devout and erudite Buddhist is perfectly aware that he or she is no authority to judge other creatures. What's more, a Buddhist who is dedicated to the path will have done away with judgmental thoughts altogether, feeling only compassion towards the fellow sufferers of the cycle. At the very worst, there is no harm in indifference, as a lack of both judgment and compassion has zero effect on one's karma.

In regards to what the suffering individual may have done in his previous lives to deserve such a fate, it really should not be a factor when perceiving these people. The vast majority of regular people are clearly unaware of their previous rebirths, so it would hardly be right to hold their present incarnation accountable for what may have happened before. The Buddha's previous lives became clear to him once he reached enlightenment, but the Buddha was hardly a regular man, despite him being made of flesh and blood. Nirvana, which he had reached, is something that most of us can only dream of in our current lives; it is something to aspire to. Until then, we are limited to our present realm and should simply do the best we can with the situation.

As you will soon learn in greater detail, the ways in which one is reborn are a matter of hierarchical order, ranging from the worst misery imaginable to life closely resembling heaven. While it's not impossible for the sufferers in this life to reach Nirvana, those who are born into opulence and joy will have something of a head-start. However, those living a life of misery have an opportunity to do well and be reborn into a better life, thus slowly working their way up.

Therefore, it is entirely possible that the Buddha himself lived many miserable lives prior to his final, enlightening one, some of which were likely caused by past misdeeds. As a matter of fact, you would be completely right to assume so. In Buddhist canonical literature, such as the Pali Canon of the Theravada tradition, there exist well over five-hundred stories of the Buddha's previous lives, otherwise known as the Jataka tales. It is generally believed by Buddhists that these stories were told by the Buddha in the course of his teaching and many sermons, but they have received substantial folkloric contributions over the centuries, of course.

The Jatakas are used by ordained Buddhists during their sermons throughout the world, and the stories tell of a huge variety of different lives lived by all kinds of people as well as animals. Far from just being a collection of stories to keep listeners entertained, the Jatakas are infused with a lot of wisdom and many important moral lessons that permeate the experiences and lives of the characters in them. Just as importantly, these tales are deeply concerned with key aspects of the Buddhist faith such as karma, which is well-illustrated and presented to the listener through the Jatakas.

This literature is very important material to study for all those who intend to gain deeper insight into the many lives that are said to have come to the Buddha under that Bodhi tree. As for the more technical details of the Buddhist belief in rebirth, we will now explore this essential topic in more depth.

Born Again and Again: Understanding Rebirth

Death is but an impermanent end to an impermanent existence.

Through powerful meditation, one has the capability to recall one's past lives. If you possess this ability, you'll be able to put your present life into a meaningful perspective.

Karma and Reincarnation provide us with a plausible explanation for inequality. It shows why some men are born rich while others are born poor, why some babies are healthy while others are handicapped. For some, this may be a pretty hard pill to swallow.

The belief in the cycle of rebirth is present in most of the major Indian religions and it is most commonly called "samsara," which means "wandering." This is also one of the core concepts of Hinduism, but Buddhism takes a somewhat different approach in regards to our position in this cycle. While Hinduism focuses much of its philosophy on the "atman," or soul, as the core of our being that is reincarnated over and over again in samsara, Buddhism rejects the idea of soul or self altogether. The belief that we possess no soul and that self is an illusion is one of the Three Marks of Existence, which we will cover in more detail soon. All things considered, although Buddhists view samsara as a painful cycle of suffering, it's important to note that each lifetime, no matter how difficult, isn't damnation. It is but a transient opportunity to turn one's future around for the better, which is one of the most important differences between the philosophy of Buddhism and that of other religions, particularly ones that profess the idea of eternal damnation in hell.

The condition to which you have been born reflects the lesson that you need to learn in this lifetime. For instance, a person may be born rich because it is most important for him to learn the value of generosity. Alternatively, a person may be born poor because it is most important for him to learn the value of hard work.

A common question asked by skeptics is this: If our souls never truly die and if we are constantly reborn in each lifetime, then how does that explain the fact that the world is more populated today than it was decades ago?

The human realm is but one of many other realms. When we pass on, we may end up in other realms. There are heavenly realms and lower realms. There are animal realms and ghostly realms. Likewise, beings from other realms may also be reborn into the human realm. Simply put, you could've been dwelling in another realm before you were reborn here in your present life. By understanding that we continuously come and go between these various realms, we gain deeper respect and empathy for other beings.

To be exact, most Buddhist teachings explain that there are six realms of existence into which sentient beings are spawned. Those are the three higher realms of gods, demigods, and humans, and three lower realms of animals, hungry ghosts, and hell, or hell beings. Sometimes, the realms are viewed as only five, with the realms of gods and demigods being one and the same, which would make the human realm the second highest one.

Without reaching Nirvana or Buddhahood, being reborn into the realm of gods is the next best outcome one can hope for, resulting from the accumulation of very good karma. There is one catch associated with this realm, though, and that is precisely the fact that it is a heavenly environment. Namely, it is said that the joy, luxury, and ease of life in this realm pose a problem in that a person is prone to getting too attached, which constitutes bad karma, of course. Therefore, if one who spawns into the godly realm is not careful and neglects their spirituality, it's quite likely that the next life will land him or her in a lower realm.

As for our human realm, even though it is largely plagued by suffering and misfortune, it is still considered a fairly fortunate outcome of one's karmic performance. This is because humans possess higher sentience and thus much more free will and independence of thought than animals, which puts us in a position of ample opportunity to make our karma better. It is said that animals suffer immensely, due to them being ruled by raw instinct that they can't control.

Of course, the last two realms are the harshest. Those who are born into the realm of hungry ghosts will find themselves as creatures of great craving, hunger, and thirst. The fact that they are reduced to existing as subtle, invisible beings is also said to cause much suffering. That still doesn't compare to the hellish realm that's reserved for those that have accumulated significant evil karma. There are many descriptions of this realm across various traditions and texts, including multiple levels of scorching or freezing areas, realms of torture and great pain, and others.

It's possible that you are wondering how one gets out of these realms, particularly since there is a lack of awareness and free will with which to conduct good karma. In essence, the demerit that one acquires through terrible karma runs a specific course and eventually is depleted. According to one's degree of wrongdoing, specific lengths of time and punishment in hellish realms will be dished out to individuals. After this punishment is complete, a being will die and be reborn into a higher realm, where they will be given a chance to move up or suffer all over

33

again depending on their conduct. Remember, nothing in Buddhism is forever, and everyone has the capacity to end their cycle of suffering.

As you can see, there is absolutely no concept of eternal damnation in Buddhism. Sooner or later, one will move up the bar ever so slightly and is presented with a chance to do better. Technically, it is possible for one to be stuck in the lower realms indefinitely, but that will always be up to them personally. And while many of the rebirths into the human realm can be quite painful and tough on people, they should always remember that unlike animals, they have the capacity to truly commit to their karmic outcome and greatly accelerate the accumulation of good karma.

At this point, there might still be some questions lingering in your mind concerning these realms. You might be wondering if that lack of free will in the lower realms means that karma can't get worse in addition to there being no way to improve it. In general, this would be a correct assumption due to that fundamental issue of free will. To put it simply, there exist multiple realms that are below and are worse than the human one primarily to account for various levels of evil karma that people acquire, not because animals or hungry ghosts can do evil deeds and get themselves reborn into an even lower realm. It is generally believed by Buddhists that animals and other, lower creatures are incapable of really doing any wrong just as they are incapable of doing good. When animals kill, they do so out of necessity and a need for food or basic survival, not because they like it or because they are following an ideology. Therefore, all there is for animals and other lower beings to do is live out their lives and wait for their bad karma to run out. It is life in one of the higher, conscious realms that determine how lowly you will be reborn, based on how evil your karma is. Animals generally can't find themselves reborn into the realms of hungry ghosts or hell. Rather, they can either remain in their realm or move up after they die.

As you can see, only humans and those in the realms above them can be as evil as to find themselves in the hellish realm, for example. If a person is careless and ends up hurting animals in their life, for instance, then that person could land into the realm of animals when they are reincarnated after death. However, if that person also remorselessly murders people for money, then their rebirth will likely pass over all the realms and lead them straight to the hellish realm, where appropriate punishment and suffering will be dished out according to the severity and degree of their atrocities.

About the Tibetan Book of the Dead

Those who have heard a few things about Buddhism in passing may have, at some point, also heard of something that is commonly referred to as the "Tibetan Book of the Dead." This piece of literature is intimately concerned with the concept of rebirth and death itself, but it's not quite as eerie as it first sounds. The Book of the Dead does not contain instructions on how to raise the dead or contact wandering spirits, but it is indeed a sort of manual.

The way that this book came to be in its current form in the West is quite a long story, but far more important are its origins and subject matter. With all its gradual additions, reinterpretations, adaptations, and revisions, this "book" is rooted in the old literature of Bardo Thodol, meaning "The Great Liberation through Hearing in the Intermediate State." Various research efforts have uncovered that Bardo Thodol was most likely authored in the 8th century, after which it was buried at some point until being unearthed and revealed to the world by Karma Lingpa, a 14th-century man who is believed to have been a Nyingma teacher.

In essence, Bardo Thodol touches upon two main subjects. Firstly, the writing teaches the beholder numerous ways of recognizing signs that the death of himself or someone else is near and how to prepare for the ordeal in a ritualistic manner. Perhaps more importantly, however, Bardo Thodol is also a kind of instruction manual meant to assist in the guidance of the dying, as well as the recently deceased, through the process of passing and moving on into rebirth. This murky, intermediate state between death and rebirth is referred to as "bardo" and it's where the consciousness of the dying individual will have many important experiences.

Bardo Thodol illustrates in great detail the many visions and other experiences that the passing individual will face during the process of dying and after the fact. In the way that these instructions were originally intended to be used, they are meant to be read to the individual in question during and after dying in hopes of helping them process the experiences in a proper way and achieve liberation.

Furthermore, this guide of death also describes the intermediate state as being divided into three main bardos or phases. Each of these is explained in great detail in Bardo Thodol, including everything that one's consciousness will encounter in this dream-like state. Throughout the whole process, both unsettling and serene experiences will intertwine, making the traversing consciousness alternate between terror and peace.

As soon as one's consciousness is detached from the body at the moment of death, the first bardo begins. This phase is characterized by one's encounter of the so-called "clear light of the reality," which, in a way, represents the essence of liberation. Through the instructions of Bardo Thodol, which are read out loud to the deceased's consciousness, he or she is encouraged and guided to fully realize and embrace this experience. However, a great emphasis is put on defeating the ego at this point. The passing individual must perceive this whole phenomenon through compassion and love of all creatures in existence, and the person must understand that "the clear light" is not there on their account, and they must let go of all selfish notions of importance. One's life and accumulated karma play an important role here, and these factors are usually what prevent most people from attaining liberation during the first bardo. This phase also has two stages, the second of which is marked by the "secondary clear light" and is where those who fail to achieve liberation in the first stage will end up for their second chance. If they fail again, their consciousness travels into the next phase.

The second bardo is for the many who fail to achieve full realization and liberate themselves in the first. And it's believed that these folks are many because the spiritual dedication to the Buddhist path, meditation, and the purity of karma required in the first bardo are rare among people from all walks of life. The second bardo is believed by Tibetan Buddhists to last for two weeks and also have two stages. A great many Buddha forms and peaceful deities are said to greet one through various visions in this phase. One Buddha form will greet the traveling consciousness on each day of the first week. The manner in which one has lived their life, as well as the way in which their consciousness interacts with each of these beings, will usually determine the next step in the course of this bardo.

The second week is said to be where the experience takes a turn for the horrific to the beholding mind. The wrathful deities encountered here will present themselves in despicable forms and a very threatening manner. It is expected and encouraged of the passing individual to face the monsters with calm and confidence in their heart and to ultimately realize that these beings are not real. It is believed that these beings are peaceful deities under their terrifying veneer, and the deceased is instructed through Bardo Thodol to understand this and refrain from fleeing the onslaught of the deities in order to attain liberation. Failure in this bardo will banish one's consciousness down to the third phase.

In the third bardo, the experiences are believed to escalate even further, with the consciousness of the deceased encountering Yamantaka, who is regarded as the lord or conqueror of death. This powerful and fearsome deity who terrifies the beholder will act as a judge of one's deeds in life. This is the phase where the dead are confronted with their good and evil karma and are expected to come to terms with all that they have done. Now, the goal for the deceased, as instructed through Bardo Thodol, is to embrace all of these deeds, fully realize the Lord of Death and all of his demons, and meditate on the clear light. This is one's last chance to achieve liberation from rebirth and reach enlightenment. After this point, the only option left to the "soul" is to be reborn.

The realm that one is reincarnated into will also depend on their journey and the way they have traversed through the bardo phases. Still, even after the possibility of liberation is lost, instructions from Bardo Thodol will be recited to the deceased in the hopes of helping them struggle to attain as favorable of a rebirth as possible at the time.

All in all, the whole idea of the dream-like state of bardo resembles a series of trials and tests, which will determine if a "soul" is to remain in the cycle of rebirth or manage to ascend to enlightenment and Buddhahood. The life that one has led will greatly impact one's journey through this state, improving or greatly reducing their odds. Nonetheless, this Tibetan Buddhist tradition is meant to give each and every deceased person an opportunity for a better future.

Back in the realm of all that is living and existing, however, we arrive at an all-important concept and set of beliefs that define Buddhism as a whole, not just the Tibetan traditions.

The Three Marks of Existence

Buddhists believe that everything that exists in this world is subject to the following:

- **Anicca**

Impermanence

Everything in this universe has its limitation. Everything exists in its own duration. When something appears, it will inevitably disappear just as surely as it had materialized.

This is where your Buddhist journey truly begins. Knowing what Anicca represents is the first step that every single Buddhist takes, no matter if he or she ends up as a casual layperson practitioner, a researcher driven by curiosity, or a full-fledged, ordained Buddhist monk that devotes his entire life to the doctrine. More so than just knowing what it is and how it is defined, you must thoroughly consider impermanence. You have to ponder what it truly implies for you, all your troubles or joy, and every single person you know and care about. Ultimately and preferably, you should also meditate on the concept, as all truly devout Buddhists do.

You look around you and you see solid objects. You derive comfort and safety from their solidity, from their permanence. However, as previously mentioned, nothing is ever as it seems. Deep inside, you *know* that nothing in this world is permanent and yet often, you choose to ignore that knowledge. That is where the problem lies. In order to successfully detach yourself from the material world, it is necessary to acknowledge Anicca. However, if you continue to nurture this kind of primordial ignorance, you will continue to fall prey to the poisons of hatred and envy.

In the usual spirit of the Buddha's teachings, this too is a concept that one can observe and draw their own conclusion as to its validity. The way things work in nature as well as human history both tell the tale of impermanence. Humans have achieved and built incredible things in their time, become attached to these creations and in the end, no matter how hard we try, everything usually falls apart and changes form. This is true of many great individuals and even empires, and although you could argue that at least their memory is permanent in the hearts and minds of others, it too will fade away given a long enough timeline. Make no mistake; impermanence isn't law only in our realm either. Buddhism teaches that Anicca holds true even in the realm of gods.

With that said, it is also a Buddhist belief that Nirvana is the one thing that is constant and permanent. Once a sentient being has achieved Nirvana, this state will never corrupt, come undone, or change in any way. Therefore, in the words of the wisdom, Nirvana is "Nicca," meaning "constant" or "permanent."

Anicca or the Buddhist doctrine of impermanence, as it is often referred to, is one of the aspects of this faith that make newcomers often misinterpret the religion as pessimistic or somehow inherently depressing. As you have surely grasped by now, Buddhism is all about the contrary, and once you start looking at it from the right angle, the doctrine of impermanence becomes yet another piece of evidence that testifies to the Buddhist aspiration toward true happiness and contentment.

What I mean by this is that impermanence is, in many regards, excellent news for you. Especially comforting is the fact that Anicca applies so broadly, both on the micro and macro levels of life. As long as you mind the concept of karma, knowing that nothing is permanent and that it ultimately does not matter can be a very powerful motivator. This realization can push you to new lengths and help you achieve what you otherwise thought you never could. Even minor life's issues such as shyness, reluctance to take risks, and tiny, everyday frustrations can be done away with once you understand with all your heart that they are all transient. So what if you embarrass yourself today while trying to achieve something you want, for instance? Even if you make a fool of yourself, the chances are good that it will be forgotten within a month, let alone in the grand scope of time.

On the flip-side, you'd be right to wonder what the point of anything is when it's all impermanent and ultimately meaningless. Why even get out of bed and go about your daily duties and tasks if nothing is permanent? This kind of thinking almost always leads to detrimental thoughts and actions, which is bound to gather bad karma over time and reflect poorly on the individual once his time in this life has come to an end. Buddhism still puts great emphasis on our obligations and responsibilities in life because fulfilling them results in accumulation of very good karma. It's necessary to harbor the right thoughts and effect meaningful action if we are to improve our position in the cycle of rebirth, let alone if we strive to reach enlightenment.

The full embrace of Anicca is thus not meant to make us give up on life. Rather, it is meant to help you detach yourself and deal with the next, all-important fact of life.

- ## Dukkha

Suffering

In essence, Buddhism teaches us that most of our Dukkha stem from Anicca. Unfortunately, the vast majority of humans have a strong urge to attach themselves to material possessions, moments, relationships, people, or ideas – things that are all transient. And because we are in a perpetual struggle to acquire these things and hold onto them, suffering is a fundamental fact of life.

However, this suffering doesn't merely pertain to our more noticeable forms of misery such as outright depression, loss, anguish, or suicidal thoughts. Less intense but still unpleasant aspects of our lives such as boredom, a feeling of emptiness, or a lack of satisfaction are all part of this human condition. If life feels overly mundane and pointless, and this feeling puts a weight on one's mind, then this is a manifestation of Dukkha. The real trouble lies with the fact that many people who find themselves in this state will look to transient, earthly answers for their problems. A lot of folks feel that buying a new car or just acquiring more money will fill the void, and even though it may feel like that for a short while after getting what you want, the sensation never lasts. Instead, you will only crave more while the emptiness grows ever larger.

As one starts to contemplate these issues, it quickly becomes apparent that this form of suffering is absolutely rampant in modern, first world societies. Never has there been such an abundance of things to buy and cling to, and yet one gets the impression that more and more people are growing depressed and anxious. Material prosperity and luxury are not bad things in themselves, but it's obvious what we are looking at quite a few matters from a faulty perspective. Buddhism thus offers the Buddhist path as an alternate means of alleviating our Dukkha. As you have and will continue to learn, this means shifting focus inward as you go about your quest to find fulfillment and peace.

Nothing is ever meant to be satisfactory. Thus, you must learn to depend on nothing, whether it's a physical object, a person, or an emotion. A happy moment, no matter how beautiful, will not last. Success will eventually fade. This mark of existence, like the previous

40

one, is closely related to the ephemeral nature of things. The Buddha teaches you to cling to nothing.

That said, it does not mean that you are not allowed to enjoy success, happiness, or prosperity. In fact, you are encouraged to relish each wonderful moment in your life. Enjoy it *but* never cling to it. Later, we will discuss Mindfulness and how it can help you live a happier, fuller life.

On a fundamental level, you can see that the Buddhist wisdom lets you have the best of both worlds and is all about shielding the follower of the path. The true beauty of the Middle Way is in that it does not prohibit or limit anything – it teaches you how to live with *it* in a way that makes you impervious to the trickery of Dukkha. That "it" is all that you own as well as everything and everyone you hold dear. The Buddha teaches you to live life to its fullest, go out there into the world and attain the good things in life, but at the same time, he teaches you to beware of letting your fulfillment, contentment, and happiness depend on those things.

Contentment and inner peace, as they are viewed in Buddhism, are not exactly what you think either. For instance, it's not about the peace that arises when you know that you have enough money not to worry about scarcity of basic necessities for you and your family. That is merely the peace of material and existential security and it refers to something that is very earthly and very human. The inner peace that Buddhism propagates is on the inside, and it is all-enveloping. It's the peace and stability of mind and spirit that endures through all tribulations, thanks to that knowledge of impermanence.

That isn't to say that you will just give up and sit back with your feet on the table when your family needs help – natural instincts will take care of that. It is to say, however, that you will remain level-headed, pure in mind, and capable of thinking in a rational and calm manner that allows effective problem solving and planning. Earthly problems of life will need solving, but an enlightened Buddhist's state of mind and spirit remains unshakeable no matter the tribulations and hardships that come to pass. And that is the finest example of how a full acceptance of Anicca can help regular people keep Dukkha at bay.

- **Anatta**

There is no "I"

There is no such thing as "the self." You are not an individual entity. Hence, you should also refrain from viewing other beings and things as separate entities. And since they are not separate entities, they can neither be owned nor controlled. Since "the self" is not real but merely an illusion, you cannot own yourself. Thus, you cannot control yourself.

Nothing in this world is permanent. That includes your "self" as you perceive it. And that which is not permanent only serves to cause you pain. Why? Because you tend to hold onto it. And when you feel that it's gone, that is, when you can no longer perceive it through your physical senses, then you experience a sense of loss, a feeling of grief.

Would you willingly place your hand on a pile of burning coal knowing that it will hurt you? Of course not! So why attempt to hold something knowing that it will only serve to hurt you in the long run? To attempt to hold, own, or control anything will inevitably lead to suffering. This is because you hold on to an illusion but the moment you lose it, you experience pain as though the object of your mourning really did exist.

Do you see now how people subject themselves needlessly every day to suffering? And it's all because they cling to delusions.

Anatta doesn't only refer to a lack of self in humans, though. It also means that no phenomena or event in life has any innate higher meaning or significance at all. Here, it becomes quite clear just how much Annata and Dukkha feed into each other.

Above, we discussed the empty feeling we experience due to our cravings and attachments to impermanent things, and how ill-advised our strife to remedy this problem through possessions is. However, our inability or, rather, unwillingness to cope and come to terms with Anatta leads to a whole new level of spiritual and emotional faltering. In fact, the sudden realization that we have no eternal soul, that we are really nobody, and that everything is essentially meaningless often leads to existential dread, which is one of the oldest, most fundamental manifestations of Dukkha.

The teachings of the Buddha are not necessary for one to start sensing the reality of Anatta either. Rather, many of us come to this realization on our own at some point in our lives. The problem is that, instead of coming to

42

terms with it, we create elaborate delusions and rationalizations or, in the worst case scenario, simply give into the suffering and carry it around willingly. Quite a few people nowadays are outspoken about their understanding of our existential disposition, yet they shoulder it as a bundle of pain instead of learning how to live happily alongside the truth of Anatta.

Living alongside that truth will necessitate that you adopt a certain attitude and way of looking at it. If you focus on Anatta as an inherently negative thing, you will most likely suffer. What's more, most people in the world have long been conditioned by their respective religions and cultures to believe that they possess a soul that is eternal. They have been conditioned to the point where it essentially feels natural that we should have a soul. This is what makes it very difficult for many newcomers to come to terms with Anatta and carry on peacefully.

The key is to stop focusing on the angle of meaninglessness and to look toward a few other things that Anatta implies. For one, looking at things from a certain perspective, the very fact that we have no soul and inherent purpose or meaning makes the phenomenon of life all that more fascinating. What are the odds of your consciousness coming to be and perceive the world, with all its beauty and wonder, just by mere accident and no particular reason? Life is so incidental yet so grand and filled to the brim with joyous moments that there's hardly any other way to look at it other than as a blessing. Add to that the Buddhist belief that life is an opportunity to attain enlightenment or be reborn into an even better realm and you will see that it's not that difficult to make peace with the Marks. These are just some of the reasons that Buddhists value and respect life, despite all its hardship.

And that is the gist of the issue: the Buddha didn't invent hot water by explaining the concept of the Three Marks and our suffering that results from them – he gave them a name, a context, and devised a path to overcoming these hard truths of life and making peace with them, despite the fact that we can change almost nothing.

But wait, didn't you just say that we are the masters of our destinies? How can we make our own fate when we cannot own and control ourselves?

What the Buddha wishes you to understand is that the absolute absence of control is the only path towards mastery. When you acknowledge the impermanence of things when you embrace the fact that the "I" does not exist, and when you learn to depend on nothing, then it is *you who controls your life* as opposed to the *illusions controlling you.*

It's with very good reason that the Buddhist teachings often refer to this journey as a path towards liberation. Our continuous refusal to come to terms with the Three Marks doesn't merely impede on our happiness, but it also enslaves us in a way. The ultimate goal of the path is to rid one's self of fear, illusions, and for our happiness to stop being dependent on that which is unsustainable.

The Four Noble Truths

Once there was a woman who was so grief-stricken by the death of her child. She wandered the streets carrying his lifeless body and asking strangers to help her bring him back to life. A sympathetic person accompanied her to meet the Buddha.

The Buddha told the woman: "Bring me some mustard seeds and I shall resurrect him. However, you must obtain them from a family who is a stranger to death."

The woman went on her way, desperately knocking from door to door. Alas, she returned in vain — for every family she had encountered had known death as well.

Finally, the woman realized the lesson that the Buddha wished to teach her. And that is: Sorrow is inescapable. If you expect to experience only happiness in your life, then you will suffer from frustration.

What are the four noble truths?

- **Suffering**

Suffering is universal. Everyone experiences it. For instance, death is inevitable. When we are ill, we feel miserable. Thus, to ask for a life devoid of disappointment would be unrealistic. The Buddha urges you to rise above self-deception and to really examine the way you live your life. The moment you wake up from your attitude of habitual denial, only then will you be able to follow the path to end suffering.

Therefore, in the simplest terms, the first of the truths is the affliction from which we suffer. This isn't simply about understanding that we sometimes suffer for one reason or the other, but about a realization that life itself is suffering in the first place, regardless of what we do. The Buddha observed that Dukkha is an integral part of life in all realms of existence, for as long as Nirvana isn't reached.

In the words of the traditional wisdom of Buddhism, birth, aging, sickness, loss, and being denied what one wants are all suffering. As you can notice right away, all of these things are unavoidable in life, which makes it quite clear that there is no hiding from pain in this life. The objective is to make peace with this fact and stop it from keeping you down. As you will see during our examination of the rest of the Four Noble Truths, the statement that there is no avoiding suffering is not exactly absolute. This is because the very objective of the Buddhist path is to liberate ourselves from Dukkha, which still doesn't change the fact that life is suffering.

This might seem contradictory at first, but once you get down into it, things start making a lot more sense. First and foremost, suffering itself is not permanent, as you could have already assumed through your newfound understanding of Anicca. Secondly, the whole idea of Buddhism revolves around reaching Nirvana, which in itself is the answer to suffering. Therefore, the Buddha never taught that everything will be suffering forever, but he taught that *life* is suffering.

Take note of that what actually implies in the Buddhist context. For one, you will notice that there is no "you" or "I" in that sentiment. The First Noble Truth is originally phrased as, "this is suffering" or "there is suffering." That means that suffering is something primordial, greater than the individual – something that doesn't necessarily concern you personally, so you should not take it as such. And then, of course, you should also understand that the crux of the first truth is simply that you will encounter suffering at every turn, just like the Buddha did, not that you can't fight it and work to lessen its effects.

In most Buddhist traditions, there is a sort of three-part formula for embracing and fully accepting the first truth: There is suffering. Suffering should be understood. Suffering has been understood.

That is more or less all there is to it, and the second truth is where the philosophy becomes much more investigative.

- **The Cause of Suffering**

We cause our own suffering. Take a look at the reasons for your own misery. How much of your unhappiness was brought about by greed? How much of it has been brought about by ignorance?

The problem with people is that they continue to seek happiness in all the wrong places. They pursue worldly pleasures that are harmful to their bodies, minds, and souls. In the end, satisfaction remains an elusive dream. For as long as you allow desire and attachment to control you, you shall never know true peace and contentment.

As mentioned above, both Anatta and Anicca are seen as the core reasons for our suffering. The key, however, is the idea that the problem lies with us, not the universe. Although all reality is transient, the problem lies with our continuous insistence on attachment. That doesn't mean that all worldly possessions and ambitions will lead us into suffering, though. In fact, it's perfectly natural and not innately detrimental for us to enjoy the fruits of success and happy moments, as long as these things aren't the very foundation of our emotional and spiritual well-being.

The Buddha teaches us to enjoy the pleasures of life without being greedy. You are urged to be sensitive to the needs of others, to take only what you need so that others will not be deprived of their share of the earth's resources.

A valuable bottom line can be drawn from this. You can enjoy all that life offers, but don't depend on it and ascribe too much value to it. This kind of attitude doesn't just help us overcome our attachment, but it also has the potential to make us a better person. People who don't have an overwhelming craving and love for their material possessions are often more magnanimous and open to helping those in need.

The formula for getting a firm grip on this truth is as follows: The root of our suffering exists, and it is our attachment and desire. One should do away with desire. Desire has been done away with and forgotten.

Keep in mind the full scope of our craving and the incredibly wide array of things and aspects of life that we are prone to cling to. Apart from just material possessions, joyous moments, happy feelings, and people, we can cling to ideas. This can be much vaguer than it first appears, and it represents a potential trap even to devout Buddhists who are already some way along their path to enlightenment. Beware that you don't begin to cling and attach yourself to the very idea of letting go of desire. Indeed, becoming overly dependent on this notion can lead to suffering just as well as materialism. This might seem counterintuitive at first, but it soon starts to make sense when you contemplate the concept some more.

Somewhat similarly, some individuals can become obsessed with their suffering, which leads them to form a strong desire to just end it and commit suicide. As you have already learned, suicide is almost always frowned upon in Buddhism, but this phenomenon often takes the form of what is known as the attachment to non-being. On the flip-side of that coin, some folks can develop a strong attachment to being. Of course, the rare cases of individuals who come to love their suffering itself and develop a taste for it are also clinging, albeit in a completely different manner.

Strange as it may seem, such folks exist, and just because one has managed to alter their state of mind to the point where their suffering brings them a warped sense of enjoyment doesn't mean they have somehow defeated the noble truth in question. Just like others who cling to desire, these individuals are depending on something that will pass. Unfortunately, people who live like this are almost always unable to enjoy actual happiness and joyous moments, which, again, leads to suffering.

- **The Termination of Suffering**

It is up to you to stop doing the things which cause suffering. The state where all suffering ceases to exist is called *Nirvana*. It is a perpetual state of peace and happiness.

According to the great Buddha, Nirvana is achieved through the extinction of desire. Nirvana is not synonymous with the concept of heaven. Instead, it is something which can be achieved right now, in this lifetime. Being Buddhist, you are called to follow a lifestyle which is free of selfishness and greed.

It's also important to note that some Buddhist texts also refer to our desire to escape suffering and the perception of pain as a form of craving. The same applies to those who come to love their current birth or the cycle itself. All of this amounts to craving and attachment to impermanent aspects of our transient lives and, as such, keeps us confined in the cycle of samsara.

Like the previous two truths, the Third Noble Truth is also to be embraced through a formula: There is a way to end suffering. This way to end suffering should be realized. The way has been realized.

This is the stage where Buddhism begins to truly shine with optimism and present answers to our problems. Once you have truly comprehended and accepted into your heart the first two truths, your next step is to rejoice and understand that an answer exists. For once, it is really as simple as it seems – you are to fully realize that suffering can end. The way it ends is our next and final Noble Truth.

- **The Path Leading to the End of Suffering**

The secret to ending all suffering is for everyone to experience enlightenment. As previously mentioned, it was in his moment of awakening when the Buddha discovered the Middle Path.

To walk on this road, one must live the Noble Eightfold Path. The Noble Path in itself is the fourth Noble Truth as well as the very essence of how and why a Buddhist navigates through life. At the end of this journey, craving and attachment will cease, and with that our suffering ends. We will explore this path into deeper detail as we proceed.

CHAPTER 3

FINDING THE
BUDDHA IN YOU

The Righteous Way of Life: The Noble Eightfold Path

Also referred to as the Middle Way, this is the path one traverses on their way towards liberating themselves from the cycle of rebirth, suffering and dying, ultimately achieving a state of Nirvana. This explanation of the Buddhist path is most characteristic of the Theravada traditions, and it is the one most commonly used to describe the road that a Buddhist walks on. The alternate name of "Middle Way" stems from the Buddha's supposed explanation of this practice. Namely, the journey constitutes a middle way because it guides the devotee right between two extremes in life – asceticism and hedonism.

To anybody familiar with these two terms, it quickly becomes apparent that this view of the Buddhist practice applies perfectly to the modern era in developed countries. Extreme asceticism, which means completely and utterly refraining from indulging in any pleasure, would have a very hard time coming into modern living. We have many responsibilities both to ourselves and others, and we can hardly do away with every single commitment to material success without completely turning our lives upside down. On the other hand, one should strive to avoid excessive indulgence and hedonism, for which the world offers ample opportunity, unfortunately. Striking a balance between these two extreme, polar opposites is where the Middle Way comes in.

Of course, just because a person makes a lot of money or owns a lot of property does not mean that he or she necessarily draws great enjoyment from these things – or any at all. Perhaps an individual has to bring in a lot of revenue because they have a big family or a lot of other people who depend on them, or maybe the person is invested heavily in charity. That hardly constitutes hedonism, of course, but asceticism does usually entail a lack of possessions for the practitioner. So, the aforementioned examples don't really fall into either category. In fact, they are perfectly agreeable to the Middle Way and they provide an excellent example of how a Buddhist in modern society can commit to the faith while engaging in business and building a career at the same time. This all just serves to illustrate to you where the Middle Way fits in between different lifestyles. The Path itself is much more detailed and instructive than that.

The Noble Eightfold Path consists of eight practices that a Buddhist embraces on the path to Nirvana, and these eight principles can, in turn, be divided into three groups or aspects of Buddhist life.

As you will probably start to understand very quickly as we proceed, the Noble Eightfold Path is not prescriptive scripture that will instruct you on a bunch of rituals, sermons, dogmatic beliefs, and supernatural assertions. The Middle Way is a guide. It is a comprehensive handbook that contains some rather straightforward and easy to grasp bits of wisdom that explain the proper way for a Buddhist to live. These are steps that everyone can follow and greatly benefit from, regardless of their level of commitment. Above all, the Middle Way is mostly very practical and applicable. The best part of all is that, in the traditional Buddhist manner that we have explained earlier, the instructions found here can be subject to a fair amount of customization and personalization in order to best suit your particular lifestyle.

Even if you completely disregard everything else that you have learned thus far and even if you cast the whole religion aside, a lot of the advice and principles of living that you will find here can help solve quite a few problems in the lives of almost everyone. As we explore these aspects of Buddhist life in detail, we will also touch upon the ways in which some of them can be applied to you and improve the quality of your own life, even if you decide completely against Buddhism.

Wisdom

The first group of principles focuses on wisdom and insight, or "prajna" in Sanskrit. That means that one should have insight into the noble truths and be well-acquainted with the true order of things in the reality that we occupy, with all its suffering, impermanence, and human dissatisfaction.

As you can see, as long as you know the Four Noble Truth and have learned all that we have covered thus far, your foot is already in the door and you have started your journey along the Middle Way. Even more importantly, that implies that you possess all the wisdom that is necessary in order to become an aspiring Buddhist devotee. It is then entirely up to you to decide how far you want to travel and to what lengths you want to study and practice the philosophy, whether it's as a layperson or a truly dedicated individual with ambitions of monastic life. Still, it is necessary to adopt the exact principles that manifest that wisdom in daily life. Namely, there are two aspects to consider in this first group, and they are as follows.

- **The Right View**

Perceive the world through wise and compassionate eyes. In other words, see it through the eyes of the Buddha.

Having the right view also means an individual has adopted the Buddhist perspective, which entails understanding a few important things. First and foremost, the right view brings one to embrace the belief that the Buddha followed a path that successfully brought him to Nirvana. This aspect also heavily revolves around the Buddhist concepts of karma and the cycle of rebirth.

Once you understand and accept into your heart that death is not the end and that your actions have repercussions both in this life and the next, you have adopted the right view. Of course, this will also mean that a follower of the path is paying heed to the Four Noble Truths.

The Four Noble Truths are really the core of the right view. In the simplest possible words, the individual who possesses the right view sees all things in this life for what they truly are, and he thus perceives the ultimate reality. Seeing as the Four Noble Truths are what describes and encapsulates this reality that we occupy, the right view then essentially boils down to understanding the Truths.

It's also important to realize that Buddhism generally differentiates between two main levels at which we understand the things we perceive and learn. Raw knowledge, memorization of information, as well as intellectual tackling of that information in our minds are all aspects of what we refer to as "understanding" in everyday life and speech. In many Buddhist traditions and scriptures, this form of understanding as we know it is considered as "knowing accordingly," or only scratching the surface of things. It is believed that there is a much deeper form of insight that penetrates to the true underlying nature of things, of which only the purest and most developed of minds are capable.

It's unnecessary to delve too deeply into how the right view can benefit the average, non-Buddhist Joe, as the right view entails understanding the essence of the philosophy, and you can simply reflect back on the Buddhist teachings you have learned thus far. After seeing which of the teachings could benefit you and provide that which is lacking in your life, it's only a matter of applying what suits you, as the Buddha himself would encourage you to do.

- **The Right Thought**

You are the product of your thoughts. Positive thoughts build positive characters.

This integral part of the path is also often referred to as right resolve or intention, and it is essentially a Buddhist's spiritual aspiration. Most importantly, having the right resolve is to do away with attachment to material possessions and any kind of ill will. In extreme cases and more stringent traditions, the right resolve means that an aspiring Buddhist has forsaken his home, material possessions, all sensory indulgence, and ill will towards any living creature, after which he or she is to embark on a journey just like that of the Buddha. In essence, this way is all about renunciation, harmlessness, and compassion.

Harmlessness and utmost compassion come together to form the doctrine of non-violence, which has been the crucial mark of many a holy man and wise teacher, hailing from many schools of thought and religions throughout history. You should take note of what Buddhism subtly implies here. As you will see very soon, the next group of principles on the Middle Way will concern morality and ethics, and yet you are reading about non-violence and goodwill under the umbrella of this group rather than that one. This tells you a lot about Buddhism and the way it perceives the world and its ills. This ancient classification implies that violence, hate, persecution, misanthropy, and many other afflictions that wreak havoc upon our world don't necessarily stem from a lack of morals, but from a fundamental lack of wisdom.

If you put aside *individuals* who hurt and murder other beings for thrills, money, or a general lack of scruples, you will see that governments, organizations, and various movements in history have often espoused morality and a supposed just cause, only to ultimately harm thousands or even millions of people. Ignorance and a profound lack of wisdom can lead to unspeakable doom, no matter how moral and righteous people might feel.

On a more personal level, you too can improve the quality of your life and possibly effect at least minor positive change in the world by adopting the right thought. Think of all the times you might have acted in a way that you quickly regretted just because you were hateful and clinging onto your ill will toward someone else for whatever reason. Ill will and hate are a tremendous weight on one's mind, they cloud judgment, and people from all walks of life and all creeds should do away with that baggage.

Moral Virtue and Ethics

Do not let what we just talked about fool you – morality is incredibly important in Buddhist life. This group too will touch upon ways of non-violence in a very concrete manner and you will be acquainted with other integral parts of moral Buddhist behavior.

This division of spiritual steps along the Middle Way consists of three aspects of Buddhist morality. These three precepts provide the basis for Buddhist ethics and are otherwise referred to by the Sanskrit word "Sila," which can be roughly translated as "good conduct," "moral conduct," or "virtue." In simplest possible terms, Sila is a code of conduct that a Buddhist must adhere to. It propagates the virtue of devotion to control and harmony, non-violence, and never causing harm. The three stages of the journey to be found here are the following.

- **The Right Speech**

Understand that your words have the power to influence others. Value the gift of speech by speaking only truthful words. Refrain from uttering hurtful words to others. Lastly, do not waste this gift by engaging in idle gossip.

The wisdom bestowed upon the follower in this stage is much deeper than it appears at first glance. Buddhism puts great emphasis on the importance of the gift that is speech while noting ways in which we abuse and squander this gift. Across most Buddhist traditions and scriptures, the right speech boils down to abstaining from precisely four verbal activities. These are lying, abusive speech or outbursts, idle chatter (including gossip as mentioned), and divisive speech.

Therefore, a Buddhist is someone who knows how to comfort others and say kind things when need be, or not speak at all. Apart from just avoiding gossip, abstaining from idle chatter is related to the quality of being a person of few words. That doesn't mean being quiet and reserved, as communication is of great importance. Rather, it means speaking only when there's something worth discussing, keeping conversations insightful and meaningful. Lastly, a Buddhist projects his desire for harmony onto other people as well. Divisive speech includes everything from talking behind people's backs, scheming, and sowing rancor between people. A true Buddhist will promote virtues of cooperation, peaceful conflict resolution, and generally positive relations between people.

It's likely that none of these moral precepts are exactly foreign to whatever religion you were born into, but the popular culture is likely a whole different story, particularly if you live in a modern, Western society. Not to isolate certain parts of the world as so much worse than others, but it's clear that the morality and *quality* of our speech nowadays is not just in a downward spiral but a thrust.

Lying, whether casual or contrived and intricate, as well as idle speech and gossip, are rampant, to say the least. Things are at a point where individuals who are completely honest and have something valuable to say are almost a rarity, usually eliciting reactions such as praise and even subtle shock from others. Of course, nobody is immune to telling lies, and we've all told a couple of white ones here and there. But should honesty and wise expressions really be a rare commodity? Honesty is absolutely deserving of praise, but society should not be in a position where it's a surprising personal trait.

If you personally notice these trends and are bothered by them, you should make absolutely sure that you are not guilty of it too. Try to always tell the truth and to speak only when you have something of value to add to the table, and make sure that when you are making points, they are backed up by knowledge and facts. Do note that the virtue of noble silence and honesty feed into each other and the rest of the aspects of right speech in one particularly important regard. Namely, honesty can be brutal and cause emotional harm to some folks, so whenever you have a potentially painful truth to speak, you should be sure that the benefits of uttering it outweigh the pain. This is the Buddhist way of striking a perfect balance. In addition to knowing when to stay silent, those harsh truths should always be followed with compassion and kind words.

Keep in mind that we are talking about valuable speech. There is a major difference between speaking out important truths that have the potential to hurt and just going around saying mean things with the intent to hurt and insult, whether or not what you say is true.

Conducting yourself in this manner can bring you untold amounts of respect and people will learn to depend on you and will start to listen to you much more than before. Honest, considerate, valuable speech has a lot of potential career-wise and can take you a long way toward getting a job and even excelling at it. Needless to say, your relationships, future and present, are bound to benefit from right speech a great deal. Abstaining from divisive speech and, in fact, being the diplomat in all situations is also indispensable in both of these areas of life.

All in all, the right speech is one of the most widely applicable principles of the Noble Eightfold Path. It is entirely based on natural human behaviors and interactions, making this principle incredibly resistant to the limits of culture and religion.

- **The Right Action**

Do harm to no one. Do not kill, steal, or engage in any form of sexual misbehavior. Instead, help and protect others. Uphold their dignity.

As you can imagine, right action pertains primarily to voluntary, premeditated, physical acts.

As far as physical harm and killing are concerned, keep in mind that this includes both humans and animals in the vast majority of Buddhist texts and schools of thought. Anything that crawls, walks, or flies is considered sentient and thus protected, which excludes only plants.

Stealing too encompasses a wide range of ways in which someone else's property is acquired. This doesn't concern only direct theft, pickpocketing, or forceful taking, but also means any form of fraud or deception as a means of taking what others don't wish to give you.

A somewhat prevalent issue that you should consider is when the line between what is and isn't stealing becomes blurred. For instance, just because there is a loophole that makes it legal to appropriate property and money from others in a way that many people know is theft deep down doesn't make it okay. Buddhism neither interferes nor is concerned with the legal order of various countries, but it's quite likely that some of the financial practices of today, which are technically legal, could constitute a breach of Buddhist morality in this regard. A person living in a modern society should keep this in mind if they are aspiring to follow the Middle Way faithfully.

The Buddhist views on sex vary from one tradition or text to the next. First of all, excessive indulgence and promiscuity are not permissible across the board. The same holds true for other sexual misdemeanors, which are considered as such in the Western societies as well, such as extramarital affairs and, of course, rape and assault. Some particularly strict traditions prescribe celibacy as an integral part of the Buddha's path, especially for monks, but such views are not as common in Buddhist circles in first world countries.

Pursuers of monastic Buddhist life are always a different story than laypersons in the vast majority of traditions, and many of them will indeed be required to give up their sexual life. Another interesting tradition that is observed in some Buddhist communities in the world concerns premarital sexual engagements. Namely, male Buddhists of all stature and commitment to the path are expected not to engage in sexual activity with women whom they have no married, especially if those women are under the protection of their family, as is the custom in quite a few communities in more rural areas. In general, the views on sex are some of the most variable matters in Buddhist parts throughout the world, and they will depend both on the specific teachings and on how conservative the community is.

Apart from the few minor matters that we have discussed, you can see that right action is almost entirely in line with virtually any country's culture and is thus easily applicable to you. One more thing that's worth mentioning is that right action often includes and encourages a follower's effort to help others uphold these values and principles. That doesn't mean you have to preach. It simply means that you should assist those who seem to be struggling by pointing out to them what it is that they could be doing wrong, thus helping them stay out of trouble. This should especially be done if someone *asks* for your guidance.

- ## The Right Livelihood

The Buddha teaches us to earn an honorable living which does not involve harming or deceiving others. Likewise, he teaches us not to pursue happiness through the sorrow of others.

Of course, virtually all cultures in the world are familiar with the fact that profiting over someone else's back is wrong. In Buddhism, there are two levels, if you will, of devotion to this step on the Noble Path.

The first version of right livelihood is less extreme and usually applies to Buddhist laypersons. Making a living by means of monetary gain and acquisition of property is acceptable as long as the means are honorable. Wrong livelihood doesn't encompass only direct harm as a means of acquiring wealth. Dealing in goods and services that have great harm associated with them, without directly hurting anyone, is still not worthy of right livelihood. Some of the activities to avoid in this regard are obvious, and they include weaponry, drugs, alcohol, human trafficking, and almost all the other business that are illegal anyway. However, in keeping with Buddhist ethics, wrong livelihood would also be trading meat and livestock, with the possible exception of dairy animals, as they are not being harmed.

Organic food production, particularly of fruits and vegetables, is thus a great way to build a profitable business and stay in line with right livelihood. Some professions in the food industry can be particularly murky and their morality is difficult to ascertain. One such line of work is butchery. At first glance, it might appear as a no-brainer that this would be forbidden, but not all butchers do the exact same kind of work. If you work in a deli, where you just cut the meat of animals that have long been slaughtered without you taking part in the deed, it may not necessarily be a breach of right livelihood.

Still, the deli makes money off the slaughter of animals, in turn paying you, which can be controversial. If you find yourself in this incredibly specific and unlikely scenario, it is best to thoroughly consult with the particular tradition you are following, as well as with an ordained, well-acquainted person of a local community.

It's possible that just working in a deli can fall under scavenging, which is quite an interesting concept in the Buddha's teachings. To take a slight digression, this matter especially concerns Buddhists who want to eat meat. The Buddha taught that scavenging, in this case of meat, is viewed as such as long as the meat one eats has not come from an animal that was slaughtered specifically for him, especially if the consumer has neither heard nor seen the killing of the animal. Many Buddhists are still vegetarian, especially in the Mahayana tradition, but it's an interesting matter to contemplate. Either way, profiting from the killing of animals is clearly just one smaller aspect of right livelihood that primarily concerns laypersons.

Now, what right livelihood entails for monks in some Buddhist traditions is a fair bit more extreme. Namely, the most devoted of followers are expected to live off of begging, with no valuable material possessions. Even then, they are not to accept more charity or food than is absolutely necessary, as fundamental Buddhist teachings recognize that even beggars are not immune to greed.

Meditation

The third and final group of steps, comprising the last three principles, is meditation, referred to by the Sanskrit word "Samadhi" in most Indian religions, including Buddhism. The word is most commonly translated simply as "concentration" or "unification of mind," which comes from successful meditation.

As the title suggests, this division of principles revolves primarily around meditation, but it still includes many other instructions and words of advice for life in general. The thing is, however, that the principles usually come down to the way in which particular detrimental forces and mistakes in life can disrupt and harm one's meditation, which still implies specific action. Nonetheless, Samadhi is where the main concern is one's mind and all the inner processes that stem from it. Things will become clearer as we delve into the subject matter.

• The Right Effort

Give your best in everything that you do. You must not entertain laziness. Likewise, you must not misuse energy on activities that bring sorrow to others.

58

The right effort focuses primarily on the contents of one's mind, as opposed to direct action. As Buddhist Sutta scriptures state, right effort is all about exerting the power of one's mind and energy as a means to prevent unwholesome states of mind and thoughts, as well as galvanize and maintain wholesome ones.

These unwholesome mental states refer to what is described in Buddhism as the five hindrances along the path. These include sensual thoughts, lack of faith in the noble path, restlessness, ill will, and drowsiness. Doing away with sensual thoughts, for example, is quite a task, especially for the most devout monks who are going all the way. Sensual thoughts, in this context, boil down to the desire for stimulation of any of the five senses. Ill-will too is quite a broad term that comprises all manner of negative emotions. A fully dedicated Buddhist monk will strive to eliminate all resentment both towards living creatures and things. This also means that all repressed anger and grievances are also to be expelled from one's mind.

The right effort is also usually broken down into four main goals to achieve in one's mind. You must always strive to prevent the aforementioned unwholesome states of thought from ever occurring in the first place, and you must also thoroughly analyze yourself and take steps to eliminate those unwholesome mental states that have already taken root in your mind prior to the fact. Then, you are expected to do your very best to bring about a change and introduce wholesome, healthy states of mind, while also constantly cherishing and perfecting those that are already there.

In the simple terms of everyday living, you can and should make every effort to control your impulses and keep anger at bay. You need to have a sit-down with yourself and see what it is about you that you need to change, and you will find that many of these things are already considered as unwholesome states of mind in the context of the Middle Way. Irritability, laziness, restlessness, and all kinds of ill will are certainly prevalent in the minds of many, so there is a lot of room for improvement through right effort.

If you are already traveling the Path and sometimes feel like you are losing faith in it, it's a good idea to take a look at how well you have really implemented it. And if you have made great efforts, you should reflect on all the subtle ways in which the Middle Way has changed your life for the better. You are likely to find that a lot of good changes have happened, some of which may not be all that subtle after all. Concrete results are always a good source of motivation to keep going.

Mastering your states of mind and being tenacious in controlling the five hindrances is crucial in the context of meditation. If you are trying to commit to meditating in any form or practice, not mastering the hindrances through right effort will put a great hurdle in your way. This is especially the case if you suffer from restlessness, which can be a real problem for one's concentration.

- **The Right Mindfulness**

In the simplest sense, mindfulness refers to being in the present. It is about paying attention to what is happening at the moment. To be mindful is to be constantly aware of what is going on with your body, your mind, and your emotions. Because you know and accept that everything is impermanent, then the only way to capture it is to live in the moment. It is only through this that you will be able to experience happiness in life and all the temporary joys it has to offer.

Do beware, however, that there is a great difference between right mindfulness and being self-absorbed. This principle doesn't imply that you should be obsessed with yourself and your feelings to the point where you start ignoring the outside world, spending entire days in aimless introspection, or feeling that everything is about you. In broad terms, right mindfulness concerns a real and objective knowledge of one's self.

The concept revolves around the four Buddhist contemplations, which are body, feelings, mind, and phenomena. Right mindfulness teaches the follower to take these things at face value. This can concern sadness, pain, tribulations, but also joy, pleasure, and prosperity. A Buddhist who is exercising right mindfulness will give no real value or meaning to any of these factors of life, leaving his mind fortified and consistent no matter what happens. The traveler on the path will thus neither cling nor dwell on life, which in itself is transient. Ultimately, right mindfulness leads the Buddhist to acquire a deeper understanding of the three marks of existence that we mentioned earlier.

Right mindfulness also often includes certain meditative practices, particularly concerning the matters of the body. One exercise that is often conducted is concentrating on one's breathing, otherwise known as Anapanasati, or mindfulness of breathing. Although an exercise of the body, this practice helps one work on their mind and improves overall mindfulness over time. We will look at some more details on the topic of meditation a bit later on.

- **The Right Concentration**

Strive to rid your mind of distractions. Achieve peace of mind by concentrating on a single thought at a time. More importantly, concentrate only on thoughts that matter.

Do note that this stage of the path is also referred to as the right Samadhi, which, as you know, entails meditation. As such, this stage is the one where a Buddhist has successfully honed their mind and made significant headway on the path. The exact meaning of right Samadhi is broad and fragmented into many different texts and teachings, but there is a bottom line: it is a state of utmost clarity and focus. This is achieved through mastering the Buddhist dhyana meditation and all of its four stages.

Some sources of teaching explain right concentration as a flawless and unhindered focus that we would have on a single object when giving that object our full attention, but without said object. In other words, right concentration is an ability to clear one's mind and make it impervious to all distractions, while essentially focusing on nothingness.

This idea might boggle your mind at first, but it should also make you understand why meditation is such a crucial part of Buddhist life, and why some monks spend their entire lives practicing and perfecting their routines. As long as one is working towards mastering their mind completely, they can be considered as being on the noble path. As a matter of fact, you will find that some Sutta texts explain that right concentration is precisely the state of having fully adopted the previous seven aspects of the noble path and integrated them into your journey towards enlightenment.

Still, the idea of concentrating on nothingness is quite appealing when thoroughly considered. That kind of power to rid the mind of clutter, of which most of us have plenty, is really a skill that anybody should hope to possess. Dhyana meditation, with all its stages, is much more advanced and intricate than you know, though. The way that this form of meditation is practiced in certain traditions is not all that accessible to beginners and casual laypersons if we are being frank. In our next

61

chapter, we will touch upon this subject in much more detail, and you will see all the stages of the practice as well as its end-goals.

For now, let us conclude by saying that the right effort, mindfulness, and concentration are the Buddhist's art. Nothing is quite as important to the Buddhist as his or her mind, and maintaining, polishing, and developing it is a life's calling for the travelers on the Middle Way, with perfected and advanced meditative practice being the crowning achievement of one's Buddhist journey. After all, the mind is where enlightenment occurs, and most traditions believe that meditation is the way to achieve it in this lifetime, as did the Buddha himself.

The Five Precepts of Buddhism

First off, it should be made clear that the five Buddhist precepts are the universal principles that apply to all non-ordained Buddhist laypersons. On the other hand, monks can have eight or ten precepts, depending on their particular monastic order (sangha). The essential Five Precepts apply to both genders, and they comprise the following.

- **Respect life.**

Do not kill.

- **Respect other people's property.**

Do not steal.

- **Respect the pure nature of human beings.**

Avoid sexual misconduct.

- **Respect honesty.**

Do not lie or gossip.

- **Respect clarity of mind.**

Do not take intoxicating substances or partake in self-destructive behavior.

The precepts that concern lying, killing, stealing, and intoxication are the base principles found in every sangha. The additional four precepts that are found in some fraternities prescribe and demand the following of their monks.

- **No sexual activity.**

- **Follow the eating schedule.**

Indeed, there are usually explicit rules regarding eating. One example is not eating after noon, especially solid foods.

- **No expression of materialism or indulgence in pointless leisure.**

This primarily concerns apparel and ornaments on one's person, such as jewelry or any pronounced clothing. Some sangha prohibit their monks to spend time on entertainment too.

- **No sleeping on tall or otherwise elevated beds.**

On top of these eight precepts, you may find a sangha that enforces two more rules, which prohibit dancing or singing, as well as taking money.

Rules will vary from one Buddhist monastery to the next, not only in the final couple of precepts but also in specific house rules. A monastery may have hundreds of additional rules on top of the core precepts, concerning decorum, apparel, grooming standards, and the like. All of these rules combined come together to form a monastery's Patimokkha or Vinaya.

It's also worth mentioning that while Buddhism has no direct punitive system for transgressing laypersons, as their punishment will be delivered by their karma; monks are liable to be punished by their monastery if they break the rules.

There is a lot of diversity in the way and degree that these punishments are dished out to monks, as well as in the offenses that warrant said punishment. In general, though, the worst punishment that can befall a fully ordained Buddhist monk is simply being excommunicated from their sangha. There is really no telling what kind of rules and penalties may be in place in the many Buddhist communities in the world, though, especially those that are fairly isolated and located in rural areas of faraway foreign lands. Whether any of them allow their monks to receive corporal punishment or other forms of physical consequences is difficult to say. Apart from the gravest offenses that warrant expulsion, however, it is generally believed in Buddhism that a monk can usually purify himself and be cleansed of his transgression.

The Roots of Evil

The following are the Three Poisons which every Buddhist must strive to avoid. They are regarded as the primary source of evil manifested through our actions, our speech, and our thoughts. They are considered as blocks to positive karma.

- **Greed**

This includes an insatiable desire for:

Riches
Fame
Sex
Food
Sleep

Overcome greed by performing genuine acts of generosity.

- **Anger**

Practice calmness and patience. Do not allow anger to dictate your actions. Once you do, you are allowing it to dictate your karma and hence, dictate the quality of your future life.

- **Ignorance**

As a Buddhist, you are urged to embrace the truth. Let go of prejudices. Stop clinging to delusions. Use your intellect and your senses to carry out observations in an objective manner.

Think of life as a wheel that turns round and round. Depending on your deeds in your past life, you may be born on top or at the bottom. And so this goes, on and on until you are finally able to experience the awakening. The purpose of reincarnation is to give you a chance to eventually escape the ever-turning wheel of life. This is done by achieving enlightenment. Accordingly, to do this means you must first successfully become free of the Three Poisons.

Remember to also apply the wheel metaphor to this very lifetime and not just the great cycle of rebirth. The suffering, temptation, and hardship that, as you have learned, come into every life are things that oscillate a great deal. Since both sorrow and happiness are subject to the doctrine of impermanence, the very life that you are traversing now is certainly also reminiscent of a great wheel, although not as great as the one of Samsara. Nonetheless, Anicca will always have you alternating between the top and bottom of the wheel, between the good times and bad, between health and sickness. Luckily, you now know how to deal with these cold facts of life, and all you have to do as a Buddhist is to strive toward enlightenment. As long as you do, you will always end up better than you started, no matter how far you manage to get.

The Four Stages of Enlightenment:

- **Arhats** are Buddhists who seek to enlighten themselves.

- A **Pratyekabuddha** is someone who retreats from the modern world in order to find enlightenment.

- A **Bodhisattva** is an aspiring Buddha, who seeks to enlighten not just himself but others as well.

- A **Buddha** refers to someone who has reached the stage of perfect enlightenment.

It is up to you to determine your degree of involvement in Buddhism. In fact, the best way to conduct your journey is to proceed at your own pace. Remember, you are free to incorporate whatever teachings work for you. Likewise, you are free to leave the ones that don't.

Keep in mind that reaching Nirvana or Buddhahood is not necessary in order for Buddhism to improve your life. It's also worth mentioning that some traditions, such as Theravada, maintain that Nirvana can only be attained by monks. On the other hand, Mahayana traditions believe that everyone can achieve this utmost enlightenment without being ordained. Either way, Nirvana is the apex of spiritual growth in Buddhism, and individuals who are recognized as having reached this point are not very common. However, millions of people practice Buddhism with only a vague aspiration towards Nirvana, while gaining much fulfillment from the lifestyle regardless.

Is being Buddhist really that easy?

Yes! These are other steps that will help you live life the true Buddhist way:

- **Be responsible for your own life.**

There is no supreme being who will be watching over you every second of your life, ready to reward or punish you as he sees fit. Unlike other religious teachers in history, the Buddha did not require his disciples to be close to him at all times. In fact, he encouraged them to wander, to meditate on their own, and to preach in different places. Then, the followers would gather once a year to listen to the Buddha's new teachings.

As mentioned at the beginning of this book, Buddhism is meant to be a way of life. As an aspiring Buddhist, you are encouraged to live life, to experience for yourself the truth in the teachings of the Buddha.

- **Receive the teachings.**

You don't have to be Buddhist in order to practice the teachings of the Buddha. As mentioned, your degree of involvement depends on you. Often, Buddhist groups and teachers of Buddhism offer classes and meditation instructions for free. They welcome anyone who is self-motivated enough to actively seek them out.

- **Gain a deeper knowledge of the teachings.**

Read more books on Buddhism. Find a teacher if you wish. However, understand that receiving someone as a teacher involves a commitment on both sides. There are different traditions of Buddhism. Before you decide to receive formal initiation, make sure that the tradition you choose is right for you. Alternatively, you may opt to remain a layperson while observing the basic precepts of the Buddhist tradition of your choice.

- **Choose a tradition.**

Theravada

Theravada is considered as one of the main branches or traditions of Buddhism, as well as the most historical. Its teachings mostly revolve around the most well-known Buddhist concepts, such as Nirvana, the Noble Eightfold Path, and escape from Samsara.

Teachers of this tradition do not claim to have any spiritual authority. Think of a fellow traveler who happens to know more about the area. He occasionally nudges you towards the right path when you lose your way. Simply put, Theravada teachers are more like mentors.

Mahayana

This is the second major branch of Buddhism, and it includes many other traditions such as the famous Zen school. Mahayana is the more adaptable form of Buddhism, and it has included numerous additional rituals and teachings over time.

A very interesting difference between Mahayana and Theravada teachings is in the way Mahayana Buddhists contemplate the idea of higher enlightenment at the end of the journey. Namely, this tradition doesn't believe that a follower will necessarily escape the cycle of rebirth but will instead remain in this state in order to facilitate and assist the awakening of others. Therefore, instead of reaching Nirvana, a follower of the Mahayana teaching aspires to attain Buddhahood by traversing the bodhisattva path, which we mentioned above.

Vajrayana

Teachers of this tradition have substantial authority over their followers. He initiates trainees and they follow his rules dutifully.

Vajrayana is the only school of thought that is sometimes considered to be the third branch, but many view it as a part of the Mahayana tradition. All the other traditions may fall under any one of the ones we mentioned thus far.

Tibetan Traditions

Instructors of Meditation may be monks or lay practitioners who assist you in developing your practice.

Lamas are teachers that are usually monks although not in all cases. They possess advanced meditation training and have disciples who revere them.

Geshes refer to teachers who possess advanced academic training. Their expertise is in interpreting and clarifying the scriptures.

Zen

Teachers of this tradition are often called "teacher" or "master." This is to signify that they possess substantial spiritual authority. Close personal training with a Zen master is an essential part of Zen practice. Aside from masters, the Zen tradition also has meditation instructors and teachers who all function under the master.

A Day in the Life of a Buddhist

Here is an example of a day in 0the life of a Vajrayana Buddhist Practitioner.

- He rises usually before six in the morning and then starts his day with meditation.

- He circumambulates around his home. All over his house are shrines with statues, sacred scrolls, and other holy objects. While walking, he fingers his mala (prayer beads) while reciting a mantra.

- Then, he offers 108 prostrations (bows) to show his devotion to the Buddha.

- After this, the Buddhist works on whichever practice his teacher had assigned to him (e.g. visualization activity with prayer).

- While he goes about his day, he chants "Om" either silently or out loud. Meanwhile, in everything that he does, he strives to show kindness and compassion to all creatures.

- In the evening, he spends a couple of hours studying the materials recommended to him by his teacher.

- Then, before he goes to bed, he meditates. He also burns incense and provides other offerings at the altar.

- Again, he prostrates himself before the altar and then finally, he utters a prayer for a long life dedicated to his teacher.

Going All The Way: Being a Buddhist Monk

When the Buddha left behind his life at the palace, he left behind his material possessions, wore humble garments, and cut off his long hair which symbolized his class in society.

Likewise, in order to be a monk, you will be asked to cut off your hair and by doing so, abandon a symbol of vanity, a source of pride and personal beauty. You will be asked to give up your clothes as well as your valued possessions. You will, in fact, strip yourself of everything which makes you an individual. Instead, you will become a part of the monastic collective. You will wear the same simple garb, eat the same food, and sleep on the same mat as all the other monks.

To receive monastic ordination means leaving behind the comforts of your old life and to be away from the warm familiarity of home, family, and friends. You are, in fact, entering a whole new world.

The Buddhist monastery is a place for Buddhists who have decided to dedicate themselves completely to the truth. Before deciding to take monastic ordination, one usually spends years as a practicing Buddhist layperson. However, it is not uncommon to encounter individuals who go from beginner to monk almost instantaneously.

If you are certain that you are meant for this kind of life, then first you would have to approach the senior monk and secure his permission. It would also be wise to consult with your spiritual teacher before going to the senior monk. You will be provided with a robe. Your head will be shaved. Ceremonies and vows will vary with different Buddhist traditions. The precepts that you will receive will also depend on the tradition and on the level of your ordination.

Buddhism lacks any real and universal system of conversion, so the rites and rituals that monks are subjected to upon initiation may not vary only according to tradition, but also the individual monastery. Of course, the real, authentic experience would be for one to renounce all he has and move to the Far East, find a monastery, and join the brotherhood. That's a little more difficult in reality, though, but there are plenty of monasteries in the West as well.

Either way, don't expect them to be watered down and more accessible just because you find yourself in the USA, UK, Germany, or wherever else. Buddhist monastic life is no joke and whether a particular monastery allows fresh laypersons to join or not, you are best advised not to rush it.

The first step you want to take is to do research and look up any Buddhist centers near you. Ask around and activate yourself with the establishment as a volunteer, if possible, or check to see if the monastic assembly you are interested in offers any kind of program for the likes of you. More often than not, they should have a system in place for people who are interested, which could include courses and classes.

Finally, it's not a bad idea to look into multiple Buddhist centers and monasteries if it is possible. As you have probably realized by now, individual collectives of Buddhists can differ quite a lot from one another in the way they view certain teachings and live. Some monasteries are definitely more difficult to fit into than others. If you are a Westerner who has only recently started getting involved with the religion, your best bet is going with the ones that are more progressive, which is not uncommon in the United States.

A Portrait of the Modern Buddhist

When people think of someone converting to Buddhism, they imagine a person leaving behind all of his material possessions and severing ties with his friends and family. For a modern Buddhist layperson, it's nothing like that at all.

It's true that renunciation is part of being Buddhist. However, this doesn't mean that you have to give up all your money or leave your promising career behind. Instead, you are asked to renounce the traditional view that happiness can be found in earthly concerns. You are asked to reject consumerism, to abandon the belief that having a bigger house or a nicer car will help you achieve contentment.

As you can see, the peaceful Buddhist renunciation of materialism occurs in the mind just as much as in the physical world. While it doesn't mean that a layperson has to give up their job and possessions, the renunciation that happens in the mind does liberate the follower of these things in a way. It's all about separating the idea of happiness from wealth acquisition. When an aspiring Buddhist achieves this in the modern world, he or she will still be able to function in a society, while simply drawing fulfillment from somewhere within, as opposed from ownership of things.

The modern Buddhist layperson is someone who embraces the unorthodox view that long-term happiness and peace can only be achieved by clearing one's mind and by getting rid of negative thoughts and emotions.

CHAPTER 4

MEDITATION AND BUDDHISM

Samadhi and Dhyana

As you have surely picked up by now, meditation is a major component of Buddhist tradition, philosophy, methodology, and lifestyle. This isn't a ceremonial ritual or a form of worship. To a Buddhist, meditation is work; it is a life's calling and a method of implementing and acting on the philosophy that was learned. Outside of Buddhist tradition itself, their meditative techniques have spread far and wide into many other practices throughout the world. This includes various circles such as yoga and meditation classes or other religions. It's also not too rare for a completely irreligious person to practice Buddhist meditation as part of their exercise routine, therapy, or simple relaxation.

We have already mentioned that "Samadhi" refers to a particular state of mind and translates into something along the lines of "unification of mind" or "mental one-pointedness." Therefore, it is a fairly inclusive term that applies to that which is achieved *through* meditation. So what, then, is Buddhist meditation really? In a word, it is dhyana. The word is most commonly translated precisely as "meditation," and since we are talking about dhyana in Buddhism, it implies the particular practice of meditation that Buddhists use, although the term can be found in other Indian religions too. It is believed that dhyana predates any major branching of the Buddhist religion, meaning that it has been there since the beginning. Since that time, though, the practice has been developed further, with many additions and contributions provided by different cultures and traditions.

In the simplest terms, Buddhist dhyana is a sequence of heightened states of mind that the practitioner must manage and master in order to attain the purity of awareness that comes at the end. The way that this meditation is conducted at first is by using an object of focus as a means of collecting and stabilizing one's thoughts and then pointing them exclusively at it. There are a few things that can play the role of this object, including one's own breathing pattern, an actual object such as an idol, a thought, mantra, or a mental image. What's important is that the object of focus is easy to comprehend and visualize.

After pure focus has been achieved, the goal is to maintain this state without a specific object to focus on. This means that a meditator will be able to retain a strong grip on his or her mind without outside interference breaking the concentration.

Different traditions perceive dhyana as having various goals, such as calmness, achieving a firm hold on one's troublesome thoughts, or gaining deeper insight into the reality of the universe, commonly referred to as "vipassana." Due to these varying views, different branches of Buddhist meditation have sprouted since the beginning, with Vipassana Meditation being one of the most popular forms. This meditation came about through the Theravada tradition and its additions to dhyana. In general, though, dhyana is viewed as having eight stages that one progresses through in a consecutive manner. These eight states of meditation are further divided into four meditations of form and four meditations that are formless. Respectively, they are called rupa dhyanas and arupa dhyanas.

The Rupa Dhyanas

The first four dhyanas are believed by some experts to have been devised by the Buddha himself, and they gradually take the practitioner towards advanced mindfulness. Generally, it is believed that these stages are the path that one must surmount in order to achieve Nirvana. Buddhist texts offer a description of what each of these stages is like for the meditator.

- **First Dhyana**

This stage is described as the one where the mind is no longer tormented by the five hindrances. This means that the spirit is reinvigorated by even stronger faith in the Noble Path, as a feeling of bliss ensues and washes away craving, ill will, and most unruly thoughts. Ultimately, the first dhyana allows one to think and deliberate with great clarity, while also experiencing the pleasure of "priti," which is often translated as "rapture." At this point, one is free and shielded from world's temptations.

- **Second Dhyana**

In the second dhyana, one's mind becomes more unified and begins to cleanse itself of all thought and intention. The meditator is then said to be washed over by a feeling of great "internal assurance," rapture, and bliss. The one-pointedness of mind also occurs at this stage, and the mind no longer needs any object to stay in focus.

- **Third Dhyana**

The sense of rapture gradually fades away in this stage, and one is left with a feeling of great equanimity and advanced mindfulness, leading to high awareness. Bliss, which the Buddha described as being composed of joy and happiness as two equal parts, loses the half that is joy in this stage, with only happiness remaining.

- **Fourth Dhyana**

Here, the meditator's mind lets go of happiness as well, leading to a pure state that knows neither pain nor pleasure. This brings a whole new level of serenity, as there is no longer any possibility of stress or any similar distraction. This is where one reaches utmost mindfulness and peace.

The Arupa Dhyanas

Earlier, we mentioned that these are the formless four stages of dhyana. Among other things, this means that this meditation is conducted without focusing on any material object. This also makes arupa dhyanas a more advanced form of dhyana, as they usually require one to have already mastered the first four. Do also note that it is largely believed that right concentration on the Noble Eightfold Path only necessitates the rupa dhyanas.

As one transitions into these last four dhyanas, the mind shifts and its focus abandons the object. They are also often regarded as "formless dimensions," each with an appropriate name.

- **The dimension of Infinite Space**

At this point, the mind perceives an infinity and emptiness of space, where the object disappears. Space ceases to have any colors or shapes.

- **The dimension of Infinite Consciousness**

It is said that the sixth dhyana is characterized by an expansion of one's mind and perception into infinity. The meditator thus transcends the previous dimension and space ceases to exist in his mind.

- **The dimension of Nothingness**

This is where even the meditator's consciousness begins to dissolve. In a way, the mind is no longer aware of its own consciousness and, instead, begins to focus on "nothingness."

- **The dimension of No Perception and Non-Perception**

And finally, if the mind reaches the last of the eight dhyanas, all perception, feeling, and thought processes will have ceased, while non-perception is not possible either. Due to such a blank state of consciousness, there exist no concrete descriptions of this dimension.

It's important to understand that this intricate, prolonged meditation process consists of many states where consciousness shrinks and wanders. The descriptions of the dhyanas are thus scarce and hard to comprehend, whether you read the Buddhist texts and canons or listen to the stories of those who ventured into the distant parts of their minds. Past the second dhyana, things can take a turn that is hard to explain. Furthermore, disagreements as to the interpretation of texts, the goals of dhyana, and other variables have led to a lot of confusion and make the whole philosophy a somewhat difficult pill to swallow.

Luckily, branches such as the Vipassana Movement have done a lot to make the practice more comprehensive and accessible, as they have greatly adapted and built upon the ancient concept of dhyana. This has made the practice spread to distant lands and make it quite popular. We will look into the Vipassana Meditation process itself a bit later on.

Mindfulness and the Modern Buddhist

Practitioners of the Zen tradition believe that monastic members and laypersons are both equally capable of achieving enlightenment. A modern Buddhist who follows the Zen tradition understands the value of mindfulness and incorporates this into his daily life. Mindfulness can be practiced while performing mundane activities like washing the dishes, taking a shower, walking or commuting to work, etc. The Mahayana tradition expresses it beautifully: *Like a lotus growing in muddy water, the modern Buddhist finds clarity in the midst of the chaos of daily life.*

Meditative awareness may be performed in every single daily activity. When you drive, feel your oneness with your car. Rather than thinking of your car and your body as separate entities, feel that the car is an extension of your body and vice versa. While taking a shower, feel every drop of water that touches your skin. Listen to the sound of the water and be aware of the sensations experienced by your body as it is being cleansed. What's the purpose of this? By accepting the truth that you're not separate from the utensils that you use, the things that you see, and the people that you encounter, you end up taking mindful care of every facet of your life. Because the world is your body and you are the world, you are disposed to take care of it.

Why is meditation so important in Buddhism?

These are the purposes of modern meditation techniques:

- *To reduce stress*

- *To promote relaxation*

- *To improve your potential*

These can easily be translated as:

- *To balance awareness*

- *To heighten awareness*

- *To expand awareness*

Contrary to what some people think, meditation is not about taking a trip away from reality. In fact, it is about calming and conditioning the mind to enable you to see and accept reality.

Meditation is not about tuning out the world. Rather, it is about tuning in. When you calm your mind, you are able to reach within yourself and find your anchor to reality. When you meditate, you become an island, immovable and imperturbable even as the rest of the world flows around you. Thus, you find an inner source of balance and stability which no external influence can destroy.

Meditation is not about emptying the mind. In any case, switching off the mind is not an effective means of alleviating suffering.

According to the Buddha, a person who does not know his own mind can be likened to a mad elephant. However, a mind which is infected by any one of the Three Poisons is even more harmful than an entire herd of wild elephants. A person with a mind like that has the potential to ruin his life as well as those of others. A group of people with minds like that can bring about destruction to the world. The way to tame the wild elephant within is through meditation.

There are many advantages of meditation. One is deprogramming the effects of habituation. When you realize that you are reacting to a certain person, situation, or object in a manner which causes you pain, anxiety, anger, discomfort, etc., practice meditation. You do this not to forget the source of your stress or anger but to change your perception and thus, neutralize the negative influences that that object, person, or situation has on you. Through meditation, you can replace greed with generosity, hatred with compassion, ignorance with wisdom, and delusional thinking with contentment.

Meditation enables you to know yourself, to accept yourself devoid of judgment or denial. Subsequently, it helps to deepen your relationship with others and to increase your capacity for love and gratitude.

More importantly, meditation enables you to live in the present. When your mind is able to awaken to the beauty of each transient but irreplaceable moment, you will experience happiness and contentment such as you never had before.

Lastly, as you let go of thoughts and emotions that are inconsequential and concentrate on the ones that really matter, you'll be able to align yourself with your true sense of purpose.

Vipassana and the Art of Accepting Reality

Vipassana Meditation is just one of the many types of meditation. Its main purpose is to teach the practitioner to accept things as they are. It will help you acknowledge more easily the things that you are unable to control. Likewise, it will help you focus on the things that you can actually change. The more you perform this type of meditation, the better you will become in accepting reality.

As we briefly mentioned, this meditative practice in the modern form is propped up by the Vipassana Movement. Vipassana Meditation focuses primarily on the importance of insight as meditation's crucial goal. This means insight into the true order of things in the universe or, as we covered earlier in this book, the Three Marks of Existence. While other traditions use meditation as a means of achieving tranquility and peace of mind above all else, Vipassana Meditation strives to provide one with sharp and deep vision into reality.

Although the practice has evolved and become adopted throughout the world to some degree, it was first introduced by The Buddha himself, with the aforementioned goals in mind. We will now take a look at the most basic steps that a beginner usually starts with.

- Select a safe and quiet environment conducive to meditation. Make sure that you wear loose, comfortable clothing. Get rid of everything that may serve to distract you, such as your mobile phone, bulky items in your pocket, etc.

- Choose a comfortable position. You've been acquainted with the concept of mindfulness so you now understand that one doesn't have to sit in the lotus position in order to achieve a meditative state. However, it is important to keep your spine erect. This is to encourage easy breathing and to prevent you from falling asleep.

- Close your eyes.

- In Vipassana Meditation, you achieve mindfulness by focusing on one thought at a time. In this case, you need to concentrate on your breathing. Relax and breathe deeply. Feel the air moving in and out of your nostrils. Each time you inhale, feel the cool air filling your lungs. Each time you exhale, feel the breath gradually leaving your system.

- Remember, you're not supposed to control your breathing. Instead, you are supposed to observe it.

- While you're meditating, your mind will inevitably wander. Whatever thoughts or emotions that arise, whether they're positive or negative, don't dwell on them. That said, you mustn't ignore them either. Instead, you should acknowledge the thought. Detach yourself from it. Observe it as though you are an outsider. And then, let it go.

- Continue with observing your breathing.

- Then, slowly step out of your meditative state.

Apply Your Inner Peace

Keep in mind what you have learned about the world from the Buddhist teachings we have covered thus far. We are all part of the same larger phenomenon, and none of it has any innate significance due to its impermanence. Why, then, should you allow petty things such as words and banal actions of others to shake you up and send even the smallest ripple through your peace and calm? It is quite striking how easily irritated a lot of people are in our society.

You can observe it virtually everywhere. Take traffic, for example, and you will remember that quite a few folks can fly completely off the handle just for being cut off. Granted, cutting people off is not a very nice thing, but if it happens to you and you lose control in an outburst of rage, you are only hurting yourself. This kind of behavior doesn't only display a lack of control – it exposes one's vulnerability. If we lose our wits and get stressed out over mundane things, what can we expect to happen when we are faced with real tribulations such as loss or disease? We cannot allow ourselves to be so vulnerable to the world's chaotic nature because this will leave us at the world's whim.

More importantly, a lack of self-control makes us enslaved to our emotions and impulses, and that reduces us closer towards the level of an animal. The same applies to our cravings and greed. While it's true that these impulses are natural, no respectable human being has the luxury to use that as an excuse. We are gifted with incredibly sophisticated minds that allow us to make concrete choices and act based on rational thinking, despite the fact that we still have our primordial instincts.

In addition to this gift, we are also presented with philosophies such as Buddhism to help us further along the way. If you struggle with controlling your cravings and this always leaves you wanting more than you have and makes you miserable, give the concepts you have learned here a thorough, logical analysis. There is also no shame in using faith as a crutch sometimes, and the vast majority of people do it with great results. Not only will you be happier and more fulfilled, but you will also avoid having to see for yourself if the Buddhists were right about the concepts of karma and lower realms.

CHAPTER 5

CONVERSION AND
TAKING REFUGE

Conversion in Buddhism

In the course of this book thus far, we have covered the actual practice of being a Buddhist in great detail. So, in regards to the Buddhist life, rituals, and all that which makes one a true Buddhist, you now have a solid understanding of things. When it comes to actually converting, however, we have only briefly touched upon the topic on a couple of occasions. You have been briefly introduced to the difference between a layperson practitioner and a monk, and we also mentioned the lack of a universally established approach to this matter. In this chapter, we will delve a little bit deeper into the matter of conversion in Buddhist traditions, giving you a clearer idea of how and why this religion differs from the rest in this regard.

One of the central questions here concerns what is meant, in practical terms, when it's said that Buddhism has no concrete means of conversion. Other major religions such as Christianity, for instance, have a rather clear stance on this matter and they prescribe physical, well-defined rituals to mark an individual's admittance into the faith. Buddhism, on the other hand, is arguably a much more personal journey and the individual is the absolute center of all that has to do with conversion into the religion. What that means is that conversion begins and ends in the aspiring Buddhist with no supreme, dogmatic authority having any real say in the matter. Therefore, according to the majority of Buddhist traditions, it's only your personal choice that matters.

As long as one truly believes in the four noble truths, accepts the precepts, and embraces the Noble Eightfold Path as we described, most Buddhist traditions nowadays will define that person as a Buddhist. As you have seen, this religion puts utmost emphasis on what's truly in your heart, and there really is no official, universal rite that's expected of you to go through. You will essentially become a Buddhist in your eyes and those of others from the moment you have fully adopted and started to uphold Buddhist morality and lifestyle.

Once upon a time, particularly during the inception of this religion, things were often somewhat different. There was a time when starting off on the Buddhist path meant a dramatic change in lifestyle where virtually any aspiring follower of Buddha had to leave his entire life behind. Then, as history went on and the religion began to spread, there were many instances of entire communities and regions converting to Buddhism, which was usually incentivized by certain powers and thus took on a much more official manner. Those times are long gone through the centuries that have passed, though, and the philosophy has evolved.

Furthermore, much of the wisdom bestowed upon Buddhists by their teachings actually goes against most forms of proactive and organized conversion effort, so Buddhism as a religion is not very missionary in that sense. You have learned that Buddhism encourages skepticism, rational thinking, and thorough analysis of presented philosophies, and this is exactly what that's all about. In fact, you can expect Buddhist communities in temples and other places of congregation, including monks, to be very open-minded, welcoming, and uncritical of those visitors who aren't even Buddhists to begin with.

Where does this leave those who do seek a certain kind of confirmation and who would actually prefer to receive a formal admission and recognition of becoming a Buddhist? Well, if merely adjusting your lifestyle and mindset is not enough for you, perhaps certain traditions can offer something to you too. Namely, it is possible to undergo a particular ritual that serves as an initiation for new adherents of the path.

Taking Refuge

In a broader sense, taking refuge simply means putting your faith into the Buddha, the dharma, and the sangha. As such, it is a spiritual orientation and decision that occurs in an aspiring Buddhist's mind. However, taking refuge can also be an actual ceremony undertaken by newcomers to the religion who wish to mark their entry with a concrete ritual.

The Buddha, dharma, and sangha, in this context, are referred to as the Three Jewels that an aspiring follower will take refuge in, above all in a spiritual sense. The ceremony of taking refuge itself is subject to certain variations according to different traditions as well as individual temples of organizations. Furthermore, the meaning of "sangha" can also vary somewhat, with some communities considering a sangha to strictly include only the ordained monks of a temple, like we discussed earlier, while others can view the sangha as the extended circle of monks and layperson practitioners on the side.

Either way, in order to undergo the Three Jewels ceremony, you must first find a temple or a Buddhist lama who has lineage and is willing to walk new initiates through the process. While many major cities in the world have their Buddhist temples, some of those temples may not hold such ceremonies because they put their emphasis on other things. Nonetheless, with enough research and inquiry, it shouldn't be too difficult to locate a place of congregation that will help you receive this formal initiation.

The temple's requirements for new initiates might differ, though, with some of them demanding certain engagement and even training with the community's lama or other spiritual authority before you can take your formal vows. And when you do, the ceremony itself can be fairly different from one sangha to another. What should be constant, however, is the core of the ceremony. In general, an aspiring Buddhist will thus have to officially vow to uphold the five Buddhist precepts and then utter a particular prayer, which usually revolves around explicitly taking refuge in the Three Jewels.

Regardless of any formal ceremony or ritual, you should always keep in mind the true nature of this religion. No matter how official the manner in which you make vows is, it won't count for much if you don't thoroughly apply the Buddhist morality to your life, and it certainly won't be enough to make you a true follower of the path. The ceremony of taking refuge generally serves as a way to help and motivate newcomers, providing them with a feeling of taking an important first step. No Buddhist sangha can really make you a Buddhist, the main and crucial part of the journey is entirely up to you.

As you can see, formal Buddhist conversion isn't really something that requires much thought and physical effort on your part. The most wholesome way of becoming a Buddhist, in the words of the many wise lamas throughout history, is taking the initiative to research and understand the philosophy before taking steps to apply it to your life in a way that makes sense. So don't fret if the nearest temples don't include any initiation ceremonies in their activities. There are many other ways to get involved with the various Buddhist communities in the world.

CONCLUSION

Thank you again for reading this book!

I hope this book was able to help you understand everything that an aspiring Buddhist should know about Buddhism, from the basic teachings of the Buddha to finding the Buddha within.

The next step is to apply this knowledge and steps to help you in becoming Buddhist — not just through philosophy but also through practice.

Do note that Buddhism is a philosophy that has now spanned across millennia, and with all the different traditions that have broken off the mainstream or simply added their own two cents in the meantime, the wisdom has grown incredibly wide. No one book will be able to teach you everything that is worth knowing about this fascinating product of human philosophy.

Luckily for you, not only do you not have to search for material on your own, but you also don't have to study on your own either. There are classes to be had and teachers of both theory and meditation to be hired in the vast majority of countries in the West, especially in the USA. The Vipassana Movement, which we mentioned recently, has a significant presence in the country, with a few prominent teachers and experts that are well-known among those who are interested in the religion.

The popularity of their insight-orientated meditational practices keeps growing since the 1980s. Some of the renowned centers are the Insight Meditation Society and Spirit Rock, while smaller ones exist as well and engage in various practices. Many Buddhist centers will provide courses in their religious practice in the form of a prolonged stay in a resort-type environment.

Whether you decide to partner up with other aspirants or not, it will be up to you to then implement all that you have learned and carry on by yourself.

Remember, the teachings of the Buddha are meant to be read and understood. But more importantly, they are meant to be lived.

Don't rush things. Continue this journey at your own pace and awaken to a state of Buddhahood in your own time.

As repeatedly mentioned throughout this book, take the teachings which suit you. Then, integrate them into your daily life as best as you can. As for the rest, leave them be.

I shall leave you with a quote from the great Buddha:

"There are two mistakes that a person can make on the road to truth. One is not going all the way. The other is not starting."

Finally, if you enjoyed this book, then I'd like to ask you for a favor, would you be kind enough to leave an honest review for this book on Amazon? It would be **greatly appreciated!**

Click here to leave a review for this book on Amazon!

Thank you and good luck,
Michael Williams

Don't forget to get your FREE Bonus Gift!

Thanks again for taking your time to read my book. I would also like for you to continue on your path to a more peaceful and enjoyable life, therefore I'm going to give you the **"Yoga For All: The Simple Guide To Yoga & Meditation"** e-book for FREE!

Go to **bit.ly/freebookyoga** to download the FREE e-book.

BUDDHISM

Beginner's Guide to Understanding & Practicing Buddhism to Become Stress and Anxiety Free

INTRODUCTION

Do you know that Buddhism is more popular now than it was half a century ago?

You can tell, based on the surge of books written about it as well as the increase in the number of Buddhist and Yoga schools, throughout the globe, notably in the west. You might even have noticed more people – from movie stars to athletes, your next-door neighbor to millionaire tycoons – that are incorporating such Buddhist practices as meditation into their everyday life.

However, many of the common questions about Buddhism remain unanswered. For instance, is it some sort of religion with its own rigid set of rules? Is it a carefree type of lifestyle? What is reincarnation? Is karma similar to fate?

If you are curious to know the answers, and if you want to learn more about Buddhism, especially with regard to becoming stress- and anxiety-free, then this book was written especially for you!

It is no secret that Buddhism is a complex topic. After all, the seed that the First Buddha planted almost three thousand years ago is now a massive tree that continues to branch out to this day. Nevertheless, this book can help you build a strong foundation for learning and practicing Buddhism.

All the fundamental questions asked by beginners are answered here, such as what Buddhism is and what its teachings are. Core subjects such as the Four Noble Truths and the Noble Eightfold Path are described clearly. Buddhist concepts such as Reincarnation, Nirvana, and Karma are also explained in a clear and concise way. Theories aside, you will also learn the practical side of Buddhism, specifically to help you achieve peace and relaxation each day.

This book is for anybody who is curious about Buddhism, particularly those who are considering it as their guide to a happy and purposeful life.

Now, the choice is yours. Clear the fog and begin your spiritual journey towards attaining peace of mind and clarity. The First Chapter awaits you!

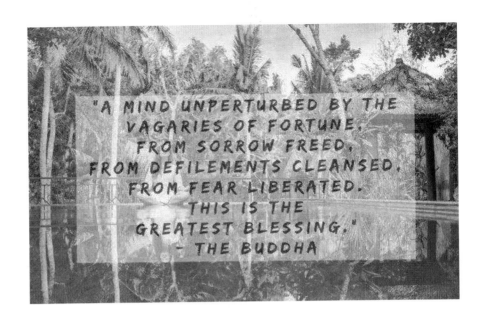

"A MIND UNPERTURBED BY THE VAGARIES OF FORTUNE, FROM SORROW FREED, FROM DEFILEMENTS CLEANSED, FROM FEAR LIBERATED. THIS IS THE GREATEST BLESSING." - THE BUDDHA

CHAPTER 1

WHAT IS BUDDHISM?

"A mind unperturbed by the vagaries of fortune, from sorrow freed, from defilements cleansed, from fear liberated — this is the greatest blessing."

— The Buddha

Hello! You must be the kind of person who is eager to learn new things every day. After all, why else would you choose this book?

You must be curious about Buddhism. You might have heard of it from somewhere, such as on social media or from a friend who is passionate about its teachings.

You might also have heard about the many ways it has helped those who find their true purpose in life, or – at the very least – find peace and calm in the midst of a seemingly fast-paced and stressful world.

A million questions might be swimming in your brain concerning Buddhism. In a while, they will be answered.

First, do take comfort in being here right now: reading this book and acquiring the knowledge that can help you find true happiness in everyday life.

One of the most essential teachings of Buddhism is an understanding that where you are at this moment is exactly where you are intended to be. As each moment passes, you are following your own course throughout life and enjoying and taking in each moment is paramount in creating a path of wisdom and understanding for yourself. Revel in each and every sentence, taking the time to fully understand what you are reading because in Buddhism every tale, every reading, and every teaching pave the way to more open, joyful, and enlightened path in life.

Look around you and notice how your body has naturally kept you alive. Your lungs continue to breathe without you having to tell it to do so. Your eyelids blink automatically to keep your eyes moist and protected. Your blood continues to flow underneath your skin, oblivious to your surroundings and thoughts.

Also, notice how you are able to comprehend the words on this page. Is that not something to be grateful? Take a moment to consider this thought.

Are you still here? Hopefully yes, because now let us answer what may be the first question in your mind: What is Buddhism?

What is Buddhism?

Would it surprise you to know that Buddhism is not a religion? At least, not in the sense wherein it is an institution that dictates how one should believe in a divine power.

In fact, there is no deity to be worshipped, although you might wonder why some seem to be worshipping the statues of the Buddha. While there indeed are those who worship his image (and erroneously so), true Buddhists merely pay respect to the memory of the Buddha. They neither worship nor pray to him. The Buddha himself is a guide and teacher for those that seek the path to enlightenment.

Many people who wake up each morning with the intention of practicing Buddhist teachings find inspiration from the gentle image of the Buddha. It is not unlike finding your motivation from the words of a successful person. His peaceful and meditative image can help you understand and remember the teachings you are following when life becomes stressful, and your mind begins to run off course.

Buddhism is a way of life that leads to the discernment of true reality. Its teachings center on developing your ability to be mindful of your thoughts, actions, and surroundings. All these lead to a life that is in tune with nature and your true self.

The practices of Buddhism – including meditation and yoga – are meant to help you unlearn your preconceived notions of yourself and the world. They serve as your guide towards embracing such qualities as kindness, love, true wisdom, and awareness.

Those who continually walk the path of Buddhism usually find themselves achieving the state of "perfect enlightenment." In other words, they become a "Buddha." A Buddha is a being who has been able to see the nature of life as it truly is. The enlightened being then continues to live life fully, all the while upholding the principles that are in line with this vision.

The idea of enlightenment can be broken down into two simple forms, the mind, and the self. The mind is that constant voice that has been molded and constructed based on the world around you in this life. Self is that inner being that is separate from the meat of your body and does not change based on any teachings or experiences that life brings you. Your real self is what can be understood to travel from life to life during reincarnation.

Each and every living being has the opportunity to become enlightened in each life they live. There is no set course or prewritten script for your life. As discussed later in this book, Karma plays a part in deciding the circumstances in which you will be born into from life to life, but your own spiritual and mental ambition are what drives each person to take one step closer to full enlightenment.

However, things get interesting here, because when you follow the path of Buddhism, you do not have an "end goal." It is a paradox for one to declare that they are going to practice Buddhism in order to reach enlightenment.

Who is The Buddha?

The word "Buddha" translates to "the enlightened one" or "the awakened being." It refers to any being who has achieved this state. However, you might be curious to know about the first Buddha.

According to legend, the first Buddha was named Siddhartha Gautama. Many believe that he was born around 563 B.C. in a land that is now found in Nepal. It is said that The Buddha was born a royal, shielded from the suffering of the kingdom of his father, who built a grand palace around him void of religion or human suffering. The King created an entire world inside those castle walls and, as he grew, led him to believe that the world was one of happiness, empathy, and joy. Later in his life, after he had married and was raised, he ventured out into the world and saw the truth of humanity. He met an old man and found that all people age, and eventually die.

At the age of twenty-nine, he found that neither his power nor his fortune brought him true happiness, and he wanted to understand the world outside of the palace walls.

Therefore, what he did was he set out to explore as many religions across the world to find the answer to the question that we all ask ourselves, "Where can one find happiness?"

Several years into his spiritual pilgrimage, the Buddha discovered "The Middle Path" while meditating under the Bodhi tree. This path is a way of balance, not of extremism, which he found only through trial and error. He sat for days under that Bodhi tree seeking the answers he had initially set out to find. During this meditation, Siddhartha had to face the evil demon known as Mara, who threatened to stand in the way of his Buddha status. He looked to the earth for guidance and the land answered by banishing Mara and allowing Siddhartha to reach full enlightenment. Such discernments led him to achieve the perfect state of enlightenment. After this life-changing experience, the Buddha then lived the rest of his days sharing what he discovered. The followers of the Buddha's teachings called his principles the *Dharma*, or "Truth."

It is thought that Buddha, or anyone who reaches the state of perfect enlightenment in their lifetime, no longer continues on the circle of rebirth. Instead, the Buddha is thought to sit outside of constant reincarnation and sends teachings and guidance to those searching for their own freedom of self. They no longer have to sit through what Buddhists believe to be an endless cycle of suffering known as life.

When you hear the word suffering, you may have images of pain and anger, come into your mind, but in Buddhism, they believe that all life is suffering. As humans, we feel the pain of loss, the emotions of sadness, happiness, disappointment, and so on. These emotions are manifestations of our mind, and they do not come from our inner selves. Because they do not come from our true self, they are thought of as suffering. False feelings created by the meat of our brains, programmed into us by what our societal view has taught.

Currently, Buddhism is increasingly becoming a popular way of life for millions of people, across the world. Even those in the Western countries seek to follow The Middle Path because they find that it speaks to their heart.

In a world where everything is always in motion, constantly forcing us to move forward at a quicker and more rapid pace, many people feel the loss of their connection with nature. Though nature is all around us, even, in the major cities, what we have done to change the pure form of earth, creates a disconnect from our minds. In Buddhism, you are connected to every natural thing in this world, and by practicing the teachings of it, you are brought back to that connection. This is an enormous draw for millions of people all over the world. You can think of it as connecting back to your roots.

Another reason why Buddhism is widespread is the fact that the Buddha never claimed to be a god. Instead, he was a teacher who shared his wisdom based on his own discernment and experiences in life. This lack of an invisible deity often speaks to those that cannot find solace or belief in other religions where God is their governing body. Though there are many tales and teachings in Buddhism, there is no one holy book such as a Bible or Quran. Instead, the "bible" of Buddhism can be found in every natural effect on the planet, from the leaves on the trees to the worms in the ground. They are the story of the past, but you don't need to look to the past to find enlightenment, you need to look at every moment that you experience.

Moreover, the belief system of Buddhism is one that can be described as "large-minded." This means that those who practice it are open to accepting the moral teachings of other belief systems. Therefore, they

94

are unconcerned with labels that pertain to specific religions, such as "Catholic," "Baptist," "Hindu," "Muslim," or even "Buddhist" itself. It is not uncommon to find those of different religious background meditating together at various Buddhist centers, especially in the western world. Enlightenment, in Buddhism, is not based on who you believe created you, but rather by opening your mind enough to allow yourself to shine through. Once that is reached, all the answers you seek on creation will be known to you. Therefore, your title of faith is of no concern, though, those that strive for enlightenment do usually find themselves identifying as Buddhist or other similar namesakes.

Buddhists neither seek an expansion of an organization nor attempt to convince others of a certain belief. Instead, they only provide an explanation if asked. The Buddha encourages one to be curious through awareness; therefore, Buddhism can be regarded more as a way of life based on discernment rather than faith.

Though Buddhism as a practice can bend and move on a scale depending on your dedication to the teachings and heritage, anyone can practice the Buddhist way of living. There is always an extreme importance put on the word empathy, throughout the teachings of Buddhas through the generations. Empathy is not just reserved for humans, but for every living creature of this world.

At this point, you must be eager to learn the different teachings of the Buddha. Keep in mind that the Buddha's teachings are vast to such an extent that it grew into many different types of Buddhism. These teachings can bring wisdom to anyone, whether seeking to find their true self through enlightenment, or those that just wish to understand the world around them a little bit better. These teachings are for the young and old alike, regardless of religion, status, gender, or heritage.

However, let us not get ahead of ourselves. For now, you can explore more about the teachings of Buddhism, which you can conveniently find in the next chapter. Before you do turn the page, though, please do remember the advice of the Buddha himself. It is to take care not to take his word for it but to test for yourself his teachings. Only by doing so would you then be able to find the true meaning of his words.

95

To check out the rest of the book that has been read by 10's of thousands of other people, simply search for the title below on Amazon or go to: **bit.ly/Buddhism2**

Buddhism: *Beginner's Guide to Understanding & Practicing Buddhism to Become Stress and Anxiety Free*

Check Out My Other Books

Below you'll find my other books that are popular on Amazon and Kindle as well. Simply enter the name of the books in the search bar on Amazon to check them out. Alternatively, you can visit my author page on Amazon to see other work done by me.

For my authorpage, go to: **bit.ly/AuthorWilliams**

- ***Chakras For Beginners*** *– How to Awaken And Balance Chakras, Radiate Positive Energy And Heal Yourself*

- ***Chakras for Beginners*** *- Awaken Your Internal Energy and Learn to Radiate Positive Energy and Start Healing*

- **Mindfulness for Beginners** - *How to Live in The Present, Stress and Anxiety Free*

- **Mindfulness:** *An Eight-Step Guide to Finding Peace and Removing Negativity From Your Everyday Life*

- **Mindfulness For Beginners** - *How to Relieve Stress and Anxiety Like a Buddhist Monk and Live In the Present Moment In Your Everyday Life*

- **Yoga For Men:** *Beginner's Step by Step Guide to a Stronger Body & Sharper Mind*

- **Empath:** *How to Stop Worrying and Eliminate Negative Thinking as a Sensitive Person*

- **ZEN:** *Beginner's Guide to Understanding & Practicing Zen Meditation to Become Present*

Resources:

https://www.thebuddhagarden.com/how-convert-buddhism.html

https://buddhists.org/a-monks-life/converting-to-buddhism/

http://viewonbuddhism.org/refuge.html

http://www.samyeling.org/buddhism-and-meditation/teaching-archive-2/choje-akong-tulku-rinpoche/the-meaning-of-taking-refuge/

https://blog.sivanaspirit.com/buddhism-and-hinduism/

http://www.historyworld.net/wrldhis/PlainTextHistories.asp?historyid=ab77

http://www.preservearticles.com/2011091613505/analyse-the-similarities-and-differences-between-jainism-and-buddhism.html

https://www.tofugu.com/japan/bowing-in-japan/

https://www.biography.com/people/buddha-9230587

https://chantamantra.com/index.php/articles/38-18-ways-to-create-good-karma

https://fpmt.org/wp-content/uploads/sites/2/2007/04/12_ways_to_create_good_karma.pdf?x25788

https://buddhism.stackexchange.com/questions/17871/is-karma-different-for-accidental-killing-than-intentional-killing

http://www.katinkahesselink.net/tibet/jatakas.html

http://www.buddha-images.com/10jatakas.asp

https://www.near-death.com/religion/buddhism/tibetan-book-of-the-dead.html

http://religion.oxfordre.com/view/10.1093/acrefore/9780199340378.001.0001/acrefore-9780199340378-e-200

http://www.buddhanet.net/4noble.htm

http://viewonbuddhism.org/4_noble_truths.html

https://tricycle.org/magazine/noble-eightfold-path/

The Bases of Human Sexual Attraction

The Bases of Human Sexual Attraction

Edited by

MARK COOK

1981

ACADEMIC PRESS

A Subsidiary of Harcourt Brace Jovanovich, Publishers

London   New York   Toronto   Sydney   San Francisco

ACADEMIC PRESS INC. (LONDON) LTD.
24/28 Oval Road
London NW1

United States Edition published by
ACADEMIC PRESS INC.
111 Fifth Avenue
New York, New York 10003

British Library Cataloguing in Publication Data
The Bases of human sexual attraction.
1. Sex
I. Cook, M.
155.3   HQ21

ISBN 0-12-187220-3

LCCCN 81-66378

Typeset in England by Dobbie Typesetting Service, Plymouth, Devon and printed by T.J. Press (Padstow) Ltd., Padstow, Cornwall

Contributors

ROXANNE M. ANDERSON, *Family Social Science, University of Minnesota, 290 McNeal Hall, 1985 Buford Avenue, St Paul, Minnesota 55108, USA*

DONN BYRNE, *Department of Psychology, State University of New York at Albany, 1400 Washington Avenue, Albany, New York 12222, USA*

MARK COOK, *Department of Psychology, University College of Swansea, Singleton Park, Swansea SA2 8PP, Wales*

KAREN K. DION, *Division of Life Sciences, Scarborough College, University of Toronto, West Hill, Ontario M1C 1A4, Canada*

WILLIAM A. FISHER, *Department of Psychology, Faculty of Social Science, University of Western Ontario, London, Ontario N6A 5C2, Canada*

CHRIS GOSSELIN, *Department of Psychology, Institute of Psychiatry, De Crespigny Park, Denmark Hill, London SE5 8AF, England*

ROM HARRÉ, *Sub-Faculty of Philosophy, 10 Merton Street, Oxford OX1 4JJ, England*

AUBREY MANNING, *Department of Zoology, University of Edinburgh, West Mains Road, Edinburgh EH9 3JT, Scotland*

B. I. MURSTEIN, *Department of Psychology, Connecticut College, New London, Connecticut 06320, USA*

RICHARD REARDON, *Institute for Behaviour Research, University of Georgia, 624 Graduate Studies Research Centre, Athens, Georgia 30602, USA*

PAUL C. ROSENBLATT, *Family Social Science, University of Minnesota, 290 McNeal Hall, 1985 Buford Avenue, St Paul, Minnesota 55108, USA*

ABRAHAM TESSER, *Institute for Behaviour Research, University of Georgia, 624 Graduate Studies Research Centre, Athens, Georgia 30602, USA*

Preface

Our awareness of all aspects of human sexuality has increased dramatically over the last dozen years. In the early 1960s psychology had little to say on the subject, unless one counted psychoanalytic speculation, or research on animals. Ford and Beach's classic *Patterns of Sexual Behaviour* contained far more information about the sexual behaviour of South Sea Islanders than about Western Europe or North America. Yet a start had been made, and the Kinsey reports had documented the frequency of sexual contacts of American men and women. Further initiatives came from the work of Ellen Berscheid and Elaine Walster on physical attractiveness, and the extensive research programme of Donn Byrne on attraction in general. Throughout the 1970s a flood of surveys, experiments and reviews came out of British and North American universities, followed by several book length reviews of the topic, including one by Cook and McHenry (1978).

So extensive has our knowledge of this field become, that the need for a different type of book has arisen — one that will examine a number of issues in the study of human sexual attraction in greater depth, rather than offer a general review. This book therefore sets out to study key issues in human sexual attraction, and falls into three main sections. Section A — Aspects of Attractiveness — is concerned with relatively specific issues. The first two issues selected for treatment in depth are familiar ones: the relationship between attitudes and sexual behaviour, analysed by William Fisher and Donn Byrne, and the relationship between sexual behaviour and appearance, analysed by Karen Dion. The third contribution by Chris Gosselin analyses an issue not previously researched — attraction in persons with "special sexual desires", namely a group of fetishists and sado-masochists.

Then follow three chapters in Section B — Models of Attraction — each dealing with the whole process of sexual attraction, but from differing perspectives. Abraham Tesser and Richard Reardon consider the cognitive and perceptual mechanisms involved; Bernard Murstein traces the stages of development of the typical relationship; the section I contribute analyses sexual attraction as a form of social skill.

Finally Section C contains three chapters looking at human sexual

attraction in a broader context. Paul Rosenblatt and Roxanne Anderson extend the study of sexual attraction beyond the narrow limits of the North American or North European college student to consider how it works for the whole of the human race. Rom Harré examines sexual relations from an "ethogenic" dramaturgical viewpoint, and Aubrey Manning offers a balanced view of what can and cannot be concluded about human sexual behaviour from the study of animal sexual behaviour, to counteract the excesses of naked ape-ism and sociobiology.

These various contributions will, it is hoped, give the reader some idea of the depth of knowledge of some aspects of human sexual attraction gained over the last 10-15 years, as well as some indication of the amount still left to be learned.

I would like to thank the contributors for producing such useful contributions so quickly, Academic Press for undertaking to publish them, and my wife for her patience while I have been working on this and other books.

February 1981   *Mark Cook*
Swansea

Cook, M. and McHenry, R. (1978). *Sexual Attraction*. Pergamon: Oxford.

Contents

Section A
ASPECTS OF ATTRACTION

1
Physical Attractiveness, Sex Roles and Heterosexual Attraction

KAREN K. DION

*Division of Life Sciences, Scarborough College,
University of Toronto, West Hill, Ontario, Canada*

During the past decade, the relation of an individual's physical appearance (specifically his or her physical attractiveness) to various interpersonal processes has received considerable research attention. One of the major issues which has been explored to date concerns the impact of attractiveness on heterosexual attraction. The present chapter examines this issue from the perspective of both traditional sex roles and some of the changing sex role patterns which have recently emerged. Most of the studies to be discussed were carried out in the context of contemporary North American society.

Attractiveness and Social-Sexual Development

During childhood, there is evidence that attractiveness is generally positively related to popularity with peers (Dion and Berscheid, 1974; Kleck *et al.*, 1974). Since the predominant pattern of peer interaction from early childhood to preadolescence has involved association with same-sex peers, relatively little research has focused on early heterosexual interaction. However, Broderick (1966) assessed attitudes toward opposite-sex peers in a large sample of middle-class children and adolescents and found that social–sexual development progressed gradually through a series of stages. Even during the late childhood phase of segregation into same-sex cliques (10-11 years old), a number of children expressed interest in opposite-sex peers. This interest mostly seemed to reflect a child's wishes and fantasies since the chosen

"boyfriend" or "girlfriend" was not necessarily informed (or even aware) that he or she was the focus of another's attention. In contrast, by the age of 14 or 15 an adolescent's choice seemed to become more realistic, involving the expectation of reciprocal feelings. By 16-17 years of age, the childhood segregation into same-sex friendship groups had disappeared, and female–male pairs became an important unit for the formation of social cliques.

Little is known about the impact of attractiveness during the transition period described by Broderick (1966). Conceivably, the basis for the "matching effect" found among young adults may be formed during this phase of heterosexual development. There is now considerable support for the matching hypothesis which suggests that, for the most part, both young men and young women choose a heterosexual partner whose level of physical attractiveness is similar to their own. Evidence supporting this hypothesis has been found in laboratory studies of dating choice (Berscheid *et al.*, 1971), in research conducted in field settings (Silverman, 1971) and among couples who were engaged or seeing each other exclusively (Murstein, 1972). The dynamics behind this effect may well emerge in early adolescence as an individual becomes increasingly aware of and sensitive about his or her physical attributes and the relative likelihood of attracting a specific potential partner.

Adolescence brings about special concerns which are related to perceived attractiveness since during this period of physical change, attention is focused on the body. Furthermore, the adolescent becomes increasingly aware of the social norms for appearance which are mediated through his/her peer group. To be different from one's peers is a sign of inferiority from the adolescent's perspective (Schonfeld, 1969; Dwyer and Mayer, 1976). A major preoccupation during this period of time concerns the "sex-appropriateness" of one's physical development. Writers spanning several decades have stressed this issue as one of focal concern during adolescence (Stolz and Stolz, 1944; Schonfeld, 1969; Dwyer and Mayer, 1976). For example, Stolz and Stolz (1944) in a longitudinal study of adolescent development found that nearly a third of the boys and two-fifths of the girls expressed concern about some feature of their development over a period of eight years. Specific areas of concern focused on skin problems, deviations in general body size, and facial features. Of particular interest however were the sex differences which emerged in these data. Stolz and Stolz stated that for the girls in their sample, "the sexually appropriate" pattern of development was quite different from what the authors referred to as the "healthy" or the

"functionally effective" pattern (p. 92), with many young women stating they would rather appear "exotic" than healthy. While interest in an "exotic" appearance *per se* may well have been specific to a particular era, more recent research suggests that for adolescent girls physical appearance continues to be a salient concern, resulting in sensitivity to this particular dimension, while males seem to be more disturbed by critical comments about physical performance or capability (Dwyer and Mayer, 1976).

As an example of a more recent investigation, differences in males versus females were also found in a study by Simmons and Rosenberg (1975) in which slightly over 1900 children and youths from two racial groups were interviewed concerning various facets of their self-image. The sample was interviewed in the late sixties (as the authors note, prior to the salience of the Women's Liberation Movement). During late childhood few sex differences were found on various components of self-image. However, by early adolescence, girls from both racial groups showed more problems with their self-image than their male counterparts — a difference that increased for white but not black girls during late adolescence. Furthermore, by adolescence, more males indicated more favourable attitudes towards their own sex. Of particular relevance for the present chapter, subjects were also asked about their own physical attractiveness. Appearance seemed to create the greatest difficulty for white girls during adolescence, especially late adolescence, when they were compared to either white boys or black girls. More members of this subgroup found themselves in the painful situation of being very concerned but at the same time less satisfied with their personal appearance. Among the black adolescents the sex differences were relatively small regarding attitudes towards one's own physical appearance. The authors feel this pattern of findings shows that the opportunities provided to the white girls are a function of her sex role, which stresses "interpersonal skills", whereas the male role focuses on "future opportunity". They note that the traditional cultural emphasis on female attractiveness, combined with the greater dissatisfaction concerning one's own appearance found among white female adolescents, would presumably leave this group more susceptible to peers' opinions, resulting in a somewhat more vulnerable self-image. Simmons and Rosenberg (1975) suggested that the black girls have a wider range of options, including the expectation that they will get a job. If so, the sex-role options for this group more closely resemble those typically associated with males.

A related analysis of the dilemma faced by the white adolescent girls can also be found in data collected by Poveda (1975), again during the late sixties. He attempted to determine the major social types present in a secondary school population, and subsequently interpreted the findings using a role model of social identity developed by Sarbin. One key feature of Sarbin's model involves the distinction between "ascribed" versus "achieved" social roles. The former role is occupied as a function of one's membership in a particular social system; little or no choice of this role takes place (for example, age roles, kinship roles). In contrast the latter type of role involves considerably more choice such as occupation, club membership, etc. In this analysis, the type of evaluation that an individual receives for fulfilling role obligations varies depending on where a particular role is located on the ascribed–achieved dimension. Achieved roles, in contrast to ascribed roles, evoke very positive evaluations for successful performance. Little credit is given to the individual for ascribed role behaviour since it is presumably expected, but strong criticism is elicited if a person does *not* fulfil the demands of an ascribed role. Following this analysis, and in light of the social types identified by his respondents, Poveda speculated that the reputation of the adolescent girl was largely based on her performance of one role, her "female social role" — which he classifies as an ascribed role, while adolescent boys appear to have a reputation as a function of achieved roles, which might take various forms. Furthermore, cross-sex relations formed a crucial component of an adolescent female's reputation with same-sex peers; but they were not as directly relevant for males. Girls' peer groups relied heavily on social control through various social cliques; thus an adolescent girl's reputation appeared to be largely a matter of information or rumour circulated about her. An adolescent boy's reputation in contrast appeared to be based much more on various behaviours which could be publicly observed or validated. In this respect his reputation among peers rested on a more autonomous foundation.

This differential emphasis on the significance of physical attractiveness for young women compared to their male peers continues to appear in the literature concerning development in late adolescence and early adulthood. As an example, in one investigation (Berscheid *et al.*, 1971) when young women were asked to rank in order appearance, personality and intelligence as to their relative importance in attracting male peers, the more physically attractive a woman was (as assessed by peer ratings), the more likely she was to indicate that her personal appearance was an important attribute in attracting men. Men however did not show this

relation; i.e. attractive men did not necessarily stress their appearance as a particularly important attribute. This contrast suggests an important sex difference in self-attribution regarding attractiveness. Attributing success in heterosexual relations to external appearance might well result in less favourable self-evaluations, at least *vis-à-vis* male peers of comparable attractiveness.

Several studies have examined the interrelation between satisfaction with one's body and other non-physical aspects of the self. A pattern of sex differences has emerged in various studies. In one investigation, satisfaction with these two components of self was significantly correlated for young women but not for young men (Berscheid *et al.*, 1971). Lerner *et al.* (1973) found a positive relation between a body satisfaction index and a self-evaluation scale for both women and men, with the correlation for women somewhat, though not significantly, higher than that for men. In another investigation (Lerner and Karabenick, 1974) a significant positive correlation was found between perceived attractiveness (based on the self-assessment of various body features) and self-evaluation for women, but not for men. Finally Lerner *et al.* (1974) asked university men and women to rate a series of body characteristics for both their attractiveness *vis-à-vis* heterosexual relations and for their effectiveness in general functioning. These two components were related for men and women. However, this correlation was higher for men than for women. Furthermore, the pattern of intercorrelations between attractiveness ratings, effectiveness ratings and self-evaluation (based on a short series of bipolar adjectives), suggested that the attractiveness ratings might be a more important correlate of self-evaluation for women, while the effectiveness ratings might be more important for men.

Finally, it appears that although young men and women agree that the most important contributors to physical attractiveness are general appearance, the face, weight distribution and general body build (Lerner *et al.*, 1973), males have stressed the importance of the attractiveness of their partners more than women (Miller and Rivenbark, 1970; Berscheid *et al.*, 1971).

Attractiveness and Social Skills: Beliefs and Behaviour

As a general cue in social encounters, an individual's physical attractiveness influences impressions formed of him or her. Many of the dimensions affected by this variable are relevant in the context of

heterosexual interaction. Dion *et al.* (1972), presented both male and female subjects with photographs of stimulus persons who were high, medium or low in physical attractiveness. Subjects were asked to rate the stimulus persons on a variety of traits, as well as to predict relevant life outcomes for them (e.g. occupational success, marriage, etc.). An "accuracy set" was used in this study; i.e. subjects were told that the investigators wished to compare the person perception accuracy of untrained university students with two other groups — graduate students in clinical psychology, and clinicians. The stimulus persons were ostensibly students at another university participating in a longitudinal study of personality development. Hence it would presumably be possible to check the validity of subjects' inferences. These instructions were devised to minimize the possibility that subjects would simply reproduce general stereotypes which they might not personally subscribe to. In essence the instructions were designed to work against subjects' tendencies to stereotype on the basis of appearance.

The results of the study indicated that a very positive general stereotype emerged which favoured highly attractive stimulus persons of both sexes. Subjects, both male and female, inferred that attractive persons possessed more socially desirable personalities than those of lesser attractiveness. The social desirability index included traits indicative of social skills relevant to heterosexual relations (sociable, poised, sophisticated, sexually warm) and traits referring to general interpersonal relations (e.g. altruistic, kind, genuine, modest). Subjects also inferred that attractive persons would be more competent spouses and have happier marriages than those of lesser attractiveness. Finally, attractive individuals were expected to lead more personally fulfilling lives and be more successful occupationally than less attractive individuals. The only dimension where attractive individuals were not expected to excel was as parents; indeed they were rated somewhat lower on this dimension than the other two groups, though the difference was not significant. No sex differences occurred in the Dion *et al.* study; attractive stimulus persons received favourable ratings from same- or opposite-sex raters, and the attractiveness stereotype did not differ as a function of the stimulus person's sex.

A study by Miller (1970) however did find interactions between the sex and the attractiveness of the stimulus person. Subjects in this study were asked to record their impressions of the stimulus person using an adjective preference scale, which consisted of 17 dimensions, each dimension containing ten pairs of bipolar adjectives in a forced choice

format. Differences were found at all three levels of attractiveness as a function of the sex of the stimulus person. Perhaps most interesting was the pattern of results at the "unattractive" level; both men and women rated unattractive males as more perceptive, curious, complex, and assertive than unattractive females. In other words it appears that unattractive males fared better on at least some dimensions than their female counterparts. The Miller study also found evidence, however, that a generally favourable set of personal traits was attributed to highly attractive people of both sexes. At the high attractiveness level, there were relatively few significant differences between male and female stimulus persons. The number of differences as a function of sex considerably increased at the medium and low level of attractiveness. In the light of this trend, Miller suggested that sex may be a more important determinant of initial impressions as one moves away from the high attractiveness level.

It is of interest to note that this set of expectations about attractive versus unattractive young men and women appears to have a long developmental history. Evidence for a set of stereotyped beliefs based on attractiveness has been found very early in childhood. Dion (1973) presented children with photographs of children they did not know personally, preselected for facial attractiveness. Pre-school subjects expressed a preference for both attractive males and females as potential friends and a corresponding rejection of unattractive children of both sexes. Furthermore, subjects inferred more frequently that attractive children were more likely to be friendly, to not like fighting or shouting and to refrain from hitting someone even if hit first. Unattractive children were seen as more likely to hit without reason, to hurt other children and to scare their peers than attractive children. No associations occurred between sex of subject or sex of stimulus person and choice of attractive versus unattractive peer for most of the items. At the conclusion of each session subjects were asked what it meant to be *pretty* or *cute*. Although these data were obviously descriptive, some distinctive patterns appeared in the type of response given by girls and boys, particularly among the older pre-schoolers. For example, girls often gave more lengthy and detailed responses than boys. Also, some of the girls' comments indicated considerable awareness of the assets associated with an attractive appearance, as illustrated in the following statement made by one pre-school girl: "It's to be the best girl in the world . . . to be a princess; everyone loves you".

In summary, there is now considerable evidence supporting the

existence of a system of beliefs and expectations about the personal characteristics of persons who differ in physical attractiveness. The evidence is particularly strong and consistent on dimensions which reflect social skills and interpersonal ease. On these dimensions, such as sociability and pleasantness, attractive individuals are regarded more favourably than less attractive persons.

Indeed there is some evidence that at least in the context of initial heterosexual encounters, attractive individuals may in fact actually be more socially skilful. Goldman and Lewis (1977) asked young adults to talk to three opposite sex peers (for 5 min) and after each telephone conversation, to rate their partner on several dimensions, including social skill. The subject's physical attractiveness was rated independently by three observers. For both men and women, physical attractiveness (as judged by observer ratings) and partners' assessment of social skills were positively related.

Another recent study also provides evidence that young adults who differ in attractiveness differ on various traits which are relevant to social skills. In this investigation (Krebs and Adinolfi, 1975), a large sample of first year students had completed several personality inventories, and the subject sample to be studied was chosen based on the sociometric ratings of peers (specifically, same-sex dorm-mates) after two months residence on campus. Four groups were identified — accepted, rejected, isolated and controls (those receiving an average number of nominations), and members of each group completed various personality measures. Attractiveness ratings were made from high school graduation photographs. Contrary to the pattern which might have been expected, the rejected group received the highest attractiveness ratings followed by the accepted, control and isolated groups respectively.

Factor analysis of the personality ratings and subsequent analysis of factor scores for the four groups helped to clarify these findings. Both young men and women in the rejected (and most physically attractive) group scored higher than the other groups on a dimension which Krebs and Adinolfi labelled "independent ambitiousness". In addition, the rejected female group scored relatively low on the need for "affectionate sociability", while in contrast, the group which was the most popular with their peers (the second most attractive group) received the highest scores on this dimension. In the isolated (and least physically attractive) group, the women received high scores on "passive withdrawal"; the males scored high on "ascetic asociability". The authors argued that, in the isolated group, the women seemed to be in more emotional difficulty

than the men at least in terms of being "more constricted, defensive and withdrawn" (Krebs and Adinolfi, 1975, p. 250). When considering these findings, it is important to keep in mind that the peer popularity ratings were made by same-sex peers, thus, as noted by the authors, a jealousy interpretation cannot be ruled out. The most attractive group seems to have been composed of assertive and autonomous individuals who did not rely on their immediate peer group for support or nurturance. This autonomy however did not preclude all types of social relationships. For example, physical attractiveness was correlated positively with one index of heterosexual popularity (number of dates on three formal social occasions) for the women but not for the men. The second most attractive group (which was popular with same-sex peers) appeared to fit most closely with the characterization of the attractive young adult, viz., sociable and approachable. This group was also rated higher in appearance than the controls. Finally, the least physically attractive group of young adults appears to have been ignored by their peers rather than actively rejected. Considering that same-sex peers were making the sociometric ratings, this group might not only have difficulty in heterosexual encounters but even in casual interaction with peers in general, resulting in less ease and skill in social interaction.

The data from the Krebs and Adinolfi study, and the Goldman and Lewis findings discussed earlier, suggest that the more physically attractive young adult may in fact be more socially skilled than his or her less attractive counterpart. There is also evidence that this differential advantage may have its origins very early in childhood. Dion (1977) found that facial attractiveness *per se* appears to have reward properties for young children (three to five-year-old age group). Peers might therefore be more likely to approach more attractive children initially, and they might also be willing to interact for longer periods with more attractive children. If so, an attractive child would be in a more favourable position to develop early on skills in peer interaction.

Examining the role which attractiveness seems to play in social–sexual development from late childhood on, there may well be both common effects and some marked discrepancies in its impact on young men and women. In the light of the research evidence reviewed, it might not be accurate to argue that attractiveness is only relevant for the social experience of women. Instead it is more heuristic to examine the meaning of the attractiveness variable in the total context of heterosexual relations and prevailing sex roles. From this perspective, attractiveness may be viewed as an important dimension for both sexes which, however, functions quite differently for each sex.

For men, attractiveness may function as a facilitative cue from childhood into early adulthood. The attractiveness stereotype leads to a set of expectations of general social skills, thus a generally favourable set of favourable attitudes from peers can be expected. At the same time, because of the performance expectations of the prevailing male sex-role, the individual is given credit for various accomplishments independently of the attractiveness dimension. In other words the male reaps a double benefit, he possesses a highly desirable personal characteristic but is not explicitly valued for it. For the young man, attractiveness may facilitate the development of competence in heterosexual interaction while still enabling the individual to feel that his personal successes are due to his own skills.

For the young woman, attractiveness would also be expected to facilitate the development of skilful interpersonal behaviour. However, during adolescence and into adulthood, attractiveness itself is a pivotal variable for the traditional female role, creating more ambiguity in heterosexual encounters. Thus, although she may possess a considerable degree of social competence, the attractive young woman may be subjectively less confident than her attractive male counterpart if she cannot as easily interpret the reasons underlying others' responses to her as reflecting an assessment of her skills and capabilities.

It is possible that physical attractiveness accentuates sex-role expectations for both sexes (Dion, 1974). In social systems where physical attractiveness is valued, attractive individuals may be expected to embody the cultural ideal for the sexes. If this is indeed the case, it might be expected that periods of sex-role ambiguity, change, or transition may result in particular stresses on attractive individuals. Accordingly, during the present period in contemporary North American society, the dilemma outlined in the preceding paragraph should be more acute for the attractive young woman who finds herself somewhere between the traditional male role, where attractiveness seems to function covertly and the traditional female role where attractiveness is overtly acknowledged as salient.

Sexuality and Attractiveness

In the subsequent section of this chapter, the interrelation between physical attractiveness, perceived sexuality and actual sexual experience will be examined. Considering the cross-cultural literature, Frumkin (1961) suggested that there appear to be certain universal aspects of

beauty, viz., health and youth — both of which are linked to sexuality. One might well therefore expect physical attractiveness and sexual attractiveness to be highly related. Consistent with this expectation, an unpublished study by Cavior *et al.* found that ratings of physical attractiveness and sexual appeal made by opposite sex peers (in the context of a sensitivity training lab) were quite highly correlated both at the beginning of the session (first impression) and at the end of the training session, after several hours of group interaction. The authors noted however that despite this correlation, the two variables seemed to reflect different dimensions, since certain facets of interpersonal communication during the session were related to judgements of attractiveness but not sexual appeal. Furthermore, the ratings for perceived sexuality showed greater variability than did the attractiveness ratings. Cavior and his colleagues concluded that measures of both variables might profitably be used in research on interpersonal attraction.

In the preceding section it was argued that while physical attractiveness is a significant dimension for both women and men, its impact differs as a function of prevailing sex-roles. The relation between physical attractiveness and perceived sexuality can also be viewed from this perspective. Traditionally, in North American society and other Western social systems, markedly different orientations toward male and female sexuality have existed. For example, Udry (1974) has noted that, at least in the context of North American society, these differences in orientation reflect distinct male and female subcultures which have a strong influence on an individual from childhood to early adulthood. With regard to sexuality, an adolescent male gains considerable status among his peers as a function of his sexual knowledge and presumed ability, and this emphasis continues into early adulthood, since sexual activity forms an important part of perceived masculinity. As Udry observes, during their early sexual experiences, young males appear to be interested in sex rather than girls, with little concern for, or awareness of, their partners' experience. In the view of the traditional male subculture, sex is something boys "do to" girls; thus girls let boys "have sex". Berg (1975) similarly notes that sexual technique, specifically finding the "right" technique, has been stressed in the male subculture. In contrast the chief preoccupation of the female in the traditional subculture has been to be sexually attractive to males, with the ultimate aim of marriage. Thus the ability to attract males based on physical characteristics has been a major preoccupation of the North American female subculture.

Udry notes that in the extreme form stated above, male and female

subcultures appear to be less powerful as cultural institutions than formerly. He cites factors such as stress on male–female companionship, earlier dating, marriage of age-peers, and co-education as contributing to the decline of the traditional sex subcultures in the United States. Presumably therefore, the contrasting views of sexuality described earlier might also be expected to have similarly declined, with the emergence of cross-sex friendships at an earlier period of development and the stress on a single standard of sexual behaviour for men and women. Some findings reported in the mid-seventies however suggest that aspects of the traditional sexual subculture may not in fact have altered appreciably among young adolescents. For example, Berg found that young adolescent males continued to assess girls' personal appeal on the basis of their physical characteristics and perceived sexuality, leading the author to conclude that while "the line has changed, the dating game remains relatively unchanged" (Berg, 1975, p. 544).

It has been suggested that in a wide variety of cultural contexts, physical attractiveness is more critical for females than for males as a determinant of perceived sexuality. Ford and Beach (1951), in their classic cross-cultural study of sexual behaviour, stated that a man's sexual attractiveness was largely attributable to "his skills and prowess", instead of his appearance *per se* (p. 86), while for a woman sexual attractiveness seemed to be defined in terms of physical characteristics, though the particular features valued varied across cultures. Frumkin (1961) too stated that "strength and health" rather than "handsome features" seemed to be more important for assessing males' sexual attractiveness (p. 218). Presumably "male beauty or handsomeness must be translated into function;" i.e. qualities such as courage or strength (Frumkin, 1961, p. 218). The cross-cultural generality of these differences warrants further empirical examination considering some of the problems encountered in interpreting ethnographic data pertaining to sexual attitudes and behaviour (see Rosenblatt and Anderson's chapter in this volume for discussion of this issue).

As noted earlier however, at least in some Western social systems, including North America, sexual assertiveness and sexual activity have formed an important part of perceived masculinity. Conceivably therefore sexual attractiveness and general physical attractiveness may not be as highly correlated for males compared to females, since the norms for masculinity stress sexual performance. Sexual attractiveness might be largely assessed on the basis of features which connote strength, vigour, stamina, fitness, etc., whether these are facial features or body

build. Following this line of argument, a male would be viewed as sexually less attractive, not because of imperfect physical features *per se*, but because of features which do not sufficiently connote the qualities listed above. Presumably therefore a man should be less likely to be concerned with facial irregularities. Paradoxically certain physically unattractive men might still be considered sexually attractive, depending on whether the gestalt of physical features is consistent with the dimensions described above. Thus physical appearance would not necessarily be irrelevant for a male's sexual attractiveness but instead the physical criteria for determining perceived sexuality would be based on features relevant to the male sex-role.

Turning now to the relation between attractiveness and perceived sexuality for women, as previously mentioned, physical attractiveness *per se* is valued as part of the traditional female sex-role and furthermore, one of the primary functions of female attractiveness is heterosexual attraction. The particular physical features stressed viz., facial appearance and overall body build (Lerner *et al.*, 1973), seem to have been emphasized for several centuries in Western cultural tradition. A similarity between contemporary criteria for women's attractiveness in North American and British society, and ideals of beauty traceable to the mediaeval period in Western history has been noted (Frumkin, 1961; Ligget, 1974). This emphasis on facial features and general form as defining criteria for female attractiveness is illustrated by an analysis of Middle English literature by Curry (1972). According to Curry the ideal female type was common to much of mediaeval literature. By mediaeval criteria a beautiful woman was

> without an exception, a blonde, whose hair is golden or like gold wine, eyes sparkling bright and light blue in color . . . red lips, white evenly set teeth . . . . Her figure is small, well-rounded, slender and graceful, with a small willowy waist . . . . The skin is everywhere of dazzling whiteness, rivaling the finest silk in softness. (1972, p. 3)

References to explicit sexual features were almost non-existent. As Curry notes in his survey of ideals of mediaeval beauty, "even when the fair one is seen nude, the natural delicacy of the poet prevents him from giving more than information concerning the whiteness of the skin, and the general loveliness of the limbs" (p. 117). In contrast to this rather ethereal description of female sexual attractiveness in mediaeval literature, accounts taken from other cultural settings have included reference to sexual characteristics more explicitly (cf. Ford and Beach, 1951). Considering this variability, the specific features stressed in a

16   *Karen K. Dion*

particular society's definition of a sexually attractive woman may well reveal a great deal about that society's attitude not only towards female sexuality but also the prevailing sex-role norms.

For a number of years, sex-role expectations indicated a marked disparity between desired physical characteristics and the functional value of these characteristics. Forty years ago, Scheinfeld (1939), a geneticist, compared a list of characteristics considered to be "socially desirable" in a North American woman with a contrasting list which would be desirable from a eugenic perspective. The former group stresses delicacy of features, general slimness (including small hips and waist), "dainty" wrists and hands, small feet and also includes the following dimensions — vivaciousness and an absence of "deep intellect". The latter list has a considerably more robust flavour, stressing "strong features", a sturdy build (including a larger waist and broad hips), strong hands, "good-sized" feet, "high intelligence" and a serious character. This discrepancy between form and function would have been much less pronounced, if not entirely absent, in the standards for male sexual attractiveness discussed earlier. The cultural norms of that period were reflected in the complaints of the adolescent girls studied by the Stolzes (discussed earlier in this chapter) who preferred looking "glamorous" or "exotic" rather than "healthy". Considering the current North American emphasis on fitness and a healthy appearance for both sexes, the concerns of these young women seem quaint in retrospect. Another examination of the list of features cited by Scheinfeld suggests however that, while characteristics such as "daintiness" and a rather vacuous vivacity do not represent contemporary ideals, other features such as slimness and at least normally proportioned (if not "delicate") facial features remain important as part of the female aesthetic ideal.

So far sexual attractiveness for women has been discussed in terms of specific physical characteristics regarded as pleasing from the perspective of heterosexual attraction; i.e. the woman's ability to attract an opposite-sex partner. As such, female sexual attractiveness exemplifies a passive form of female sexuality. The behavioural or performance component, which seems to be an important feature of sexual attractiveness for the male, has been absent in traditional Western concepts of female sexual attractiveness. Thus for the male implied or inferred sexual skill seems to be inherent in the concept of attractiveness in a heterosexual context, while for the female, the relation between attractiveness and inferred sexual skill (as opposed to a more passive sexual stimulus value) is

ambiguous. There is some evidence that physical attractiveness is positively related to reported sexual experience among young undergraduate women (Kaats and Davis, 1970; Curran *et al.*, 1973). Surveys of reported sexual behaviour frequently, however, simply examine whether or not an individual has ever engaged in specific sexual behaviours, thus providing little or no information on the quality of sexual experience, a person's perception of his/her sexuality, etc. It is thus unclear how sexual experience and sexual skill are related to female sexual attractiveness. The undergraduate women in the Kaats and Davis (1970) survey continued to perceive their immediate social environment (friends, family) as disapproving of sexual intercourse (for unmarried women) despite the fact that a number of these women had experienced sexual intercourse. This type of ambivalent attitude towards female sexuality might well include an ambivalent attitude concerning attractiveness and sexual experience. If, however, active rather than passive female sexuality is increasingly seen as desirable from the perspective of young adults, norms for sexual attractiveness might well focus more on sexual behaviour with less emphasis on a particular group of physical attributes regarded as sexually arousing.

Attractiveness and the Social System

The interrelation between attractiveness and sex-role expectations discussed in the preceding sections has implications, not only at an interpersonal level, but also from a broader societal perspective. An investigation by Elder (1969) strikingly illustrates the link between physical attractiveness and opportunities for socioeconomic advancement by marriage for American women during the years between 1920-1960. Drawing on longitudinal data collected as part of the Oakland Growth Study, Elder compared the relative influence of attractiveness, education and intelligence on a woman's upward socioeconomic mobility by marriage. The women participating in the project were born in the early 1920s, studied during the thirties, and had at least one follow-up interview after that time. Physical attractiveness judgements were based on ratings made by observers during adolescence for each subject. Mobility by marriage was assessed by comparing the status of the subject's family origin in 1929 (viz., father's occupation) with husband's occupational status in 1958.

During adolescence the more physically attractive girls were not found to be more intelligent nor more achievement-oriented as a group than less

attractive peers. However, as their lives progressed, the former were more likely to be upwardly mobile via marriage. This finding characterized both working- and middle-class women, although the relation between attractiveness during adolescence and husband's occupational status was somewhat stronger for the working-class women. Furthermore, fewer working-class women who were upwardly mobile retrospectively reported sexually permissive or liberal behaviour during adolescence compared to women who were not upwardly mobile (e.g. the percentage for women reporting sexual intercourse when they were in high school was 10% versus 70% respectively). In contrast to the findings obtained for attractiveness, the correlation between both the woman's I.Q. and her academic achievement in adolescence (specifically during high school) and her husband's status was negligible. Further analysis suggested that intellectual ability and academic achievement did have an impact on her husband's status but largely through an indirect route; viz., a bright woman might enter the higher education system more readily — where she would have the opportunity to meet the males who had the potential to become future high-status mates. Elder noted that the attractive, bright woman was particularly fortunate. Presumably her less attractive, bright counterpart had the same opportunity to encounter high-status youths, but this opportunity was not "embedded in physical qualities which are valuable in mate selection" (Elder, 1969, p. 530). Underscoring this point, internal analyses indicated that wives with more education than their husbands were more often found in the less physically attractive group of women. The pattern of findings which Elder obtained therefore vividly illustrates the impact which female sexual attractiveness has had on certain facets of social history in contemporary North American society.

Why might a woman's attractiveness be important for marriage to a higher-status man? As mentioned earlier, physical attractiveness traditionally has been the critical component of sexual attractiveness for women. In addition, however, a woman's attractiveness may also affect how her partner is perceived. Sigall and Landy (1973) provided support for a "radiating beauty" effect by finding that a young woman's physical attractiveness can contribute to the favourability of the impression made on observers by her male companion. Young adults of both sexes were asked to rate a male stimulus person who was presented as either the boyfriend of, or unassociated with, a female confederate, who was made to appear physically attractive or unattractive. The male (who was average in appearance) was most favourably evaluated when associated

with an attractive woman. Furthermore, the specific dimensions affected mostly reflected social skills; viz., perceived friendliness, self-confidence and likeability. Thus, when considering the value of attractiveness for heterosexual relations, one must consider the contextual effect of association with attractive individuals.

Further research along these lines was conducted by Bar-Tal and Saxe (1976) who asked university students for their impressions of attractive and unattractive persons after viewing two slides, where the male and female were presented as a married couple. Subjects viewed different types of pairings of attractive or unattractive individuals. The stimulus persons were rated on a number of dimensions, adapted from the Dion *et al.* (1972) measures; viz., the social desirability scale and several indices of personal and professional success. The investigators noted that a young woman's ratings on most of the scales was independent of her "spouse's" physical attractiveness while a man's ratings (especially for unattractive men) did seem to be influenced by his "spouse's" appearance. An unattractive man paired with an attractive woman was seen as likely to have the highest income, the most professional success and the highest occupation status — a pattern which did not emerge when an unattractive woman was paired with an attractive man. Women seemed to be judged based on their attractiveness *per se*, regardless of their presumed partner's appearance. Thus men saw the attractive women as having the more socially desirable characters compared to the unattractive women. It appears therefore that the "radiating beauty" effect may only apply, or at least applies more strongly, for men than for women paired with attractive partners.

In contrast to the literature presented so far, a case history presented by Seidenberg (1973) exemplifies a changing perspective on sex-role expectations, particularly with regard to attractiveness. The case cited was that of a good-looking young woman who undertook therapy because of sexual problems with her fiance. Seidenberg notes that even in the context of classic psychoanalytic therapy a woman's concern with her physical appearance has been interpreted as reflecting "her basic innate narcissism", instead of being seen as a response to "a societal imperative" (p. 67). In this particular case, despite parental approval and encouragement of her pending marriage (to a medical student), as the time approached for her wedding, the young woman found that sexual intercourse with her fiancé was becoming repugnant, and, unable to change this unfortunate feeling, she entered therapy. As her past history emerged, it became apparent that the young woman had undergone a

number of procedures, including facial surgery, to improve her physical appearance. These drastic measures had their hoped for effect when she reached university level, culminating in her engagement to a highly intelligent prospective physician. However her fiancé was "no movie star"; he had residual acne, a "receding chin" and was noticeably shorter than she was (Seidenberg, 1973, p. 69). As therapy progressed, it became apparent she deeply resented that her fiancé did not have to "improve" his appearance for anyone — "he had the luxury of continuing with the face that he and his friends were used to" (p. 69). In contrast, she seemed to be valued largely, if not solely, for those physical qualities which were so obviously irrelevant for her prospective mate.

When considering the findings reported by Elder (1969) and the case history discussed by Seidenberg (1973) together, a question which comes readily to mind is the following: does the dilemma faced by the young woman symbolize a gradual change in acceptance of societal norms concerning differential emphasis of attractiveness for men and women? Or, alternatively, is the case study simply an isolated illustration of one young woman's rebellion?

If the pattern found by Elder is changing, what is the direction of this change? Seidenberg speculates that women who become more professionally and financially autonomous might begin to stress the importance of an attractive physical appearance in prospective male partners. Currently, traditional benefits (i.e. socioeconomic mobility) noted by Elder can be achieved by the individual woman — thus obviating the need for vicarious status conferred by a male partner.

Concluding Remarks

Throughout this chapter it has been argued that the impact of physical attractiveness on heterosexual relations is mediated by sex-role norms and expectations. This perspective integrates findings from a diverse array of studies in the area of attractiveness and attraction. Most of the research described was conducted during the previous twenty years. The 1980s should provide an excellent opportunity to study both continuity and change in the impact of physical attractiveness compared to previous eras, particularly in a time of transition where elements of traditional sex-roles co-exist with more recently emerging norms for women and men.

1. References

Bar-Tal, D. and Saxe, L. Perceptions of similarly and dissimilarly attractive couples and individuals. *Journal of Personality and Social Psychology*, 1976, **33**, 772-781.

Berg, D. H. Sexual subcultures and contemporary heterosexual interaction patterns among adolescents. *Adolescence*, 1975, **10**, 543-548.

Berscheid, E., Dion, K. K., Walster, E. and Walster, G. W. Physical attractiveness and dating choice: a test of the matching hypothesis. *Journal of Experimental Social Psychology*, 1971, **7**, 173-189.

Broderick, C. B. Socio-sexual development in a suburban community. *Journal of Sex Research*, 1966, **2**, 1-24.

Cavior, N., Jacobs, A. and Jacobs, M. The stability and correlation of physical attractiveness with sex appeal ratings (unpublished paper).

Curran, J. P., Neff, S. and Lippold, S. Correlates of sexual experience among university students. *Journal of Sex Research*, 1973, **9**, 124-131.

Curry, W. *The Middle English ideal of personal beauty*. New York: A.M.S. Press, 1972.

Dion, K. K. Young children's stereotyping of facial attractiveness. *Developmental Psychology*, 1973, **9**, 183-188.

Dion, K. K., Children's physical attractiveness and sex as determinants of adult punitiveness. *Developmental Psychology*, 1974, **10**, 772-778.

Dion, K. K. The incentive value of physical attractiveness for young children. *Personality and Social Psychology Bulletin*, 1977, **3**, 67-70.

Dion, K. K., Berscheid, E. and Walster, E. What is beautiful is good. *Journal of Personality and Social Psychology*, 1972, **24**, 285-290.

Dwyer, J. and Mayer, J. Psychological effects of variations in physical appearance during adolescence. *Adolescence*, 1976, **11**, 353-376.

Elder, G. Appearance and education in marriage mobility. *American Sociological Review*, 1969, **34**, 519-533.

Ford, C. S. and Beach, F. A. *Patterns of sexual behavior*. New York: Harper, 1951.

Frumkin, R. M. Beauty. In Ellis, A. and Arbarbanel, A. (Eds), *The encyclopedia of sexual behavior*. Vol. 1. New York: Hawthorn Books, 1961.

Goldman, W. and Lewis, P. Beautiful is good: evidence that the physically attractive are more socially skillful. *Journal of Experimental Social Psychology*, 1977, **13**, 125-130.

Kaats, G. R. and Davis, K. E. The dynamics of sexual behavior of college students. *Journal of Marriage and the Family*, 1970, **32**, 390-399.

Kleck, R. E. and Rubenstein, C. Physical attractiveness, perceived attitude similarity and interpersonal attraction in an opposite-sex encounter. *Journal of Personality and Social Psychology*, 1975, **31**, 107-114.

Kleck, R. E., Richardson, S. A. and Ronald, L. Physical appearance cues and interpersonal attraction in children. *Child Development*, 1974, **45**, 305-310.

Krebs, D. and Adinolfi, A. Physical attractiveness, social relations and personality style. *Journal of Personality and Social Psychology*, 1975, **31**, 245-253.

Lerner, R. M. and Karabenick, S. A. Physical attractiveness, body attitudes, and self-concept in late adolescents. *Journal of Youth and Adolescence*, 1974, **3**, 307-316.

Lerner, R. M., Karabenick, S. A. and Stuart, J. L. Relations among physical attractiveness, body attitudes and self-concept in male and female college students. *Journal of Psychology*, 1973, **85**, 119-129.

Lerner, R. M., Orlos, J. B. and Knapp, J. R. Physical attractiveness, physical effectiveness and self-concept in late adolescents. *Adolescence*, 1976, **11**, 313-326.

Liggett, J. *The human face*. London: Constable, 1974.

Miller, A. Role of physical attractiveness in impression formation. *Psychonomic Science*, 1970, **19**, 241-243.

Miller, H. and Rivenbark, W. H. Sexual differences in physical attractiveness as a determinant of heterosexual liking. *Psychological Reports*, 1970, **27**, 701-702.

Murstein, B. Physical attractiveness and marital choice. *Journal of Personality and Social Psychology*, 1972, **22**, 8-12.

Poveda, T. G. Reputation and the adolescent girl: an analysis. *Adolescence*, 1975, **10**, 127-136.

Scheinfeld, A. *You and heredity*. New York: Frederick A. Stokes, 1939.

Schoenfeld, W. A. The body and body-image in adolescents. In Caplan, G. and Lebovici, S. (Eds), *Adolescence*. New York: Basic Books, 1969.

Seidenberg, R. Psychosexual adjustment of the unattractive woman. *Medical Aspects of Human Sexuality*, 1973, 60-77.

Sigall, H. and Landy, D. Radiating beauty: the effects of having a physically attractive partner on person perception. *Journal of Personality and Social Psychology*, 1973, **28**, 218-224.

Silverman, I. Physical attractiveness and courtship. *Sexual Behavior*, 1971, 22-25.

Simmons, R. G. and Rosenberg, F. Sex, sex roles, and self-image. *Journal of Youth and Adolescence*, 1975, **4**, 229-258.

Stolz, H. R. and Stolz, L. M. Adolescent problems related to somatic variations. In Henry, N. B. (Ed.), *The forty-third yearbook of the National Society for the Study of Education. Part I. Adolescence*. Distributed by Department of Education, University of Chicago, Chicago, Illinois, 1944.

Udry, J. R. *The social context of marriage* (3rd edn). New York: Lippincott, 1974.

2
Social Background, Attitudes, and Sexual Attraction

WILLIAM A. FISHER
Department of Psychology,
University of Western Ontario, London, Ontario, Canada
and
DONN BYRNE
Department of Psychology, State University of New York at Albany,
Albany, New York, USA

Introduction

This chapter discusses how social background factors and attitudes may influence sexual attraction. As a point of departure, we note several different approaches to the study of sexual attraction and arrive at a working definition of this phenomenon. Relevant data are reviewed which link social class, religiosity, generational differences, and attitudes with sexual attraction, and a tentative conceptual framework is proposed for understanding these relationships. Based on our analysis, suggestions are made for future research on social determinants of sexual attraction.

Orientations to the Study of Sexual Attraction

Across history a continuing fascination with sexual attraction has been expressed in a variety of ways. During the Early Stone Age, sexually oriented cave paintings and carvings in bone were used as magical fertility charms, and in accord with religious convention, Greek art as early as the seventeenth century B.C. portrayed explicit scenes of copulation (Eitner, 1975). Literature dating back to Ovid's *Heroides* (tenth century B.C.) and the biblical Song of Solomon has idealized erotic attraction (Purdy, 1975). English authors from at least the

fourteenth century onwards have pursued the subjects of physical and emotional love with great vigour (Kronhausen and Kronhausen, 1959; Purdy, 1975). In addition, western religions have promulgated standards for sexual conduct (cf. Rosenheim, 1978; Sporken, 1978; van Gennep, 1978) and thus exert a significant influence on who could and should be attracted to whom (cf. Hunt, 1974). In recent years, film makers have suggested a wide spectrum of possibilities for erotic relationships, from mate swapping with *Bob and Carol and Ted and Alice*, to themes of promiscuity and sexual violence (*Looking for Mr. Goodbar*), and the print media and the public at large have devoted considerable energy to extolling — or damning — certain forms of sexual expression.

Despite this longstanding preoccupation, there has often been resistance to the scientific study of sexuality, and research on this topic has been a marvel of circumspection. Long before it was acceptable to examine the mating habits of ordinary individuals, for example, clinical workers were able to publish descriptions of "aberrant" sexual practices including masturbation and fellatio (Krafft-Ebing, 1894); others offered detailed commentary on the erotic predilections of non-white native peoples (e.g. Dr Iwan Bloch's *Strange Sexual Practices of All Races in All Ages*, reprinted in 1974); and still others reported data on the amatory behaviour of non-human primates (e.g. Ford and Beach, 1951). When such indirect approaches gradually gave way to studies of sexual behaviour in representative human populations, reaction was swift and it was sometimes severe. The Kinsey research team, for instance, encountered

> attempts by the medical association in one city to bring suit on the ground that we were practicing medicine without a license, police interference in two or three cities, investigation by a sheriff in one rural area, and attempts to persuade the University's Administration . . . to dismiss the senior author (Kinsey *et al.*, 1948, pp. 11-12).

Fortune was even less kind to Senji Yamamoto, the first sex researcher in Japan, who had the temerity to circulate questionnaires about sex among university students in 1922. According to Asayama (1976), he was discharged from his teaching post, became a politician, and was assassinated in 1929 by ultranationalists "who denounced his thoughts and actions" (p. 371).

Notwithstanding the occasional (but less violent) denunciation of thought and action, a substantial literature on various aspects of sexual attraction has developed during the past several decades. It is possible to

divide this research into a number of categories. First, there are the large-scale surveys of sexual behaviour which tabulate frequency and incidence of petting, pre- and extramarital intercourse, and the like, and analyse these data in terms of social class, religion, and other demographic variables. This tradition began in earnest with the Kinsey volumes on male and female sexuality (Kinsey *et al.*, 1948, 1953) and has continued with up-dates on patterns of sexual behaviour in the 1960s and 1970s (e.g. Hunt, 1974; Schofield, 1965; Sorensen, 1973; Tavris and Sadd, 1978; Wilson, 1975; Zelnik and Kantner, 1977). Secondly, there have been studies of sexual attitudes, and of the relation of such attitudes to behaviour (e.g. Byrne, 1971; Byrne *et al.*, 1973; Christensen and Gregg, 1970; Mosher and Cross, 1971; Reiss, 1967). Thirdly, there have been efforts to study the role of sexual intimacy in interpersonal relationships, including premarital dating (Ehrmann, 1959; Kirkendall, 1961; Peplau *et al.*, 1977) and marriage (Ard, 1977; Davis, 1929, republished 1972; Hamilton, 1929). Fourthly, there have been a number of experimental studies concerning factors that may elicit heterosexual attraction, including research on the role of physical attractiveness (e.g., Dion *et al.*, 1972; White, 1980), sexual arousal (Griffitt, 1979; Griffitt *et al.*, 1974), attitude similarity (Byrne *et al.*, 1970; Touhey, 1972), and playing (or being) "hard to get" (Driscoll *et al.*, 1972; Walster *et al.*, 1973). Experimental methods have also been used to study sexual arousal, which is presumably a fundamental part of sexual attraction; research has focused on responses to various erotic stimuli (Brady and Levitt, 1965; Clark, 1952; Clark and Sensibar, 1955; Commission on Obscenity and Pornography, 1970; Schmidt and Sigusch, 1970), and on physiological manifestations of sexual arousal (Geer, 1975; Geer *et al.*, 1974; Masters and Johnson, 1966, 1970; Wincze *et al.*, 1977). Finally, a number of investigators have conducted studies of romantic or emotional love (cf. Berscheid and Walster, 1974; Kanin *et al.*, 1970; Rubin, 1970, 1973; Swensen, 1961).

While research on sexual attraction has thus employed both survey and experimental strategies to study a variety of sub-topics in this area, several limitations on the scope of this literature are apparent. Of primary concern to the present chapter, it should be noted that only the large-scale surveys of sexual behaviour have concentrated attention on the role of social background factors in sexual attraction. These surveys emphasize the result of attraction (i.e. sexual behaviour) much more than they do the processes which lead to overt sexual expression. Such surveys suffer from a variety of methodological flaws, including self-selection of

subjects, bias in favour of Caucasian, American respondents, and ambiguities in the wording of questionnaire items and in the analysis of results. Secondly, while heterosexual attraction is obviously an interpersonal process, most behavioural scientists — across the sub-areas listed above — have studied individuals, not dyads; consequently, the reciprocal interactions which may lie at the centre of sexual attraction have largely been ignored. Finally, the process of sexual attraction would seem to be an accumulative one; past experience and learning may shape the future course of sexual attraction, but longitudinal studies that track erotic relationships across time are scarce. Naturally, our discussion of the literature will reflect these limitations. It is hoped, however, that the present overview and analysis of the findings will provide some basis for future work on these missing links in the chain of evidence regarding sexual attraction.

From the preceding discussion, it is clear that sexual attraction has many referents, some of which have been the subject of research, and some of which have not. In view of this diversity, it seems appropriate to attempt to define this phenomenon. We conceptualize sexual attraction as involving a series of approach responses that increase the probability of overt sexual behaviour, typically resulting in orgasm. Thus, sexual attraction consists of two phases: preliminary, pre-orgasmic responses (i.e. emotional responses, courtship rituals, light petting, etc.) and overt, orgasmic (or potentially orgasmic) behaviours (i.e. cunnilingus, fellatio, coitus, etc.). The task at hand involves understanding how social background and attitudes may influence such behaviours. It should be noted that sexual attraction is defined as a longitudinal, interpersonal process. Sexual attraction may occur with respect to opposite-sex others (heterosexual attraction), same-sex others (homosexual attraction), or even with respect to one's self (autoerotic behaviour), although we will confine our discussion largely to heterosexual attraction. Finally, we propose that while sexual attraction typically occurs in the context of liking or loving relationships, it may also arise in neutral or even antagonistic settings. The relation of sexual attraction and the interpersonal context in which it exists is an important research question, but we do not regard sexual attraction and emotional love, for example, as *necessarily* related. Having briefly considered such definitional issues, we will now turn to a survey of empirical findings on sexual attraction in relation to social background and attitudes.

Sexual Attraction in Relation to
Social Background and Attitudes

The links that are observed between social background, attitudes, and sexual attraction are meaningful on two levels. Ideally, such data should describe who is becoming sexually attracted to whom, with what frequency, at what point in time, and in what manner this process develops, in terms of variables such as social class, religion, attitudes, and the like. These descriptions should also provide a basis for theorizing about how differences in social background and attitudes are translated into distinctive patterns of sexual attraction. The present section provides an overview of research on the relationship of sexual attraction to social class, religious devoutness, generational differences, and attitudes, and the concluding portion of this chapter proposes a conceptual framework for understanding these relationships.

Sexual Attraction as a Function of Social Class

Survey research has often focused on differences in social class in efforts to explain observed variations in sexual behaviour. Social class has frequently been defined in terms of respondents' educational background or the occupational class which they (or their parents) have achieved. These operationalizations share many common referents; occupational class (i.e. professional, unskilled, etc.) has educational concomitants (although the relationship is not perfect), and both educational background and occupational status carry with them differences in age of marriage and vocational entry, access to social power, mobility, etc. As we shall see below, educational and occupational status are also correlated with fairly distinct styles of sexual expression.

Social Class and Sexual Attitudes

It has been argued that attitudes regarding premarital coitus are more permissive in the lower than in the middle class. In contrast, the lower class is said to be *less* permissive with respect to non-coital or "unorthodox" sexual behaviours (i.e. masturbation, homosexuality, etc., Bell, 1966; Schmidt, 1978), although Hunt (1974) and Schmidt (1978) propose that the social classes are now converging in these regards.

Data reported by Kinsey and his associates (Kinsey et al., 1948) provide some support for the notion that lower class persons have more permissive attitudes regarding premarital coitus. For example, it was found that college (versus high school or grade school) educated men reported more moral objections to premarital intercourse, they were more likely to fear adverse public opinion or possible pregnancy in conjunction with premarital intercourse, and younger college educated men desired more often to marry a virgin. Interestingly enough, Kinsey's better educated men were also more likely to report that they lacked opportunities to engage in premarital sex, and it seems possible that their negative attitudes could be something of a reaction to involuntary chastity.

In contrast to the findings of Kinsey et al. (1948), more recent survey data show a uniform trend for better educated persons to have more positive attitudes towards premarital coitus and other sexual behaviours. Using large, representative US samples, Glenn and Weaver (1979) found that with few exceptions, better educated men and women were most permissive with respect to premarital, extramarital, and homosexual relations. Concerning other sexual practices, Wilson (1975) reported that college educated men and women (versus respondents with high school or elementary educations) had less restrictive views on masturbation, and Hunt (1974) found that better educated males were less likely to agree that the man should always take the lead during coitus. Thus, recent findings suggest that better educated persons have more liberal attitudes towards a range of sexual practices. Some interesting behavioural parallels to these social class differences in sexual attitudes are considered next.

Social Class and Autoerotic Behaviour

Survey studies show fairly consistent social class differences in autoerotic behaviours such as masturbation and sexual fantasy. Kinsey et al. (1948, 1953) found, for example, that better educated men, and those of higher occupational status, reported more frequent masturbation. In addition, better educated women were more likely to have masturbated to orgasm. Recent findings (Wilson, 1975) also show that college educated men and women (versus those with secondary or elementary education) report that they begin to masturbate at an earlier age. These differences in masturbatory behaviour parallel social class differences in attitudes regarding this subject.

There are also some data which suggest the presence of educational level differences in sexual fantasy and related behaviours. Wilson (1975) found that college and high school (versus elementary) educated men and women report that they more often dream about sex and that they more frequently fantasize, during coitus, that they are having sex with someone other than their partner. In addition, Kinsey *et al.* (1948) found that men with some college education, and those of higher occupational status, reported more frequent nocturnal emissions than men with no college education or those of lower occupational classes. According to Kinsey *et al.*, "It may be that the paucity of overt socio-sexual experience among upper level males accounts . . . for their nocturnal dreaming" (1948, p. 340).

Social Class and Heterosexual Attraction

Social class seems to have a general relationship to patterns of petting behaviour, premarital, marital, and extramarital coitus, and even to subjective satisfaction with one's sex life. With respect to premarital petting to the point of orgasm, Kinsey *et al.* (1948) reported that males with some college education were more likely to indicate that they had petted to the point of orgasm (61%) than were men with high school (32%) or grade school (16%) educations, and a similar tendency existed for higher occupational status men to report more often that they had petted to climax. Kinsey's female sample (Kinsey *et al.*, 1953), however, did not show such differences; in fact, there is a trend for less well educated women to pet to orgasm at an *earlier* age than their better educated counterparts. This tendency, however, seems to depend upon the fact that less well educated women may marry (and presumably begin petting) at a younger age. Within groups of women who married at about the same age, Kinsey did not observe educational level differences in frequency or incidence of petting to orgasm. Similarly, Kinsey found little correlation between women's occupational class background and frequency of petting to orgasm.

The specific techniques employed in premarital petting, Kinsey and his colleagues found, show distinct variations at different educational levels. College (versus high school or grade school) educated men were more likely to report that they had engaged in manual and oral manipulation of the females' genitals, and they were more often fellated in the context of premarital petting. Women with college or postgraduate (versus high school) educations were also somewhat more adventurous in

petting; the better educated females in Kinsey's sample were more likely to report that they had received oral stimulation of their breasts and that they had manually and orally stimulated their partners' genitals during premarital petting. It is interesting to note that recent surveys have not closely examined the relation of social class and premarital petting; evidently, the significance of such behaviour has diminished, relative to premarital coitus, both in the view of investigators and the general public. Hunt (1974) does suggest, however, that social class differences in petting are becoming less noticeable, with more lower class persons engaging in petting during foreplay, and more middle class persons moving on quickly from premarital petting to coitus.

While better educated men and women seem to engage in a greater variety of petting behaviours than the less well educated, they are not more likely to engage in premarital coitus. Among males, Kinsey and his associates (1948) found that by the age of 20, 86% of the elementary educated respondents had engaged in premarital intercourse, compared to 76% of the high school and only 44% of the college educated sample. According to Kinsey, less well educated men also have more frequent premarital intercourse. Hunt (1974), in an effort to up-date these figures, reports a major increase in the incidence of premarital coitus for college men, and a smaller increase for those who do not attend college. Hunt's data suggest that — at least through age 17 — less well educated men are still more likely to engage in premarital coitus. For women, the Kinsey *et al.* (1953) data are somewhat less clear; at age 20, more elementary and high school (versus college) educated females report that they have had premarital coitus, but ultimately — by age 35 — more college women have done so. According to Kinsey *et al.*, these relationships are due to the fact that women at different educational levels tend to marry at different ages. When Kinsey examined the incidence of premarital coitus for women who married at similar ages, educational level differences were few. More recent findings on women's educational background and premarital intercourse experience are reported by Tavris and Sadd (1978), in a survey of *Redbook* magazine readers, and these data show that less well educated women are still likely to begin premarital coitus at an earlier age. Tavris and Sadd also found that ultimately about 80% of women at each educational level engage in coitus prior to marriage.

There is one other set of findings, reported by Kanin (1960), that sheds interesting light on premarital sexual behaviour in dating dyads. Kanin found that the social class of the female — but not of the male — was reliably associated with the incidence and intensity of premarital erotic

expression. In particular, only 31% of the upper middle class women reported that they had engaged in premarital intercourse, compared to 41·6% of the middle class and 82·5% of the lower class women. Moreover, during the month prior to their marriage, upper-middle class women were more likely to increase the frequency of their most intimate sexual activity (44%) than were middle and lower class women (21%). Upper-middle class women — who were least permissive with respect to premarital coitus — apparently felt secure enough just before their wedding day to increase somewhat their sexual activity (Kanin, 1960). In a related vein, Ehrmann (1959) found that among college students, most dated persons perceived as belonging to the same social class. Social class lines were crossed on occasion, however, most often by males who crossed class lines to date females they viewed as lower in social class. With respect to sexual behaviour of the students in Ehrmann's sample, it was determined that

> the degree of physical intimacy among the females was greatest with males of the same social class, intermediate with those of a higher, and least with those of a lower social class; whereas among males it was greatest with females of a lower social class, intermediate with those of the same, and least with those of a higher social class (Ehrmann, 1959, p. 149).

It should be noted, however, that a recent study by DeLamater and MacCorquodale (1979) failed to replicate these findings linking perceived social class of partner with sexual behaviour.

Highly educated persons begin to have coitus at a relatively late age, but they do not have entirely lackluster sex lives. In fact, with respect to marital coitus, better educated persons seem to employ more variations for this behaviour than do the less well educated. Kinsey *et al.* (1948, 1953) found that high school or college (versus grade school) educated men more often have marital coitus in the nude, and use the female above, side by side, and rear entry positions more frequently (although college men used standing or sitting positions less often). And, college educated females in Kinsey's sample reported having marital coitus while nude more frequently than did high school educated women, and better educated women, as well as those from higher occupational status backgrounds, were more often orgasmic. (In relation to this last point, it should be noted that Hunt (1974) did not find a strong relation between social class and frequency of orgasm.) In addition, Hunt (1974) has found that fellatio and cunnilingus are used in a greater proportion of marriages that include college (versus high school) educated men and women. And, at least one study (Wilson, 1975) suggests that college (versus high school

or elementary) educated men and women may have intercourse somewhat more often, although neither Kinsey's (1948, 1953) data nor Hunt's (1974) show increased coital frequencies at higher levels of education.

While better educated individuals seem to be a bit more adventurous in terms of coital and oral sex techniques, their spirit of adventure seems to be limited — at least initially — to the confines of marriage. For example, Kinsey and his colleagues found a tendency for fewer well educated men to engage in extramarital coitus. This trend is strongest through about age 35, after which it begins to reverse (i.e. after age 35, more better educated men engage in extramarital coitus). Hunt (1974) suggests that this situation has not changed appreciably in recent years. For the females studied by Kinsey, after about age 30, there was a tendency for more better educated women, and those of higher occupational status background, to engage in extramarital coitus. More recent survey data (Levin, 1975) corroborate this trend: before age 40, college (versus high school) educated women are less likely to engage in extramarital sex, while after age 40, the reverse is true.

Given these social class differences in patterns of sexual behaviour, it would be interesting to know whether persons at various social levels report differential subjective satisfaction with their sex lives. Data on this topic are difficult to find, but Rainwater (1966) has provided some interesting comparisons. In particular, middle and upper-lower class spouses were more likely to report great interest and enjoyment with their sexual relations than were lower-lower class husbands and wives. Rainwater has proposed that such differences may derive from the greater mutuality of higher social class marriages, in contrast to the social role segregation that may characterize lower class marriages. And, at least for younger (i.e. under 35) persons, satisfaction with marital sex seems to be consistent with the likelihood of engaging in extramarital coitus; higher social class individuals express more satisfaction with marital sex and are less prone to engage in extramarital sex, while lower class persons are less satisfied with marital sex and are more likely to seek extramarital alternatives.

According to a recent analysis (Schmidt, 1978), the crucial class difference with respect to sexual satisfaction occurs between the unstable versus stable working classes. Among the unstable working class — unskilled persons with insecure jobs — women are viewed (and see themselves) as asexual, while for men, sexual success is important for achieving social status. Among the stable working class — individuals

who are at least semi-skilled and somewhat secure — sexual relations are presumed by men and women to be at least potentially satisfying. In Schmidt's (1978) view "a certain socioeconomic level is a prerequisite for emotionally satisfying and mutual sexual relations enjoyable for both partners" (p. 289).

At this juncture, a brief summary of social class differences in sexual expression would seem to be useful (see Table I). Indications are that

Table I

Summary of patterns of sexual behaviour as a function of social class, religious devoutness, and generational differences

	Social class Middle (versus lower)	Religiosity Devout (versus non-devout)	Generation Present (versus past)
Sexual attitudes	More permissive	Less permissive	More permissive
Autoerotic behaviour	More, earlier masturbation, More fantasy activity	Less or later masturbation	More masturbation
Heterosexual behaviour			
Premarital petting	More likely to pet to orgasm (males only)	Less likely to engage in light or heavy petting	More heavy petting
Premarital intercourse	Premarital coitus occurs at a later age	Less premarital intercourse	More premarital intercourse, more frequent orgasm in premarital intercourse (women only)
Marital intercourse	More varied techniques		More frequent, more positions
Extramarital intercourse	Less extramarital coitus early in marriage, more extramarital coitus later in marriage	Less extramarital coitus	More extramarital coitus
Satisfaction	More subjective satisfaction with marital sex	Less subjective satisfaction with *premarital* sex More subjective satisfaction with *marital* sex	Less guilt concerning premarital intercourse among college students

As the reader is aware, the relation of social background and sexual attraction is a complex one, subject to certain qualifications that are discussed more thoroughly in the text. Therefore, this summary table might best serve as a supplement to the accompanying discussion.

middle (versus lower) class persons hold more permissive attitudes towards premarital and extramarital coitus, and the middle class is also more positive towards masturbation, female initiative in coitus, and homosexual relations. With respect to sexual behaviour, lower class men and women begin to have premarital coitus at an earlier age, while middle class individuals are more likely to masturbate, to pet (males only), and to employ greater variation in petting and in coitus, and to engage more often in sexual fantasy. Compared to younger persons of the lower class, those of the middle class are less likely to engage in extramarital coitus, but this relationship is reversed for older men and women. Finally, middle (versus lower) class spouses are more likely to report satisfaction with their marital sex relations. Discussion will now turn to the relationship of religious devoutness and sexual expression.

Sexual Attraction as a Function of Religious Devoutness

At first glance, it seems obvious that adherents of different faiths should also differ in their sexual practices, since each religion has unique guidelines for sexual behaviour (cf. Rosenheim, 1978; Sporken, 1978; van Gennep, 1978). Indeed, variations in sexual behaviour by nominal religious classification have been found; for example, Tavris and Sadd (1978) report that 80·6% of the Protestant women in their sample had engaged in premarital intercourse, compared to 78·3% of the Catholics and only 68·6% of the Jewish women. Religious preference, however, does not indicate how closely an individual identifies with and practises the tenets of a specific faith. Consequently, many researchers have focused on religious *devoutness*, often measured in terms of frequency of church attendance, to understand differences in sexual behaviour. Possibly the best way to study the relationship of religion and sexual behaviour would involve focus on both the religious group a person belongs to (in order to understand the content of specific guidelines on sex) and the devoutness of the adherent (to assess the intensity of his or her commitment to a particular doctrine; cf. Kinsey *et al.*, 1948, 1953; Tavris and Sadd, 1978). For a number of reasons, however, much of the research has looked primarily at links between devoutness (rather than religion *per se*) and sexual behaviour. Perhaps because indices of devoutness provide at least a crude measure of the centrality of religion in a person's life, and because Western faiths have many common sex-related dogma, religious devoutness has proved to be a useful

concept for understanding variations in sexual behaviour. We will now turn to an overview of findings for links between religious devoutness and sexual expression.

Religious Devoutness and Sexual Attitudes

In view of the fact that Western faiths traditionally proscribe masturbation, premarital sex, and certain other sexual activities, it would not be surprising to find differences in sexual attitudes as a function of devoutness, regardless of the particular religion in question. Reiss (1967), for example, found that men and (to an even greater extent) women who attended church frequently (i.e. more than once a month), compared to infrequent church attenders, were less permissive on Reiss's Premarital Sexual Permissiveness Scale. DeLamater and MacCorquodale (1979) have recently confirmed these relationships, and Hunt (1974) has also provided data which suggest that differences in sexual attitudes as a function of devoutness may persist in recent years, although the attitudinal gap between devout and non-devout persons seems to be narrowing.

Religious Devoutness and Autoerotic Behaviour

The difference between devout and non-devout persons carries over into the domain of autoerotic behaviour. Kinsey and his colleagues (1948, 1953) found that a smaller percentage of devout (versus non-devout) men and women report masturbation, and for men (but not for women) greater devoutness was also correlated with less frequent masturbation. More recent data (Hunt, 1974) suggest that while devout women, compared to non-devout, are still less likely to masturbate, most men at each level of devoutness today eventually do so. Nonetheless, devout men in Hunt's sample were still likely to begin to masturbate at a later age than were non-devout men. With respect to links between devoutness and sexual fantasy or dreams, there are very few contemporary data. Kinsey's (1948, 1953) findings are intriguing, however: for men, religious devoutness was not correlated with incidence or frequency of nocturnal emission, but for women, the religiously devout were less likely to report that they had experienced nocturnal dreams that resulted in orgasm.

Religious Devoutness and Heterosexual Attraction

Religious devotion has been found to be linked with sexual attitudes and autoerotic activity, and in the current section we will consider the relationship of devoutness with heterosexual behaviour. For example, the Kinsey volumes provide some interesting findings concerning religiosity and premarital petting. Religiously active (versus inactive) males in the Kinsey sample were somewhat less likely to engage in premarital petting to the point of orgasm, although it is noted that the effects of religion are more minor than those of social class. For females, within each of the major religions, highly devout women were also less likely to report that they had petted to orgasm. Survey data collected by Mahoney (1980) has confirmed that relatively devout college students are less likely to engage in light or heavy petting. In addition, Kinsey *et al.* (1948, 1953) reported that increasing religious devoutness (especially for women, but among men as well) was associated with a lower incidence and frequency of premarital coitus. What is more, recent survey data (Hunt, 1974; Mahoney, 1980; Tavris and Sadd, 1978) indicate that religious devoutness remains linked with lower levels of premarital intercourse experience. An additional finding reported by Peplau *et al.* (1977) is also informative with regard to the role of religiosity in the dynamics of premarital intercourse. These investigators asked members of dating couples to indicate when (if ever) they had begun to have coitus, and these couples were also asked for self-ratings of how religious they were. It was found that couples that delayed coitus were more likely to include a relatively religious woman, while the male's devoutness was not related to the timing of premarital intercourse. Not only does this result suggest the importance of religion *vis à vis* premarital intercourse, but together with Kanin's (1960) data, shows that women may play a decisive "gate keeper" role in controlling premarital sexual intimacy.

With respect to marital sex, there are interesting links between religious devoutness, marital and extramarital coitus, and satisfaction with one's own sexual experiences. Kinsey and his colleagues found that marital coitus was more frequent among non-devout (versus devout) men, although this analysis was limited to highly educated, Protestant men. For women, little relation of devoutness and frequency of marital coitus (or orgasm in coitus) was found. More recent findings (Hunt, 1974) show that devoutness is still linked with frequency of marital coitus, but it now appears that devout *women* report lower coital frequency than the non-devout, while no differences in marital coitus

frequency were seen for devout and non-devout men. (In relation to this last point, it should be noted that Tavris and Sadd (1978) did not find any difference in the frequency of marital coitus reported by devout and non-devout women.)

According to research that spans the last 30 years, extramarital coitus is less common among devout (versus non-devout) persons. Kinsey *et al.* (1948, 1953) found this to be the case for both men and women, and more recent data show that, while the gap between devout and non-devout individuals may be narrowing, it is still fairly substantial. For example, Tavris and Sadd (1978) report that only 15% of the very religious women in their sample had extramarital affairs, compared to 36% of the non-religious women, and Hunt (1974) reports that extramarital coitus remains less common among religiously devout (versus non-devout) males.

In view of the relationship observed between religious devoutness and sexual expression, it would be interesting to find differences in subjective satisfaction with sex for persons who differ in devoutness. The limited amount of data on this issue, in fact, do paint a fairly consistent picture. For example, Tavris and Sadd (1978) found that very religious women (versus moderately and non-religious females) reported higher levels of satisfaction with marital sex *and* more frequently reaching orgasm. This link between relative devoutness and sexual satisfaction, interestingly enough, may be limited to *marital* sex. Hunt (1974), for example, found that single men and women who were regular churchgoers (versus non-attenders) were less likely to report that intercourse was very pleasurable — a reversal (at least for women) of the effects observed for marital sex. (In regard to this last finding, it is interesting to note that relatively religious college men studied by Mahoney (1980) also reported less enjoyment of sex.)

In summary, it appears that there are regular differences in sexual behaviour for devout and non-devout persons, and these differences seem to persist even in the more recent surveys on this topic. These findings are summarized in Table I. Compared with less devout individuals, the religiously devout have non-permissive attitudes regarding sexual behaviour, they are less likely to report that they masturbate, and fewer religious women indicate that they have had nocturnal sex dreams that result in orgasm. Devout men and women are also less likely to report that they have engaged in petting or in premarital intercourse, and relatively religious women seem to wait longer before permitting premarital coitus to occur in a relationship. Data suggest that religious (versus non-religious) men and women may have marital coitus less

frequently (but religious women may have orgasm within such coitus *more* often), and fewer religious persons engage in extramarital coitus. Finally, religiously devout (versus non-devout) women seem to be more satisfied with their marital sex relations, but some data hint that devout men and women may enjoy non-marital intercourse less.

Sexual Attraction as a Function of Generational Differences

According to contemporary folk wisdom, western society has been undergoing a sexual revolution during the past 20-odd years. Naturally, social scientists have begun to study this highly touted phenomenon, and they have adopted two different approaches to investigating differences in sexual behaviour across time. Some have compared the sexual attitudes and behaviour of persons of the same age who were born at different points in time (e.g. Bauman and Wilson, 1976; Christensen and Gregg, 1970; Finger, 1975; King *et al.*, 1977); such research indicates generational differences in sexuality, but in most cases only for a particular age range (e.g. 20-year-olds in 1960 versus 1970). Other investigators have examined the sexual behaviour of persons of different ages at a given point in time (e.g. Hunt, 1974; Kinsey *et al.*, 1948, 1953; Tavris and Sadd, 1978; Wilson, 1975), and these studies may reveal age differences in sexual behaviour, somewhat confounded with differences in generation of birth. Perhaps the ideal method for studying generational and age effects on sexual behaviour would involve tracking the same persons across the life span (to detect age and maturational influences) and to do so for multiple decade of birth cohorts (to investigate generational differences), but such research has not been undertaken. In the present section, we will consider differences in sexual behaviour and attitudes that have been reported for persons of the same age at different points in time (generational differences), and variations in behaviour for individuals of different ages at the same point in time (age or maturational effects, confounded by generational differences).

Generational Differences in Sexual Attitudes

Survey data provide consistent evidence that sexual attitudes have become quite a bit more liberal in recent years. In research reported by Christensen and Gregg (1970), mid-western US college students were surveyed in 1958, and similar groups of students responded to the same

questionnaire items again in 1968. Across this ten-year span, attitudes shifted to a markedly more liberal position on issues such as censorship, acceptance of non-virginity in a marriage partner, and approval of premarital coitus. Using similar procedures, King and his associates (1977) surveyed students at a southern US university in 1965, 1970, and 1975. Compared to the 1965 groups, the 1975 samples of men and women were less likely to indicate the belief that premarital sexual relations are sinful or immoral. Changes in sexual standards across a period of time as brief as four years have been documented by Bauman and Wilson (1976), who found that college men and women in 1972 (versus 1968) were more permissive with respect to petting and intercourse. In each of these surveys, a tendency is observed for women to show greater changes towards permissiveness than do men, and the sexes seem to be converging towards a single standard for sexual behaviour. It is also worth noting that, using large representative samples drawn during the 1970s, Glenn and Weaver (1979) have confirmed recent changes towards permissiveness in regard to premarital coitus. At the same time that the public is getting more liberal about premarital intercourse, however, Glenn and Weaver report uniformly low levels of acceptance of either extramarital or homosexual relations across the 1970s. The authors conclude that the revolution in sexual attitudes has been largely confined to liberalization of standards for premarital coitus.

An indirect measure of generational change in sexual attitudes has been provided by Farr and Gordon (1975). These investigators surveyed sexual graffiti in public restrooms in Pennsylvania, and compared the incidence of erotic inscriptions with the percentages reported by Kinsey *et al.* (1953). For women, the prevalence of sexual graffiti seems to have markedly increased; 44% of women's restroom inscriptions were of an erotic nature in 1973 (the year of Farr and Gordon's data collection) compared to only 25% in Kinsey's day; the corresponding figures for men show but a modest increase (89% in 1973 versus 86% in the Kinsey survey).

With respect to age differences in sexual attitudes, findings generally show that younger men and women profess more liberal views on such topics as masturbation, premarital intercourse, anal intercourse, and the like (Wilson, 1975; Hunt, 1974). Whether these differences are due to age *per se*, or differences in decade of birth, however, is difficult to gauge.

Generational Differences in Autoerotic Behaviour

In general, the Kinsey findings for masturbatory behaviour reveal that more recent generations of men are more likely to have masturbated, and to do so more frequently, than earlier generations of men (Downey, 1980). Concerning nocturnal dreams to orgasm, "the youngest generation appears to have begun dreaming to orgasm slightly earlier than their predecessors, but to have quickly tapered off to a lower incidence level than any of the earlier generations" (Downey, 1980, p. 284). With respect to women, Kinsey and his associates (1953) found that a greater number of the most recent generation of women ultimately masturbated, and compared to females who were born earlier, they were also somewhat more likely to report nocturnal sex dreams which resulted in orgasm. In the same vein, Finger (1975) has presented comparisons of masturbatory behaviour of university men in the years 1943–44 and 1967–73. Compared to a group of college men surveyed in 1943–44, those queried in 1967–73 did not show much of an increase in the percentage who report that they have masturbated (92·8% versus 95·4%, respectively), nor did the age at which these men first masturbate differ (13·3 years in both generations). The frequency of masturbation apparently *has* changed markedly, however, with a mean of 36·0 occasions a year in 1943–44, compared to 105·8 times a year in 1967–73. Other data (Wilson, 1975) are consistent with the general finding for increased masturbation in the present generation, and cross-cultural comparisons show that this trend is not limited to the West. Asayama (1976), for example, surveyed Japanese students in 1960 and in 1974, and found that by the age of 18, 92% of the 1974 males (versus 74% of the 1960 males) had masturbated; for females, 24% of the 1974 sample of 18-year-olds had masturbated, compared to only 6% of the 1960 sample. With respect to sexual fantasy, very little data concerning generational or age differences are available, although Hunt (1974) and Wilson (1975) do provide some suggestive findings. Hunt asked respondents to indicate how many of nine possible themes appeared in their masturbation fantasies. Younger men indicated an average of 3·3 themes (compared to 1·7 themes for men over 55), and younger women indicated an average of 2·6 themes (compared to 1·1 themes for women over the age of 55). Wilson (1975) also reports that younger men and women are more likely to dream about sex, and to fantasize, during coitus, that they are having sex with someone other than their partner. Again, it is not clear whether these are age differences *per se*, or age differences confounded with generational differences. Taken together, however, these data suggest

increases in autoerotic behaviour and sexual fantasy among members of more recent generations and among younger persons generally.

Generational Differences in Heterosexual Attraction

With respect to petting and premarital intercourse, survey data suggest that there have been consistent increases during the past several years. For example, in the King *et al.* (1977) survey of college students in 1965, 1970, and 1975, there were uniform decreases in light and medium petting from 1965 to 1975, accompanied by consistent increases in heavy petting and premarital intercourse. Similar increases have been found in Vener and Stewart's (1974) surveys of Michigan high school students in 1970 and 1973. Across this short interval, Vener and Stewart found fairly sizable increases in coitus and coital experience with more than two different persons. In the 1973 group of high school males, 33·4% reported that they had coitus (versus 27·8% in 1970), and 19·4% reported coitus with more than two partners (versus 14·2% in 1970). For women in the 1973 sample, 22·4% reported coitus (versus 16·1% in 1970), and 8·9% reported coitus with more than two partners (versus 5·7% in 1970). Findings for increased premarital coitus in succeeding generations of college students have also been reported by Bauman and Wilson (1974), Bell and Chaskes (1970), Finger (1975), and Asayama (1976, for Japanese students); Zelnik and Kantner (1977) report increases in the prevalence of premarital coitus in national probability samples of US women taken in 1971 and 1976. Hunt (1974), Tavris and Sadd (1978) and Wilson (1975) also present data from non-student samples of men and women which suggest that the younger generation may have coitus at an earlier age than did previous generations. Moreover, according to Tavris and Sadd (1978), more women in the present (versus past) generation have reached orgasm during their premarital coitus. Evidence from a number of sources has thus converged to show an earlier onset and greater prevalence of premarital coitus in the present (versus past) generation.

With respect to frequency of marital coitus, Kinsey and his colleagues (Downey, 1980) reported few differences between older and younger generation men. For women, Kinsey *et al.* (1953) found that females of the younger generation engaged in somewhat less frequent marital coitus than those of the older generation, but women of the younger generation reported that their coital experience more often resulted in orgasm. More recent data collected by Hunt (1974) attempt to compare Kinsey's data on marital coitus with Hunt's own findings, and this analysis suggests

that there has been an increase in the frequency of marital coitus, for all age groups, since the time of Kinsey's research. Moreover, for Kinsey's male and female samples (Downey, 1980; Kinsey et al., 1953), and in Hunt's (1974) survey, a trend is observed for more men and women of the younger generation to employ a greater variety of positions in marital coitus.

Turning to generational differences in extramarital coitus, Kinsey and his associates (Downey, 1980) found that, in general, more men of recent generations have engaged in extramarital sex, but they tend to do so less frequently than their older generation counterparts. For women, the Kinsey et al. (1953) findings suggest that more of the women of the younger generation have had extramarital sex, but those who do so do not engage in this behaviour more frequently than those in older generations. Hunt (1974) has compared his findings with those of the Kinsey research, and suggests that changes in incidence of extramarital coitus have only occurred among those below the age of 25. The percentage of under-25 males who have engaged in extramarital coitus has increased slightly since Kinsey's studies, but the percentage of under-25 women who have done so has increased three-fold (according to Hunt's recalculations, only 8% of the under-25 women in Kinsey's sample had extramarital coitus, compared to 24% in his own sample). Tavris and Sadd (1978) present evidence for an age trend in extramarital coitus; older women are more likely than younger to report that they have had extramarital intercourse. It seems quite likely that this result reflects, in part, the greater amount of time that older women have had to develop extramarital relationships. It is also interesting to note that Tavris and Sadd (1978) detected a pronounced tendency for full-time employed women (versus housewives) to report that they have had extramarital coitus; at age 40 or older, 47% of the full-time employed women, but only 33% of the housewives, report that they have engaged in this behaviour. Given the increasing number of women now entering the work force, it seems possible that this factor may play a role in increasing extramarital sex for future generations of women.

Very little data are available regarding subjective sexual satisfaction across the generations, but some interesting observations have been provided by Bell and Chaskes (1970) and Christensen and Gregg (1970). In 1958 and again in 1968, these investigators asked college men and women who had experienced premarital intercourse about their feelings regarding this experience. Compared to those surveyed in 1958, students who were questioned in 1968 were less likely to report that they had felt

obliged or forced to have premarital sex, and fewer men and women in the 1968 sample felt that they had "gone too far" or expressed guilt or remorse over having had premarital intercourse. These data suggest that, at least for college men and women, the recent generation may have a more accepting view of its sexual behaviour.

In sum, there appear to have been rather consistent changes in sexual expression in recent years (see Table I). Compared to earlier generations, young men and women today seem to have more liberal, sexually permissive attitudes, and such changes have been tracked across intervals as short as four years. Findings also indicate that the younger generation may masturbate with somewhat greater frequency, and there are some indications that younger persons, more than old, engage in sexual fantasy. There is also evidence that increases in heavy petting and premarital intercourse have occurred in recent years, and women of the younger generation more often have orgasm during premarital coitus. Findings also suggest that the frequency of marital coitus and the variety of positions used in coitus may have increased as well. In addition, members of recent generations seem to be more likely to engage in extramarital coitus than in times past. Finally, there is some suggestion that the present generation may feel less regret over its sexual involvements. This completes our overview of social class, religious, and generational differences in sexual expression, and discussion will now turn to the relationship of sexual attitudes and sexual attraction.

Sexual Attraction as a Function of Attitudes

In the preceding section it was observed that differences in social background were associated with differences in sexual attitudes. For example, middle class persons, the non-devout, and recent generation of birth individuals were all relatively permissive in their sexual attitudes. Moreover, there were numerous behavioural parallels to such differences in sexual attitudes. The relation between sexual attitudes and behaviour, however, has not yet been considered directly. We have consistent evidence linking social background factors with sexual attitudes, and if it is possible to establish a firm link between such attitudes and behaviour, there might be some basis for higher order conceptualization. For instance, it could be speculated that social background differences result in variations in attitudes, which in turn mediate the differences in sexual behaviour that are characteristic of a particular social background. Before considering such links, however, it will be necessary to demonstrate directly the

relationship between sexual attitudes and behaviour, and the present discussion will address this topic in brief detail.

Linking Sexual Attitudes and Sexual Behaviour

Social psychologists have been studying the relationship between attitudes and behaviour for at least half a century (cf. Allport, 1935; Fishbein and Ajzen, 1975). There seems to be fairly consistent evidence, with respect to sexual topics, that an individual's evaluations are related to his or her behaviour. Several points in this connection must be emphasized at the outset, however. First, the attitude–behaviour concordance which is typically observed is far from perfect. Secondly, the question of *causal* attitude–behaviour links is an open one; some propose that attitudes are causally related to behaviour (e.g. Fishbein and Ajzen, 1975), while others argue that our behaviour, in fact, informs us of our attitudes (e.g. Bem, 1965). To establish cause and effect for sexual attitudes and behaviour would presumably require experimental manipulation of sexual attitudes, and for obvious ethical reasons, researchers are reluctant to do this. With these issues in mind, let us turn to research on the links between sexual attitudes and behaviour.

An interesting case of sexual attitude–behaviour correlation has been reported by Christensen and Gregg (1970). They compared subjects' approval or disapproval of premarital sex with self-reports of their behaviour in this regard. In samples taken in 1958 and in 1968, the concordance of attitudes and behaviour was substantial; for instance, in the 1968 sample, 74% of the men who approved of premarital coitus had engaged in this behaviour, while 79% of those who disapproved had *not* done so, and attitude–behaviour agreement was great for women as well. It is also interesting to note that such concordances were somewhat stronger in 1968 than in 1958; it seems possible that the generally more permissive atmosphere of the late 1960s may have freed people to behave (or not to behave) more in accord with their personal inclinations.

Additional evidence regarding a sexual attitude–behaviour link has been developed in a variety of research contexts. For example, Peplau *et al.* (1977) compared attitudes regarding sexual permissiveness among dating couples who either abstained from intercourse, had intercourse early in the relationship, or engaged in coitus somewhat later. Not surprisingly, the abstaining couples were more sexually conservative than the other couples, and those who had sex later in their relationship were more conservative than those who had sex earlier. It is also worth

noting that women's sexual attitudes were found to be better predictors of the timing of coitus than were men's attitudes; presumably, it is still the male who attempts to initiate sexual relations, and the female who regulates such behaviour. In related research on sexual attitudes and behaviour, Reiss (1967) has found a relationship between premarital sexual standards and the extent to which a person may engage in behaviour which violates these standards. In one of Reiss' samples, most of the students who were opposed to anything but kissing reported that their most extreme involvement was in kissing; those who accepted petting attitudinally were more likely to pet than to go farther; while those whose attitudinal standards included coitus were most likely to engage in this behaviour. Reiss also presents data to suggests that violations of these attitudinal standards result in guilt feelings.

There are additional studies which have employed general dispositional measures to demonstrate a relationship between one's evaluation of sexuality and one's sexual behaviour. Mosher (1966, 1968) has developed an index to assess a trait disposition towards sex guilt — "a generalized expectancy for self-mediated punishment for violating or for anticipating violating standards of proper sexual conduct" (Mosher and Cross, 1971, p. 27). Males who scored low (versus high) in sex guilt were more likely to report that they had manually or orally manipulated women's genitals and that they had been masturbated by a woman, while females who scored as low (versus high) in sex guilt were more likely to indicate that they had received manual manipulation of their breasts, or had masturbated — or been masturbated by — a male (Mosher and Cross, 1971). Schill and Chapin (1972) found that men who spent much of their time reading *Playboy* or *Penthouse* while waiting for an experimenter (versus men who spent little time doing so) scored lower in sex guilt, and Schwartz (1973) reports that men and women with low (versus high) sex guilt showed more retention of birth control information when quizzed after a lecture on this subject. And, Griffitt and Kaiser (1978) found that, in a discrimination learning task, subjects with low sex guilt acquired responses that were instrumental in increasing their exposure to erotic stimuli, while subjects with high sex guilt learned responses which resulted in less exposure to erotic stimuli. Utilizing a measure of positive versus negative attitudes about sex, White *et al.* (1977) found that men and women with relatively negative sexual attitudes reported more negative emotional responses to a series of erotic slides, and persons with negative attitudes also reported that they masturbated less often and had fewer premarital sex partners than did those with positive attitudes. Employing the

same attitude measure, Miller and Byrne (1978) reported that, among subjects with negative sexual attitudes, a stranger who was represented as possessing contraceptives was rated as immoral; subjects with positive sexual attitudes did not judge contraceptives to be indicative of immorality. These findings have confirmed the sexual attitude-behaviour link in a variety of settings. On the basis of such evidence, it appears that attitudes towards sex may reflect an approach–avoidance gradient with regard to sexual behaviour.

Since attitudes seem to be an important correlate of sexual behaviour, it seems worthwhile to comment briefly on factors that may determine sexual attitudes. One theoretical approach (Byrne, 1971, 1977; Clore and Byrne, 1974) proposes that, via simple association with reward and punishment, sexual stimuli become capable of eliciting affective responses. Stimulus elicited affect, in turn, is viewed as mediating evaluative responses — such as attitudes — to the stimulus and to other associated cues. The quality of elicited affect (positive or negative) is assumed to determine the direction of the evaluative response (i.e. positive to negative attitudes). It has been proposed that such evaluative responses may serve to justify for individuals the emotions with which they react to sex. Empirical data from a number of sources have been consistent with these assumptions. For example, Fisher and Byrne (1978) found that subjects who reported having restrictive histories of socialization to sex — involving fear, guilt, and religious proscription — showed the most negative emotional responses to an erotic film. And, subjects who responded to the film with these negative emotions also expressed negative attitudes towards a variety of sexual topics, in addition to rating the erotic stimulus as relatively pornographic. In another study, Byrne *et al.* (1974) demonstrated that emotional responses to erotic slides predicted subjects' evaluations of the pornographic quality of these stimuli, as well as opinions about placing legal restrictions on such material. Other studies (Fisher *et al.*, 1977, 1979) have shown a relationship between emotional orientation to sexuality and attitudes about contraception. While these findings do not establish causal relationships, they are in accord with the assumption that stimulus-elicited affect may mediate evaluational responses in the form of attitudes. And, as discussed earlier, there appears to be a consistent link between such sexual attitudes and behaviour.

Attitudes in Sexual-Interpersonal Relationships

So far we have seen that sexual attitudes may reflect an approach–avoidance gradient with respect to behaviour. In addition to this,

attitudes also appear to play a central role in the development of interpersonal — and heterosexual — attraction. In particular, it has been repeatedly observed that attitude similarity may be associated with interpersonal attraction, both in observational research (cf. Galton, 1870/1952; Newcomb, 1956, 1961; Schuster and Elderton, 1906; Terman and Buttenwieser, 1935a, b) and experimental investigations (cf. Byrne, 1961; Byrne *et al.*, 1970, 1971; Byrne and Nelson, 1965). Presumably because the expression of similar attitudes by others may confirm our own views of reality, it has been found that similar attitudes may serve as positive reinforcers (Byrne *et al.*, 1966; Golightly and Byrne, 1964) which elicit positive emotional responses (Byrne and Clore, 1970; Clore and Gormley, 1974; Meadow, 1971), and result in positive evaluations — including interpersonal attraction or "liking" (Byrne, 1961; Byrne *et al.*, 1970, 1971). Attitude dissimilarity, in contrast, appears to serve as a negative reinforcement, eliciting negative affect and resulting in low levels of attraction or in interpersonal dislike.

The link between attitude similarity and attraction has frequently been observed in the context of sexual-interpersonal relationships such as dating dyads and married couples. For example, Wallin and Clark (1958) surveyed 459 married couples with respect to husbands' and wives' ratings of marital satisfaction, their perceptions of how often their spouse wishes to have coitus, and their own preferred coital frequency. Results showed that husbands and wives who had high marital satisfaction were also most likely to perceive their preferences for coital frequency as similar. Wallin and Clark report that the link between marital satisfaction and perceived similarity held, for the most part, even among couples whose preferences for coital frequency were in fact different. Apparently, the perception of similarity with respect to sexual preferences — even when differences actually exist — may be associated with a satisfying marriage. Levinger and Breedlove (1966) and Byrne and Blaylock (1963) have also found that perceived similarity along various dimensions may be associated with ratings of marital satisfaction. And, in a study of married couples, Ard (1977) found that spouses who reported disagreement on sexual issues indicated that such disagreement had made their marriage less happy. In order to gain further insight into husband-wife similarity on sexual issues, Byrne *et al.* (1973) exposed married couples to a series of 19 erotic slides, and assessed subjects' responses to these stimuli. Husbands' and wives' sexual arousal responses to these stimuli were found to be correlated, as were their ratings of how pornographic the stimuli were and their opinions about placing legal restrictions on such material. On a number of sexual attitude dimensions, then, husbands and wives show a consistent tendency to be similar, and

marriages that are rated as happier are associated with greater perceived agreement on sexual issues.

The correlational evidence regarding attitude similarity and sexual-interpersonal attraction is consistent, and what is more, several investigators have conducted experimental research which has confirmed these correlational findings. For example, Byrne (1971) reports a study in which male and female undergraduates responded to a series of sexual and non-sexual attitude statements. Later, these subjects were given a copy of the same questionnaire which supposedly had been filled out by a person of the same, or opposite, sex. These bogus responses were arranged so that the sexual items were either similar or dissimilar to subjects' own attitudes. After reading the stranger's attitude scale, subjects were asked to indicate their attraction for him or her. Results showed that sexual attitude similarity (versus dissimilarity) resulted in higher attraction responses, and in the case of opposite-sex strangers, this effect was especially pronounced. In a more elaborate setting, Touhey (1972) surveyed the attitudes of 250 undergraduate men and women, and created "computer date" matches that were either similar or dissimilar in their sexual attitudes, or were randomly matched (other attitude dimensions were also used as bases for matching but these procedures are irrelevant to the present discussion). Subjects who had met their dates were asked to complete a paper and pencil measure of heterosexual attraction, and the pattern of results in general shows that sexual attitude similarity — especially for males — resulted in higher ratings of heterosexual attraction than did sexual attitude dissimilarity or random matches. In a still more elaborate setting, Byrne et al. (1970) arranged "computer dates" for undergraduate men and women on the basis of similarity or dissimilarity of attitudes and beliefs along several dimensions; dates met in the laboratory, at which time they were given 50c and instructed to have a "coke date" at the student union. Following this, subjects returned to complete a measure of heterosexual attraction. Results show that attitudinally similar (versus dissimilar) dates indicated higher levels of heterosexual attraction, and rated their partners as higher in intelligence and more desirable as a date and marriage partner. As an indirect measure of heterosexual attraction, the physical proximity of the dating couple to one another was measured at the end of the experiment, and attitudinally similar (versus dissimilar) couples were found to stand closer together at this time.

In summary, this overview has suggested that attitudes may play two somewhat different roles in the process of sexual attraction. First,

sexual attitudes appear to represent a general approach-avoidance tendency with respect to sexual behaviour. It was observed that sexual attitudes and overt behaviour are rather consistently linked, and the question of antecedent-consequent (or reciprocal) links between sexual attitudes and behaviour would appear to be an important subject for future research. Secondly, attitudes seem to serve as reinforcing stimuli in the process of sexual attraction; presumably because attitude similarity may serve to validate one's own views and to facilitate reciprocal reinforcement in a couple, both correlational and experimental evidence suggest that attitude similarity may be an important determinant of heterosexual attraction.

Preliminary Suggestions for Understanding the Influence of Social Background and Attitudes on Sexual Attraction

The links that were observed between social background, attitudes, and sexual attraction have described, within limits, who becomes sexually attracted to whom, with what frequency, and in what manner, in terms of variables such as social class, devoutness, attitudes, and the like. These observations also provide a basis for speculation regarding *how* social background and attitudes may affect the sexual attraction responses of individuals. The present section considers one such conceptualization.

It is proposed that sexual attraction is, in important respects, conditioned by prior learning and by the contingencies present in the current interpersonal field. And it is our view that social background and attitudes may represent critical influences on what a person has learned about sexual attraction and on the social context in which this process is likely to take place. We will now turn to a tentative formulation for understanding sexual attraction. This model identifies factors that are thought to determine attraction, and we will discuss the ways in which social background and attitudes may work through these factors to affect individual behaviour with respect to sexual attraction.

The Sexual Behaviour Sequence

Recently, Byrne (1977) has proposed a preliminary model for the study of sexual behaviour, the Sexual Behaviour Sequence. This formulation does not, at present, comprise a thoroughly articulated predictive theory; rather, it presents conceptual guidelines for research on psychological

factors that may influence sexual behaviour. It is therefore regarded as useful to the extent that it may guide our thinking about sexual attraction, generate testable hypotheses, and ultimately lead to accurate predictions of behaviour; this conceptualization is of course subject to change.

The Sexual Behaviour Sequence is presented in Fig. 1. Each box represents a basic psychological concept, the solid arrows indicate proposed antecedent–consequent links, broken arrows suggest relationships between constructs, and the dot–dash arrow represents a feedback loop whereby the rewarding and/or punishing outcome of a resulting sexual behaviour may alter the elements of the system and thus modify future responses. We will discuss the proposed determinants of sexual attraction from the standpoint of this model and consider how social background and attitudes may enter the system and shape the sexual attraction responses of individuals.

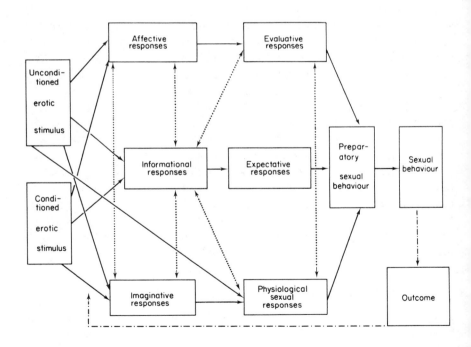

Fig. 1. *The Sexual Behaviour Sequence (after Byrne, 1977)*

Sexual Arousal Responses

Straightforward elicitation of physiological sexual arousal may occur when an individual is exposed to an Unconditioned erotic stimulus. Such stimuli, which lead to arousal without the benefit of prior learning, include tactile stimulation of the genitals (in human beings) and chemical scents called pheromones (in males of some species, and possibly in human males; cf. Comfort, 1971). Physiological sexual arousal is signalled by changes in blood flow to the genitals (cf. Geer, 1975; Geer *et al.*, 1974), and aroused individuals are usually motivated to act in some way that eventually leads to the reduction of this arousal. Such actions are termed Preparatory sexual behaviours in the model, and these can be expressed as preliminary sexual attraction responses which will increase the probability of an orgasm. An aroused individual can choose from any number of such responses which, if successful, will lead to the performance of an overt, orgasmic sexual behaviour. Ordinarily, this will constitute a positive Outcome that will feed back into the system to increase the future likelihood of similar responses. It can happen, however, that circumstances are such that this outcome is negative, and this will decrease the probability of such responses in the future or will alter some aspect of the stimulus–arousal–preparatory response sequence.

While this chain of events seems to be relatively uncomplicated, we propose that each stage of this sequence is subject to extensive social elaboration. For example, it is obvious that sexual arousal in humans is not wholly dependent upon direct tactile stimulation of the genitals. The Sexual Behaviour Sequence suggests that, by simple association, almost any discriminable stimulus that is paired with an Unconditioned erotic stimulus may itself acquire the capacity to elicit physiological sexual arousal. Observation suggests that individuals may learn to become aroused by Conditioned erotic stimuli as diverse as pictures of same and opposite sex nudes, rock music, small children, garter belts, and (depending on which culture and generation one lives in) facial tatoos, small feet, flat or full bosomed women, and bearded or clean-shaven men. Experimental research (e.g. Rachman, 1966) has in fact demonstrated that sexual arousal may be classically conditioned to objects such as boots by pairing such stimuli with nude photos of the opposite sex. We do not have a great deal of evidence regarding differences in cues for arousal for those of varying social background or attitudes, but some of the data are suggestive. Working back from observed differences in autoerotic behaviour and extramarital coitus, we might speculate that religiously

devout persons and those born in earlier generations have *not* learned to become aroused in response to their own bodies or the bodies of persons to whom they are not married; in contrast, the non-devout and the younger generation may have learned to become excited by such cues. In any event, systematic research on social background or attitudinal factors that influence what one finds arousing may be crucial to understanding differences in behaviour, since arousal may act to initiate a chain of sexual attraction responses.

Not only may the cues for sexual arousal be affected by social background and attitudes, but just what one does once he or she has become aroused, and what kind of an outcome this course of events leads to, may also be a function of background and attitudes. The psychological mechanisms that may translate differences in background and attitudes into variations in such behaviour are discussed next.

The Role of Information and Expectancies

The Sexual Behaviour Sequence proposes that, in addition to eliciting sexual arousal, erotic cues also activate a class of acquired beliefs and expectancies regarding sexual behaviour. Informational responses to erotic cues (e.g. "The sexual act in that picture is a sin") and expectancies ("If I did that, I'd feel terrible") may be accurate or inaccurate, but both types of information are assumed to guide behaviour so long as the individual in question is confident that they are true (cf. Fishbein and Ajzen, 1975).

Background factors such as social class, religious devoutness, and even generation of birth may be important sources of beliefs and expectancies about sex. For example, a highly devout individual may become sexually aroused, but this individual may believe that engaging in an overt sex act is morally wrong, and may expect to be punished for such behaviour by the self (e.g. sex guilt) and by others (e.g. devout parents, clerics in the confessional, God, etc.). Consequently, the person may decide *not* to engage in a preliminary sexual attraction response, but rather to distract him or herself cognitively so as to mitigate arousal (as has been demonstrated experimentally by Geer and Fuhr, 1976) or to initiate incompatible stimulus-response sequences (as in the proverbial cold shower). Or, the person may be persuaded — by self or others — to engage in preparatory behaviours that lead to an overt sex act. Still guided by religiously determined beliefs and expectancies, however, the choice of a sexual behaviour (e.g. masturbation is less wrong than

premarital intercourse, which is less wrong than extramarital sex, etc.) and the frequency with which it is engaged in, may be relatively restrained. Finally, beliefs and expectancies may also affect the individual's appraisal of the outcome of such behaviour. For example, the occurrence of orgasm in premarital sex could prove troubling for a devout person, since it makes the "sin" a success; in contrast, marital orgasm may be especially positive, since it may mark the sacred union of marriage a success. The data on religious devoutness and sexual attraction which were surveyed, in fact, are generally consistent with these assumptions. We know that religiously devout persons have non-permissive sexual standards (Hunt, 1974; Reiss, 1967), that they are less likely to masturbate or to engage in premarital sex and to wait longer before doing so (Hunt, 1974; Kinsey *et al.*, 1948, 1953; Peplau *et al.*, 1977; Tavris and Sadd, 1978), and they may enjoy non-marital sex less, but marital sex more, than non-devout persons (Hunt, 1974; Tavris and Sadd, 1978). These concordances suggest the utility of research that bears *directly* on the impact of religious devoutness, through beliefs and expectancies, on sexual behaviour and the appraisal of such behaviour.

It also seems likely that social class and generational differences in sexual attraction could be understood in terms of characteristic variations in beliefs and expectancies. For example, lower social class and less well educated persons were consistently found to engage in premarital coitus at a relatively early age, while middle class, better educated persons tend to delay this behaviour and to masturbate and pet more often in the interim. Conceivably, some of these differences could be accounted for in terms of social class differences in beliefs and expectancies. It might be found that lower-class youth — quite accurately — believe that others like themselves engage in premarital coitus at an early age. They may expect to marry younger, and hence initiate premarital intercourse earlier, and they may anticipate fewer negative sanctions for doing so. Middle-class youth, in contrast, may accurately perceive premarital sex as less normative, they may expect to marry later and hence postpone premarital involvement, and they may anticipate that the risks (e.g. pregnancy, early marriage, etc.) of premarital coitus could seriously complicate plans for extended education, etc. Similarly, generational shifts toward sexually permissive behaviour may also be traced to shifts in the perceived normativeness of sexual activity and expectancies concerning the likely outcome of such behaviour. While the parent generation may have regarded premarital intercourse as somewhat deviant and likely to result in significant difficulties, today's youth —

who have not often seen the public shaming of unwed mothers but who do know about the pill and legal abortion — may perceive such behaviour as more normative and as less likely to have negative consequences. In an analogous way, class differences in such acts as cunnilingus may simply reflect class differences in the beliefs and expectancies associated with that activity. To the extent that social class and generational differences are linked with variations in beliefs and expectancies, the Sexual Behaviour Sequence would predict concomitant differences in sexual behaviour and in the positive or negative outcome of such behaviour. Beyond the speculative and oversimplified examples provided above, research is needed that directly focuses on how social background may work through beliefs and expectancies to affect behaviour.

The Role of Affect and Evaluation

In addition to evoking arousal, beliefs, and expectancies, the Sexual Behaviour Sequence proposes that erotic stimuli may also elicit positive and negative Affective responses. As discussed earlier, it is assumed that such emotional responses are acquired via simple association of reward and punishment with erotic cues during one's socialization history (cf. Byrne, 1971, 1977; Fisher and Byrne, 1978). And, emotional responses to erotic stimuli are regarded as mediating similarly valenced Evaluative responses to these cues, such as positive or negative attitudes (cf. Byrne *et al.*, 1974). According to the model, this affective–evaluative subsystem may influence the entire Sexual Behaviour Sequence. Individuals who respond to sex with primarily negative (versus positive) affect and evaluations, for example, should be less likely to engage in preparatory sexual attraction responses. And, the research surveyed showed that persons with a negative affective–evaluative disposition toward sex seem to have less premarital sexual experience (Christensen and Gregg, 1970; Mosher and Cross, 1971; White *et al.*, 1977), to delay coitus in dating relationships (Peplau *et al.*, 1977), to act in accord with their non-permissive standards (Reiss, 1967), and to avoid contact with erotica (Griffitt and Kaiser, 1978; Schill and Chapin, 1972). With respect to the dynamics of sexual attraction, it has also been found that persons with a negative emotional and evaluative orientation toward sex find it relatively aversive to communicate about this topic with others (Fisher *et al.*, 1980).

The affective–evaluative subsystem appears to influence sexual attraction and overt behaviour, and it may influence one's beliefs and expectancies about sex as well. It has been suggested, for example, that

persons with negative (versus positive) feelings about sex may know and retain less information about sexual topics (cf. Schwartz, 1971), and such persons may also expect others to disapprove of various sexual behaviours, including the use of contraception (Fisher, *et al.*, 1977, 1979, 1980; Miller and Byrne, 1978). Presumably, beliefs and expectancies may also have reciprocal effects on the affective-evaluative subsystem. A devout person who believes that premarital sex is sinful but that marital sex is sacred may report differential evaluations of such experiences, as noted earlier (cf. Hunt, 1974; Tavris and Sadd, 1978), and a person in the permissive 1960s may feel less guilty about sex than a similar individual in the more restrictive 1950s (cf. Bell and Chaskes, 1970; Christensen and Gregg, 1970). Such direct and interactive effects of affect and evaluations, then, seem to influence sexual attraction, the choice and timing of sexual behaviour, and appraisal of the outcome of such behaviours. According to the proposed model, such effects should feed back into the system to shape future behaviour.

It was consistently observed that social class, devoutness, and generational differences have relatively homogeneous attitudinal concomitants. For example, religiously devout individuals are attitudinally opposed to many forms of sexual behaviour, while non-devout persons, members of the middle class, and those born in more recent generations, seem to have more positive feelings about sex, etc. Behavioural parallels to differences in attitudes that are characteristic of various social backgrounds were often seen as well, and research that has directly examined the subject indicates clear sexual attitude-behaviour consistencies. The Sexual Behaviour Sequence proposes that to the extent social background affects emotional and attitudinal responses to sex, corresponding differences in behaviour and appraisal of behaviour will occur. What is needed now is research that directly considers how social background factors may work, through emotional and attitudinal responses, to affect sexual attraction.

The Sexual Behaviour Sequence indicates that attitudes may play an additional role in the process of sexual attraction. As discussed earlier, the expression of similar attitudes is positively reinforcing and leads to interpersonal attraction; attitude dissimilarity, in contrast, acts as a negative reinforcement that elicits unpleasant emotions and interpersonal dislike. In a sexual-interpersonal context, the emotional and evaluative consequences of attitude similarity should have effects that reverberate throughout the Sexual Behaviour Sequence. Positive beliefs and expectancies may more often occur with respect to an individual whose

attitudes are reinforcing (i.e. positive), and such a person will be more likely to elicit sexual attraction responses, overt sexual behaviour, and positive sexual outcomes. Such responses, in contrast, should be less likely to occur with respect to an individual whose attitudes are negatively reinforcing (i.e. dissimilar). The literature which was surveyed, in general, is quite consistent with these assumptions. It was observed, for example, that married persons tend to have similar attitudes about sexual issues (Byrne *et al.*, 1973) and that perceived similarity of sexual preferences was associated with marital satisfaction (Ard, 1977; Wallin and Clark, 1958). And, experimental manipulation of attitude similarity was also found to result in heterosexual attraction (Byrne, 1971; Byrne *et al.*, 1970; Touhey, 1972). This chain of evidence, incidentally, suggests another role of social background in the process of sexual attraction. To the extent that social background factors mediate development of similar attitudes — or convey the impression of similarity — it seems likely that persons of similar backgrounds will find each other relatively reinforcing and relatively sexually attractive. Such an effect would most likely be compounded by the influence of propinquity, since persons of similar social class, religion, etc., may be more likely to encounter one another during their sexual careers. Hence, the Sexual Behaviour Sequence suggests dual roles of attitudes in sexual attraction. First, they are part of an affective — evaluative subsystem that may comprise an approach — avoidance gradient with respect to specific aspects of sexuality. Secondly, similar attitudes may act as reinforcers that lead to heterosexual attraction. Future research may investigate the role of social background factors in shaping attitudes and trace the effect of such attitudes throughout the Sexual Behaviour Sequence.

The Role of Fantasy and Imagination

One additional factor in the Sexual Behaviour Sequence remains to be discussed, and that involves the construct of sexual fantasy or Imaginative responses. We have reviewed data which suggest that individuals who are middle class, non-devout, or of the younger generation may be the most likely to engage in sexual fantasy, but unfortunately, we have very little information regarding the relation of sexual fantasy to other elements in the proposed model. We do know that erotic stimuli may serve as cues for sexual fantasy, and that such imaginative responses may result in sexual arousal (Byrne and Lamberth, 1971). Many individuals report that they engage in sexual fantasy during

masturbation and coitus (cf. Clifford, 1978; Hariton and Singer, 1974; Hunt, 1974; Wilson, 1975) and at least one experiment found that directed sexual fantasy led to higher levels of arousal than did exposure to erotic stimuli that depicted scenes like the ones subjects were asked to imagine (Byrne and Lamberth, 1971). Less is known about the links between sexual fantasy, beliefs and expectancies, affect and evaluation, and overt sexual behaviour. Byrne (1977) has noted that a person's beliefs and expectancies may appear in their sexual fantasies, and the possibility also exists that individuals who have negative emotional and evaluative responses to sex may fantasize less often and in less detail than those who are more positively disposed.

With regard to fantasy-behaviour links, still less is known. It is possible to speculate that those with active fantasy lives will become motivated to engage in overt sexual behaviour, but it is equally plausible that persons with impoverished sex lives may employ fantasy as a surrogate for reality. In sum, data exist to suggest that social background may affect sexual fantasy, but until more is learned about the role of fantasy in the process of sexual attraction, the question of how such differences in fantasy may affect other responses remains open (Kelley and Byrne, 1978). It seems possible that research on the effects of social background and attitudes on fantasy, and research on fantasy-behaviour links, could converge in the future to improve our general understanding of sexual attraction.

Directions for Future Research

In this chapter, we have surveyed different ideas about sexual attraction, provided a descriptive overview of links between social background, attitudes, and sexual attraction, and proposed a conceptualization to help understand these relationships. It is our belief that theory is needed to integrate research in this area, and the Sexual Behaviour Sequence provides one such conceptual guide. According to this model, social background factors and attitudes work through basic psychological processes to affect sexual attraction. We have proposed that future research consider more directly the impact of social background on what stimuli a person finds arousing, on beliefs and expectancies, and on emotions, attitudes, fantasy, and behaviour. A special emphasis in this regard could involve focus on such responses in interpersonal, dyadic settings, which have so far received little empirical attention. It is hoped that such approaches may provide further insights into social determinants of sexual attraction.

2. References

Allport, G. W. Attitudes. In Murchison, C. (Ed.), *Handbook of social psychology.* Vol. 2. Worcester, Massachusetts: Clark University Press, 1935.

Ard, B. N., Jr. Sex in lasting marriages: A longitudinal study. *Journal of Sex Research*, 1977, **13**, 274-285.

Asayama, S. Sexual behavior in Japanese students: Comparisons for 1974, 1960, and 1952. *Archives of Sexual Behavior*, 1976, **5**, 371-390.

Bauman, K. E., and Wilson, R. R. Sexual behavior of unmarried university students in 1968 and 1972. *Journal of Sex Research*, 1974, **10**, 327-333.

Bauman, K. E. and Wilson, R. R. Premarital sexual attitudes of unmarried university students: 1968 vs. 1972. *Archives of Sexual Behavior*, 1976, **5**, 29-37.

Bell, R. R. *Premarital sex in a changing society.* Englewood Cliffs: Prentice-Hall, 1966.

Bell, R. R. and Chaskes, J. B. Premarital sexual experience among coeds, 1958 and 1968. *Journal of Marriage and the Family*, 1970, **32**, 81-84.

Bem, D. J. An experimental analysis of self-persuasion. *Journal of Experimental Social Psychology*, 1965, **1**, 199-218.

Berscheid, E. and Walster, E. A little bit about love. In Huston, T. L. (Ed.), *Foundations of interpersonal attraction.* New York and London: Academic Press, 1974.

Bloch, I. *Anthropological studies in the strange sexual practices of all races in all ages, ancient and modern, oriental and occidental, primitive and civilized.* New York: Anthropological Press, 1933. (Republished, New York: AMS, 1974.)

Brady, J. P. and Levitt, E. E. The relation of sexual preferences to sexual experiences. *Psychological Record*, 1965, **15**, 377-384.

Byrne, D. Interpersonal attraction and attitude similarity. *Journal of Abnormal and Social Psychology*, 1961, **62**, 713-715.

Byrne, D. *The attraction paradigm.* New York and London: Academic Press, 1971.

Byrne, D. Social psychology and the study of sexual behavior. *Personality and Social Psychology Bulletin*, 1977, **3**, 3-30.

Byrne, D. and Blaylock, B. Similarity and assumed similarity of attitudes between husbands and wives. *Journal of Abnormal and Social Psychology*, 1963, **67**, 636-640.

Byrne, D. and Clore, G. L. A reinforcement model of evaluative responses. *Personality: An International Journal*, 1970, **1**, 103-128.

Byrne, D. and Lamberth, J. The effect of erotic stimuli on sex arousal, evaluative responses, and subsequent behavior. In *Technical report of the Commission on Obscenity and Pornography.* Vol. 8. Washington, D.C.: US Government Printing Office, 1971.

Byrne, D. and Nelson, D. Attraction as a linear function of proportion of positive reinforcements. *Journal of Personality and Social Psychology*, 1965, **1**, 659-663.

Byrne, D., Young, R. K. and Griffitt, W. The reinforcement properties of attitude statements. *Journal of Experimental Research in Personality*, 1966, **1**, 266-276.

Byrne, D., Ervin, C. R. and Lamberth, J. Continuity between the experimental study of attraction and real-life computer dating. *Journal of Personality and Social Psychology*, 1970, **16**, 157-165.

Byrne, D., Baskett, G. D. and Hodges, L. Behavioral indicators of interpersonal attraction. *Journal of Applied Social Psychology*, 1971, **1**, 137-149.

Byrne, D., Cherry, F., Lamberth, J. and Mitchell, H. E. Husband-wife similarity in response to erotic stimuli. *Journal of Personality*, 1973, **41**, 385-394.

Byrne, D., Fisher, J. D., Lamberth, J. and Mitchell, H. E. Evaluations of erotica: Facts or feelings? *Journal of Personality and Social Psychology*, 1974, **29**, 111-116.

Christensen, H. T. and Gregg, C. F. Changing sex norms in America and Scandinavia. *Journal of Marriage and the Family*, 1970, **32**, 616-627.

Clark, R. A. The projective measurement of experimentally induced levels of sexual motivation. *Journal of Experimental Psychology*, 1952, **44**, 391-399.

Clark, R. A. and Sensibar, M. R. The relationship between symbolic and manifest projections of sexuality with some incidental correlates. *Journal of Abnormal and Social Psychology*, 1955, **50**, 327-334.

Clifford, R. E. Development of masturbation in college women. *Archives of Sexual Behavior*, 1978, **7**, 559-573.

Clore, G. L. and Byrne, D. A reinforcement-affect model of attraction. In Huston, T. L. (Ed.), *Foundations of interpersonal attraction*. New York and London: Academic Press, 1974.

Clore, G. L. and Gormly, J. B. Knowing, feeling, and liking: A psychophysiological study of attraction. *Journal of Research in Personality*, 1974, **8**, 218-230.

Comfort, A. Likelihood of human pheromones. *Nature*, 1971, **230**, 432-433, 479.

Commission on Obscenity and Pornography. *The report of the Commission on Obscenity and Pornography*. Washington, D.C.: US Government Printing Office, 1970.

Davis, K. B. *Factors in the sex life of twenty-two hundred women*. New York: Harper and Brothers, 1929. (Republished, New York: Arno Press and The New York Times, 1972.)

DeLamater, J. and MacCorquodale, P. *Premarital sexuality: Attitudes, relationships, behavior*. Madison: University of Wisconsin Press, 1979.

Dion, K., Berscheid, E. and Walster, E. What is beautiful is good. *Journal of Personality and Social Psychology*, 1972, **24**, 285-290.

Downey, L. Intergenerational change in sex behavior: A belated look at Kinsey's males. *Archives of Sexual Behavior*, 1980, **9**, 267-317.

Driscoll, R., Davis, K. E. and Lipetz, M. E. Parental interference and romantic love: The Romeo and Juliet effect. *Journal of Personality and Social Psychology*, 1972, **24**, 1-10.

Ehrmann, W. *Premarital dating behavior.* New York: Holt, 1959.
Eitner, L. The erotic in art. In Katchadourian, H. A. and Lunde, D. T., *Fundamentals of human sexuality* (2nd edn). New York: Holt, Rinehart and Winston, 1975.
Farr, J. H. and Gordon, C. A partial replication of Kinsey's graffiti study. *Journal of Sex Research*, 1975, 11, 158-162.
Finger, F. W. Changes in sex practices and beliefs of male college students over 30 years. *Journal of Sex Research*, 1975, 11, 304-317.
Fishbein, M. and Ajzen, I. *Belief, attitude, intention, and behavior: An introduction to theory and research.* Reading, Massachusetts: Addison-Wesley, 1975.
Fisher, W. A. and Byrne, D. Individual differences in affective, evaluative, and behavioral responses to an erotic film. *Journal of Applied Social Psychology*, 1978, 8, 355-365.
Fisher, W. A., Fisher, J. D. and Byrne, D. Consumer reactions to contraceptive purchasing. *Personality and Social Psychology Bulletin*, 1977, 3, 293-296.
Fisher, W.A., Byrne, D., Edmunds, M., Miller, C. T., Kelley, K. and White, L. A. Psychological and situation-specific correlates of contraceptive behavior among university women. *Journal of Sex Research*, 1979, 15, 38-55.
Fisher, W. A., Miller, C. T., Byrne, D. and White, L. A. Talking dirty: Responses to communicating a sexual message as a function of situational and personality factors. *Basic and Applied Social Psychology*, 1980, 1, 115-126.
Ford, C. S. and Beach, F. A. *Patterns of sexual behavior.* New York: Harper, 1951.
Galton, F. *Hereditary genius: An inquiry into its laws and consequences.* 1870. (Republished, New York: Horizon, 1952.)
Geer, J. H. Direct measurement of genital responding. *American Psychologist*, 1975, 30, 415-418.
Geer, J. H. and Fuhr, R. Cognitive factors in sexual arousal: The role of distraction. *Journal of Consulting and Clinical Psychology*, 1976, 44, 238-243.
Geer, J. H., Morokoff, P. and Greenwood, P. Sexual arousal in women: The development of a measurement device for vaginal blood volume. *Archives of Sexual Behavior*, 1974, 3, 559-564.
Glenn, N. D. and Weaver, L. N. Attitudes towards premarital, extramarital, and homosexual relations in the U.S. in the 1970s. *Journal of Sex Research*, 1979, 15, 108-118.
Golightly, C. and Byrne, D. Attitude statements as positive and negative reinforcements. *Science*, 1964, 146, 798-799.
Griffitt, W. Sexual stimulation and sociosexual behaviors. In Cook, M. and Wilson, G. (Eds), *Love and attraction: An international conference.* Oxford: Pergamon, 1979.
Griffitt, W. and Kaiser, D. L. Affect, sex guilt, gender, and the rewarding-punishing effects of erotic stimuli. *Journal of Personality and Social Psychology*, 1978, 36, 850-858.
Griffitt, W., May, J. and Veitch, R. Sexual stimulation and interpersonal

behavior: Heterosexual evaluative responses, visual behavior, and physical proximity. *Journal of Personality and Social Psychology*, 1974, **30**, 367-377.

Hamilton, G. V. *A research in marriage*. New York: Albert and Charles Boni, 1929.

Hariton, E. B. and Singer, J. L. Women's fantasies during sexual intercourse: Normative and theoretical implications. *Journal of Consulting and Clinical Psychology*, 1974, **42**, 313-322.

Hunt, M. *Sexual behavior in the 1970s*. Chicago: Playboy Press, 1974.

Kanin, E. J. Premarital sex adjustments, social class, and associated behaviors. *Marriage and Family Living*, 1960, **22**, 258-262.

Kanin, E. J., Davidson, K. R. and Scheck, S. R. A research note on male-female differentials in the experience of heterosexual love. *Journal of Sex Research*, 1970, **6**, 64-72.

Kelley, K. and Byrne, D. The function of imaginative fantasies in sexual behavior. *Journal of Mental Imagery*, 1978, **2**, 139-146.

King, K., Balswick, J. O. and Robinson, I. E. The continuing premarital sexual revolution among college females. *Journal of Marriage and the Family*, 1977, **39**, 455-459.

Kinsey, A. C., Pomeroy, W. B. and Martin, C. E. *Sexual behavior in the human male*. Philadelphia: Saunders, 1948.

Kinsey, A. C., Pomeroy, W. B., Martin, C. E. and Gebhard, P. H. *Sexual behavior in the human female*. Philadelphia: Saunders, 1953.

Kirkendall, L. A. *Premarital intercourse and interpersonal relationships*. New York: Gramercy, 1961.

Krafft-Ebing, R. von. *Psychopathia sexualis*. Philadelphia: F. A. Davis, 1894.

Kronhausen, E. and Kronhausen, P. *Pornography and the law. The psychology of erotic realism and pornography*. New York: Bell, 1959.

Levin, R. J. The Redbook report on premarital and extramarital sex. The end of the double standard? *Redbook*, Oct. 1975, 38, 40, 42, 44, 190, 192.

Levinger, G. and Breedlove, J. Interpersonal attraction and agreement: A study of marriage partners. *Journal of Personality and Social Psychology*, 1966, **3**, 367-372.

Mahoney, E. R. Religiosity and sexual behavior among heterosexual college students. *Journal of Sex Research*, 1980, **16**, 97-113.

Masters, W. H. and Johnson, V. E. *Human sexual response*. Boston: Little, Brown, 1966.

Masters, W. H. and Johnson, V. E. *Human sexual inadequacy*. Boston: Little, Brown, 1970.

Meadow, B. L. The effects of attitude similarity-dissimilarity and enjoyment on the perception of time. Unpublished master's thesis, Purdue University, 1971.

Miller, C. T. and Byrne, D. Affective orientation to sexuality and attributions of contraceptors. Paper presented at the meeting of the Midwestern Psychological Association, Chicago, Illinois, May 1978.

Mosher, D. L. The development and multitrait-multimethod matrix analysis

of three measures of three aspects of guilt. *Journal of Consulting Psychology*, 1966, **30**, 25-29.

Mosher, D. L. Measurement of guilt in females by self-report inventories. *Journal of Consulting and Clinical Psychology*, 1968, **32**, 690-695.

Mosher, D . L. and Cross, H. J. Sex guilt and premarital sexual experiences of college students. *Journal of Consulting and Clinical Psychology*, 1971, **36**, 27-32.

Newcomb, T. M. The prediction of interpersonal attraction. *American Psychologist*, 1956, **11**, 575-586.

Newcomb, T. M. *The acquaintance process.* New York: Holt, Rinehart and Winston, 1961.

Peplau, L. A., Rubin, Z. and Hill, C. T. Sexual intimacy in dating relationships. *Journal of Social Issues*, 1977, **33**, 86-109.

Purdy, S. B. The erotic in literature. In Katchadourian, H. A. and Lunde, D. T., *Fundamentals of human sexuality* (2nd edn). New York: Holt, Rinehart and Winston, 1975.

Rachman, S. Sexual fetishism: An experimental analogue. *Psychological Record*, 1966, **16**, 293-296.

Rainwater, L. Some aspects of lower class sexual behavior. *Journal of Social Issues*, 1966, **22**, 96-108.

Reiss, I. L. *The social context of premarital sexual permissiveness.* New York: Holt, Rinehart and Winston, 1967.

Rosenheim, E. Sexual attitudes and regulations in Judaism. In Money, J. and Musaph,, H. (Eds), *Handbook of sexology*. Vol. 1. New York: Elsevier, 1978.

Rubin, Z. Measurement of romantic love. *Journal of Personality and Social Psychology*, 1970, **16**, 265-273.

Rubin, Z. *Liking and loving. An invitation to social psychology.* New York: Holt, Rinehart and Winston, 1973.

Schill, T. and Chapin, J. Sex guilt and males' preference for reading erotic magazines. *Journal of Consulting and Clinical Psychology*, 1972, **39**, 516.

Schmidt, G. Working-class and middle-class adolescents. In Money, J. and Musaph, H. (Eds), *Handbook of sexology*. Vol. 1. New York: Elsevier, 1978.

Schmidt, G. and Sigusch, V. Sex differences in responses to psychosexual stimulation by films and slides. *Journal of Sex Research*, 1970, **6**, 268-283.

Schofield, M. *The sexual behaviour of young people.* London: Longmans, Green, 1965.

Schuster, E. and Elderton, E. M. The inheritance of psychical characters. *Biometrika*, 1906, **5**, 460-469.

Schwartz, S. Effects of sex guilt and sexual arousal on the retention of birth control information. *Journal of Consulting and Clinical Psychology*, 1973, **41**, 61-64.

Sorensen, R. C. *The Sorensen report. Adolescent sexuality in contemporary America. Personal values and sexual behavior ages thirteen to nineteen.* New York: World, 1973.

Sporken, P. Marriage and sexual ethics in the Catholic church. In Money, J.

and Musaph, H. (Eds), *Handbook of sexology.* Vol. 1. New York: Elsevier, 1978.

Swenson, C. H., Jr. Love: A self-report analysis with college students. *Journal of Individual Psychology*, 1961, **17**, 167–171.

Tavris, C. and Sadd, S. *The Redbook report on female sexuality. 100,000 married women disclose the good news about sex.* New York: Dell, 1978.

Terman, L. M. and Buttenwieser, P. Personality factors in marital compatibility: I. *Journal of Social Psychology*, 1935a, **6**, 143–171.

Terman, L. M. and Buttenwieser, P. Personality factors in marital compatibility: II. *Journal of Social Psychology*, 1935b, **6**, 267–289.

Touhey, J. C. Comparison of two dimensions of attitude similarity on heterosexual attraction. *Journal of Personality and Social Psychology*, 1972, **23**, 8–10.

van Gennep, F. O. Sexual ethics in Protestant churches. In Money, J., and Musaph, H. (Eds), *Handbook of sexology.* Vol. 1. New York: Elsevier, 1978.

Vener, A. M. and Stewart, C. S. Adolescent sexual behavior in middle America revisited: 1970–1973. *Journal of Marriage and the Family*, 1974, **36**, 728–735.

Wallin, P. and Clark, A. Marital satisfaction and husbands' and wives' perception of similarity in their preferred frequency of coitus. *Journal of Abnormal and Social Psychology*, 1958, **57**, 370–373.

Walster, E., Walster, G. W., Piliavin, J. and Schmidt, L. "Playing hard to get": Understanding an elusive phenomenon. *Journal of Personality and Social Psychology*, 1973, **26**, 113–121.

White, G. L. Physical attractiveness and courtship progress. *Journal of Personality and Social Psychology*, 1980, **39**, 660–668.

White, L. A., Fisher, W. A., Byrne, D. and Kingma, R. Development and validation of a measure of affective orientation to erotic stimuli: The Sexual Opinion Survey. Paper presented at the meeting of the Midwestern Psychological Association, Chicago, Illinois, May 1977.

Wilson, W. C. The distribution of selected sexual attitudes and behaviors among the adult population of the United States. *Journal of Sex Research*, 1975, **11**, 46–64.

Wincze, J. P., Hoon, P. and Hoon, E. F. Sexual arousal in women: A comparison of cognitive and physiological responses by continuous measurement. *Archives of Sexual Behavior*, 1977, **6**, 121–133.

Zelnik, M. and Kantner, J. F. Sexual and contraceptive experience of young unmarried women in the United States, 1976 and 1971. *Family Planning Perspectives*, 1977, **2**, 55–71.

3
The Influence of Special Sexual Desires

CHRIS GOSSELIN
Department of Psychology, Institute of Psychiatry,
De Crespigny Park, London, England

Introduction

From the evidence so far presented in this book, it is clear that at least some of the bases on which sexually average people are attracted to one another are known. At the risk of inadvertently demonstrating inadequate literature coverage, however, it would seem to me that the bases on which the sexually *unaverage* man or woman is attracted towards a partner have been rather less well studied.

There are three reasons for this. The first is that nearly all the attention directed at those whose sexual patterns are different from the norm is confined to the clinical setting, with its emphasis on change to be wrought upon this minority of a minority. The second barrier to knowledge is simply that the stigma still seemingly attached to even the most modest sexual variation makes the possessor difficult to find: except in special circumstances, he is also often reluctant to talk openly of his predilection. The third barrier is that such studies as do exist of non-clinical variants have only indirectly been concerned with discovering the bases or criteria of attraction that they use. We have in fact only just begun to examine the broad non-clinical spectrum of variant populations.

Some examination of clinical findings and views, both psychodynamic and otherwise, will nevertheless not go amiss, largely because what is sauce for the clinical goose *might* also be sauce for the non-clinical gander. This examination will confine itself to three sexual variations, namely, fetishism, sadomasochism and transvestism, partly because certain of the findings can be compared with the new data to be discussed in the present chapter which has been obtained from non-clinical groups

practising these variations, and partly because this triad of behaviours seems to be regarded as almost "acceptable" to society (in contra-distinction to, say, pedophilia, necrophilia or coprophilia) and might therefore have a real-life impact on the choice of a sexual partner.

Psychoanalytic Approaches

Psychoanalytic theorists generally consider sexual variations as serving some sort of defensive function, warding off anxiety about conventional sexual contacts or about other sexual beliefs, whether misguided or not. Because there is no way of testing those theories, however, ideas about what lies behind these defences have proliferated wildly. The fetish object, for example, is said by different writers to represent the means by which the phallic woman is created, a defence against castration anxiety, the vagina, a substitute for the mother's "lost" penis, a means of damping down sadistic impulses, a perceived bodily defect, the female breast, the father's penis, the parent's anal tract, parental faeces or a concrete image compensating for a lost sense of security.

Sadomasochism is more generally thought of as the adult expression of infantile hostility due to sexual frustration, though whether masochism is self-directed sadism or an independent instinctual drive or behaviour seems never to have been settled. Meanwhile, when an individual experiences a situation which is severely traumatic in the sense that his ego resources are nearly overwhelmed, it may lead to recapitulation of that experience (rather than repression), either in fantasy or by acting out, in the form of a sadistic ritual which seeks to master the cause of the trauma or a masochistic one which seeks to appease the cause of the trauma. Since the trauma does not easily disappear under such circumstances, the repetition can occur again and again (Freud, 1924). This concept has been explored and developed by Stoller (1970), who points out with admirable pragmatism that the trauma playout must be modified so that the affect becomes bearable yet is still powerful enough to induce arousal. The attainment of this balance and the sense of triumph thus engendered is then celebrated with a masturbatory orgasm — an experience which militates towards further repetition on subsequent occasions. Some writers (e.g. Sack and Miller, 1975) have also moved towards the idea of sadomasochism being an interpersonal relationship rather than a definable behaviour, designed to increase attachment and dependence: unfortunately, however true this may be, it allows sadomasochism as a concept to escape from the almost totally

sexual orbit in which popular images put it, and give it a sense of perfusing real life which contrasts with the ritualistic aspect stressed not only by Smirnoff (1969) in his telling analysis of Sacher-Masoch's novel *Venus in Furs*, but also by many "professionals" who specialize in, and cater for, a masochistic clientele. It is nevertheless possible that this perfusion tells us more about the bases of attraction used by the masochist than does a purely objective appraisal of his sexual behaviour: the almost poetic statement of Karen Horney (quoted in Barbara, 1974) may well be pertinent to what the masochist seeks in his relationships. To him,

> Love must and does appear as the ticket to paradise, where all woe ends; no more loneliness; no more feeling lost, guilty and unworthy; no more responsibility for self; no more struggle with a harsh world for which he feels hopelessly unequipped. Instead, love seems to promise protection, support, affection, encouragement, sympathy, understanding. It will give him a feeling of worth. It will give meaning to his life. It will be salvation and redemption.

and, of course, it matters not to the masochist that the way to this Nirvana is strewn with whips and manacles.

The psychoanalytic interpretation of transvestism has been formally stated by Storr (1964), who holds that

> the homosexual replaces his love for his mother by an identification with her: the fetishist refuses to acknowledge that a woman has no penis. The male transvestite assumes both attitudes simultaneously. He fantasises that the woman possesses a penis, and thus overcomes his castration anxiety, and identifies himself with the phallic woman.

Such an interpretation may nevertheless be over-complex: Havelock Ellis (1936) attributed transvestism to no more than an exaggeration of the tendency to identify oneself with a beloved person. The difficulty here may be that, as Benjamin (1966) has pointed out, transvestites are probably not a homogeneous group, but may be divided into "fetishistic" and "femmiphilic" types: the first cross-dress in order to increase sexual arousal, the clothes chosen being often theatrically female, whilst the second group cross-dresses in order to relax, using "ordinary" female attire and feeling that they belong, psychologically, to the opposite sex. Incidentally, this attitude may seem similar to that of the transsexual, but the femmiphilic transvestite seldom makes any physical attempt to "cross the barrier" by taking female hormones — except, perhaps, experimentally — or making enquiries about sex-change surgery.

Whatever the interpretations and theories proposed by psychoanalytic

writers to "explain" sexual variation, however, there seems to be some consensus as to some characteristics of those who practise it. Case histories often depict the sexual variant as shy, neurotic, introverted, lacking in conventional sexual experience and sometimes brought up under circumstances which seem likely to stunt his sexual and emotional growth. True, the judgements are virtually always subjective, but even putting aside such pejorative reporters as Krafft-Ebing (1886/1965) — "patient comes of a degenerate family", "of tainted stock", "history of pollutions", "coarse and peculiar" are phrases of a type liberally sprinkled about his case-histories — one cannot merely disregard the cumulative psychoanalytic view.

Behaviourist Approaches

The alternative view of sexual variation stems largely from the behaviourist school, who see it as a maladaptive learned behaviour acquired by both classical and operant conditioning. Whether such conditioning (or, for that matter, any psychodynamic trauma) takes root preferentially within a brain pre-prepared by genetic messages or by lesions is at present poorly evidenced: fortunately, however, such a question is virtually irrelevant to the present discussion of the bases of sexual attraction. Evidence for the role of learning stems first from Rachman and Hodgson (1968), who showed that the sexual arousal which occurred when subjects viewed slides of naked women could be conditioned to a slide showing a pair of women's knee-length boots, and that the response generalized to similar objects such as high-heeled shoes and boots of a different colour. In fairness, however, the response was comparatively weak and transient — though whether this was because the experiment was carried out on adults rather than on children of a more vulnerable age, or whether the response was not the same in the long term simply because a "real" fetish had in fact not been generated, is of course unknown.

The second type of evidence that conditioning plays a part in channelling sexual behaviour in a particular direction stems from the now large number of reports detailing the comparative successfulness of learning theory approaches in *removing* unwanted sexual variations of the types under discussion (see, for example, Bebbington, 1977; Marks *et al.*, 1970; Davison, 1968; for different techniques). It may nevertheless be inadvisable to claim that because sexual variations can be removed in adulthood by conditioning methods, this is how they were acquired in infancy in the first place.

Finally, it is fairly easy to construct a two-process learning theory model of how a fetishist or a fetishistic transvestite acquires his liking, with a high-salience stimulus initially becoming conditioned to fortuitous or even inadvertent high arousal, and its subsequent association with genital pleasure (so much easier to notice in the male than in the female, thanks to the almost biofeedback-like response from the penis), the associated pleasure being increased during masturbation using the fetish object as the crux of a fantasy. Certainly the power of fantasy and masturbatory pleasure in creating or setting a sexual pattern must not be underestimated, as is evidenced by Marquis's (1970) use of it in therapy. Marquis instructed his patients to masturbate using their favourite variant fantasy until orgasm was inevitable, whereupon they were to switch to a fantasy previously agreed upon as more desirable. After doing this a number of times (and thus classically conditioning the "desirable" fantasy to orgasmic pleasure) the desirable fantasy could without loss of pleasure be switched in earlier and earlier in the masturbatory sequence until the variant fantasy was no longer necessary to gratification.

Emphasis on the power of masturbation to a fantasy in developing a variant behaviour is in fact the basis of the theory of McGuire *et al.* (1965), who suggest that an initial experience or set of experiences (contact with a salient object or a traumatic event) forms the basis for a fantasy that is used in masturbation, the resulting orgasm acting as an operant conditioning reinforcement. Since that fantasy may be imperceptibly modified to maximize its effectiveness, the eventual story-line might be somewhat different from the original precipitating event — and, incidentally, may well as a result prevent any patient undergoing psychoanalytic treatment for sex variation from recognizing his "original event" even is he does have it brought to his attention. Such a theory allows one to deal with the objection sometimes raised against straight classical conditioning theories that they may be adequate where a definite conditionable stimulus object exists (as in fetishism), but are hard to apply when an attitude or a belief such as "I want to submit to a woman" or "I feel I am a woman" is concerned. At the same time, such a theory produces a sequence not unlike that of Stoller's idea of a trauma revamped into manageable form and celebrated with an orgasm at every visualization. Without the McGuire concept, indeed, the paradox of approaching an aversive stimulus (as in masochism) is only rendered plausible by postulating that is it engendered during a hypothesized "imprinting period" and noting that during the imprinting period of animals, punishing behaviour emanating from the object of imprinting *increases* attachment rather than decreasing it (see

Sack and Miller (1975) for a general review of the evidence on this point).

Details apart, however, learning theory approaches emphasize that those who enjoy variant behaviour seem to have shown themselves more susceptible to conditioning than those who have not learned such behaviours. The association between ease of conditioning and introversion is evidenced by Eysenck (1965), whilst the similarity between the obtrusiveness (to the possessor) of a variant liking and an obsessive–compulsive neurosis is well marked. Couple this with the additional finding of McGuire *et al.*, that over half the patients examined believed themselves incapable of a normal sex life due to guilt, repressive upbringing, previous aversive experience with girls and feelings of physical, social or sexual inadequacy, and the picture of the variant as shy, introverted, neurotic and sexually inexperienced and inadequate mirrors the image created in psychodynamic writings to a considerable extent.

Surveys of Non-clinical Populations

All this, however, is derived from experiment with clinically-presenting subjects, and may by no means apply to those who find their variant behaviours enjoyable rather than a burden. It is therefore time to look at one or two typical papers devoted exclusively to non-clinical variants.

Purely as examples of such papers (and *pace* those others whose work is just as important, but was not selected), mention will be made later of the work of Prince and Bentler (1972) on transvestites, Spengler (1977) on sadomasochists and Gosselin (1979) on a group of fetishists. Two points arise which are relevant both to these studies and to the data to be presented in this chapter. It may first be argued that because each of the groups studied was made up of people who chose to respond to an invitation to participate, rather than being dragooned into ensuring 100% coverage, the groups might not be representative of the population of transvestites, sadomasochists or fetishists as a whole. However, since the riposte might be that the sample stands a far better chance of being representative of the population in question than one made up of clinically-presenting people could ever be, the criticism is not felt to be damaging.

The second question raised is simply that of the degree of truthfulness in replies given to questions dealing with what is probably a quite sensitive subject. Questionnaires asking such questions are nevertheless

returned anonymously, so there would in theory seem to be no *a priori* reason why respondents should be untruthful unless they have some difficulty in even admitting to themselves (by formally putting it down on paper) what they feel or do. The only bias that is thought to occur inadvertently, as illustrated in the paper on fetishists, is the possibility of answers being biased towards social acceptability. However, it has been noticed by the writer that many sexual minority groups are only too eager to find out why they are what they are, so great care is often taken by these respondents to ensure that the answers given are true to their best belief.

Prince and Bentler's work with transvestites gives no direct information about bases of attraction, but certain probabilities can be read between the lines. The authors found that 86% of their 504 transvestites had an average or above average sexual interest in women, 78% were married, 74% were fathers: in such respects they were thus behaving similarly to those whose sex lives were more or less conventional, and are thus likely to have used the same bases of attraction. Seventeen per cent were either presidents or owners of a company or business, thus contradicting the idea that men of this persuasion are necessarily weak or follower types.

It will nevertheless be remembered that there are at least two types of transvestite. The first cross-dresses because the apparel gives him sexual excitement in the same way as any other fetish object arouses the fetishist: the second type cross-dresses because he feels, in part at least, as if he belongs to the opposite sex and therefore wears female clothes as a natural accompaniment to this belief, finding the process relaxing rather than arousing. Other research to be discussed later makes it seem likely that, for the fetishistic cross-dresser, a predominantly masculine set of bases of attraction is always operating, even when cross-dressing is being used as a stimulant, whereas a man who feels himself to be primarily expressing the female side of his nature uses — even if only temporarily! — more traditionally feminine criteria such as those found by Centers (1972). Achievement, leadership, occupational ability and economic competence come before the male criteria of physical attractiveness or erotic ability. It may incidentally be helpful at this stage to point out that the non-fetishistic transvestite should not be confused with the homosexual taking the passive role: both may have fantasies of being made love to by a man, but whereas the homosexual will require another homosexual as his partner, even in fantasy, the transvestite requires a heterosexual man as his dream partner, and finds the idea of a homosexual partner distasteful.

72   *Chris Gosselin*

Spengler's (1977) empirical study of 245 West German male sadomasochists who either placed appropriate advertisements in contact
magazines or who belonged to sadomasochistically oriented clubs
(unspecified in nature) contains no details of the bases of attraction
particular to the group, unless one counts the search for relevant partner
behaviour as a basis in itself, the subject in effect saying "One of my
criteria of attraction is that the partner I am seeking will be willing to let
me beat her/willing to tie me up/do XYZ with me". If, however, such a
criterion is used, it seems to be seldom fulfilled: only 33% of the group
had actually met with like-minded people, for sadomasochistic entertainment, in the last year; 79% nevertheless interacted by writing
sadomasochistic letters to their "pen-partners". Much of the remaining
frequency data is difficult to interpret in terms of our particular quest: to
say that, during the previous year, 15% of the group had never had
sadomasochistic sex with a partner, 20% had had it 1-3 times, 28% had
had it 4-6 times, 19% had had it 7-24 times and 18% had had it yet more
often, tells us little about the extent to which it influences the choice of a
partner. The quest for such activity would not seem, however, to be a
very important criterion, for the sheer physical impossibility of carrying
out many of the practices described in sadomasochistic pornography
without killing one or other of the partners makes it likely that this
variation is more relegated to fantasy than are many other sexual likings.

Research Data

Rubber Fetishists

My earlier work (Gosselin, 1979) on rubber fetishists shows them to be
marginally more introvert and neurotic than control males and very little
different from them in terms of masculinity or self-rated sexual
excitability. They were nevertheless rather more shy, significantly more
prudish and impersonal, had a higher frequency of sexy thoughts and a
greater physical excitement arising from such fantasies. As mentioned
earlier, they also had a greater desire for social acceptability, if high
scores on the "Lie Scale" in the Eysenck Personality Inventory can be
interpreted thus. From these findings one can perhaps infer that this
group have not so much a different basis on which they build their
criteria for sexual attractiveness, as a slightly imperfectly developed one,
an impression also gained during interviews with members of this group.
It seems as if the high sensory salience, amounting almost to theatricality,

of fetishistic articles such as high heels, black shiny garments, masks and suchlike, emphasizes the sexual cues of the wearer to a point where he or she can with greater confidence be accepted.

Personality of Leather Fetishists, Transvestites, and Sadomasochists

Some recent research by Gosselin and Wilson (1980) may, however, be able to throw light on the subject of what bases of attraction the heterosexual variant might use — apart from those which we all use. An extended sample of fetishists, another of sadomasochists and a third of transvestites were studied by means of questionnaires concerning personality, sexual fantasy and performance preferences, upbringing and present situation, followed up in certain cases by interviews. Although no questions directly aimed at elucidating any particular bases of attraction in such groups were asked, the picture that emerges of these variant groups allows us to draw at least some conclusions (especially by examination of their sexual fantasies) as to the special bases of attraction that press upon them. At the same time, comparison of these groups with control and with one other group (made up of ladies who, for one reason or another, partnered certain of the males during their sex fantasy playouts) allows an examination of the points at which the sexual variant appears different from his sexually more conventional counterpart.

The fetishists actually comprised two nominally different subgroups: 38 of them were predominantly biased towards leather as the stimulant material, and belonged to a correspondence club run by the owner of a company selling fetishistic leather and vinyl garments, whilst 80 more belonged to a society for rubber fetishists and their wives or girlfriends. The transvestite group comprised 269 members of the Beaumont Society, the leading UK society for transvestites and transsexuals. The 133 sadomasochists studied belonged to a group formed exclusively for those of their persuasion, which acted as a correspondence and contact system but did not hold group meetings.

Measurements of psychoticism, extraversion, neuroticism and the Lie Scale from the Eysenck Personality Questionnaire for each group are of interest for two reasons. For a start, if the average value for each group on each of those variables is much the same as that of the control group of sexually conventional males, then the chance of variants possessing a radically different basis for attraction from that applying normally is probably quite small. Secondly, some theorists have supposed that variants have acquired their predilections because they have difficulties

in social interaction, or lack the skills or good looks shown (Wilson and Nias, 1976), to attract members of the opposite sex, or have had experiences with adults during upbringing which have prejudiced them against sex relationships (McGuire *et al.*, 1965). Such ideas imply that people with variant sex patterns will be introverted in personality. Additionally, introverts seem to lend themselves more readily to conditioned emotional fixations such as fetishism, as well as to other idiosyncratic predilections.

With regard to neuroticism, it might be expected that those who are anxious, guilt-ridden or otherwise unhappy with their sexual pattern would score higher on this variable than controls — hence the traditional association of clinical sex devision with neuroticism. Many of the variants here studied were, on the other hand, happily enjoying their variation (for example, only 20% of Spengler's (1977) sadomasochists stated that they would/could give up their predilection if it was made easy for them to do so). In such a situation, would sexual variants manifest any more neuroticism than controls? Psychoticism is associated with masculinity, both in the Eysenckian sense of males having a higher P-score, on average, than women of the same age, and in the clinical sense that associates psychoticism with androgen levels and notes that, below the age at which females stop producing oestrogen, males with psychotic disorders such as schizophrenia outnumber females with such disorders (for details of this and other evidence associating psychoticism with masculinity, see Eysenck and Eysenck, 1976). As a result, higher scores might be found in sadists rather than in masochists and in leather fetishists rather than in rubberites, for traditional sexual folklore has always given a more "macho" image to the leatherite: transvestites might be expected to have rather lower scores on this variable than controls.

Results in fact did not entirely confirm these predictions. Transvestites have psychoticism scores similar to those of control males (and significantly higher than those of control females), are significantly more introvert than both male and female controls, and score significantly higher than male controls (but similar to female controls) in terms of neuroticism. The Lie Scale scores were unexceptional. Leather fetishists were not significantly different from male controls on any of the variables concerned, whilst rubber fetishists, although slightly more introvert and neurotic than controls, were not significantly so. Psychoticism scores on this last group were not available: Lie Scale scores were significantly higher than those of controls. (Figures for rubber fetishists were derived from Gosselin (1979).)

Sadomasochists present an interesting, if confusing, picture. Taken as a single group, their psychoticism is unexceptional, but they are significantly more introvert and neurotic than the controls. If, however, the group is split into sadists and masochists on the basis that sadists have more frequent dominant fantasies (as measured in the Wilson Sex Fantasy Questionnaire, q.v. later) than submissive fantasies, while masochists exemplify the reverse situation, it becomes clear that sadists are slightly (though not significantly) higher than masochists on psychoticism, slightly less neurotic, but far more extravert. In fact, sadists have virtually the same extraversion score as the controls: it is the masochists (91 out of the total 133 in the sadomasochistic group) who show significantly more introversion than the controls. Summing up, then, it would seem that fetishists show only minor differences on these personality variables from controls, whereas transvestites and masochists tend towards introversion and neuroticism. Should it therefore be postulated that a basis of attraction for such types is that the partner should have a similarly introverted and neurotic personality, following the findings of Sinberg *et al.* (1972), that congruence in terms of sober/happy-go-lucky, confident/apprehensive, and relaxed/tense 16PF factors were more associated with the married state?

There are two objections to such a conclusion. The first is that members of the groups have "defined" themselves as sadomasochists, fetishists and so on, by joining a specific society. However, sado-masochists can be fetishistic, fetishists can enjoy transvestism, transvestites can enjoy both, as will be seen when the results from the Sex Fantasy Questionnaire are examined. However, a study of the correlations between the frequency of masochistic fantasies among the leather fetishists (who, it will be remembered, most closely resembled the control group in terms of the personality variables mentioned) shows that masochism as a trait tends to predispose the possessor towards introversion and neuroticism. There appears, however, to be no relationship between the frequency of transvestite fantasies and the personality variables for this group.

Sexual Fantasy and Special Sexual Desires

The second objection to accepting personality traits as predicting (on the congruency principle) the bases of attraction lies in the extremely powerful fantasy image of the ideal sex partner, formed by many sexual variants of the types at present under consideration. This ideal image

Table I

Differences between variant and control groups in fantasy frequency on different themes. (+ = significantly higher frequency than controls: - = significantly lower frequency than controls.)

	Transvestite group	Rubber fetishistic group	Leather fetishistic group	Sado-masochistic group
Making love out of doors in a romantic setting	-		-	-
Having intercourse with a loved partner				
Intercourse with a known but untried partner	-			
Intercourse with an anonymous stranger	-			
Sex with two other people				
Participating in an orgy				
Being forced to do something	+	+	+	+
Forcing someone to do something		+	+	+
Homosexual activity				+
Receiving oral sex	-			
Giving oral sex	-			
Watching others have sex	-			
Sex with an animal				
Whipping or spanking someone		+	+	+
Being whipped or spanked	+	+	+	+
Taking someone's clothes off	-		-	
Having your clothes taken off				+
Making love elsewhere than in the bedroom	-			
Being excited by material or clothing	+	+	+	+
Hurting a partner		+		+
Being hurt by a partner	+	+	+	+
Mate-swapping				
Being aroused by watching someone urinate		+		+
Being tied up	+	+	+	+
Tying someone up		+	+	+
Having incestuous sexual relations				
Exposing yourself provocatively				
Wearing clothes of the opposite sex	+	+	+	+
Being promiscuous				
Having sex with someone much younger than yourself	-			
Having sex with someone much older than yourself				
Being much sought after by the opposite sex				+

Being seduced as an "innocent"	+		+
Seducing an "innocent"			
Being embarrassed by failure of sexual performance			
Having sex with someone of different race	-		
Using objects for stimulation (e.g. vibrator, candle)	+	+	+
Being masturbated to orgasm by a partner	+		+
Looking at obscene pictures or films			+
Kissing passionately			

emerges on examination of data from the Wilson Sex Fantasy Questionnaire (Wilson, 1978). The Wilson Questionnaire asks subjects to rate the frequencies with which they fantasize on each of 40 themes, ranging from having sex with a loved partner to being aroused by watching someone urinate. This questionnaire measures differences between variant and control groups as well as the similarity between the sadomasochistic and fetishistic groups and their partial dissimilarity from the transvestite group. The results are shown in Table I: a positive sign indicates that the group in question had an average fantasy frequency significantly higher than the controls, whilst a negative sign indicates that the variant group had a significantly lower fantasy frequency than the control group.

These differences spotlight first the fact that the transvestites have a fair number of themes about which they fantasize *less* than the controls, whereas the other three groups are distinguished by having *more* fantasies on a variety of themes than do the controls. This may be partly a function of differences in libido between the groups: the correlation between total fantasy output and other measures of libido, such as self-rated sex drive, frequency of orgasm, and number of past sexual partners, is fairly high. Even so, the fantasy themes showing individual differences in frequency between variant and control groups are of interest. The transvestites show two general trends: they avoid even marginally exploratory themes (the more daring exploratory themes being frequently avoided by controls as well, so that differences between the groups fail to show up), and they enjoy submissive fantasies.

The fetishists and sadomasochists, on the other hand, avoid very little that is not also turned down by the control group. They both nevertheless enjoy each other's themes — and the transvestite theme as well! Little wonder that North (1970) was able to devote his book

to this trio of variations without finding a need to separate them for discussion purposes.

Examination of the size of the differences between variant and control groups nonetheless reveals that, as with the transvestites, submissive themes have a greater frequency amongst fetishists and sadomasochists than do dominant or sadistic themes. In fact, if the differences are ranked in order of significance and across groups, the ranked order for the "top ten" most popular fantasies among the variant groups is

(i) Being forced to do something,
(ii) Wearing clothes of the opposite sex,
(iii) Being whipped or spanked,
(iv) Being tied up,
(v) Being hurt by a partner,
(vi) Being excited by material or clothing,
(vii) Whipping or spanking someone,
(viii) Tying someone up,
(ix) Using objects for stimulation,
(x) Forcing someone to do something.

This submissive bias goes against the familiar idea that sadomasochism is a unitary phenomenon: such a bias towards submission is nevertheless shown by all the variant groups, a state of affairs mirrored by the greater popularity of male-masochistic than male-sadistic pornography. Further work on this data in fact showed that (a) masochistic fantasy frequency correlates significantly with fetishistic and transvestite fantasy frequencies, whilst sadistic fantasy frequencies show virtually zero correlation, and (b) as total fantasy output increases, masochistic themes increase in frequency at a higher rate than do sadistic themes; it is thus felt that the preponderance of masochistic fantasy in variants is a real phenomenon rather than an experimental or sampling artefact.

From this, therefore, it is not implausible to conclude that variants tend to be more submissive than dominant, and (from the high scores on the "being excited by material or clothing" and "using objects for stimulation" themes) somewhat impersonal. This links in with the admittedly rather slender generalized findings from the personality questionnaire data which, because of the introversion and neuroticism associated with the transvestite and sadomasochistic groups at least, infers a reservedness, a shyness, an aloofness and perhaps consequent difficulties in sociosexual interaction experienced by the variant. In short, he seems to prefer to withdraw into himself and to submit, perhaps a little more than his partner might expect.

Item Analysis of Personality Data

By returning to certain individual questions in the Personality Questionnaire, some confirmation or clarification of this outlook on life may now be afforded. Here, unfortunately, data can only be obtained from one of the two fetishistic groups (the leatherites), for, as was previously mentioned, data on the rubberite group were obtained on a slightly different version of the questionnaire. However, the questions asked of all the remaining groups gave additional clues.

It was found that members of the variant groups tended to feel more lonely and had a less active sense of humour than their control counterparts. They also were more often depressed, though this may be more a question of moodiness than a pathological state of being continually "down". Additionally, transvestites and sadomasochists tended to keep more in the background on social occasions, and stated that their feelings were more frequently hurt than did controls. Lastly, transvestites (but not the other groups) worried more than usual about their looks, though this answer may well have been highly influenced by the necessity for members of this group to look good as a female as well as presenting a reasonable male appearance. Perhaps one of the surprising additional findings was that only the transvestites showed a heightened sense of guilt about their general life-style — a finding confirmed when the rubber fetishists were tested on this point *en passant* by me during my previous work with that group. Perhaps we all feel somewhat guilty about some part of our sex-lives: 44% of the control group stated that they were "often troubled" by guilt feelings.

To sum up this section, then, the reservedness, the seriousness and the sense of being alone which have been noticed before obtrude once more. These feelings press harder upon the transvestite than upon the sadomasochist, and upon both more than upon the fetishist. Has this more to do with upbringing, family background and environment than with biological factors? Or has the variant learnt to be what he is? These questions will be considered in the next section.

The Origins of Special Sexual Desires

Inheritance

Twin study methods have shown (see Eysenck and Wilson, 1979) that homosexual orientation is partly due to genetic factors, as is the level of

libido. When it comes to the variations with which this chapter is mostly concerned, however, information is thinner on the ground. One or two case studies have been reported in which remarkably similar fetishistic or transvestic behaviour has been observed in identical twins, each of whom was apparently unaware of the other sharing the proclivity which he enjoyed (see, for example, Gorman, 1964), but a classical twin study designed to test the importance of genetic factors in the development of fetishism, sadomasochism or transvestism has yet to be carried out. All that can be reported at present is the beginnings of such a study being carried out at the moment by Glenn Wilson at the Institute of Psychiatry, involving asking pairs of identical and fraternal male twins to complete the previously mentioned Sex Fantasy Questionnaire, then correlating the ratings for each pair on certain key items. Table II shows the results, together with those for self-rated sex drive and self-rated sexual satisfaction.

Table II
Intraclass correlations of identical and fraternal male twins on key fantasy items, self-rated sex drive and overall sexual satisfaction (n = 14 pairs in each group).

	Identical twins	Fraternal twins
Being whipped or spanked	0·36	0·13
Being excited by material or clothing	0·37	0·50
Wearing clothes of the opposite sex	0·80	0·53
Sex drive	0·42	0·02
Sexual satisfaction	0·52	0·17

The results are interesting, even bearing in mind the small sample studied so far. It points to the possibility of genetic factors being implicated in transvestism (and non-fetishistic transvestites often declare their predilection to be a question of differing gender identity) and in sadomasochism, where individual differences in aggression and submission (which have at least some biological basis) are all-important. Fetishism seems from these results to be far more a matter of learning and experience — probably within the influential orbit of family upbringing. Certainly this ties up with the fact that it is far easier to build a classical and/or instrumental conditioning model to explain fetishism, with its implication of a definite conditionable stimulus, than it is to try and explain an unusual gender identity or a submissive attitude by this simple means.

The relevance of this slender twin study to the present quest is

nevertheless not simply to suggest that some less usual bases of attraction might be genetically influenced, but to offer a possible explanation of why fetishists seem to be less trammelled by introversion, neuroticism and associated difficulties than are sadomasochists and transvestites. The answer may simply be that it might be hard to offset a position dictated by biological influences, but rather easier to come to terms with what the clinician might term "maladaptive learning". As a result, the fetishist may to some extent brush his puzzlement aside and get on with living, whereas the transvestite or the sadomasochist, finding their liking somewhat more ingrained or immutable, might be more troubled about it as a result, especially if an excessive tendency to worry is one of the traits built into them anyway.

Family Dynamics

Clinicians nevertheless find it only too easy to discern special circumstances of upbringing and environment which can plausibly account for their patient's behaviour, so it is clearly also necessary to examine the present and past environments of these groups in order to discern what influence, if any, such factors may have had on them. Present and past must equally be looked at, for, as one clinician has put it to me, "I often think I can see how and why they have acquired their special liking: what I am rather more uncertain of, however, is why they have bothered to retain it".

The exercise may also help to support or demolish some favoured tenets of sexual folklore. For example, it is frequently believed that the prime requisite for the creation of sexual variants is a physically or emotionally dominant mother and a physically or emotionally absent or weak father. Such a dyad is also said to create delinquents and geniuses, but that is by the way. Prince and Bentler's (1972) transvestite group showed no particular evidence of this, however, although there was no control group with which to compare the transvestites: 51% stated that the father was the dominant parent, 72% said that the father's image was masculine and good. The present research did not ask the same question, but to the question "Was your mother a good woman?", transvestites gave an 83% "Yes" answer while sadomasochists gave a 93% affirmative, as against the control group's 95%. Only the leather fetishists upset the picture, with only 37% agreeing that mother was good. Does the child starved of mother love turn to an immediate inanimate substitute for the mother such as the strip of blanket often carried about by young

children, and thus create his fetish? Surely that idea is doubtful, for if it were so, there would be many more wool fetishists than rubberites or leatherites.

Popular sexual folklore also associates the ideas of childhood and punishment, especially when variant sexuality is at issue. Sadomasochists particularly seem to believe that their predilection arose directly from their experience of punishment at home or at school. One might therefore predict that they would recall more frequent punishment in childhood than those who did not enjoy that variation; indeed, since submissive or masochistic fantasies are enjoyed more frequently than usual by all of the groups studied, one might predict that they would all recall a preferentially high incidence of corporal punishment. In fact, however, the recalled incidence was virtually the same for both variant and control groups. The sadomasochists report slightly more beatings than the controls, but the difference is insignificant (Gosselin and Wilson, 1980). In spite of this, however, it cannot be said that punishment is not an important precipitatory cause of variant sex behaviour, because other aspects of the act besides frequency might be important. Walters *et al.* (1972) have pointed out that the manner in which the punishment was delivered, the intensity, the relationship between the punisher and the person punished, the circumstances, costs and pay-offs are all important aspects of punishment. More important, punishment may only be associated with the development of variant sexuality if linked with sex activity in the first place.

Interestingly, when investigating a sample of sexually adventurous *women* (see later) it was noted that, while such ladies did not report a higher frequency of punishment than their own (female) control group, a reasonably powerful association was found between punishment frequency and the incidence of both intimate and sadistic (but not masochistic) fantasies. Speculation as to why these categories of fantasy should correlate with experience of punishment may be fruitless, though one could postulate that, following frequent punishment, the female tries to obtain either loving reassurance — via the intimate activity — or vengeance via sadistic activity, on encountering a sexual approach. The fact that the female might have been punished by a female when young need not stand in the way of such a hypothesis, for a very high correlation was found between the incidence of punishment and the incidence of lesbian fantasies for this group. Now, West (1967) points out that adolescent and pre-adolescent males who get into trouble with authority generally do so for offences not involving sexual behaviour, and

seldom for offences with a sexual connotation. Adolescent and pre-adolescent girls, on the other hand, are more often in trouble as a result of sexually-oriented activities — a conclusion also reached by Work (1972) — and are sometimes placed into care at a younger age because they are regarded as more exposed to sexual influences than boys. It is therefore worth postulating that, as might be expected on a conditioning basis, the relationship between punishment and sexuality only holds when the punishment arises as a result of, or is associated with, sexual behaviour or inferences.

Punishment is one aspect of childhood; what behaviour is permitted is another, especially in the sexual field. The child who is discouraged from expressing sexuality in any form may have grave difficulty in expressing himself sexually in later life: conversely, one of the most consistent findings to come out of clinical research on sexual deviation is that those who develop variant sexual behaviour, and find the result disturbing enough to find themselves seeking help in the management of that behaviour, are likely to have had a more restrictive upbringing. The present findings confirm this, in that all the variant groups appear at least to regard their own upbringing as fairly strict by comparison with the controls. The differences are small, but it must be remembered once again that non-clinical subjects are being studied who are coping with, and even enjoying, their activites: perhaps only the really repressed become troubled enough to have recourse to the clinic. Additionally, it must be remembered that the concept of variant behaviour being allied to restrictive upbringing is well-known by the subculture concerned, and it is possible that this might have affected their view of the upbringing which they received.

The findings nevertheless link with the concept so far developed of an imperfectly developed system of sociosexual skills: if the child is told nothing and is discouraged from sexual experiment and experience of even the most simple kind, one can hardly expect him to choose without difficulty the correct goals, cues and sequences pertaining to sexual interaction. As a result, one would expect even the variant himself to rate himself as more inhibited than his non-variant counterpart. Does he in fact do so?

The present research would seem to indicate that he does not, unless he is a transvestite, in which he might feel inhibited largely because he lacks the freedom to express himself by wearing female clothes. The leather fetishists, indeed, regard themselves as less inhibited than the controls. The reason for this may lie in the fact that in conversation with

those of this variant persuasion, they are often convinced that their behaviour hallmarks them as "way out" in comparison with those of more conventional sexual behaviour, much as other groups may adopt an unusual style of dress in order to proclaim to the world their belief, not always well-founded, that they are less inhibited than those who do not belong to their group. Pursuing the thread of a poorly learned set of sociosexual skills, it may be logical to try to check whether in fact the variant has found it harder to find or keep a sexual partner than does the man of more orthodox sexual tastes. Merely by checking the percentage of each group who had a stable sexual partnership, it was found that the percentage is indeed lower for each of the variant groups than for the controls although, as usual, the difference is significant for the sadomasochists and the transvestites but not for either of the fetishist groups. Unfortunately, the finding is open to alternative interpretations: it could be that variant likings impair their owner's ability to acquire a steady partner or maintain a steady relationship, *or* that he does not need a partner because his variant activities are enough to content him sexually, *or* that he deliberately avoids acquiring a partner in order that his variant life should not suffer interference, *or* that the lack of a partner (however caused) encourages the maintenance of variant behaviour. To use the vernacular, you pays your money . . . .

The Role of the Female Partner

Final clues as to the bases of attraction in variants stem first from a brief look at their ideal fantasy partner and then from an examination of a group of females who are partnering variants sexually and/or socially. Admittedly, not every variant has the same type of fantasy partner. The non-fetishistic transvestite, who cross-dresses because he feels himself to belong at least in part to the opposite sex will seldom conjure up the dream partner to be described below but will prefer a conventional but good-looking heterosexual male. Neither will every one of the remaining males that have been studied either fantasize about, or be partnered in reality by, this dream woman. It is nevertheless clear from conversation with variants, from their folklore, from their pornography and from their favourite fantasies, that one image of the ideal sexual partner persists. She is beautiful, aloof, serene, imperious, theatrical, to some extent cruel and, behind a mask of disdain for sex, she is almost permanently sexually aroused. She is outgoing and accomplished at communicating her sexual wants, in that she uninhibitedly says what she desires and what she does

not desire (and she always *does* desire something, even if it is only a cup of coffee, with sufficient vehemence to arouse the man with whom she interacts), and commands him to fulfil those desires. She is, in fact, very much the inverted mirror image of the fantasist who creates her, searches for her and gives her the attributes of everything that he lacks. She is beautiful, he is unexceptional in appearance: she is aloof, he is obsessionally involved: she is imperious, he is submissive. Her command is his comfort and security, for by totally obeying her, he is absolved from responsibility and from the possibility of doing anything wrong. Her demonstration, by attitude and costume, of her arousal lulls his fear that he can offend her by displaying the sexual arousal he feels within himself, giving him confidence that his own desire will not only be tolerated but encouraged. Her outward-going directness compensates for his introversion and imperfectly-formed sociosexual skills, her confidence and serenity anchors his emotionality and anxiety. This type of woman fulfils, in fantasy at least, his main bases of attraction.

It now only remains to ascertain whether in reality the variant's partner possesses any or all of the attitudes ascribed to the fantasy image. This, in fact, has been impossible to discover, and obtaining a representative sample of such ladies obviously presents grave difficulties. Any attempt to reach variants' partners would clearly largely have to be made through the male variants themselves, and success in doing so is only likely to be achieved if the lady is sympathetic towards her man's predilections. Returned questionnaires are thus likely to come only from more sympathetic females, thus biasing the sample.

Data has nevertheless been received from 25 female members of the groups studied. Female-to-male transvestism (as opposed to female-to-male transsexualism) is virtually unknown, as is female fetishism, except for that produced by a sort of operant conditioning wherein wearing the man's fetish preference (or allowing him to wear it) results in good sex, so after a while the garments also arouse the female. Female sadomasochists are by no means unknown, however, and some of these are included in the sample. Other members of the group are wives and girlfriends of the male subjects, and yet another sub-set consists of professional or semi-professional "mistresses" — a term preferred to the traditional one of prostitute because the former seldom give intercourse for money. Instead, they create a scenario for their partners which they themselves nearly always also enjoy: herein lies a most interesting difference, for both in answers to one of the questionnaire items and in interviews it is clear that, unlike the "straight" prostitute, these specialists virtually

always enjoy their work. Additionally, they are not always totally commercially oriented, but will accept on occasion a gift of quite trivial monetary value, an evening out or shared refreshment in lieu of cash.

Results from this group were compared with an equal-sized, age-matched control group of females without any particular predilection in terms of the Sex Fantasy Questionnaire, and with the age-matched group norms provided by Eysenck in his Personality Questionnaire Manual. These results, limited by size and source though they may be, show how well the fantasy image created by their male partners is born out in practice.

In personality terms, these ladies score highly significantly above the average, for either the male or the female control group, on the psychoticism scale. In terms of extraversion, they again average higher than the controls and thus score significantly higher than their partners as a group.

With respect to neuroticism, the group value is only slightly higher than that of the female control group. Perhaps amusingly, however, the average value for the professional "mistresses" alone — who frequently advertise themselves within the pages of their specialist contact magazines as creatures of tempestuous and unpredictable mood — is significantly higher than that of even their non-professional sisters.

Lie Scale figures for this group, which average less than any of the other groups studied, seem to offer further evidence for the interpretation of this scale as a social conformity measure: surely this group is a prime example of those who disdain the power of social pressure and have little regard for the establishment view. Data from the Sex Fantasy Questionnaire show this group to have a very high frequency and range of fantasies indeed, having a higher fantasy rating than the female controls on all but three of the themes cited, significantly so on at least half the themes. Intercourse with an anonymous stranger, troilism and orgies, receiving oral sex, being excited by materials or clothing, all the sadomasochistic themes, mate-swapping, excitement from watching urination, sex with someone much older or much younger, seducing (and being seduced as) an innocent, having sex with someone of a different race, using objects for stimulation and viewing erotica all serve to help act as distinguishers between this group and their controls.

On examination of the demographic and attitudinal self-ratings shown by these ladies, however, it is perhaps surprising how small are the differences between them and their controls. They are less often married,

but are more satisfied with their steady partner, if any, than are the controls. They rate their sex lives as slightly more satisfactory, have a slightly higher frequency of orgasm, a little higher self-rated sex drive, a rather greater number of partners, a fractionally less permissive upbringing, slightly less sexual inhibition and a slightly lower estimated frequency of punishment as a child, but none of these differences are anywhere near significant. In these respects, the "superbitch" (as she sometimes calls herself) seems much the same as anyone else.

A general review of this data thus shows that the members of this group resemble the male variant's image of the ideal sexual woman quite well, seeming to him (to paraphrase Dr Reuben) to be "what you always wanted from a woman but were too scared to ask". On the occasions when it became possible to observe wives and girlfriends of group members within a natural (i.e. non-interview) context, it must nevertheless be admitted that some of them were rather less extreme than the data may have made out. However, the variant who seeks to translate his dreams into reality by using the dominant personality and sexual uninhibitedness of this ideal as bases for attraction may be arming himself with a two-edged sword. If perhaps unscientific quotation may be permitted at this stage, it is felt that two views might have relevance here. The first is from one of the professional "mistresses" interviewed: "It's never got to be taken seriously," she said, "for if you start dominating for real, you end up despising for real — and that's fatal to a relationship". The second quotation stems from a variant who realized a sad fact about his partner. "The trouble is," he said ruefully, "that she dominates me everywhere but in the one place where I would enjoy it — in bed".

3. References

Barbara, Dj. A. Masochism in love and sex. *American Journal of Psychoanalysis*, 1974, **34**, 73-79.

Bebbington, P. E. Treatment of male sexual deviation by use of a vibrator: a case report. *Archives of Sexual Behaviour*, 1977, **6**, 21-24.

Benjamin, H. *The transsexual phenomenon.* New York: Julian Press, 1966.

Centers, R. The completion hypothesis and the compensatory dynamic in intersexual and love. *Journal of Psychology*, 1972, **82**, 111-126.

Davison, G. C. Elimination of a sadistic fantasy by a client-controlled counterconditioning technique: a case study. *Journal of Abnormal Psychology*, 1968, **73**, 84-90.

Ellis, H. *Studies in the psychology of sex*. New York: Random House, 1936.

Eysenck, H. J. *The structure of human personality* (3rd edn). London: Methuen, 1970.

Eysenck, H. and Eysenck, S. B. G. *Psychoticism as a dimension of personality*. London: Hodder and Stoughton, 1976.

Eysenck, H. J. and Wilson, G. D. *The psychology of sex*. London: Dent, 1979.

Freud, S. The economic problem of masochism. In *Standard edition of the complete psychological works*. Vol. 19. London: Hogarth Press, 1955.

Gorman, G. F. Fetishism occurring in identical twins. *British Journal of Psychiatry*, 1964, **110**, 255-256.

Gosselin, C. C. Personality characteristics of the average rubber fetishist. In Cook, M. and Wilson, G. D. (Eds), *Love and attraction: proceedings of an international conference*. Oxford: Pergamon, 1979.

Gosselin, C. C. and Wilson, G. D. *Sexual variations*. London: Faber, 1980.

Krafft-Ebing, R. von *Psychopathia Sexualis*. New York: Stern and Day, 1965.

Marks, I. M., Rachman, S. and Gelder, M. G. Methods for assessment of aversion treatment in fetishism with masochism. *Behaviour Research and Therapy*, 1965, **3**, 253-258.

Marquis, J. N. Orgasmic reconditioning: changing sexual object choice through controlling masturbation fantasies. *Journal of Behaviour Therapy and Experimental Psychiatry*, 1970, **1**, 263-271.

McGuire, R. J., Carlisle, J. M. and Young, B. G. Sexual deviations as conditioned behaviour: a hypothesis. *Behaviour Research and Therapy*, 1965, **2**, 185-190.

North, M. *The outer fringe of sex*. London: Odyssey Press, 1970.

Prince, V. and Bentler, P. M. Survey of 504 cases of transvestism. *Psychological Reports*, 1972, **31**, 903-917.

Rachman, S. and Hodgson, R. J. Experimentally induced sexual fetishism: replication and development. *Psychological Record*, 1968, 18, 25-27.

Sack, R. L. and Miller, W. Masochism: a clinical and theoretical overview. *Psychiatry*, 1975, **38**, 244-257.

Sinberg, R. M., Roberts, A. F. and McClain, D. Mate selection factors in computer matched marriages. *Journal of Marriage and the Family*, 1972, **34**, 611-614.

Smirnoff, V. N. The masochistic contract. *International Journal of Psycho-analysis*, 1969, **50**, 665-671.

Spengler, A. Manifest sadomasochism in males: results of an empirical study. *Archives of Sexual Behaviour*, 1977, **6**, 441-456.

Stoller, R. J. Pornography and perversion. *Archives of General Psychiatry*, 1970, **22**, 390-499.

Storr, A. *Sexual deviation*. Harmondsworth: Penguin, 1964.

Walters, R. H., Cheyne, J. A. and Banks, R. K. *Punishment*. Harmondsworth: Penguin, 1972.

Wilson, G. D. *The secrets of sexual fantasy*. London: Dent, 1978.

Wilson, G. D. and Nias, D. K. B. *The mystery of love.* New York: Quadrangle, 1976.

Work, H. W. Sexual deviations. In Freedman, A. M. and Kaplan, H. I. (Eds), *The child: his psychological and cultural development.* Vol. 2. New York: Athenaeum, 1972.

Section B

MODELS OF
ATTRACTION

4
Perceptual and Cognitive Mechanisms in Human Sexual Attraction

ABRAHAM TESSER

and

RICHARD REARDON

Institute for Behaviour Research, University of Georgia,
624 Graduate Studies Research Centre, Athens, Georgia, USA

Recently, a number of related concepts emphasizing the role of human beings as social information processors have appeared in the social psychological literature. These concepts, whether they be called "schematic processing" (Taylor and Crocker, 1979), "script processing" (Abelson, 1978), or "implicit personality theory" (Schneider, 1973), share a common recognition of the importance of cognition. They also share common origins, deriving from cognitive psychology on the one hand and developmental psychology on the other.

It may seem odd to the reader to think of human sexual attraction in cognitive terms. After all, cognition seems cold and "rational" while sexual attraction is passionate and "irrational". In the pages to come we hope to show that cognitive variables are worthy of consideration in this domain. They can capture, characterize, and help us to understand passion; and, cognitive processes are often and predictably non-rational. However, by way of introduction, let us turn to a brief review of some of the background geneology of the social cognition approach.

As mentioned above, this background comes from cognitive and developmental psychology. It is our thesis that perception of social situations necessarily involves the intake, classification, and storage of information. These processes have been examined in situations which would seem to be

quite removed from the present topic. Indeed, while much of the research that will be cited in this chapter is not directly concerned with sexual attraction, we hope to show how sexual attraction can be understood in terms of the general cognitive principles illustrated by these studies.

Consider, first, some cognitive psychological background. Obviously our feelings about a particular individual are going to be conditioned by what we remember about the individual and the way we represent him/her in our heads. One of the more interesting findings in memory research has been the tendency for subjects to impose organization on seemingly unrelated information.

What is the basis for this subjective organization? Tulving (1972) has made a distinction between episodic and semantic memory. Episodic memory records and stores information about temporally dated episodes or events and temporal–spatial relations among these events. For example, I might recall the dance I went to with Mary Merry on 14 Nov. last year, at which she was wearing a low-cut red dress, and at which the drummer got sick. Note that this memory, when stored in the episodic system, is stored only in terms of its perceptible properties and in terms of its autobiographical relationship to the already existing contents of the store. Thus an item, such as the dress in the example, is remembered only in terms of the item preceding it and the item following it on input.

In contrast to the example, as noted previously, individuals sometimes impose subjective organization on what they remember. In discussing Mary Merry, I remember that she is very much like the women I was seeing two or three years ago in terms of her mannerisms, sense of humour, preference for low-cut red dresses, and so on, and I wonder if this is not what attracted me to her. The fact that individuals subjectively organize memory cannot be attributed to the episodic system. Rather, it is more likely a function of what Tulving (1972) and others have called semantic memory; i.e. semantic memory is the organized knowledge a person possesses about persons, symbols, events, their meanings and referents, and the relations among them. Further, it specifies the rules and formulations for the manipulation of information about the persons, symbols, events, and relations.

Input into semantic memory comes from two sources: perception, as in episodic memory; but also thought. That is, inputs into semantic memory are in contact with an existing cognitive structure. The store itself is capable of inferential reasoning, generalization, and the application of rules. Not only do I remember what dress Mary Merry

was wearing that night, but I am able to make inferences about her from my knowledge of persons in general, my ideas about what kinds of women wear low-cut red dresses (e.g. my old girlfriend), the ease with which I made a date with her, etc.

Developmental psychology helps us understand how semantic memory is formed. Piaget (1963) and his students have talked of development in terms of the twin adaptive processes of assimilation and accommodation. Children have a tendency, they observed, to employ a behaviour pattern which has "worked" in the past, in new though similar situations (assimilation). Whether the pattern was successful again depended on how well the child had restructured the new situation, i.e. on how well the child was able to see the old and new situations as similar. To the extent that the pattern did not work in the new situation, the pattern would be modified (accommodation).

Flavell (1963) points out that these processes are also operating at the cognitive level. "Assimilation refers to the fact that every cognitive encounter with an environmental object necessarily involves some kind of cognitive structuring (or restructuring) of that object in accord with the nature of the organism's existing intellectual organization." However, the individual must still deal with the special properties of the object encountered. Flavell notes that reality is not infinitely malleable. An individual assimilates an object, giving it meaning consistent with existing notions, and he accommodates his intellectual organization to the object's novel features. In the case of Mary Merry, for instance, I might expect certain behaviours of her based on her dress and on my past experience with women who have dressed similarly (assimilation). Should Mary behave differently, my cognitive construction about low-cut red dresses and women who wear them would have to be modified (accommodation). Failure to modify would result in over-assimilation, yielding probable future maladaptive behaviour on my part.

The picture emerging from cognitive and developmental psychology seems to suggest the following: over time, people encounter new phenomena actively rather than reactively. The organization they impose on what they encounter is consistent with existing cognitive structures. In a real sense, then, the existing structures provide us with a rule system that helps us deal with questions like: What is it? Do I need to know more about it? How can I learn more about it? The structures provide machinery for generating inferences about phenomena from experience. The gamble inherent in making these inferences often pays off. However, the potential is also there for losing the gamble:

phenomena are not always consistent, though we may judge them to be so.

In this chapter we will elaborate and apply some of the ideas offered in this introduction: we discuss variables that make us think of sexual partners (real or potential). We examine in some detail the effects of thought on human sexual attraction, and in doing so we introduce the notion of a cognitive schema. We discuss the question of conscious awareness in cognitive processing. Finally, we use the schema concept to provide an alternative perspective in trying to understand other variables that have been shown to be important in attraction research, i.e. similarity, physical attractiveness, and arousal.

Focusing Attention

If thought has a central role in an understanding of cognitive processes, then the factors that make a person think of one thing as compared to another are also central. The relevant literature has suggested two classes of variables that determine the focus of one's attention. One class may be termed perceptual factors and the other affective/motivational factors.

Perceptual Factors

There a number of factors which cause persons to focus their attention on objects in the physical environment. Such things as novelty, brightness, movement, intensity, etc. certainly command our attention. There are data indicating that similar variables work in focusing attention on other persons. Langer *et al.* (1976) examined the effects of novelty on the extent to which subjects looked at pictures of others. They suggest that persons will attend more to novel persons than normal persons if given a "free" opportunity to do so. That is, there is a norm which prohibits one from staring at handicapped or pregnant persons, for example. As predicted, they found that when subjects believed they were not being observed, they spent more time looking at handicapped and pregnant persons than non-handicapped, non-pregnant people. Conceptually similar outcomes have been obtained when novelty is varied in terms of "solo-status", i.e. having a single male in an all female group, or a single female in an all male group; a single black in an all white group (Taylor *et al.*, 1977); and a person dressed differently from the other members of his group (McArthur and Post, 1977).

Novelty of others is not the only perceptual factor that arrests our

attention. McArthur and Post (1977) examined several other determinants of attention. In one study, people viewed two others interacting, one who was in a bright light while the other was in a dim light. A second study was concerned with the effects of movement; people observed two interacting persons, one who was rocking in a rocking chair and the other who sat relatively still in a stable chair. In another study, pattern complexity was varied by having one of the actors wear a boldly striped shirt and the other actor a solid grey shirt. In each case, the manipulation affected attention as measured by causal attributions.

What this short review suggests is that the potential sexual partners who arrest our attention are likely to be persons who are in some way like physical objects upon which attention is focused, i.e. novel, bright, moving, etc. Physically attractive and "sexy" potential partners also attract our attention; at least, that is what advertisers believe. For example, Sexton and Haderman (1974) found a 21% increase in the use of "decorative" female models in print ads from 1959 to 1971; the use of "obviously alluring" models increased from 10% to 27% in this same period. Indeed, the presence of a sexy or decorative model does bring more attention to an advertisement and make it more memorable, but, incidentally, it does not necessarily make the brand name itself more memorable (Chestnut *et al.*, 1977; Steadman, 1969). In sum, there are a number of perceptual variables that call our attention to potential sexual partners and make those partners grist for the cognitive mill.

Motivational Factors

The particular person attended to, or even whether any person at all will be attended to, as a sexual partner may be a function of our own state, rather than the physical figure-ground display in which the stimulus person is imbedded. That is, we may attend to a certain other person because we are experiencing a specific need and that person is relevant to that need. If an individual is experiencing a need, e.g. sexual desire, she/he will attempt to satisfy that need through instrumental behaviour — finding a sexual partner. Failure to satisfy the need will result in symbolic processes, i.e. thought, fantasy. These symbolic processes will deal with persons relevant to the need; that is, persons who have been associated with satisfying the need in the past (i.e. a positive love object), or a person seen as being the agent of the current lack of satisfaction (i.e. a negative attitude object).

Freud (Hall and Lindzey, 1957) has suggested that the developing individual's earliest responses to a need is primary process thinking in which the organism fantasizes about those objects which would satisfy its needs. As the individual matures and his ego develops, he becomes more rational and reality-oriented (secondary process thinking). Needs now produce reality-based instrumental behaviour. Continued frustration, however, can result in regression and a reversion to primary process thinking. Thus, classical Freudian theory would predict that unsatisfied needs lead to primary process thought concerning relevant objects. For Freud, the relevant objects are only those associated with satisfaction, while the present thesis holds that they may also be those objects responsible for the frustration.

There are some empirical data consistent with the idea that people think about need-*satisfying* objects under conditions of high need. For example, Sanford (1936) found that subjects tended to give more food responses to a word association before a regular meal than after it. In their study of semi-starvation, Brozek *et al.* (1951) noted that "During starvation the thoughts of food, in all its ramifications, came to dominate the men's minds" (p. 250). McClelland *et al.* (1949), using the Thematic Apperception Test (TAT), found that the arousal of a need for achievement increased the number of stories containing references to positive affect as a result of achievement. Thus, a person experiencing a sexual need should focus thought on others who can satisfy that need.

There are also data consistent with the notion that an unsatisfied need produces thought about the agent responsible for the dissatisfaction. For example, Atkinson and McClelland (1948) studied responses to the TAT as a function of food deprivation. They found that incidence of central themes concerned with shortage or blocking of food by an external agent increased; "Friendly Press" and actual eating (Goal activity) decreased. (It is noteworthy that one of their conclusions is that fantasy does *not* serve the function of partially gratifying unfulfilled desires.) Under conditions designed to arouse a need for achievement, McClelland *et al.* (1949) found an increase in TAT themes in which the protagonist is having long-term achievement difficulty.

We have said that symbolic (cognitive) processes are more likely to manifest themselves when efficacious instrumental responses are unavailable. That is, we would argue that the individual is less likely to dwell on unavailable relevant persons when instrumental behaviours exist that will lead to actual need satisfaction. Again, such a proposition is consistent with Freudian theorizing. In the mature individual, need

satisfaction is under the direction of the ego operating by means of secondary process thinking. Needs tend to be satisfied through realistic external instrumental responses. It is only after this does not work that the individual regresses and becomes likely to engage in primary process thinking — fantasy concerned with wish-fulfillment.

There is also some empirical evidence to suggest that an unsatisfied need increases the extent to which an individual tends to think about instrumental behaviour. For example, Atkinson and McClelland (1948) found that greater hunger resulted in greater incidence of TAT responses which included a reference to successfully overcoming a source of food deprivation. Similarly, McClelland *et al.* (1949) found an increase in references to successful instrumental acts in TAT stories when need achievement had been aroused.

On a more reality-oriented level, the motives of predictability and control have been given special emphasis in trying to understand what directs our attentional processes in perceiving others in general (e.g. Kelly, 1972), and in perceiving potential sexual partners in particular (e.g. Berscheid and Graziano, 1979). The argument is that we try to render our environment and the persons in it predictable. If we know what to anticipate in the environment, we can adjust our own behaviour. Thus, our attempt to make the environment predictable is in the service of our need to control the environment so as to maximize our own outcomes. If this is the case, it follows that we will pay attention to other persons who have the greatest potential for affecting our own outcomes since we most need to predict the behaviour of such persons. Thus, the greater the dependence one has on another, the more likely is the possibility that that person will be the focus of our attention.

Although there are other relevant studies (e.g. Tesser and Johnson, 1974), perhaps the best evidence for this hypothesis can be found in a fine study by Berscheid *et al.* (1976). Subjects in this study agreed to date only the person(s) assigned to them over a five-week period. Each of the subjects was given the name and telephone number of a date. Dependence was manipulated by leading some subjects to believe that they would have to date that particular person exclusively for the five weeks, or that they would have to date that particular person only once over the five weeks. Subjects were then exposed to a three-person videotaped discussion. One of the discussants was the subject's date and the other two discussants were non-dates. In order to see the videotape, the subject had to depress any one of three switches. Regardless of which switch was depressed, the subject could hear the complete audio portion.

However, each switch allowed only one of the three discussants to be visible. Thus, by keeping track of the amount of time each switch was depressed, it was possible to keep track of the relative amount of attention given to each discussant.

The results provided strong confirmation for the hypothesis. Subjects' outcomes are more dependent on the person they anticipate dating than the persons they do not anticipate dating. Thus, they spend significantly more time viewing dates ($\bar{x}$ = 41%) than non-dates ($\bar{x}$ = 30%), and remember and recognize more information about dates than non-dates. Also, persons are more dependent on those others they will date exclusively for five weeks than persons they will date only once, and they spend more time viewing the former ($\bar{x}$ = 43%) than the latter ($\bar{x}$ = 38%). These data indicate that our dependence on a sexual partner will affect our attention to such a partner, and that the exclusiveness of a relationship is important in focusing attention. (We might speculate that cultural variations in the extent to which sexual relationships are exclusive should affect attentional processes, and such processes tend to lead to idealization as we will see in later sections of this chapter. If this is the case, one might expect differences in the extent to which cultural products, i.e. literature, art, etc., idealize sexual partners, with greater idealization evident in cultures marked by greater exclusivity in relationships.)

Personal commitment to exclusivity or circumstances that increase exclusivity, such as few potential partners, should also increase attention. Above, in talking about perceptual factors in attention, we reviewed evidence that novelty and "solo-status" increases attention. An exclusive sexual partner is novel in a sense, but the locus of the novelty resides in the relationship between the perceiver and the partner rather than the statistically novel aspects of the physical stimulus array. Further, in this section, we are arguing that it is not only the novelty, *per se*, that is affecting attention, but rather the motivational significance of the fact that exclusive sexual partners can affect one's costs and rewards to a greater degree than non-exclusive partners.

In sum, there are a number of factors that determine where our attention is focused. These include perceptual factors such as novelty, brightness, movement, and physical attractiveness. Motivational processes also play a role in attentional processes. For example, increases in sexual need will focus attention on potential partners, instrumental acts or persons/things that tend to block satisfaction. On a more realistic level, persons tend to exhibit a need to predict and control their

environment so as to maximize their outcomes. Thus they attend to others on whom they are highly dependent, such as exclusive sexual partners.

The Effects of Thought on Sexual Attraction

We have mentioned some of the factors involved in directing our attention and selecting persons/objects to think about. In this section, we discuss the role of thought, *per se*, on sexual attraction.

The Relationship between Beliefs and Feelings

Many social psychologists (e.g. Isen *et al.*, 1978; Rosenberg, 1956; Fishben, 1965), and clinical psychologists (e.g. Meichenbaum, 1976; Ellis, 1962) have theorized about the role of cognition in feeling states. Rosenberg (1956) has shown that one's feelings about a particular entity are a function of the extent to which that entity is believed to block or facilitate one's values. For example, if a particular woman values outdoor vacations, liberal causes, and big families, she will be attracted to a particular man if she believes he will facilitate those values, i.e. he will help her attain outdoor vacations, support liberal causes, and have a big family. She will not be attracted to him if she believes he will block the attainment of those values. Beliefs about persons and things have been measured in many different ways, but they are invariably related to feelings.

Not all of an individual's beliefs affect his/her feelings. An individual may have a large number of beliefs about his/her lover, but only a few will be salient at a given time. It is this transient sub-set of *salient* beliefs that determine the individual's current feelings about his lover. This point has been demonstrated by Salancik (1974) in a classroom context rather than a romantic one. He had students rate the extent to which they remembered engaging in a number of behaviours relevant to a particular course. Some of the behaviours had to do with intrinsic aspects of the course (e.g. did non-required reading, discussed material with friends), and some of the behaviours had to do with extrinsic aspects of the course (e.g. did the assigned homework). Following this, his subjects responded to a series of questions which were phrased so as to make salient either the intrinsic aspects of the course or the extrinsic aspects of the course. Finally, subjects' feelings about the course were measured. He found that only salient beliefs were related to feelings: for subjects whose intrinsic

beliefs about the course were made salient, their previously measured recollection of intrinsic behaviours was correlated with their feelings, but their previously measured recollection of extrinsic behaviours was not. On the other hand, for subjects whose extrinsic beliefs about the course were made salient, previously measured memory of intrinsic behaviours was *not* correlated with the course, but previously measured recollection of extrinsic behaviour was correlated with the course.

Although salient beliefs affect attitudes, all salient beliefs do not have equal impact. Suppose an individual was to learn something new about her lover. Would this new knowledge affect her feelings? A young person may have learned her parents' arguments against her lover quite well without that knowledge negatively affecting her feelings about her lover (Driscoll *et al.*, 1972). Greenwald (1968) did a relevant experiment dealing with persuasion using three persuasive communications. One contained arguments in favour of the issue, one against the issue, and one contained arguments for and arguments against the issue. There were five experimental groups: there was a separate group that learned each of the three communications, a fourth group that was exposed to all arguments but asked to learn only the pro-arguments, and a fifth group that was exposed to all the arguments but asked to learn only the anti-arguments. Subjects did indeed learn what they were asked to learn. Now, what about feelings? Persons who were exposed to and learned only the pro-arguments felt significantly more positive than subjects who were exposed to and learned only the anti-arguments. The most interesting results, however, are for the subjects who were exposed to all the arguments. The attitudes of these subjects did *not* differ regardless of what they had learned. That is, if they had been exposed to all arguments, the feelings of subjects who had learned the pro-arguments did not differ from the feelings of subjects who had learned the anti-arguments. In a further study, Love (reported in Greenwald, 1968) had subjects record their reactions to a persuasive communication while reading it. He then assessed their feelings about the topic. He also measured what they had learned from the persuasive communication. Results showed that persons' final feelings about the topic were predictable from their *own* cognitive reactions to the communication, but not from what they had learned from the communication (to the extent that this was independent). In sum, it appears that credible and/or self-generated beliefs are particularly important in affecting feelings. In the romantic context, this means that self-generated beliefs about the partner will be consequential.

Thought and Idealization

We have suggested that an individual's salient, self-generated beliefs about his lover affect his feelings. Many beliefs are the results of acquiring external information. One acquires information by being with one's lover, interacting with one's lover, or by learning something from other sources such as friends. Changes in feelings as a result of these kinds of changes in beliefs are, at least on the face of it, not difficult to understand. What happens, however, when an individual has no new external information about his lover, but begins to think about her? Will feelings change? If so, how? It is to these questions that we now turn.

There are a number of guesses one might make about the effects of thought on sexual attraction. Aristotle suggests that "The brain tempers the heat and seething of the heart" (625b). While the smart money is usually on Aristotle, we are inclined to disagree with him in this case. It seems to us that with thought about a sexually attractive partner, those things that are appealing become more so — her body becomes more shapely, her face more beautiful, her smells, gestures, and responses all become more perfect. These shifting cognitions produce increased rather than decreased passion. This process can work in the opposite direction as well. Suppose an individual begins to think about someone who is sexually unattractive. With thought, her body smells will become more offensive, her behavioural style more annoying, her physical imperfections become exaggerated. In this case, thought-generated cognitions can change a mild aversion into a downright repulsion. In short, we would expect thought, at least over a short period of time, to result in the polarization of feelings rather than the depolarization of feelings.

There are experimental and correlational data which are consistent with the expectation that simply thinking about someone can polarize feelings about that individual. In one study (Sadler and Tesser, 1973), pairs of subjects were split up and put into separate cubicles. They were told that the study concerned forming impressions of one another. Each subject was given an opportunity to prepare to describe himself to the other. The first subject then described himself to the second subject over an intercom. In actuality, both subjects thought they were the first subject and the intercom was connected to the experimenter's room. Further, the second subject was in actuality one of two previously prepared tape recordings. In the Nice-Other condition, the tape recording complimented the subject on his presentation and was

generally intended to simulate a likeable person. In the Nasty-Other condition, the person simulated by the tape recording criticized the subject, bragged about himself, and generally presented himself as a dislikeable person. Half of the subjects were exposed to the Nice-Other and half to the Nasty-Other. Within each of these conditions, half of the subjects were distracted from thinking about the other person by doing an irrelevant task, while the remaining half of the subjects were encouraged to think about the other person. Finally, subjects recorded their impressions of the other person. It was not surprising to learn that the Nice-Other was liked more than the Nasty-Other. More interesting was the significant interaction between thought and kind of other person. Subjects who thought about the Nice-Other liked him better than subjects who were distracted from thinking about the Nice-Other. Subjects who thought about the Nasty-Other disliked him more than subjects who were distracted from thinking about the Nasty-Other.

In the study just described, participants were all males, and heterosexual attraction was not directly at issue. However, the finding that thought tends to polarize feelings appears to be rather general and has been found in a variety of contexts including romantic attraction. For example, polarization of feelings about various attitude issues has been found to increase monotonically with thought over the time interval from 30 s to 3 min (Tesser and Conlee, 1975). Thought has resulted in polarization of feelings about paintings (Tesser, 1976), football tactics and women's fashions (Tesser and Leone, 1977), and even one's self (Ickes *et al.*, 1973). More to the point is a study by Tesser and Paulhus (1976). Using a correlational design, they found that over the immediately preceding two weeks, the more an individual thought about the person she/he had dated, the greater his love (Rubin, 1970) for that person. We will have more to say about this study later. For now, the point we wish to make is that in the absence of any new external information, thought will intensify feelings about one's partner. If one is sexually attracted to the partner, thought will tend to increase that attraction; if one is sexually repelled by the partner, thought will tend to increase that repulsion.

Thought Idealization Mechanisms

One way of construing one's feelings toward a sexual partner is in terms of that partner's psychological distance or dissimilarity to an ideal partner. If the partner is close to one's ideal, the partner is liked; if the

partner is far from one's ideal, the partner is disliked. We know that thought results in idealization — likeable partners become more likeable, disliked partners become more disliked. How might this idealization come about? Thought might result in shifts in one's conception of the ideal partner, or in shifts in one's perception of one's partner such that the partner is rendered more or less similar to the ideal, or in shifts both in the conception of the ideal and the perception of the partner. A "least effort" principle would tend to argue against shifts in the ideal, since such shifts would result in wholesale attitude change. That is, there would be a change in feelings about all persons who are compared to the ideal. Therefore, we hypothesized that thought would result in shifts in the perception of one's partner.

In order to test this hypothesis, Valenti and Tesser (1981) recruited 40 female subjects for a study on impression formation. They were shown seven cards, each containing a four-adjective personality description, plus an eighth card with the words "Ideal Date" written on it. Subjects were given all possible (28) pairs of the eight cards and were asked to indicate the similarity of each pair with respect to how much they would like to date the person described. A moderately attractive target date, i.e. moderately similar to the ideal, was selected for each subject. Subjects were exposed to the target and asked to form an impression. Half the subjects were then given 90 s in which to think about the target person, while the remaining subjects were given an anagram task to distract them from thinking about the target during this interval. Following this, subjects were again asked to make similarity judgements for each of the 28 pairs of descriptions.

As expected, thought was more likely to result in polarization of feelings than distraction. (In this case, polarization is scored if a subject indicates that the target and the ideal are more similar on the post-test than on the pre-test.) If this polarization was a result of the conception of the ideal becoming more similar to the target date, we should find that the distance between the ideal and the descriptions that were initially similar to the ideal increased with thought, and the distance between the ideal and the descriptions initially similar to the potential partner decreased with thought. Neither of these changes was observed. On the other hand, if the polarization was a result of changing one's perception of the target date by making it more like the ideal, we should find that the distance between the target date and the descriptions initially close to the target date increased with thought, and the distance between the target date and the descriptions initially near the ideal decreased with thought.

While there was no significant change in the latter distance, thought did significantly ($p < 0.05$) increase the distance between the target date and the descriptions initially similar to the target date. Thus, there is no support for the hypothesis that the ideal moves as a result of thought. On the other hand, there is some suggestive evidence that the perception of the target partner moves as a result of thought. We turn now to the question of what may mediate such thought-generated movement.

The Microprocess of Thought-induced Change in Cognition

We have seen that thought about one's partner or potential partners often intensifies one's initial feelings. And there is some evidence that in this process, rather than change our notions of what an ideal partner is, we change our beliefs about our partner to make him/her more (or, in the case of dislike, less) like the ideal. Now we would like to focus more specifically on how this happens.

Suppose an individual is moderately sexually attracted to a particular partner. He begins to think about her. What can happen to his beliefs to make her more like the ideal? There are several possibilities. First, he can add positive beliefs; for example, if he has had no sexual experience with her, he might come to believe that she is a very good lover. Or, in spite of the fact that he has never met her friends, he could convince himself that they are just the kinds of people he likes. There is evidence from the Sadler and Tesser (1973) study described earlier for the generation of new beliefs. Subjects wrote their thoughts about their partners. A content analysis revealed significantly more beliefs consistent with their feelings (like or dislike) given thought rather than given distraction.

We would assume, however, that adding consistent beliefs is not always equally easy. Consider the game of 20 questions. It is easy to make guesses in the beginning when little is known. But as you learn more and more, each succeeding guess becomes more difficult because the new guesses have to be consistent with more information. We assume that the same thing is true when one thinks about a sexual partner. The more one knows about the partner, the more difficult it will be to generate new beliefs in the idealization process. This assumption suggests a way of testing the hypothesis that adding new beliefs is part of the idealization process.

Tesser and Cowan (1975) gave subjects either four or eight pieces of information about other persons. Some subjects were instructed to think about, and some subjects were distracted from thinking about, a person's

description that was either moderately likeable or moderately dislikeable. Assume that the more information one has, the harder it is to add new information. If the idealization process depends on adding new cognitions, we would expect greater polarization due to thought (compared to distraction) where there are four cognitions (easy to add more) than where there are eight cognitions (harder to add new ones). This is precisely what was found. These data suggest that the more we know about a romantic partner, the less likely we are to add, i.e. to idealize her/him.

A second way in which a likeable partner can be idealized is to change or reinterpret the known negative things about her/him. For example, her/his refusal to go out when asked might be interpreted to mean that she/he is hard-working rather than that she/he is not overly fond of the idealizer. Or, a tasteless statement might be interpreted as overzealous honesty rather than impoliteness or lack of sensitivity.

Tesser and Cowan (1977) reasoned that it is easier to reinterpret the meaning of something ambiguous than something unambiguous. If reinterpretation of meaning is involved in the idealization that is produced by thought, then to the extent that there are ambiguous aspects of another person, thought should produce polarization. These ideas were tested by developing descriptions of persons using four trait adjectives. Three of the adjectives were favourable (or unfavourable) and the fourth was neutral. The neutral adjective was either unambiguous (low variability in ratings) or ambiguous (high variability in ratings). After rating the descriptions, some subjects were encouraged to think about the persons described while others were distracted from thinking. After thinking about each person (or distraction) subjects re-rated their feelings and also evaluated the neutral adjective.

The results fully supported the hypothesis that reinterpretation is involved in the idealization process. Thought produced more idealization than distraction, and this effect was significantly stronger ($p < 0.01$) when the neutral adjective was ambiguous, making reinterpretation easier. Further, the ratings of the neutral adjective showed context effects, i.e. it was rated more positively when appearing with favourable adjectives than when appearing with unfavourable adjectives. This effect was stronger given thought rather than distraction, and when the adjective was ambiguous rather than unambiguous. Another way in which we idealize our partners, then, is to interpret ambiguous information about them in a biased way.

Besides adding beliefs and reinterpreting beliefs, there are other ways

in which thought can change the cognitive representation of a potential sexual partner. For example, thought can result in the repression or elimination of inconsistent beliefs. There is some evidence that persons have a harder time remembering things which are inconsistent with their attitudes (e.g. Levine and Murphy, 1943), but we have no evidence that this happens as a result of thought.

Cognitive Schemas: the Blueprint for Change

Thought about a sexual partner often results in idealization. Whether one is attracted to, or repelled by, that partner, there is a tendency for thought to intensify the feeling. This change of feeling is a result of changes in one's salient beliefs about the partner. That is, one adds, or reinterprets, or drops out beliefs, so as to make the salient cognitive representation of the partner more likeable or dislikeable. Obviously these changes in beliefs are not haphazard or random. If the changes were unbiased, with likeable attributes and dislikeable attributes equally likely to end up in the set, there would be no systematic change in feeling. Indeed, there is good evidence to show that beliefs are retrieved and organized along affective lines (Isen *et al.*, 1978). However, we would like to go a step further and suggest that thought-related changes in beliefs are not only constrained by their affective content but by their meaning content as well. In thinking about an attractive, potential sexual partner not just any positive belief will do. We have an *ideal* conception of a good lover in our heads and it is this ideal which directs our thought process. Consequently, self-generated beliefs will be consistent with the ideal.

Let us elaborate. In earlier work (e.g. Tesser, 1978) we have used the term cognitive schema to refer to structures like "ideal lover". A cognitive schema is a naive theory of some stimulus domain and it functions much like a scientific theory. Scientific theories tell the scientist what he should attend to and what he should ignore regarding some entity. Similarly, a particular cognitive schema will make only selected aspects of a stimulus salient. Scientific theories provide inference rules: if a scientist observes some value on dimension X, he can infer a particular value on dimension Y. Similarly, a cognitive schema provides an inference structure: if an individual observes some aspect of a stimulus, to the extent that other aspects are unknown (or ambiguous), he will infer those aspects in a way which is consistent with the schema (Minskey, 1975). Inferences from scientific theories are subject to empirical test. Similarly, inferences about a particular stimulus on the

basis of cognitive schemas are bound by "reality constraints". Finally, different scientific theories can be used to deal with the same phenomenon. Human sexual attraction can be understood using a biological theory, a reinforcement theory or a cognitive theory. Similarly, different schemas can be tuned in for thinking about the same stimulus object: one can think of another person as a lover, work partner, or companion. Using different schemas results in different aspects of the stimulus being salient and leads to different inferences (see Taylor and Crocker (1979) for an excellent overview of the schema research in social psychology). Since feelings are at least partially dependent on one's salient beliefs, changing the schema for thinking about a particular stimulus will change one's feeling about it *in spite of the fact that the stimulus itself has not changed in any way*. Below we look at the evidence for some of these implications and we relate them more directly to human sexual attraction.

Well Developed vs. Poorly Developed Schemas

We have argued that idealization is the result of cognitive changes resulting from thought. Further, schemas direct those cognitive changes. Since most of us have a well developed schema for "lover" and therefore a well developed means for making inferences, thought results in idealization. Suppose, however, that we did not have a well developed schema for "lover". If we started to think about someone as a "lover" we wouldn't have a clear idea of what to focus on and we wouldn't know what to infer from what we already know. In the absence of systematic changes in beliefs, thought should not be associated with changes in feeling. If this line of reasoning is correct, we would expect to find that, in general, there will be less idealization when a person thinks about a stimulus for which she/he has a well developed schema than if she/he thinks about a stimulus for which she/he does not have a well developed schema. In short, one is less likely to idealize a partner if one does not have a well developed schema to direct the process.

There is some evidence for this line of theorizing. Tesser and Leone (1977) assumed that men have better developed cognitive schemas for thinking about the game of football than for thinking about women's fashions. On the other hand, women have better developed schemas for thinking about women's fashions than for thinking about the game of football. This being the case, thought should produce more idealization of football than fashion for men; and thought should produce more

idealization of women's fashions than football games for women. To test this, men and women were exposed to videotaped sequences of well-executed/poorly-executed football tackles and attractive/unattractive women's outfits. Some of the subjects were encouraged to think about an example of each stimulus type while the remaining subjects were distracted from such thought. The results confirmed the hypothesis: idealization co-varied with the presumed degrees of development of the cognitive schema. Among men there was a greater difference between thought and distraction for football games than for women's fashions; among women, there was a greater difference between thought and distraction for women's fashions than for football matches.

The Tesser and Leone (1977) study showed that the extent of idealization depends on how well developed a schema for thought is. In the present context, this generalization implies that the extent and direction of self-generated changes in beliefs and feelings about a sexual partner are going to depend on the content of, and the extent to which, a person has an articulated relevant schema. When it comes to sexual partners we suspect that well developed schemas are almost universal. Almost everyone has to deal with others in this kind of relationship. Further, while there are certainly individual and subcultural variations, we suspect that such schemas are almost always provided by one's culture through books, movies, stories, etc. Consequently we would expect a great deal of within-culture commonality in idealization.

Changing Schemas for Thought

We have suggested that it is possible to tune in different schemas for thought. Thus, thinking about an individual as a co-worker will lead to a particular kind of idealization. One might be concerned with efficiency, competence, training, etc. On the other hand, if one's relationship to that co-worker changed to a potential sexual partner, thought will lead to a different kind of idealization. Here the concern might be with appearance, fidelity, similarity of values, etc. With initial positive feelings, in both cases thought will produce greater positivity. However, since different schemas are involved, the specific thought-generated changes in beliefs will be different in spite of the fact that the stimulus person hasn't changed and the affective direction is the same.

In the first stage of their study, Clary *et al.* (1978) had one group of subjects list the characteristics of a good salesman and another group list the characteristics of a good book-keeper. They then isolated the most

widely agreed upon characteristic for each. Such characteristics, in a very rough sense, represent schemas for book-keepers and for salesmen. In the second stage, new subjects were asked to role-play the personnel officer of a company and to look over a set of résumés in order to hire either a salesman or book-keeper. Half the subjects were then given an opportunity to think about a candidate they were moderately favourable toward, and half were distracted. They then re-rated their favourability toward the candidate and wrote a description of the candidate.

The results were consistent with expectation. As usual, thought produced greater idealization (i.e. favourability) than distraction, and this was equally true for salesmen and book-keepers alike. The more interesting finding concerns the descriptions subjects wrote. Each description was compared with the list representing the salesman schema and the list representing the book-keeper schema, and the number of matches were noted. The number of matches with the book-keeper list was unaffected by the experimental variables. However, the number of matches with the salesman list were affected by the treatments as expected. (Recall that regardless of whether focus was on a salesman or book-keeper, the résumés themselves came from the identical pool.) First, the number of matches with the salesman list was greater when the person was being considered for salesman than when being considered for book-keeper. Further, this difference was significantly more pronounced with thought than with distraction.

The results of this study provide good support for the hypothesis that self-generated beliefs are consistent with a *particular* schema. That is, feelings about the potential book-keeper and the potential salesman became equally more favourable, but they did so on the basis of different cognitive changes. Thought produced not just more favourable beliefs but beliefs that were at the same time more consistent with the particular schema. In a like manner, the implication is that idealization of a co-worker and a sexual partner are based on quite different changes in beliefs.

We have seen how changing a schema for thinking about a particular person can change the kinds of beliefs one generates about that other, even while the affective change is in the same direction. Can changing a schema also result in different *affective* change? Absolutely. A new schema will make salient new beliefs and provide new rules for generating beliefs. Thus, tuning in a new schema might make salient attributes that are evaluatively different from the old schema and thus result in immediate affective change. With continued thought the *new*

affective direction will become accentuated. Suppose one thinks of one's mate as a good spouse. Much of what is salient will be positive and thought will tend to increase that positively. Now, there is convincing evidence that the spouse has been unfaithful. This information is negative in itself and we would expect it to result in lowered affect. Further, it should tune in a new schema for thought. Rather than increased positivity, thought should now produce increased negativity in affect. Thinking about the unfaithful spouse should increase negativity. In short, not only does tuning in a new schema result in different thought generated changes in cognitions, but it can also alter the direction of affective change.

There is evidence for such a process. Tesser and Danheiser (1978) used a paradigm similar to that of Sadler and Tesser (1973). Subjects described themselves and listened to the self-description of their "partner". As in the earlier study the "partner" was really a tape recording prepared by the experimenter to be either likeable or dislikeable. Subjects then rated their first impression of their partner. Following this, subjects were told that they would either be competing with their partner or that they would be cooperating with their partner. Let us tie these operations back to our earlier speculation. We have subjects encountering either a likeable person or a dislikeable person initially. Subjects are then induced to adopt a cooperative schema (analogous to loving spouse) or a competitive schema (analogous to unfaithful spouse). Some of the subjects are encouraged to think about their partner and others are distracted from thinking. Lastly, they give their final impression of their partner.

What happened? In the studies described previously, there was no change in schema, and thought intensified feelings in the initial affective direction, positive or negative. Such polarization was not found here. Although the initial likeability manipulation was highly successful — the likeable partner was better liked than the dislikeable partner on the first impression measure — affect *change* was in the direction of the new schema. With no other new information, when subjects learned that they would be cooperating with their partner, their feelings became more positive toward their partner; when they learned they would be competing, their feelings became more negative toward their partner, regardless of their initial feeling. Further, thinking about one's partner intensified these changes in feeling.

What these data point out for romantic attraction is the lability of feelings persons can have for their partner. If feelings about a sexual

partner are a function of the schema one uses to think about that partner, and if one can tune in different schemas for thought, then one has the potential for many different feelings. These feelings can change quickly in direction and can be intensified by thought. One would expect that there are certainly individual differences in the number and variety of schemas which can be brought to bear. But, certainly most of us have a repertoire containing schemas which would tend to be associated with both positive and negative attributes, and which lead to both positive and negative cognitive changes.

The changing of schemas can be rapid and oscillating. Such a process could look like ambivalence toward the partner. If circumstances lead to the adoption of different schemas in rapid succession, or the rapid back and forth exchange of two different schemas, the result will be fluctuating changes in feelings. It is not ambivalence in the sense that the individual is experiencing positive and negative affect *at the same time*. Indeed, if one assumes that feelings are enduring entities, then the presence of both positive and negative feelings toward a particular person implies ambivalence. However, from our perspective, feelings are not necessarily enduring; they are the product of one's momentary salient cognitions and cognitive constructions. Thus, we see no need for an "ambivalence" construct.

Does Absence Make the Heart Grow Fonder?

In our analogy we compared cognitive schemas to scientific theories and suggested that just as scientific theories are subject to empirical verification, so self-generated beliefs are subject to reality constraints. That is, we assume that cognitive changes (i.e. additions, changes, or deletions) as a result of thought will not be maintained in the face of compelling evidence that they are false. This does not mean that one's search or exposure to evidence is unbiased, but rather that when confronted by strong, incontrovertible evidence, the change will be abandoned.

Consider the case of a couple who are very much in love. They think about each other often and they see each other often. Each can only distort the attributes of the other to a limited extent. He can't convince himself that she has a beautiful body because everytime he sees her he is confronted by 170 pounds of woman on a 5 ft 5 in frame; she can't convince herself that he does not drink too much because almost everytime she sees him he ends up drinking. Now, his business takes him

out of town for an extended period of time. They are still in love and they still think of one another often. In this case, however, greater distortions are possible since there are no constraints on the process. Now, she can forget about his drinking and he can fantasize about her as being a beauty queen.

What all this suggests is that absence has the *potential* for making the heart grow fonder. This potential is there because absence reduces the reality constraints on self-generated changes in beliefs and, therefore, feelings. But absence holds only the potential for greater positive change for two reasons. First, we have argued that idealization is a function of thought, so if absence is not accompanied by thought we would expect little, if any, intensification of feeling. Secondly, the idealization process is bidirectional. That is, without a change in schema, thought will tend to intensify the initial affective direction whether it is positive *or* negative. Thus, given both an initially negative feeling and thought, rather than increasing fondness, absence will make the heart grow colder.

There are some relevant data. Tesser (1976) had his college student subjects express their feelings about works of art. Some subjects were encouraged to think about a particular work while the work was in front of them. Others were encouraged to think about the work when the work was absent. The presence of the work puts "reality constraints" on the potential level of change and hence should retard the change process. A final group of subjects were distracted from thinking about the work. For female subjects, our hypotheses were confirmed. Not only did thought produce greater idealization of the work than did distraction, but thought in the absence of the work (i.e. no reality constraints) produced more idealization than thought in the presence of the object. In short, absence did make the heart grow fonder, but only when the initial feeling was positive and there was focused attention on the absent object.

External Information Processing and Schemas

Our discussion of people's responsiveness to "reality constraints" may make the process appear more unbiased than we believe it actually is. Indeed, there are several recent studies indicating that information search and its subsequent recollection are clearly influenced by the schema itself. For example, Snyder and Uranowitz (1978) had subjects read a detailed life history of a woman. Some subjects subsequently learned that the woman was living a lesbian life-style and others learned that she was living a heterosexual life-style. One week later, subjects were given a

multiple choice test of memory about the woman's life. There was clear evidence of constructive processes in their memories. Subjects given the lesbian schema remembered more facts and made more errors consistent with this schema than did subjects given the heterosexual schema. The latter subjects remembered more facts and made more errors consistent with a heterosexual schema than did the former subjects. On the other hand, in spite of its constructive nature, the recall was not a complete fabrication.

The fact that schemas can produce a bias in memory is not surprising. It is consistent with all the work we have reviewed so far. Do schemas also influence our transactions with external "reality" to produce biased information? There is evidence that they do. That is, if we have a schema that leads us to suppose that our potential partner is alluring, sexually attractive, and receptive, our information search procedures will produce evidence biased toward confirming the supposition. Snyder and Swan (1978) have done a relevant experiment. An introvert schema was described to subjects and they were asked to find out if another person's beliefs, attitudes, and behaviours were consistent with this schema. An extrovert schema was described to others and they were also asked to find out if the schema held. Subjects chose 12 questions from a large list of questions they were given. They tended to choose to ask questions which were biased in the direction of the schema they were trying to verify. That is, subjects trying to verify the extrovert schema asked questions which *presupposed* the accuracy of that schema, e.g. "What would you do if you wanted to liven things up at a party?", while subjects trying to verify the introvert schema asked questions which presupposed the accuracy of the introvert schema, e.g. "What things do you dislike about loud parties?"

Does such a biased search for information result in biasing the actual information obtained? When dealing with human relationships it appears to. If we think a particular partner is attracted to us, we will behave toward that partner in a way that will make the partner respond as if she/he is indeed attracted to us. On the other hand, if we think that our partner is hostile, our behaviour might actually produce hostile behaviour in our partner. For example, when randomly paired persons were asked the questions selected by the subjects in the Snyder and Swan experiments described above, judges, who heard *only* the answers, judged those questioned by subjects in the extrovert condition as extroverted and those questioned by subjects in the introvert condition as introverted.

Perhaps the most interesting demonstration of schema confirmation from the perspective of a chapter on sexual attractiveness comes from an ingenius study by Snyder *et al.* (1977). There is a schema for physical attractiveness. "Physically attractive people, for example (are) perceived to be more sexually warm and responsive, sensitive, kind, interesting, strong, poised, modest, sociable, and outgoing than persons of lesser physical attractiveness" (Berscheid and Walster, 1974). Thus if we believe our partner is physically attractive, there are a number of ways in which that belief can be confirmed behaviourally, i.e. we can get our partner to behave as if she/he is physically attractive. Male subjects were randomly paired with female subjects. They never saw one another but were instructed to get to know one another via a ten-minute telephone conversation. Before the conversation took place, the male was presented with what he believed was a photograph of his partner. The photograph was not actually a picture of his partner but rather was intended to make a randomly selected half of the males think their partner was physically attractive, while the remaining half thought their partner was physically unattractive. The conversation was tape recorded. Regardless of their partner's actual attractiveness, males who believed their partners were physically attractive made their partners behave as though they *were* physically attractive! That is, judges who had neither seen the girl nor the photograph and who listened to *only* the girl's track of the tape rated the girl as more beautiful if her male partner thought she was beautiful than if her male partner thought she was unattractive.

In short, we have seen that distortion takes place in the absence of relevant information, i.e. "reality constraints". Here we see that it is often the case that even actual "reality" can be "manipulated" to fit our schematic view of the world. Obviously, there are limits to such distortion processes, but such processes clearly exist.

Putting It All Together

Up to this point we have tried to spell out some of the factors that affect when we will think about a potential sexual partner, the consequences of thinking about that partner (generally, idealization), and the conditions under which the consequences are facilitated or attenuated (the absence and presence of reality constraints). The following study was an attempt to put all these factors together in a natural setting to examine how they work as a system over a two-week period of time.

We assume that people tend to like the persons they date, so our

(Tesser and Paulhus, 1976) first hypothesis (a) was that thought about a prior date would have a positive causal impact on love for that date. We have previously argued that affect is a potent determinant of the schema for thinking one tunes in. Thus, our second hypothesis (b) was that love (affect) for a prior date would have a positive causal impact on thinking about the prior date. We have also suggested that "reality constraints", i.e. knowledge inconsistent with one's schema-generated beliefs, will constrain polarization. It follows then that (c) reality constraints will have a negative impact on love. One cause of reality constraints is the presence of the object itself, so we hypothesized (d) that dating frequency would have a positive causal impact on reality constraints. Finally, we hypothesized (e and f) that dating and loving would be reciprocally, causally related. These hypotheses are summarized in Fig. 1.

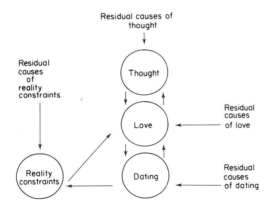

Fig. 1. *Summary of hypothesized relations between thought, love, dating, and reality constraints*

In order to test these hypotheses, we used a panel of college students. On the first administration of our questionnaire, respondents identified the last person they dated. Their love for that individual was measured using Rubin's (1973) love scale. All the other variables were measured retrospectively over the prior two weeks, e.g. how often did you think about _____? (Thought); . . . (did) new information confirm or contradict your expectations? (Reality constraints); . . . how many times have you dated this person in the last two weeks? (Dating frequency). On a second occasion, two weeks later, respondents answered the same questions about the same person.

We used temporal order to infer causal direction. Within administrations we assume that the retrospectively measured variables are causally prior to love. We assume that variables measured on the first occasion are causally prior to variables measured on the second occasion. Finally we assume that each variable is causally dependent on its own prior state. These assumptions and our hypotheses (in Fig. 1) allowed the specification of a model to be tested with path analysis (Land, 1969).

The resulting path diagram, with all non-significant paths deleted, is shown in Fig. 2. The path diagram can be used to "predict" the original

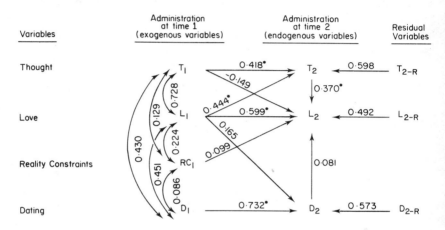

Fig. 2. *Path diagram showing observed relations between thought, love, dating, and reality constraints, at times 1 and 2*

intercorrelation matrix. The closer the fit, the more adequate the model. In this case the "predicted" and obtained correlation matrices do *not* differ beyond chance. Thus, overall, the hypotheses receive some support.

Now let us examine the diagram more closely. First, it is not surprising to learn that the largest (measured) cause of each variable at time 2 is that same variable at time 1. (This much "inertia" or stability in the system makes it difficult to detect other relationships.) The hypothesis (a) that thought would produce love was supported. Thought immediately preceding the measurement of love had a substantial impact on love (0·370). Although the direct delayed effect of thought on love was negative (-0·155), its *indirect* effect through L_2 was positive and of about equal magnitude (0·172), making the *total* causal effect negligible. In

short, thought has a substantial immediate effect on love but no (*net*) delayed effect. Furthermore, love has a direct impact on thought (0·444) as predicted by the hypothesis (b).

Dating did not have a significant impact on Reality constraints as expected (d) and Reality constraints did not have an *immediate* impact on love. These two non-significant paths were deleted in Fig. 2. Reality constraints did, however, have a delayed impact on love (0·092 — the Reality constraints variable is inverted, thus the coefficient is positive), thereby providing some support for the hypothesis (c). It may also be worth noting that there was some support for the hypotheses that loving causes dating (e) and dating causes loving (f).

In sum, although the data are not totally unequivocal (cf. Bentler and Huber, 1979; Smith, 1977; Tesser and Paulhus, 1978), this study provides evidence that thought affects romantic attraction even in periods up to two weeks. Affect has a reciprocal impact on thought. Reality constraints, at least after a delay, seem to retard the polarization process.

The Issue of Awareness

In this chapter we have emphasized cognitive process (i.e. thought and cognitive structure (i.e. schemas), but have not dealt explicitly with the extent to which persons are aware of these processes and structures. The issue of awareness is an old one, but has recently received renewed attention and some interesting data have been brought to bear on the question. There are at least two related issues: one deals with the question of whether apparently thoughtful responses are indeed thoughtful and conscious, or whether they are "automatic", requiring little in the way of conscious thought (i.e. are our behaviours and feelings with respect to a sexual partner thought out or are they rather automatic?). The second deals with the question of whether persons have conscious access to their own thought processes (i.e. are we able to give the "real" reasons for our behaviour and feelings toward our sexual partners?).

The "Automatic" Nature of Some Behaviours

In the earlier sections of this chapter we examined in some detail the effects of conscious thought on feelings about potential sexual partners. In this section we explore the possibility that much of our behaviour toward potential sexual partners is "automatic" (Shriffrin and Schneider,

1977), or "top of the head" (Taylor and Fiske, 1978), or "mindless" (Langer *et al.*, 1978), rather than being the result of conscious, in-depth processing and integration of new information with old information. The work of Taylor and Fiske (1978) demonstrates that often what is most salient at a particular moment accounts for our beliefs. For example, the person we are directly facing in a discussion is more salient than the person sitting to our side. When actual contributions are held constant, we tend to see the person facing us as having shown greater leadership and as being more internally directed in his/her behaviour (Taylor and Fiske, 1971). When a person in a group has "solo-status", e.g. only dark-skinned or only female, that person is more salient. Again, holding actual contribution constant, that person is seen as more of a leader, more internal in their behaviour, and more typical of the schema (i.e. stereotype) we have of that person's group (Taylor *et al.*, 1978). Thus, it appears that the mere salience of individuals, including sexual partners, can affect our judgements about them.

Langer's work provides some nice demonstrations of "mindless" social behaviour. She makes creative use of the notion of a cognitive script (Abelson, 1978; Schank and Abelson, 1977), a concept very much like the schema concept we have developed here. It refers to an overlearned sequence of behaviours to be expected or enacted in a particular situation. According to Langer (1978), given the appropriate stimuli to enter a particular script, scripted behaviour often emerges automatically and without conscious thought on the part of the actor. For example, a "favour script" might have as its entering conditions "makes request" and "gives reason for request". If these conditions are met, the actor will enact the favour. On the other hand, if these formal conditions are not met, the person will think about the favour before doing it. Further, if enacting the favour is potentially costly, the person will think before acting.

To test these ideas, Langer *et al.* (1978) had an experimental accomplice approach persons about to use the Xerox machine at a library. In the *request only* condition, the accomplice said, "Excuse me, I have _____ pages. May I use the Xerox machine?" In the *placebic information* condition, the second sentence read: "May I use the Xerox machine because I have to make copies?" Notice that this condition has both elements for entering the script — a request and a reason — but the reason is non-informative. That is, what else would one do with a Xerox machine if not make copies? In the *real information* condition, the second sentence was: "May I use the Xerox machine because I'm in a rush?"

This last condition contains the necessary request plus reason, but here the reason provides new information.

The investigators reasoned that if a reason plus request elicited the script, and if scripted behaviour was performed without thought, then there should be no difference between the placebic and the real information conditions. Since both contain the necessary elements, they should both produce more compliance than the request only condition. If people do think before acting, then the request only and placebic information conditions should not differ because they both contain exactly the same "actual" information, and they should both produce less compliance than the "real information" condition. When the favour was small, i.e. few pages to copy, compliance appeared "mindless": placebic information = real information > request only. On the other hand, when the favour was large, compliance did appear to reflect thoughtful attention: real information > placebic information = request only. Langer *et al.* (1978) and Langer and Abelson (1972) provide further evidence for "mindlessness" in other social behaviour.

It appears that at least under some circumstances, our behaviour is not based on well-thought-out plans of action but proceeds rather automatically under the control of schema-like cognitive structures. Such behaviour is certainly likely to be found in romantic encounters as well. We have well-learned "scripts" for dealing with the initial acquaintance process and encounters in well-frequented settings. Behaviours are likely to be enacted rather automatically under such circumstances. When the enactment of some behaviour is likely to be costly, i.e. marriage, divorce, affairs, etc., conscious thought is more likely to be involved.

Are Persons Aware of Their Own Cognitive Processes?

Bob and Barbara have just announced their engagement. We interview them to get at the reasons for their decision to marry. Bob tells us that he is tired of being a bachelor, Barbara is a great cook and will make a great mother, and that he and Barbara share a deep religious commitment. Barbara tells us that Bob is fun to be with, has a good job with a bright future, and is a person whose character she can really admire. Are these the real reasons that Bob and Barbara decided to marry? Maybe yes, maybe no. There is much evidence to suggest that persons' reports about their own cognitive processes are often not very accurate. While persons are perfectly capable and willing to provide "accounts" for their feelings

about another person, those accounts are often not consistent with what systematic observation reveals to be the true causal factors.

An early dating study by Tesser and Brodie (1971) illustrates the problem. Their subjects filled out questionnaires about a "computer date". The questionnaire asked them to rank in order the following attributes in terms of their importance for a date: personality, intelligence, physical attractiveness, and character. They also rated their date in terms of these attributes, and indicated how attracted they were to their date. Subjects' rankings indicated that the most important attribute in a date is "personality" and the least important is "intelligence". If the subjects are accurately reporting the basis of their feelings, the ratings of their attraction to their date should be most strongly correlated with ratings of their date's "personality" and least strongly correlated with ratings of their date's "intelligence". This was not the case. While attraction was least strongly associated with rated "intelligence" (r = 0·39) is was most strongly associated with rated physical attractiveness (r = 0·69), an attribute that was rated as next to lowest in importance. These data suggest that subjects may not be fully aware of the determinants of their feelings about potential sexual partners.

Nisbett and Wilson (1977) have recently pointed out the pervasiveness of this lack of awareness. For example, persons are often unaware that their attitudes have changed and are unable to reproduce their original attitudes (e.g. Bem and McConnel, 1970; Goethals and Reckman, 1973); in the tradition of "subliminal perception", persons are often unable to report even the presence of stimuli that affect their feelings (e.g. Wilson, 1975); creative problem solutions often appear at times when there is no conscious attention being paid to the problem (e.g. Ghiselin, 1952); and persons often cannot report the cues that triggered the solution (e.g. Maier, 1931).

Obviously, individuals' reports of what influences their feelings are not always inaccurate. For example, Nisbett and Bellows (1977) varied the appearance, academic credentials, clumsiness, accident history and likelihood of meeting a stimulus person. Subjects made judgements of the stimulus person that included intelligence and likeability. They were also asked to report how influential each of the independent variables (e.g. appearance, clumsiness) were in affecting their judgement. Nisbett and Bellows then compared the extent to which each independent variable *actually* affected the subjects' judgements with the subjects' self-reports of the effect of each. Subjects were quite accurate in the domain of judgements of intelligence and quite inaccurate in the domain of

likeability. Self-reported influence was correlated 0·94 with actual influence in the former case but correlated -0·31 in the latter case.

Why is it that people sometimes appear to be accurate in their reports and sometimes inaccurate? Nisbett and Wilson (1977) suggest that people simply do not have access to their own cognitive processes, but they do have available culturally shared, implicit causal theories. (Such theories are like consciously held schemas.) When asked for an "account" of their feelings or judgements, persons simply read off their conscious schema or implicit theory rather than interrogating the actual cognitive process. Thus, if the implicit theory is correct, the self-report will appear to be correct, e.g. judgements of intelligence; if the implicit theory is not correct, e.g. attraction, the self-report will appear to be incorrect.

If, indeed, persons are simply reading off their implicit theories rather than interrogating their own cognitive processes, then one would expect that persons with similar implicit theories would give the same reports of the influence of various factors, *both accurate and inaccurate*, even though they never made the relevant judgements, i.e. intelligence and likeability. This was the case in the Nisbett and Bellows study. Ratings of the influence of the independent variables by persons who did not make actual judgements of the stimulus person, were accurate in the case of intelligence, inaccurate in the case of likeability, and highly correlated with the reports of persons who actually did make the judgements (r = 0·99 for intelligence, r = 0·89 for likeability).

Although Nisbett and Wilson's (1977) thesis can be criticized (e.g. Smith and Miller, 1978), they provide compelling evidence to suggest that at times we are unaware of the kinds of things that actually affect our feelings. In trying to understand our feelings and the causes of our decisions and actions, we will be guided by consciously held schemata. Such a process could be consequential to persons involved in a relationship. For example, if Bob felt his decision to marry Barbara was based on shared religious values, whether that was true or not, he might become more religious (e.g. Ross *et al.*, 1975). Barbara might feel, rightly or wrongly, that a negative change in her feelings towards Bob was based on Bob's not spending enough time with her. Even though Bob might subsequently spend more time with Barbara to the detriment of his vocational pursuits, the added time would not necessarily affect Barbara's negative feelings.

Up to this point, we have examined some of the determinants of thought about sexual partners and some of the consequences of thought. In this section we have tried to balance this presentation. Here we have

argued that often what appears to be well thought out and planned in our behaviour is not. Our behaviour with the opposite sex, especially that which is potentially non-costly, is sometimes rather automatic. Our judgements and feelings about sexual partners and potential sexual partners are sometimes based on factors which are not consciously accessible. However, even these processes appear to be governed by schema-like variables. That is, automatic behaviour seems to follow a "script", and accounts of judgements and feelings seem to be directed by implicit causal theories. Below, we use the schema construct to deal with other variables that research suggests is important in human sexual attraction.

The Role of Schemas in Physical Attractiveness, Similarity and Arousal

Physical Attractiveness

The physical attractiveness–attraction link is a fairly reliable experimental phenomenon (Berscheid and Walster, 1974; Tesser and Brodie, 1971; Walster *et al.*, 1966). One rather simplistic explanation for this relationship is that physical attractiveness brings direct aesthetic rewards based on culturally determined criteria (Walster *et al.*, 1966). While aesthetic rewards are a factor, it appears that the role of attractiveness is considerably more complex than this.

Schematic processing allows for more efficient use of social information; but, as Taylor and Crocker (1979) note, it also has its potential liabilities. Remember that, to help a perceiver fill out a stimulus configuration, schemas direct both the search for new information and the generation of inferences. These functions, however, are not performed objectively. There are built-in biases towards (a) generating inferences consistent with the schema invoked; (b) accepting new information if it is schema-consistent; (c) distorting new information to make it schema-consistent; and (d) underevaluating the importance of disconfirming information. There also seems to be a tendency, over time, to treat the inferences generated as "hard data", making the stimulus configuration further resistant to disconfirmation.

As noted earlier, persons have a schema dealing with physical attractiveness. The physical attractiveness schema has been found to contain positive attributes such as sexual warmth and responsivity, poise, sociability, desirability of personality, future

perceived marital and parental competence, likelihood of marriage, future high occupational status, and likelihood of future happiness (Berscheid and Walster, 1974; Dion *et al.*, 1972). Clearly, if we have no information about some potential date besides physical attractiveness, our schema will lead us to infer numerous positive attributes and we will be quite attracted to that person.

What if information beyond physical attractiveness becomes available? Some information processing models of person perception hold that one's evaluation of another is some additive or averaged function of the weighted pieces of information (e.g. Anderson, 1970; Fishbein and Ajzen, 1975). If this were true, additional positive information should bolster the effects of attractiveness, while additional negative information should attenuate attractiveness effects. According to the schematic processing model, positive information is likely to be schema-consistent, and bolstering may occur. However, negative information is likely to be schema-inconsistent, and will be distorted, undervalued, or rejected. In fact, there is evidence that attractiveness effects *do* persist beyond the initial impression regardless of additional negative information (Huston and Levinger, 1978).

Except in psychological experiments, it is rarely the case that physical attractiveness is the only information available to the social perceiver. Furthermore, in the "real world", it is not likely that people would be satisfied with only attractiveness information if they were anticipating an actual date. In other words, in the laboratory, where there are few, if any, consequences for their actions, subjects are likely to engage in automatic processing. In the real world, consequences for choosing a potential partner are profound, and one would expect more careful, controlled processing. More information should be sought, and inferences generated should be more cautious. Indeed, two studies show this pattern clearly. In the first, people were asked to rate the relative importance of a variety of characteristics at various levels of interpersonal involvement in a hypothetical relationship. Results showed that superficial attributes such as appearance were seen as important in the initial stage of a relationship, while personality variables were seen as important in relationships at more advanced levels of involvement (Levinger and Snoek, 1972). The second (Stroebe *et al.*, 1971) involved a paper and pencil study of attraction and attractiveness. Subjects were asked to rate pictures of physically attractive and unattractive opposite sex persons as potential dates, friends, or marriage partners. The authors found that attractive stimulus persons were rated more highly as potential dates; no

attractiveness effect was found when the ratings were for potential friends or marriage partners. Thus, attractiveness was important for a pencil and paper date, but when subjects were forced to think in terms of a potential partner, the importance of attractiveness diminished.

If one were expecting a real date with another person, rather than a paper and pencil date, one might be more aware of the potential consequences of the encounter, and weigh available information carefully (Berscheid and Graziano, 1979). In this case, the correlation between attractiveness and desirability as a date becomes less perfect. In fact, in real dating situations, the evidence suggests that people generally try to match their potential partner's attractiveness with their own (Berscheid and Walster, 1974).

As with automatic processing, in controlled processing, once a stimulus configuration has been filled out, it becomes resistant to disconfirmation. Further, once a potential partner has been selected, the partner's attributes will be perceived as more positive. Interestingly, though one might have chosen a somewhat plain looking person to go out with, that person is likely to be perceived as more attractive over time (Berscheid and Graziano, 1979; Sears and Taylor, 1977).

Similarity

The relationship between similarity and attraction may be even more complex than that between physical attractiveness and attraction. While it is generally conceded that similarity does, in some cases, lead to attraction, demonstrations of this effect are often a function of particular research strategies and experimental arrangements. These, in turn, are often biased by particular philosophical outlooks.

For instance, Byrne and his colleagues have taken a reinforcement approach. Similarity of attitudes and personality traits is rewarding because it is evidence that our attitudes and traits are valid. To illustrate his position, Byrne created the "bogus stranger" paradigm (e.g. Byrne, 1969). Subjects are asked to fill out a general attitude questionnaire to be given to another subject for that person's evaluation. The subject also gets a questionnaire to rate which he believes was filled out by still another subject. Actually, each subject is given a questionnaire reflecting attitudes consistent or inconsistent with his own. Typically, subjects have indicated greater liking for the person represented by the attitude consistent questionnaire. Similar results were also found by Stroebe *et al.* (1971).

In a field test of the model, Byrne *et al.* (1970) set up a simulated computer dating situation. Couples either high or low in attitude similarity were sent on a 30-min "coke date". While not exposed to each other's questionnaires, subject pairs were told that they were either attitudinally similar or dissimilar. The authors found that similarity had a positive effect on ratings of one's partner's desirability as a date or marriage partner. This effect was enhanced substantially if one's partner was also rated as physically attractive. Together, attractiveness and similarity were also found to predict the likelihood that partners spoke to each other and remembered each other's names two to three months post-experimentally.

Not all research has supported the similarity–attraction relationship. Curran and Lippold (1975) conducted two studies, each the replication of the other. Again, a "computer date" cover story was used. Subjects filled out an attitude questionnaire and were rated in physical attractiveness (without their knowledge) by judges. They were matched according to approximately equal physical attractiveness. The male of each pair was given the phone number of his prospective partner, and no limits were placed on the type or duration of the date. Curran and Lippold found a small similarity effect in one study, and no similarity effect in the other. A possible explanation offered for the discrepancy of these results with the Byrne *et al.* (1970) results had to do with subjects' awareness of the similarity: the Byrne *et al.* subjects were made aware of the similarity; the Curran and Lippold subjects were not. In a single encounter, subjects may never have discovered the similarity on their own.

As Ajzen (1977) suggests, similarity, like attractiveness or any other variable, affects attraction only in so far as similarity information is available, and noticed, at the time a judgement is made. Thus, the influence of any single variable, like similarity, will be minimized if (a) it is not salient, and/or (b) it is not washed out by the presence of more and/or "heavier" variables. Since similarity is the *only* information available in the bogus stranger paradigm, and it and attraction are the only information available in the coke date paradigm, it is not surprising to Ajzen (1977) that there is a similarity effect. In the Curran and Lippold (1975) studies, there was no control over what variables might have operated during the date, and similarity was not made known. If there was a similarity effect, it may have been obscured by other variables. Ajzen (1974), for example, gave subjects two kinds of information: similarity (high vs. low) of Other and Other's bogus evaluation (positive or negative) of the subject. There was no similarity

effect; but, there was a strong increase in liking when Other gave the subject a positive evaluation.

A schematic processing interpretation of the similarity-attraction link has elements of the reinforcement model, and also takes into consideration some of the points made by Ajzen (1977). As noted earlier, we assume that persons are motivated toward prediction and control of their environment — a motive that sounds very much like Byrne's (1969) effectance motive. The use of schemas in the service of this motive tends to make salient specific inferences and aspects of the environment which are combined to determine affective responses. We illustrate below.

The bogus stranger paradigm is functionally equivalent to the more spartan physical attractiveness experiments discussed in the previous section. That is, a single variable is made salient and all others are controlled. Subjects are implicitly asked to consider the possibility of encountering the stimulus stranger. Persons have well developed self-schemas (Markus, 1977). If we assume that persons are motivated to predict and control their environment, subjects should become more attracted to the high similarity stranger because (a) knowing that he/she is like them increases their ability to predict his/her behaviour, and (b) if they feel reasonably good about themselves, they can generate other positive inferences about the stranger (since they will see their own positiveness in the stranger).

Likewise, in the computer date paradigms, awareness of similarity is induced (e.g. Byrne *et al.*, 1970) or it is not (e.g. Curran and Lippold, 1975). When the information is available, it has the same effect as in the bogus stranger situation. A single piece of positive information is parleyed into a positive expectancy about the date. Information consistent with the expectancy is weighted highly; inconsistent information is underweighted or rejected. The result is increased attraction.

Locus of Similarity

We have argued that similarity has its effect on attraction by rendering the stimulus person more predictable and thus controllable. If this argument is correct we would expect that information about similarity which leads to greater predictability and control should also lead to greater attraction. For example, knowledge that a potential partner's preferences for their own activities are similar to one's own such preferences, is less informative about predictability/controllability than

knowledge that both you and the partner agree on how *others* should behave. The latter foretells that, should a relationship begin, both partners can predict and adjust these interpersonal behaviours to maximize one another's outcomes. Research by Santee (1976) supports this reasoning. His subjects were put through the bogus stranger paradigm. However, the degree of similarity was crossed with the *type* of similarity. Subjects were asked to fill out a questionnaire in which they were to indicate attitudes towards themselves as actors (intrapersonal attitudes), or towards others as actors (interpersonal attitudes). At a follow-up session, they received, and were asked to evaluate, the questionnaires of bogus individuals. The questionnaires of these other individuals were also either intra- or interpersonal. Attraction was most affected by degree of similarity when subjects both filled out and received an interpersonal questionnaire. It was least affected when both the questionnaires of the subjects and the other individuals were intrapersonal.

If predictability mediates the relationship between similarity and attraction, and schemas are an important element in predictability, then *patterns* of similarity/dissimilarity should affect attraction because patterns of similarity provide information about similarity of schemas. Suppose, for example, that an important dimension in Alice's schema for evaluating potential vacations is a Bucolic/Urbane dimension. She is in favour of vacations in New York and San Francisco and not enthusiastic about vacations in Yellowstone Park or the Grand Canyon. Now she is confronted with Albert who is in favour of vacations in New York and the Grand Canyon but not in favour of vacations in San Francisco or Yellowstone Park. Albert's pattern of responses provides evidence that his schema for evaluating vacations is not the same as Alice's, i.e. he seems to be ignoring the Bucolic/Urbane dimension. Since schema similarity increases predictability, Albert should be seen as less predictable and less well-liked than others who disagree with Alice the same number of times but do not provide evidence of schema-dissimilarity. Using the bogus stranger paradigm, Tesser (1971) independently varied the number of similar attitude statements and the pattern of similar attitude statements. As predicted, he found main effects for both types of similarity on attraction. Additionally, he found that "others" high in schema similarity were judged by subjects to be more predictable, more consistent, and more likely to look at items in the same way. Importantly, then, subjects were able to detect differences in schema similarity. All of these results were later replicated (Tesser, 1972).

In another study, Johnson and Tesser (1972) manipulated evaluative and structural similarity as above. They also included a situational manipulation in which subjects (a) believed that they would engage in a task in which they would have to predict the responses of the other (prediction situation), or (b) believed that their task was to match opinions with the other (representative situation). Results showed that evaluative similarity was more positively related to attraction in the representative situation than the predictive situation, and structural similarity was more positively related to attraction in the predictive situation than in the representative situation. Thus when we wish to predict another's behaviour, we would prefer to know how that person structures the world. In some cases, however, agreement itself is the goal of an encounter, perhaps because the other's behaviour will be seen as representative of one's own. In these cases, similarity without regard to pattern becomes more important.

Arousal

According to Schachter (1964), emotional states are the joint product of a change in one's level of arousal and cognitions. Physiological arousal is undifferentiated. Its interpretation depends on the current situation and past experiences in similar situations. If the origin of the arousal state is ambiguous, persons will seize whatever cues are available to label the state and reduce the ambiguity. The same state of arousal might be labelled fear if the person experiencing it was standing on a cliff; or it might be labelled passion if the person was with someone of the opposite sex.

Walster, Berscheid and their associates have applied Schachter's theory to sexual attraction. Their position, as stated in Walster (1971), is that sexual attraction can result from a state of physiological arousal and proximal cues indicating that passion or love is an appropriate label. Consider the examples below.

Dutton and Aron (1974) conducted a series of experiments designed to see if subjects would be more sexually aroused by the presence of a female under conditions of high fear or anxiety. Two of the experiments were conducted in the field. The task involved crossing a bridge. All the subjects were male. For half of them, the bridge was steady and fairly close to the ground. For the other half, the bridge was very high, swayed in the wind, and generally appeared unstable. Either a male or female interviewer, actually an accomplice, approached each subject on one of

the bridges. As predicted, subjects in the high fear condition demonstrated more attraction to the female accomplice than to the male; this attraction to the female in the high fear condition was much greater than that to either male or female in the low fear condition. Further, subjects in the high fear-female condition also exhibited more sexual imagery to administration of the TAT.

Returning to the laboratory, Dutton and Aron led male volunteer subjects to anticipate either a mild or severe shock. In half of each of the severity conditions, a female confederate posing as a fellow subject was either present or not. Results showed that subjects reported more attraction to the present female in the severe shock condition, and some sexual imagery in response to TAT cards. Similar results were obtained by Jacobs *et al.* (1971) using verbal attack as the arousal-producing stimulus.

Recently, a compelling argument for a reinforcement interpretation of the misattribution stand was made by Kenrick and Cialdini (1977). Their position is this: attraction in the situations above is not due to the misattribution of physiological arousal, but to the reward value placed in one who relieves an aversive state. They point out that the existence of ambiguity regarding arousal in much of the misattribution research is questionable. For example, it is doubtful that Dutton and Aron's high bridge subjects could not directly attribute their arousal to fear of its height and instability. The female confederate reduced their anxiety directly by her mere presence.

However, the reinforcement interpretation fails to adequately account for the operation of some important cues. Consider again the Dutton and Aron study. Subjects were more attracted to female than male confederates in the high fear condition. A reinforcement position does not allow for differences due to the sex of the confederate unless it admits that persons have schematic beliefs regarding masculine and feminine behaviour. Namely, since women are generally not high risk takers, the presence of a woman on the bridge indicates that the bridge is safe; since males are prone to take risks the presence of a male does not necessarily indicate that the bridge is safe.

Recently, Kenrick *et al.* (1979) reported four attempts to replicate the laboratory half of the Dutton and Aron (1974) study. They found, as speculated by Kenrick and Cialdini (1977), that subjects were able to correctly attribute their arousal to the situation. More importantly, they did *not* find increased attraction to a female confederate (or male confederate for that matter) in either high or low fear conditions. One

wonders, on the basis of these results, whether both misattribution and reinforcement explanations are inappropriate.

How can we reconcile the failure of Kenrick *et al.* (1979) to find attraction in high fear conditions with Dutton and Aron's (1974) successful demonstration of the effect? There is a schematic processing interpretation that does not require the assumptions of the misattribution or reinforcement positions. The latter two interpretations assume, in terms of Dutton and Aron's (1974) results, that the high bridge female was the informational cue regarding (a) a bodily state, or (b) the safety of the bridge. The schematic processing interpretation works in the other direction: instead of the female providing information about the safety of the bridge, it is the bridge which provides information about her. Each of us has a schema for members of the opposite sex. In the absence of specific information, this schema is likely to be some sort of average, or "typical" cluster of attributes. More specific informational cues allow us to make more specific inferences. In other words, as situations change, our schemas for a particular stimulus may also change. Thus, the low bridge situation provided Dutton and Aron's (1974) low bridge subjects no new information beyond that which could typically be inferred. In the high bridge situation, no new information was obtained regarding the male accomplice since the male accomplice was engaging in behaviour not inconsistent with the "average male" schema. However, the high bridge situation did provide additional information about the female accomplice, namely that she was daring, willing to take risks, and so forth. Perhaps subjects were more attracted to the high bridge female because they could make schematic inferences about her, such as her social and sexual boldness. This would certainly explain subjects' greater TAT sexual imagery in the high bridge-female condition.

It would be difficult for the subjects of Kenrick *et al.* (1979) to infer anything about the female accomplice in that study. She was there in her role as fellow subject, or experimenter; i.e. she was there because she had to be there. In Dutton and Aron's (1974) experiment, the presence of the female on the high unsteady bridge would likely have been perceived of as an act of choice, and therefore could be taken as representative of her other behaviours. (We should point out that there have been difficulties replicating Schachter and Singer's (1962) original misattribution findings. It appears that an ambiguous state of arousal (given that such states can be produced in the laboratory — see our earlier discussion) may produce a bias toward negative affect (Maslach, 1979; Marshall and Zimbardo, 1979).)

The Role of Schemas in Long-term Relationships

We have seen that single variables such as arousal, attractiveness, and similarity are related to attraction. These links have been demonstrated in experiments which have, for the most part, treated individuals as passive responders. Further, the experimental situations have often been ahistorical. Subjects do not know the stimulus person, real or bogus, to whom they are exposed (or about whom they are informed), and in most cases they are not likely to have extended contact with that person. Processing in these cases is rather automatic: A single piece of positive (or negative) information is presented, and an array of positive (or negative) inferences is generated. However, we have also seen that as soon as some element of history is added to experiments, such as anticipation of an actual encounter, these simple "A causes B" microtheories sometimes break down. This seems to be the case when subjects are confronted with, or asked to consider, real consequences for their responses.

The single variable microtheories may only explain some relationship initiation attempts. For example, they offer an adequate explanation for the "love at first sight" phenomenon. However, as Burgess and Wallin (1953) have pointed out, love at first sight is by far the exception to the rule. Most relationships, better than 90% according to Burgess and Wallin, develop between persons who have known each other for some time. Romantic relationships begin between people who already know much about each other. Neither person need even be aware of the particular moment when the relationship began.

The schematic processing model, therefore, must be able to account for long-term factors in romantic attraction. The earlier part of this chapter dealt with those long-term factors that can be attributed to thought *per se*. Now we turn briefly to factors of a more interpersonal nature.

Behavioural Confirmation

As we have pointed out earlier, one's selected partner is likely to be the object of inference generation and perceptual distortion. Thinking schematically performs these feats for us and allows us to form expectancies about a stimulus person's behaviour. These expectancies may be based on actual information (i.e. hard data), and/or valid, reasonable inferences. Because schematic thinking is not an unbiased process, expectancies may also be based on incorrect inferences.

Whatever the case, our expectancies about another person's behaviour affect the way we interact with that person. They, in turn, may respond differentially to different sets of expectancies. Evidence for this was presented earlier under the heading External Information Processing and Schemas (see p. 114). For example, consider the man who has a rather plain looking female partner. Through mechanisms discussed earlier, he may, over time, come to increase his estimation of her attractiveness. In response, when around him, she may come to exhibit those attributes associated with the physical attractiveness schema. That is, she will become more sociable, outgoing, sexually responsive, etc., than she was earlier in the relationship. Among other people, she will likely retain her old habits.

Exchange

Some theorists have attempted to interpret attraction in terms of exchange. Partners in a relationship are said to provide each other with rewards, but also to exact costs. The pleasantness of the relationship is reflected in the degree to which a person's rewards exceed his costs (cf. Walster *et al.*, 1973). Rewards and costs are exchanged according to a norm of reciprocity (Gouldner, 1960). Violation of the norm also jeopardizes the relationship.

However, other authors have questioned whether principles of exchange are appropriate for explaining romantic relationships. Clark and Mills (1979), for instance, have distinguished between exchange relationships and communal relationships. In the former, a benefit is given with the expectation of receiving a benefit in return. In turn, the receipt of a benefit incurs an obligation on the part of the receiver to provide a benefit. In communal relationships, the concern of members is not how much they have received from, or owe to, each other, but with each other's welfare. There are no debts or obligations. Each person responds to the other's needs. Members of a communal relationship simply *appear* to be operating according to exchange principles. Indeed, according to Mills, the perception that benefits are given and received according to rules of exchange can actually undermine a communal relationship. Such a perception would challenge the motives of one or both of its members. One partner might ask, for example, whether the other really has his or her needs and interests at heart. A romantic relationship is such a communal relationship.

To test the exchange–communal distinction Clark and Mills (1979)

conducted the following studies. In the first, unmarried male under-graduate subjects performed an experimental task while an attractive female subject (actually a confederate) performed a similar, but apparently more difficult task. The males could see the woman by way of a television monitor. When the male completed his task, he was given a credit point and allowed to send task materials to the woman. The woman was given four points upon completion of her task.

The males were then given a bogus thank-you note from the woman (no benefit), or a bogus thank-you note accompanied by one of her points (benefit). They were then informed that the woman was married (exchange) or unmarried (communal). Clark and Mills found that when the woman was unmarried, she was liked more when she did not give a benefit than when she did. The opposite was true when she was thought to be married. In the second study, Clark and Mills approached the question from the point of view of the expectation of a benefit. Female subjects were benefitted, or not, as above. However, the confederate (also a female) then either requested, or did not request, a benefit in return. As predicted, when an exchange relationship was anticipated, liking for the other was higher when the other requested a return benefit. The opposite was true when the subject anticipated a communal relationship.

One wonders whether a romantic relationship, as Clark and Mills (1979) conceptualization suggests, operates according to principles qualitatively different from exchange. Perhaps romantic relationships' adherence to principles of exchange is more than just apparent. Tedeschi (1974) has taken what appears, at first, to be a position similar to Clark and Mills'. Rewards must be perceived of as having been given intentionally, not as a repayment of debt, and not with the expectation of repayment. However, Tedeschi qualifies his argument by emphasizing that this perception of altruistic motives on the part of the other is just that — a perception. The giving and receiving of benefits may in fact be instrumental. However, to be attracted to another, one must learn to disattend to the planned aspect of his/her behaviour since the other's motives are essentially selfish. Likewise, one's own behaviour must *appear* altruistic to the other to increase the other's liking. In actuality, the reciprocity norm still holds. As Tedeschi points out, "That attraction is not simply a matter of altruism is demonstrated when failure to reciprocate disrupts a friendship" (1974, p. 21).

At this point, we might reconsider the argument we made in the section about awareness of one's own cognitive processes (p. 119). People have a conscious schema, or implicit causal theory in Nisbett and

Wilson's (1977) terms, about romantic relationships. One aspect of this schema is the notion that the giving and receiving of benefits is altruistic, not instrumental. Thus people may like to believe that romantic relationships are altruistic, and may espouse altruism in romantic relationships, yet may actually be behaving according to principles of exchange.

Explicit acknowledgement of the exchange nature of costs and benefits is inconsistent with the romantic schema. When this occurs, especially before initiating a relationship, it could change the construed nature of the relationship and reduce attraction. Perhaps this is what occurred in the Mills studies. Even before a relationship began, the rules of exchange for the relationship were made explicit or not, with the latter resulting in greater attraction.

Self-disclosure

Self-disclosure, the revealing of one's private self to another (Jourard, 1971), has usually been considered a special case of exchange. According to Worthy *et al.* (1969), attraction is mediated by reciprocal self-disclosure. In a loving relationship, disclosure is rewarding to another because it makes that person worthy of receiving intimate information, raising that person's self-esteem. This encourages the other to reciprocate by offering information at equal levels of intimacy. Once so engaged, the tendency is for the couple to proceed with continuously more intimate cycles of rewarding disclosure.

Self-disclosure may actually be partners' attempts to fill out each other's "romantic partner" schema. In a sense, then, partners are informationally dependent on one another. Both need to know about the other to improve predictability. Yet each must have some of what Kelvin (1974) has called "tolerance of vulnerability". One must give a little information to get a little information. To disclose too much to a potential partner is to decrease predictability by (a) suggesting maladjustment, and/or (b) norm violation. To disclose too little is to withold information. To withold information is to decrease predictability, and to leave one's partner susceptible to exploitation. Miller and Steinberg (1975) point out that self-disclosure can be used as a conscious strategy by one partner who wishes to deepen his or her involvement with another. This may be true, but only if the strategies are subtle. There is also the potential for impression management; partners may provide each other with false intimate information. Thus they maintain predictive control

over the other, yet avoid such control over themselves by the other.

An interesting parallel can be drawn between disclosure and some of the single variable research. When there is no potential for future interaction, people may disclose much intimate information about themselves (Rubin, 1973). The risks of exploitation disappear and caution need not be exercised.

In sum, we have tried to suggest that schematic processing does have a role beyond relationship initiation. It allows us to generate expectancies about another's behaviour which then influences the way that person interacts with us. It explains why, though we eschew exchange notions in romantic relationships, we actually behave according to exchange principles. Finally, the schematic processing model provides a useful framework in which to consider mutual self-disclosure.

Summary

It has been our thesis that thought plays a central role in human sexual behaviour. To focus thought processes on a potential partner, however, means that the partner must first be attended to. Attention is directed towards another through perceptual and motivational factors. By perceptual factors, we mean the particular figure-ground relationship that makes one person stand out from among other potential partners. By motivational factors we mean one's own state, such as sexual and companionship needs, but including the need to know and predict a partner's behaviour in order to maximize rewards and minimize costs in a relationship.

Once attention is focused on a particular potential partner. What is the role of thought? One's beliefs about a partner are the result of external information. Further, beliefs, particularly salient beliefs, affect one's feelings towards that person. Thus feeling states are dependent on information. Research on self-generated attitude change suggests that should the flow of external information be interrupted, thought will operate alone to polarize existing feelings about the partner. How is this possible? We have answered this question by adopting the cognitive schema concept. Schemas are naive theories people have about particular stimulus domains. They operate like scientific theories by directing information searches, telling people which information to ignore, and generating inferences based on available information. One such schema may be that of "ideal lover". In the absence of disconfirming external

information (i.e. "reality constraints"), if one applies the ideal lover schema to one's partner, the schema would direct the addition, deletion, or reinterpretation of existing cognitions to make the overall pattern of cognitions schema-consistent.

Schematic processing is sometimes "mindless" or "automatic", and people may not be aware of their own cognitive processes. When asked about these processes, they may respond by reading off a conscious, culturally defined schema, appropriate for the situation.

The schematic processing model also sheds light on the role of cognition in other variables associated with attraction research — physical attractiveness, similarity, and arousal. Physical attractiveness itself may define a schema. Knowing that another is attractive leads persons to fill in informational gaps about the other with positive attributes. Most people have self-schemas; knowledge of another's similarity leads to the generation of schema-consistent attributes. This causes attraction because people basically like themselves, and because it makes the other seem more predictable. People may also be similar with respect to schemas. Schema-similarity provides knowledge of how another constructs his/her world, thus rendering the other even more predictable. Arousal itself may not be as important as the informational cues available about the experimental stimulus person in the situations in which arousal is induced.

Single variables, such as similarity or attractiveness, may only explain relationship initiation. Schemas also enter into factors in long-term relationships. A schema formed around one's partner creates expectations about him/her, which influence the way one interacts with the partner. The partner, in turn, will behave in ways that confirm these expectations. Romantic relationships appear to operate according to exchange principles, yet partners seem to disavow reward–cost explanations of their relationship in favour of altruistic explanations consistent with a romantic relationship schema. Finally, since partners in a relationship require information about each other for the relationship to be mutually predictable, reciprocal self-disclosure may be their attempts to fill out each person's data base for the other.

4. References

Abelson, R. P. *Scripts*. Invited address to the Midwestern Psychological Association, 1978.

Ajzen, I. Effects of information on interpersonal attraction: Similarity versus affective value. *Journal of Personality and Social Psychology*, 1974, **29**, 374-380.

Ajzen, I. Information processing approaches to interpersonal attraction. In Duck, S. (Ed.), *Theory and practice in interpersonal attraction*. New York and London: Academic Press, 1977.

Anderson, N. H. Integration theory and attitude change. *Psychological Review*, 1970, **77**, 153-170.

Aristotle. *De partibus animalium*. Book 2, Chapter 7, 652b.

Atkinson, J. W. and McClelland, D. C. The effect of different intensities of the hunger drive on thematic apperception. *Journal of Experimental Psychology*, 1948, **38**, 643-658.

Bem, D. J. and McConnell, H. K. Testing the self-perception explanation of dissonance phenomena: On the salience of premanipulation attitudes. *Journal of Personality and Social Psychology*, 1970, **14**, 23-31.

Bentler, P. M. and Huba, G. J. Simple minitheories of love. *Journal of Personality and Social Psychology*, 1979, **37**, 124-130.

Berscheid, E. and Graziano, W. The initiation of social relationships and interpersonal attraction. In Burgess, R. L. and Huston, T. H. (Eds), *Social exchange in developing relationships*. New York and London: Academic Press, 1979.

Berscheid, E. and Walster, E. Physical attractiveness. In Berkowitz, L. (Ed.), *Advances in experimental social psychology*. Vol. 7. New York and London: Academic Press, 1974.

Berscheid, E., Graziano, W., Monson, T. and Dermer, M. Outcome dependency: Attention, attribution, and attraction. *Journal of Personality and Social Psychology*, 1976, **34**, 978-989.

Brozek, J., Guetzkow, H., Baldwin, M. V. and Cranston, R. A quantitative study of perception and association in experimental semi-starvation. *Journal of Personality*, 1951, **19**, 245-264.

Burgess, E. W. and Wallin, P. *Engagement and marriage*. Philadelphia: Lippencott, 1953.

Byrne, D. Attitudes and attraction. In Berkowitz, L. (Ed.), *Advances in experimental social psychology*. New York and London: Academic Press, 1969.

Byrne, D., Ervin, C. R. and Lamberth, J. Continuity between the experimental study of attraction and real life computer dating. *Journal of Personality and Social Psychology*, 1970, **16**, 157-165.

Chestnut, R. W., LaChance, C. C. and Lubitz, A. The "decorative" female model: Sexual stimuli and the recognition of advertisements. *Journal of Advertising Research*, 1977, **17**, 11-14.

Clark, M. S. and Mills, J. Interpersonal attraction in exchange and communal relationships. *Journal of Personality and Social Psychology*, 1979, **37**, 12-24.

Clary, E. G., Tesser, A. and Downing, L. L. Influence of a salient schema on thought induced cognitive change. *Personality and Social Psychology Bulletin*, 1978, **4**, 39-43.

Curran, J. P. and Lippold, S. The effects of physical attraction and attitude

140   *Abraham Tesser and Richard Reardon*

similarity on attraction in dating dyads. *Journal of Personality*, 1975, **43**, 528-539.

Dion, K. K., Berscheid, E. and Walster, E. What is beautiful is good. *Journal of Personality and Social Psychology*, 1972, **24**, 285-290.

Driscoll, R., Davis, K. and Lipetz, M. Parental interference and romantic love: The Romeo and Juliet effect. *Journal of Personality and Social Psychology*, 1972, **24**, 1-10.

Dutton, B. G. and Aron, A. P. Some evidence for heightened sexual attraction under conditions of high anxiety. *Journal of Personality and Social Psychology*, 1974, **30**, 510-517.

Ellis, A. *Reason and emotion in psychotherapy.* New York: Lyle-Stuart, 1962.

Fishbein, M. A consideration of beliefs, attitudes, and their relationships. In Steiner, I. D. and Fishbein, M. (Eds), *Current studies in social psychology.* New York: Holt, Rinehart and Winston, 1965, pp. 107-120.

Fishbein, M. and Ajzen, I. *Belief, attitude, intention, and behavior: An introduction to theory and research.* Reading, Massachusetts: Addison-Wesley, 1975.

Flavell, J. H. *The developmental psychology of Jean Piaget.* Princeton, N.J.: Van Nostrand, 1963.

Ghiselin, B. *The creative process.* New York: Mentor, 1952.

Goethals, G. R. and Reckman, R. F. The perception of consistency in attitudes. *Journal of Experimental Social Psychology*, 1973, **9**, 491-501.

Gouldner, A. W. The norm of reciprocity: A preliminary statement. *American Sociological Review*, 1960, **25**, 161-179.

Greenwald, A. G. Cognitive learning, cognitive response to persuasion, and attitude change. In Greenwald, A. G., Brock, T. C. and Ostrom, T. M. (Eds), *Psychological foundations of attitudes.* New York and London: Academic Press, 1968, pp. 147-170.

Hall, C. S. and Lindzey, G. *Theories of personality.* New York: John Wiley, 1957.

Huston, T. L. and Levinger, G. Interpersonal attraction and relationships. *Annual Review of Psychology*, 1978, **29**, 115-156.

Ickes, W. J., Wicklund, R. A. and Ferris, C. B. Objective self-awareness and self-esteem. *Journal of Experimental Social Psychology*, 1973, **9**, 202-219.

Isen, A. M., Shalker, T. E., Clark, M. and Karp, L. Affect, accessibility of material in memory, and behaviour: A cognitive loop? *Journal of Personality and Social Psychology*, 1978, **36**, 1-12.

Jacobs, L., Walster, E. and Berscheid, E. Self-esteem and attraction. *Journal of Personality and Social Psychology*, 1971, **17**, 84-91.

Johnson, M. J. and Tesser, A. Some interactive effects of evaluative similarity, structural similarity and type of interpersonal situation on interpersonal attraction. *Journal of Experimental Research in Personality*, 1972, **6**, 154-161.

Jourard, S. M. *The transparent self.* (revised edn). New York: Van Nostrand, 1971.

Kaplan, K. J., Firestone, I. J., Degnore, R. and Moore, M. Gradients of

attraction as a function of disclosure probe, intimacy, and setting formality. *Journal of Personality and Social Psychology*, 1974, **30**, 638-646.

Kelley, H. H. Attribution in social interaction. In Jones, E. E., Kanouse, D. E., Kelley, H. H., Nisbett, K. E., Valins, S. and Wiener, B., *Attribution: Perceiving the causes of behavior*. Morristown, N.J.: General Learning Press, 1972.

Kelvin, P. Predictability, power, and vulnerability in interpersonal attraction. In Duck, S. (Ed.), *Theory and practice in interpersonal attraction*. New York and London: Academic Press, 1977.

Kenrick, D. T. and Cialdini, R. B. Romantic attraction: Misattribution versus reinforcement explanations. *Journal of Personality and Social Psychology*, 1977, **35**, 381-391.

Kenrick, D. T., Cialdini, R. B. and Linder, D. E. Misattribution under fear-producing circumstances: Four failures to replicate. *Personality and Social Psychology Bulletin*, 1979, **5**, 329-334.

Land, K. C. Principles of path analysis. In Borgatta, E. F. (Ed.), *Sociological methodology 1969*, Chapter 1. San Francisco: Jossey-Bass, 1969, pp. 3-37.

Langer, E. J. Rethinking the role of thought in social interaction. In Harvey, J., Ickes, W. and Kidd, R. (Eds), *New directions in attribution research*. Vol. 2. Potomac, Maryland: Laurence Erlbaum Associates, 1978.

Langer, E. J. and Abelson, R. P. The semantics of asking a favor: How to succeed in getting help without really dying. *Journal of Personality and Social Psychology*, 1972, **24**, 26-32.

Langer, E. J., Taylor, S. E., Fiske, S. T. and Chanowitz, B. Stigma, staring, and discomfort: A novel stimulus hypothesis. *Journal of Experimental Social Psychology*, 1976, **12**, 451-463.

Langer, E. J., Blank, A. and Chanowitz, B. The mindlessness of ostensibly thoughtful action: The role of placebic information in interpersonal interaction. *Journal of Personality and Social Psychology*, 1978, **36**, 635-642.

Levine, J. M. and Murphy, G. The learning and forgetting of controversial material. *Journal of Abnormal and Social Psychology*, 1943, **38**, 507-517.

Levinger, G. and Snoek, J. Y. *Attraction in a relationship: A new look at interpersonal attraction*. Morristown, N.J.: General Learning Press, 1972.

Maier, N. R. F. Reasoning in humans: II. The solution of a problem and its appearance in consciousness. *Journal of Comparative Psychology*, 1931, **12**, 181-194.

Markus, H., Self-schemata and processing information about the self. *Journal of Personality and Social Psychology*, 1977, **35**, 63-78.

Marshall, G. D. and Zimbardo, P. G. Affective consequences of inadequately explained physiological arousal. *Journal of Personality and Social Psychology*, 1979, **37**, 970-988.

Maslach, C. Negative emotional biasing of unexplained arousal. *Journal of Personality and Social Psychology*, 1979, **37**, 953-969.

McArthur, L. and Post, D. Figural emphasis and person perception. *Journal of Experimental Social Psychology*, 1977, **13**, 520-535.

McClelland, D. C., Clark, R. A., Roby, T. B. and Atkinson, J. W. The effect

of need for achievement on thematic apperception. *Journal of Experimental Psychology*, 1949, **37**, 242-255.

Meichenbaum, D. By way of introduction. *Cognitive-Behavior Modification*, 1975, **1**, 1-2.

Miller, G. R. and Steinberg, M. *Between people: A new analysis of interpersonal communication*. Chicago: SRA, 1975.

Minsky, M. A framework for representing knowledge. In Winston, P. H. (Ed.), *The psychology of computer vision*. New York: McGraw-Hill, 1975.

Nisbett, R. E. and Bellows, N. Verbal reports about causal influences on social judgments: Private access versus public theories. *Journal of Personality and Social Psychology*, 1977, **35**, 613-624.

Nisbett, R. E. and Wilson, T. D. Telling more than we know: Verbal reports on mental processes. *Psychological Review*, 1977, **84**, 213-259.

Piaget J. *Psychology of intelligence*. Patternson, N.J.: Littlefields, Adams, 1963.

Rosenberg, M. J. Cognitive structure and attitudinal affect. *Journal of Abnormal and Social Psychology*, 1956, **53**, 367-372.

Ross, L., Lepper, M. R. and Hubbard, M. Perseverance in self-perception and social perception: Biased attributional processes in the debriefing paradigm. *Journal of Personality and Social Psychology*, 1975, **32**, 880-892.

Rubin, L. B. *Worlds of pain: Life in the working class family*. New York: Basic Books, 1976.

Rubin, Z. Measurement of romantic love. *Journal of Personality and Social Psychology*, 1970, **16**, 265-273.

Rubin, Z. *Liking and loving: An invitation to social psychology*. New York: Holt, Rinehart and Winston, 1973.

Sadler, O. and Tesser, A. Some effects of salience and time upon interpersonal hostility and attraction during social isolation. *Sociometry*, 1973, **36**, 99-112.

Salancik, J. R. Inference of one's attitude from behavior recalled under linguistically manipulated cognitive sets. *Journal of Experimental Social Psychology*, 1974, **10**, 415-427.

Sanford, R. N. The effect of abstinence from food upon imaginal processes. *Journal of Psychology*, 1936, **2**, 129-136.

Santee, R. T. The effect on attraction of attitude similarity as information about interpersonal reinforcement contingencies. *Sociometry*, 1976, **39**, 153-156.

Schachter, S. The interaction of cognitive and physiological determinants of emotional states. In Berkowitz, L. (Ed.), *Advances in experimental social psychology*. New York and London: Academic Press, 1964.

Schachter, S. and Singer, J. Cognitive, social, and physiological determinants of emotional state. *Psychological Review*, 1962, **69**, 379-399.

Schank, R. C. and Abelson, R. P. *Scripts, plans, goals, and understanding: An inquiry into human knowledge structures*. Hillsdale, N.J.: Lawrence Erlbaum Assoc., 1977.

Schneider, D. J. Implicit personality theory: A review. *Psychological Bulletin*, 1973, **79**, 294-309.

Sexton, D. E. and Haderman, P. Women in magazine advertisements. *Journal of Advertising Research*, 1974, **14**, 41-46.

Shiffrin, R. M. and Schneider, W. Controlled and automatic human information processing: II. Perceptual learning, automatic attending, and a general theory. *Psychological Review*, 1977, **84**, 127-190.

Smith, E. R. Specification and estimation of causal models in social psychology: Comment on Tesser and Paulhus. *Journal of Personality and Social Psychology*, 1978, **36**, 34-38.

Smith, E. R. and Miller, F. R. Limits on perception of cognitive processes: A reply to Nisbett and Wilson. *Psychological Review*, 1978, **85**, 355-362.

Snyder, M. and Swann, W. B. Hypothesis-testing processes in social interaction. *Journal of Personality and Social Psychology*, 1978, **36**, 1202-1212.

Snyder, M. and Uranowitz, S. W. Reconstructing the past: Some cognitive consequences of person perception. *Journal of Personality and Social Psychology*, 1978, **36**, 941-950.

Snyder, M., Tanke, E. D. and Berscheid, E. Social perception and interpersonal behavior: On the self-fulfilling nature of social stereotypes. *Journal of Personality and Social Psychology*, 1977, **35**, 656-666.

Steadman, M. How sexy illustrations affect brand recall. *Journal of Advertising Research*, 1969, **9**, 15-19.

Stroebe, W., Insko, C. A., Thompson, V. D. and Layton, B. D. Effects of physical attractiveness, attitude similarity, and sex on various aspects of interpersonal attraction. *Journal of Personality and Social Psychology*, 1971, **18**, 79-91.

Taylor, S. E. and Crocker, J. Schematic bases of social information processing. In Higgins, E. T., Herman, P. and Zanna, M. P. (Eds), *The Toronto Symposium in Personality and Social Psychology*. Vol. 1. Hillsdale, N.J.: Lawrence Erlbaum, 1979.

Taylor, S. E . and Fiske, S. T. Point of view and perceptions of causality. *Journal of Personality and Social Psychology*, 1975, **32**, 439-445.

Taylor, S. E. and Fiske, S. T. Salience, attention, and attribution: Top of the head phenomena. In Berkowitz, L. (Ed.), *Advances in Experimental Social Psychology*. Vol. 11. New York and London: Academic Press, 1978.

Taylor, S. E., Fiske, S. T., Close, M., Anderson, C. and Ruderman, A. Solo status as a psychological variable: The power of being distinctive. Unpublished manuscript, Harvard University, 1977.

Taylor, S. E., Fiske, S. T., Etcoff, N. L. and Ruderman, A. J. Categorical and contextual bases of person memory and stereotyping. *Journal of Personality and Social Psychology*, 1978, **36**, 778-793.

Tedeschi, J. T. Attributions, liking, and power. In Huston, T. L. (Ed.), *Foundations of interpersonal attraction*. New York and London: Academic Press, 1974.

Tesser, A. Evaluative and structural similarity of attitudes as determinants of interpersonal attraction. *Journal of Personality and Social Psychology*, 1971, **18**, 92-96.

Tesser, A. Attitude similarity and intercorrelations as determinants of interpersonal attraction. *Journal of Experimental Research in Personality*, 1972, **6**, 142-153.

Tesser, A. Thought and reality constraints as determinants of attitude polarization. *Journal of Research in Personality*, 1976, **10**, 183-194.

Tesser, A. Self-generated attitude change. In Berkowitz, L. (Ed.), *Advances in experimental social psychology*. Vol. 11. New York and London: Academic Press, 1978.

Tesser, A. and Brodie, M. A note on the evaluation of a "computer date". *Psychonomic Science*, 1971, **23**, 300.

Tesser, A. and Conlee, M. C. Some effects of time and thought on attitude polarization. *Journal of Personality and Social Psychology*, 1975, **31**, 262-270.

Tesser, A. and Cowan, C. L. Some effects of thought and number of cognitions on attitude change. *Social Behavior and Personality*, 1975, **3**, 165-173.

Tesser, A. and Cowan, C. L. Some attitudinal and cognitive consequences of thought. *Journal of Research in Personality*, 1977, **11**, 216-226.

Tesser, A. and Danheiser, P. Anticipated relationship, salience of partner, and attitude change. *Personality and Social Psychology Bulletin*, 1978, **4**, 35-38.

Tesser, A. and Johnson, R. D. Thought and dependence as determinants of interpersonal hostility. *Bulletin of the Psychonomic Society*, 1974, **2**, 428-430.

Tesser, A. and Leone, C. Cognitive schemas and thought as determinants of attitude change. *Journal of Experimental Social Psychology*, 1977, **13**, 340-356.

Tesser, A. and Paulhus, D. L. Toward a causal model of love. *Journal of Personality and Social Psychology*, 1976, **34**, 1095-1105.

Tesser, A. and Paulhus, D. On models and assumptions: A reply to Smith. *Journal of Personality and Social Psychology*, 1978, **36**, 40-42.

Tulving, E. Episodic and semantic memory. In Tulving, E. and Donaldson, W. (Eds), *Organization of memory*. New York and London: Academic Press, 1972.

Tyler, T. R. and Sears, B. O. Coming to like obnoxious people when we must live with them. *Journal of Personality and Social Psychology*, 1977, **35**, 200-211.

Valenti, A. and Tesser, A. On the mechanisms of thought-induced attitude change. *Social Behavior and Personality*, 1981, **9**, in press.

Walster, E. Passionate love. In Murstein, B. I. (Ed.), *Theories of attraction and love*. New York: Springer, 1971.

Walster, E., Aronson, V., Abrahams, D. and Rottman, L. Importance of physical attractiveness in dating behavior. *Journal of Personality and Social Psychology*, 1966, **4**, 508-516.

Walster, E., Berscheid, E. and Walster, G. W. New directions in equity research. *Journal of Personality and Social Psychology*, 1973, **25**, 151-176.

Wilson, W. R. Unobtrusive induction of positive attitudes. Unpublished doctoral dissertation, University of Michigan, 1975.

Worthy, M., Gary, A. L. and Kahn, G. M. Self-disclosure as an exchange process. *Journal of Personality and Social Psychology*, 1969, **13**, 59-63.

5
Social Skill and Human Sexual Attraction

MARK COOK

Department of Psychology, University College of
Swansea, Singleton Park, Swansea, Wales

Ask a psychologist what the bases of human sexual attraction are, and the list you'll get will include similarity (or complementarity) of personality, intelligence, social background, proximity, and appearance — the topics covered in the other sections of this book. All these are important, but they do not form the whole picture. They may well be necessary conditions, but they are not themselves sufficient. Being good-looking, intelligent, and close to someone of similar background, personality and attitudes sets the scene for getting on with that person, but does not by itself guarantee attraction. For one thing a lot of the variance is still unaccounted for; people who ought, according to all the literature on determinants of attraction, to be highly attracted, often are not. Secondly, and the point of this chapter, starting a sexual relationship with someone is not an instantaneous process and does not occur magically and automatically, given the right degree of similarity, proximity, etc. Establishing a sexual relationship involves a complicated, long drawn-out sequence of moves, directed by an overall plan, and triggered by what each person's previous actions were. The focus of this chapter will be what happens between the first meeting of a couple, and the establishment of a relationship.

Some theories of sexual attraction take account of this fact; many do not; and some make a partially successful attempt. Reiss's (1960) "wheel" theory of attraction has four "spokes", the first of which is "rapport". Reiss' theory lacks precision and, as Murstein notes in his section, also lacks empirical support. A similar vagueness mars other accounts. Rapoport (1965) refers to "establishing a mutually satisfactory

mode of communication", while Lewis (1972) includes a number of headings like "ease of communication" and "achievement of role-taking accuracy". Neither theorist tries to make either of these very general statements more precise, even though we now have a very extensive body of research on what actually goes on in social encounters, and the makings of an account of how some people fail to establish "rapport" with the opposite sex.

Introduction

The idea of social skill is an old one and not even special to psychology; the social skill model is a more recent development. The model depends on an analogy between social behaviour and motor behaviour such as typing, playing ball games, or operating machine tools. As a model or analogy it has no predictive power, but should be judged rather according to its usefulness and its power to impose order on a diverse and confused area of research.

Making friends with someone is a skilled performance in the same sense that typing a letter, returning a serve in tennis, or driving a car are skilled performances. All depend on summing up the initial state of the object. All depend on knowing what to do next to bring the object nearer the desired state; then doing it; then observing the effect. The analogy between motor and social skill was drawn explicitly by Argyle, Kendon and Crossman (Argyle and Kendon, 1967) in the form of a diagram of a simple feedback loop (Fig. 1). It includes four headings or boxes. The person initially Perceives the other individual and decides what to do to achieve his Goal (Translation). He then does it (Response), and looks at the effects (Perception again).

For example the man's goal might be to persuade a woman to have sexual intercourse with him (while not committing himself to any longer lasting relationship). He sees that the woman is unwilling, because (he thinks) she is afraid of the possible consequences, so he assures her that he will use contraceptives. He observes continued unwillingness which he now attributes to a fear that she will acquire a bad reputation, so he assures her — almost certainly falsely (*v. infra*) — that he will not tell anyone. Continued unwillingness may lead the man to give up — i.e. change his goal — or resort to other tactics, such as professing love for the woman, suggesting they become engaged, or threatening to blacken her reputation if she does not cooperate. (These methods are taken from accounts of their courtship methods volunteered to Kirkendall (1961) by American men — *v. infra*).

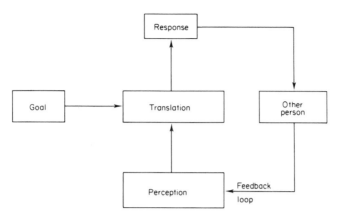

Fig. 1. *The social skill model*

Argyle (1967) distinguishes two levels at which the social skill model operates: a higher level of conscious "plans" and a lower level of automatic habitual responses. (This distinction corresponds roughly to that made by Harré in his section on "The Dramaturgy of Sexual Relations" between "autonomisms" and "automatisms" (see Chapter 8 of this volume).) Choosing to be nice to someone is a plan; putting the plan into effect depends in part on responses which may not be made consciously, like smiling, agreeing, or deferring in the right places.

In his various discussions of the model Argyle (1967; and Argyle and Kendon, 1967) makes little reference to attraction, social or sexual, and does not discuss whether the model might apply better to some relationships than to others. A useful distinction can be drawn between goals that are "extrinsic" to an encounter (such as getting information, or giving it, or borrowing money) and goals that are "intrinsic" (such as making friends with someone, talking to someone for the sake of talking). Sexual attraction generally comes into the "intrinsic" category, with the exception of brief encounters geared to sexual exploitation.

Most of the samples of social skill discussed so far (borrowing money, selling something, getting or giving information) last only a short time. Does the social skill model apply to longer lasting relationships? Clearly a person who lacks social skill will have difficulty establishing any long-term relationships, but what of the person who already has a partner? Does the social skill model still apply? Presumably he or she will not cease to operate at the lower "automatism" level of the system — perceiving reactions, desire to speak, etc. One might predict that this lower level will function more efficiently in a well established couple,

since the signs will have become that much more familiar; this prediction needs empirical test however, since research has shown that established or married couples may not be any better at reading each other's opinions.

However, social skill seems most important in the early stages of the relationship, and should perhaps be seen as a first filter (Duck, 1973). People who lack social skill will not get on, but once the relationship is established it ceases to be very important. (Unless for some reason, such as the onset of senility or mental breakdown, social skill deteriorates in one of the parties.)

Looking at attraction as an exercise in social skill usually leads to the objection that people are not aware of going through the moves of assessing the other, choosing a tactic from a repertoire of such, putting it into effect, then sitting back to observe its effects. This is an old, and irrelevant, criticism; most perceptual processes work too fast for the perceiver to be aware of their operation as well as of their effects.

In effect the social skill model is no more than the minimum necessary to explain how sexual attraction, and other social encounters, happen at all. It provides a convenient set of headings for studying the formation of relationships, and by the same token a set of headings for studying why some people have trouble translating feelings of attraction for another person into an established relationship.

Perception

It is a truism that people respond to the world as they see it, not to the world as it really is. The discrepancy between the two is often large enough to make the distinction very important. For example the actual similarity of outlook in established couples is really rather modest — so much so that one wonders how computer dating agencies actually pair off their clients — but the degree of assumed similarity is much greater. Byrne and Blaylock (1963) found an actual correlation between husbands and wives on the Rokeach Dogmatism Scale of 0·30 to 0·44, but assumed similarity of dogmatism ranging from 0·69 to 0·89, showing that the couples shared far fewer opinions than they thought they did.

Too much person perception research has studied perceptions formed by people, who have no pressing need to form them, about people they have little contact with, and will never meet again outside the laboratory. A courting couple are in a much better position to get to know each other, besides having much stronger reasons for needing to. A number of

studies of how clearly couples see each other have yielded mixed results. Even before male meets female, both partners have serious misconceptions of the other's wants and intentions. Hewitt (1958) found that 69% of men wanted women friends who were "ambitious and industrious", but only 48% of women thought men valued these qualities, while 80% of men thought women regarded the man's physical appearance as crucial, when only 21% of women actually thought this. Balswick and Anderson (1968) asked a number of college students what they expected should happen on a first date, and what they thought the other person would expect should happen. College men were asked if they expected a woman to let them kiss her after a first date, and college women if they expected a man to want to; slightly more than half said yes to these questions. Next the subjects were asked to predict what the other sex thought should happen, to see if the women think the men expect a kiss, and if the men think the women expect them to try. The results showed that the two sexes misunderstand each other, in a particularly significant way. Whereas only half the men and women actually expected or wanted a kiss after a first date, rather nearer than three-quarters thought it expected of them. If they act on this false impression, a perfect example of the self-fulfilling prophecy results. Similarly another study by Jackson and Potkay (1973) found that college women generally underestimated rather than overestimated the proportion of their peers who were still sexually inexperienced; on average they thought less than half of college women were still virgin, when in fact rather more than half were.

Kirkpatrick and Hobart (1954) found that the ability of couples to predict each others' answers to a Family Opinion Survey was higher, if they were married, as opposed to engaged, and higher in engaged couples than in dating couples. This finding might be dismissed as a demonstration of the obvious, if it were not that the size of the difference Kirkpatrick and Hobart found was rather small, and that subsequent research has not always been able to find even modest correlations between length of relationship and accuracy of perception within it. Udry (1963) found that most of the variance in couples' predictions of each others' 16 PF questionnaire answers was accounted for by random error, with assumed similarity and accurate prediction each accounting for about 10–15%. Murstein (1972) found a modest but reliable tendency for inaccurate perception of each other's completion of the Marital Expectation Test to predict poor "courtship progress". On the other hand, Udry, using the possibly less relevant 16PF, was unable to relate the outcome

of a liaison — break-up or marriage — to accuracy of perception. Attempts to prove that happy marriages are characterized by the partners seeing each other's point of view clearly — an eminently plausible hypothesis — have not generally been very successful either. Corsini (1956), using Q sorts, and Clements (1967), using rank orders of marital grievances, found no differences between stable happy marriages and unstable unhappy ones. Dymond (1954) found a very modest advantage — 38 against 33 correct out of 55 predictions — for happy couples, while Murstein and Beck's (1972) best correlation, out of 48, between adjustment and accuracy of perception, was only 0·37.

One of the explanations for these apparently puzzling effects has been mentioned already — assumed similarity. Many couples seem to live together quite happily for periods of years, unaware that their opinions on important issues differ. Steiner (1955), in a curiously neglected paper, points to another reason; he argues that it is not always necessarily beneficial to be able to see clearly what other people think about you. Such an insight could instead lower self-confidence and discourage social initiatives.

First Impressions

Perception really takes two forms — first impressions and feedback. The first impression takes in a number of things. In most relationships people look for someone who is attracted to them, with the possible exception of short term sexual encounters where sexual willingness matters more. Some preliminary assessment of personality, outlook, and social background will also be made — to try to "place" the other person. Also a more subtle evaluation gets made — whether the other person falls into the same status range as the perceiver. Zetterberg (1966) called this the "secret ranking"; a relatively unattractive or unpopular person who tries to make a sexual partner of someone much more popular or attractive is likely to suffer a rebuff. Part, at least, of the "secret ranking" is visible; Dion's section summarizes the literature on similarity of attractiveness in courting and married couples (see Chapter 1 of this volume).

The "secret ranking" — together with factors of social similarity, proximity and so on — allow one to make an indirect estimate of who is likely to be a suitable partner. However it is still possible for two apparently compatible people to dislike each other; there is a lot of variance left unaccounted for. When two people meet they can start trying to decide if the other actually likes them — partly using non-verbal

cues. Sociometric research early on started looking at how good people were at seeing who likes who. Tagiuri (1958) summarized a series of studies noting that people can generally perceive who likes them, but are less good at seeing who dislikes them. In fact people tend to assume that anyone they like returns their liking. Tagiuri's work dealt with non-sexual attraction; an experimental account of accuracy of perception of sexual interest has still to be offered.

There is an extensive literature on the correlates of sexual attitudes and sexual behaviour. Questionnaires can be used to type people into those who believe in absolute freedom, those who believe in premarital intercourse only if the couple are emotionally involved, those who disapprove of sex before marriage for anyone, and those who subscribe to the "double standard". Not surprisingly permissiveness diminishes with age; Reiss (1967) found it decreased particularly in parents, and reached an especially low point for parents of girls in their late teens. Woman at all ages are less permissive, whereas American blacks are more permissive. Not surprisingly deeply religious people are less permissive.

However, attitudes and sexual behaviour are not always entirely consistent. Kaats and Davis (1970) found that although very attractive women were twice as likely to be sexually experienced, their attitudes to premarital intercourse were no more liberal than those of less experienced women. Mercer and Kohn (1979) found sexual attitudes, sexual behaviour, and general outlook were more closely "integrated" in women than in men, in that authoritarianism, drug use, and liberality of sexual behaviour were unrelated in males, but positively correlated in females. As Mercer and Kohn say, this possibly reflects the fact that females tend to control males' sexual opportunities, so that men whose outlook permits them free sexual expression may nevertheless be unable to find a partner, whereas a woman with a liberal outlook is less likely to find its expression frustrated.

The person who wants to decide how experienced his or her possible partner is has essentially two sources of information — gossip and inference. If the couple inform a social scientist, they provide information for inferences; if they inform their friends and relations they provide information for gossip. Carns (1973) found that college students certainly do not keep their sexual experiences to themselves. Only one in five men did *not* tell anyone about their first experience of sexual intercourse, and only one in four of the women did not. Men tended to broadcast the information — over half told five or more of their friends — whereas only one in five of the girls did so. As Carns (1973) notes, these

figures imply that "a woman's decision to enter coitus also implies that she is creating for herself a sexual status which will have a relatively pervasive distribution".

Actual sexual behaviour and its correlates have been exhaustively studied by the Kinsey reports (Kinsey *et al.*, 1948, 1953) and their numerous successors. Decade of birth is one factor; regardless of age, the longer ago a woman was born, the less likely she is to have had premarital intercourse. The effect has continued and accelerated since the 1950s; Bell and Chaskes (1970) found a marked increase in sexual experience among college women between 1958 and 1968, particularly in more casual liaisons. The most recent survey to hand, by Bauman and Wilson (1974), showed that premarital intercourse is getting steadily more general in American college youth. By 1972 three-quarters of students, both male and female, had experienced sexual intercourse, and the overall sex differences had at last vanished, although more women than men — 45% against 32% — still confined their experience to a single partner.

Of late national differences have been studied extensively. Luckey and Nass (1969) found quite large differences between American and Danish students, while Vener *et al.* (1972) looked at student samples in the USA, Canada, Germany, Norway, and England, and produced some surprising results. About 60% of American men, aged 20 to 22, had had premarital intercourse, as did a similar proportion of Canadian men, slightly fewer German men, rather more Norwegian men — 67% — and three-quarters of English men. The picture for women was similar but not identical; around 40% American and Canadian women had had premarital intercourse, just over half the Norwegian women, and around 60% of German and English women. The most striking results were the answer to a question about intercourse with casual partners; here the English sample were far more experienced than any other, especially the women, where a third said they had had such experience, opposed to 12% in Norway and under 10% for the other nationalities.

Other recent research has used a standard personality test, such as the Eysenck Personality Inventory (EPI). Giese and Schmidt (1968), in a survey of West German students, found large differences in the sexual behaviour of introverts and extroverts of both sexes. The extrovert group were more likely to have had sexual intercourse, had done so at an earlier age, had had sexual intercourse with more people, had experimented with a greater variety of coital positions; and were also more likely to have tried oral sex. Eysenck (1971a) studied people with

high "psychoticism" scores and found "an interesting combination of promiscuity, pre-marital sex, and curiosity, with hostility and lack of satisfaction".

In a further analysis of his data Eysenck (1971b) looked at the sexual behaviour of 100 students with "hysterical personalities" — high scorers on both extraversion and neuroticism. An extravert wants stimulation and variety in his or her sex life, and tends to get it, while someone with a high neuroticism score tends to worry about sex. When Eysenck compared his 100 "hysterics" with 100 stable introverts, the hysterics emerged as more experienced but also guilt-ridden. Twice as many "hysterical" women — 50% — had experienced intercourse, compared with a stable introvert group, but despite this — or perhaps because of it? — neither they, nor the hysterical men, were contented, and a high proportion suffered from guilt feelings.

Signs of sexual status can be more specific; for example smoking and drinking can be quite good cues to teenagers' sexual experience. Schofield (1965) found in particular that British teenage girls who smoked more than 20 cigarettes a day were hardly ever virgins. Arafat and Yorburg (1973) found that 62% of female drug users — American college students — were sexually experienced, as opposed to 49% of those that did not use drugs. Furthermore, girls who smoked marijuana tended to have, or have had several sexual partners, rather than just one steady partner. Two surveys (Teevan, 1972; Mirande, 1968) suggest these may be reference group effects; three times as many students whose friends were sexually experienced were experienced themselves. Dion's section summarizes the evidence on physical attractiveness as a cue to sexual experience.

Evidence of the sort just summarized allows one to make a general, actuarial type assessment of an individual's sexual attitudes and behaviour. However systematic evidence on how good people are at making such predictions is presently lacking. Contact between cultures also sometimes leads to misunderstanding; Cohen (1971) reports that Arab teenagers in the Israeli occupied territories believe that Israeli girls are sexually uninhibited and have intercourse readily with Israeli males, but not with Arabs.

First impressions are often stereotyped. Skipper and Nass (1966) found that medical students thought nurses sexually promiscuous, and went on to suggest that the prophecy to some extent became self-fulfilling in that nurses who were unwilling to live up to it, didn't receive as many invitations from men. Weinstein and Brook (1978) studied a rather small

sample of 30 female nurses in New York City and did not find their attitudes any more permissive. Quite specific (and false, or only partly true) predictions are made on the basis of appearance. McKeachie (1952) found that a woman wearing a lot of lipstick was seen as more frivolous and flirtatious, while Thornton (1944) found that men wearing glasses were judged more intelligent. (Subsequently Jahoda (1963) demonstrated that this was one of the stereotypes that had a grain of truth, and later still Argyle and McHenry (1971) found that the stereotype was limited to first impressions, vanishing after as little as five minutes interaction.) Gibbins (1969) found that people were ready to make quite specific predictions about women wearing different types of clothing, even down to whether they smoked or not.

More recently Davis and Cross (1979) reported the first investigation of a long held stereotype — that black males are more sexually potent; drawings of black men, by white men and women, tended to include a larger than average penis, and ratings of their potency were higher.

Several investigations of stereotyped perceptions of male homosexuality have been reported. Levitt and Klassen (1974) described a pattern of attitudes which they termed "homosexphobia", consisting of a distrust of homosexuals, belief that their behaviour is feminine, belief that homosexuality is an illness, and hence curable, and a feeling that homosexuals should be barred from certain occupations. Such belief, not surprisingly, are commoner in authoritarian individuals (McDonald and James, 1974). Plummer (1979) analyses stereotyped, and often incorrect, views held about pedophile men.

Feedback

One of the most useful features of the social skill model is the way it takes account of the sequential nature of perception. The first impression suggests an initial response that has some effect on the other person; and this effect is observed and acted on, producing further changes; and so on. The process is continuous and circular for as long as the interaction lasts. Responses may be made specifically to produce a response, as when questions are asked to clear up uncertain points. Another feature of skilled performance — motor or social — is the development of overlapping perception and response; while the person is responding to what he has seen, he is already looking ahead to the next part. Argyle and Cook (1976) describe how gaze direction is used socially to do several things at once — collect information about the other person, tell the

listener that the speaker is or is not about to finish speaking, and convey the speaker's opinion of the listener.

Feedback during a social encounter occurs on a number of levels. At the lowest level is what Argyle and Kendon (1967) term "regulation", or the "maintenance" of the interaction. Gaze and postural cues are used to start the encounter as well as to finish it. Melbin (1972) remarks on the use by one person, e.g. a charity collector, of gaze to get another person's attention, and on the avoidance of gaze by someone who does not want to get involved. Goffman (1977) describes how a code of glances opens, or refuses to open, sexual encounters at parties, dances, and in public places.

> Males who are present show broadcast attention to females held to be desirable, and await some furtive sign that can be taken as encouragement of their interest. . . . "Civil inattention" allows male and female a quick mutual glance. Her SECOND quick look can serve as a signal of encouragement to him.

Kendon and Farber (1973) found a standard sequence of greeting and recognition in a field study at an open air party; eye contact was made at a distance, accompanied by a wave, then broken until just before the host and guests met to embrace or shake hands.

Presumably these interchanges are learned and culturally variable, although one or two occur sufficiently frequently to permit the suggestion that they might be innate. Eibl-Eibesfeldt (1975) has found that the "eye-brow flash" — a swift raising and lowering of the eye-brow — occurs as a sign of greeting or recognition in many cultures.

Another form "regulation" takes is the interchange of the role of the speaker. A well-known study by Kendon (1967) showed that a speaker approaching the end of his utterance looks up at the other person and remains looking steadily. If he has merely paused for thought and hasn't finished, he doesn't look up. Kendon's data implied that looking up is a definite signal; when the speaker neglected to give it, the other person took a significantly longer time to realize it was his time to speak. Kendon's subjects were "getting to know each other"; Beattie (1978), studying gaze and speech in college tutorials, didn't find that gaze was used to regulate turn-taking. The study of Arkowitz *et al.* (1975) comparing successful and unsuccessful male daters found avoidance of silences distinguished the two, which suggests that fluency and/or command of turn-taking cues are especially important.

Most people are unaware of reacting to the other person's gaze patterns in these sorts of ways, but this is not surprising; most people are unaware

of the perceptual processes involved in motor skills too. In fact calling people's attention to the role of gaze in "regulation" often makes them very self-conscious, having the same disruptive effect that is often produced by making someone think about a tennis shot or a gear change while driving. The rapidity of perception of "regulation" and the fact of it being largely below the level of awareness led Argyle and Kendon to postulate a second, parallel channel, giving the more complex social skill model, illustrated in Fig. 2.

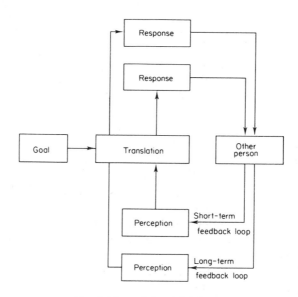

Fig. 2. *Expanded social skill model*

Gaze also plays a key part in a third type of regulation — the maintenance of an emotional equilibrium. Argyle and Dean (1965) argue that there is an appropriate "level of intimacy" for any given type of encounter; they went on to suggest that the right level of intimacy is both maintained and communicated by non-verbal behaviour: the distance people are from each other and the angle between them, the amount of time they look at each other, what they talk about, whether they touch each other — all set the emotional tone. A person who wants to make friends — and particularly someone who wants to put relations on a sexual footing — will be working towards increasing the emotional tone, whereas a person who wants to keep things distant and formal will try to

negate the other's moves, in the ways documented by Argyle and Dean and others since (e.g. Bakken, 1979). Thus greater proximity may be countered by reduced eye-contact (Argyle and Dean, 1965) or increased smiling by reduced eye-contact (Kendon, 1967). Argyle and Cook (1976) point out that not all cues may be used in this way; perhaps some cues are used to try to increase the intimacy of the encounter, whereas others are used primarily to counter such efforts.

The next level of feedback during interaction is generally above the level of awareness — the perception of moods, emotions, reactions, and the anticipation of what the other person is going to do next. Both have received extensive study, very little of it however directly related to sexual attraction. Thus research on facial expression has used still photographs as stimuli and given subjects the task of naming the emotion expressed using a check list or rating scales. Research on tone of voice has used tape recordings of standards sentences or of "content-free" speech. The objections to this type of research have been stated more than once (Cook, 1979); perhaps the most serious is that subjects are probably being asked the wrong questions. Extreme emotions, like disgust, fear, and anger, probably figure less in building up social relations than relatively subtle variations in approval, interest, and animation. Psychophysiological research reviewed by Zuckerman (1971), and the work of Masters and Johnson (1966), show that there is no pattern of physical changes specifically associated with sexual interest, other than changes to the genitals. Hence there is no such thing as a tone of voice or facial expression of sexual interest.

Recent research, reviewed by Hall (1978) and Hoffman (1977) has re-opened the old issue of sex differences in sensitivity to others. Tagiuri's (1969) review had found a tendency for women to be better judges of emotional expression, where sex differences were found, which was only in the minority of studies. Hall (1978) in a statistically more sophisticated analysis concluded that there was a genuine, if modest, tendency for women to be better judges; and that the tendency was more marked when visual and auditory information together was being judged, rather than visual or auditory on their own. Hammond's review shows that women have consistently greater "empathy", defined as sharing another's emotional response, not just observing or naming it. Rosenthal and DePaulo (1979), in a series of complex studies, found that, while women were better at perceiving non-verbal cues to emotion, their superiority was less marked for cues given fleetingly, or unintentionally — non-verbal "leakage". Rosenthal interprets this as an expression of female sex

role learning — to be more accommodating and polite in social encounters. His finding also implies that women's greater sensitivity might be more apparent in laboratory studies, where the task is made explicit, than in real life, where as element of "eavesdropping" is often present.

The prediction of what someone is going to do next has not been studied in directly relevant setting. Cline (1964) developed a "Behaviour Post-diction Test" in which judges had to predict which of four responses a person would make, in for example a violent argument. Dailey (1971) used a similar task and found that his judges could make on average 50% correct predictions in answers to three-choice questions — not much above chance level.

The list of things to be perceived before and during talking to someone is long and diverse, so it is not surprising to find that people who are good at observing one thing are not necessarily good at perceiving another. What is surprising — at least to people who still believe in personality traits — is that there seems little transfer from one type of perception to another. Cline and Richards (1960) found only modest correlations — the highest of 21 calculated being 0·44 — between different perceptual tasks, all completed after seeing a filmed interview, while Crow and Hammond (1957) found no correlation at all between ability to judge opinions and personality, and ability to perceive attraction in a group.

Goal

The suggestion that social encounters have goals is an idea that strikes many as cold and manipulative. Some encounters do have fairly specific goals (e.g. getting or giving information) but others have vaguer and more long-term aims, like making friends. A number of tests have been constructed to measure the extent and nature of an individual's desire to relate to his fellows. One example is Schutz's FIRO — Fundamental Interpersonal Relationships Orientation — which yields measures of inclusion, affiliation, and control, both wanted from others, and expressed towards others.

In a sexual encounter the goal is more obvious, at least at a superficial level, namely marriage and/or sexual satisfaction. If one asks why people want to get married or otherwise pair off, the answer is again sexual satisfaction, plus the same sorts of things that people get from friendship. Various surveys (e.g. Casler, 1970) have asked people — usually college

students — what they look for in marriage and marriage partners, and have drawn up lists of reasons like "security", "desire for home and family", "happiness and contentment". Less articulate samples, like the British working class couples surveyed by Slater and Woodside (1951), were unable to introspect on their motives, and could not offer any account of their choice of partner.

In some encounters one of the parties may have quite different goals; he or she may not wish to get involved sexually, or at all, so the goal becomes *not* attracting or being attractive to the other; or steering a relationship away from a sexual basis; or making it clear from the outset that it is not to be on a sexual footing. Doing all this, and avoiding offending the other person, probably requires a lot more social skill than a straightforward proposition. Knowing when and how to break off a relationship that is no longer rewarding — either in the early stages, or after some years together — can be very difficult too.

Probably more nonsense has been written about human sexual motivation than about any other topic in psychology. Some individuals probably do seek a succession of joyless mechanical seductions because they are uncertain of their own sexuality, but the obvious reason why men seduce women and vice versa is because they enjoy it. Despite the efforts of psychoanalysis, not a lot seems to be known about human sexual motivation — apart from the obvious facts that there are large individual differences, a point emphasized by Eysenck (1979), and that hormone levels do not seem to have much to do with it. A study by Larsen (1971) found that length of deprivation hardly correlated with feelings of sexual tension nor with the arousal produced by watching a pornographic film. Amount of previous (enjoyable) experience, measured by a short questionnaire containing items like "I find a variety of different partners makes sex more interesting", did correlate moderately with tension and arousal.

Translation

In the light of what the person sees, and what he or she wants, the person next decides what to do — which in the social skill model is the box labelled "Translation". To take a simple motor skill example, the driver who wants to turn left turns the steering wheel in an anti-clockwise direction. To give a social skill example, Inbau (1942), in a standard manual of police interrogation methods, points out that appeals to

conscience, or attempts to minimize the seriousness of the offence, will work on first offenders, but will cut no ice with professional criminals, who can only be made to confess by playing on the fear that their accomplices will confess first — the so-called "prisoner's dilemma". Specifically sexual examples are relatively hard to find. Symonds (1972) gives one, being "willing to generalise that with the male propositioner the directness of the proposition is positively correlated with his perception of the chances of acceptance". Amis (1969) offers another — "every minute a girl is allowed to spend in official ignorance of man's intentions means two minutes extra build-up when the time comes".

The essence of the notion of translation, in Argyle and Kendon's original model, was that the individual has a repertoire of different social techniques, from which he or she selects one seen as appropriate for his or her goal, or for the type of person he or she is dealing with. On this analogy a man courting a nervous inexperienced woman will use a different approach from a man courting a worldly, experienced woman; and a woman seeking to attract a man at a party would set about it differently from the same woman trying to attract a man at her workplace. One wonders how far people are actually able to vary their approach in this way; certainly many people seem to have only one way of approaching the opposite sex. Which, so long as they remain within their own subculture, and are not put off too much by the odd rebuff, may not matter very much.

Response

Kirkendall (1961) interviewed a number of young men about their approaches to women, and found one who thought he had got it to a fine art. It is worth describing some of his tactics, to illustrate sequence and strategy in courtship. Kirkendall's informant started by locating a partner and creating a good first impression; working in a woman's clothes shop took care of the former and possessing a good wardrobe of smart clothes ensured the latter. (Kirkendall's data was collected in the 1950s; it would be interesting to know whether clothes are as important today.) On the first date he impresses the woman by his car, his experience of motor racing, by demonstrating how many friends he has. He asks her for small favours and takes willingness to oblige as a good sign. By the second date he has succeeded in getting her in the right frame of mind to steer the conversation to more intimate topics and soon after that, but not before, to make sexual advances.

Others of Kirkendall's 200 informants rely on verbal arguments, persuading the woman she really has no grounds for refusing, telling her that "all the college girls are doing it", or accusing her of letting her parents think for her. Others claim to be in love or say that intercourse will strengthen the relationship; or they may plead special cases, like impending call up; many of course try to allay the woman's fear of pregnancy, or of being found out by her parents. Other men use a radically different approach, summed up by one who said: "If you begin by talking you'll talk yourself right out of it. I never talk . . . I just work slowly, but always go a little further each time". Some couples who worked on this basis had intercourse regularly without ever referring to the fact, before or after. In Kirkendall's sample, the men who seduced by talk were heavily out-numbered — three to one — by the ones who seduced by touch; Kirkendall does not report which approach was more "successful".

The more rigorous type of psychologist tends to be suspicious of data like Kirkendall's, calling it "anecdotal"; yet it is hard to see how else one can gain information about courtship ritual — short of bugging public places, which would be unethical.

Some of Kirkendall's other informants report cruder tactics, ranging from accusing an unwilling female of being dominated by her parents, to threatening to blacken her reputation. A series of studies by Kanin (1969) found that many American college men resorted to force quite readily; 56% of women reported experiencing repeated acts of "sex aggression". Surprising — at least to men — are the women's reactions to the aggression; only 3 of 163 who had been attacked complained to police or authority, and only 30% broke off the relationship with their attacker. In fact many of the attacks came from "steady" male-friends, or fiancés, not all from casual dates or strangers.

More systematic, experimentally-based accounts of the response "box" of the social skill model come from Argyle (1969) or Berscheid and Walster (1969). Argyle emphasizes particularly the role of non-verbal behaviour. Interest in another person can be communicated by standing closer to the other person (Byrne *et al.*, 1970), looking at him or her more (Exline and Winters, 1965; Cook and Smith, 1975), smiling (Argyle *et al.*, 1972), "openness" of posture (Mehrabian, 1969), as well as in less obvious or deliberate ways. Hess (1965) suggests that pupil dilation can express liking or sexual interest. Males found a photograph of women, in which the pupils had been enlarged by photographic re-touching, looked attractive. The interest of this finding is that pupil dilation is not subject

to voluntary control. Shelley and McKew (1979) replicated Hess' study with less exaggerated stimuli, and found a reliable effect, specific to adult males; adult females, and 11-year olds of either sex did not prefer photographs of females with enlarged pupils.

Ekman and Friesen (1969) introduce the concept of "leakage"; attempts to suppress feelings, such as dislike on the one hand, or sexual interest on the other, are not always successful. Fragmentary expressions of the person's true attitude may "leak" through. Thus Haggard and Isaacs (1966) found "micromomentary" facial expression, detectable only by frame-by-frame analysis of cine-films; these changes — filmed during psychotherapy sessions — were thought to indicate repressed hostility to the therapist "leaking" through, before being rapidly suppressed. Scheflen (1965) describes gestures and postures of "quasi-courtship", which could be regarded as forms of leakage. A man often reacts to the sight of a woman, and gives away his interest in her by "preening" movements — straightening the tie, smoothing the hair, etc.

Comfort (1971) claims that humans attract each other sexually by "pheromones" or sexual odours. Brody (1975) identifies the armpit as one source of human pheromones, and cites the example of Austrian peasants using handkerchiefs previously stored in the armpit to attract partners. It is obvious, as any pet-owner will have noticed, that odours play an important part in the sexual behaviour of animals. The case for human pheromones rests largely on the argument — further discussed by Manning (see Chapter 9 of this volume) — that what animals do, man does, perhaps in disguised or symbolic form, and on the argument that man has pheromone producing bodily structures, such as the armpit. Rogel (1978) and Clegg (1979) are sceptical.

Some non-verbal cues can be used to communicate interest in someone other than the person one is talking to. Gaze of course is one such cue; according to Scheflen (1965), posture can do the same. A man or woman talking to one person can indicate his or her greater interest in someone else by angling the lower part of his or her body towards the third person rather than towards the speaker. Scheflen (1965) also claims that "palm presentation" — facing the palm outwards — is used by American middle class women to indicate sexual availability.

Of course non-verbal behaviour is not the only way to communicate — or create — attraction. More elaborate sequences of behaviour have been described and experimentally studied, including the research on ingratiation by Jones (1964), which demonstrates that the most obvious tactics for winning favour may not always work precisely because they

are obvious. Figley (1979) gives a good review of research on ingratiation, and "tactical self-presentation". An example of a subtle way of making oneself liked may be derived from the "pratfall" experiment (Aronson *et al.*, 1966). It was reasoned that while people prefer others of superior ability and accomplishments, they are also a little wary of them; hence if a superior person were humanized by being seen — heard in fact since a tape recording was used — to make a clumsy blunder, then he would be judged more favourably. The experiment supported the hypothesis; the clumsy but accomplished person was seen more favourably than the accomplished, careful person. The same was not found for a person of average ability — who lost esteem by committing a blunder.

A similarly ingenious study by Walster (1965) has examined the role of self-esteem in courtship. It is a reasonable hypothesis that the higher a woman's opinion of herself the more particular she will be about accepting invitations. Walster found that "failing" a test made a woman much more favourably inclined towards a man she met shortly afterwards, indicating that passing mood — open to manipulation — partly determines the attractiveness of others. A series of studies by Walster *et al.* (1973) showed that "playing hard to get" was not — contrary to folklore — a good tactic for women to follow. Men were not attracted to women who were reluctant to accept invitations, nor likely to return to a prostitute who told her clients she only accepted men she liked.

Rules

A person making a chair leg is free to use whatever methods he thinks best, but there are strict limits on one's choice of approach when seeking to attract a sexual partner. Both law and custom impose numerous restrictions on one's initial choice of partner; on the places one can visit to find a partner; and on the things one can do and say to gain his or her interest. There are even social constraints on what one can be seen to notice about others, which Goffman (1963) named the norm of "civil inattention".

Rules imposed by law — the age of consent for example — are clearly stated and known to all; rules imposed by custom are often much less obvious, and some can only be uncovered by "rule-breaking" or by cross-cultural comparisons. Garfinkel (1967), a sociologist, pioneered the "rule-breaking" technique; it can show that a rule is very basic, yet taken so much for granted that people are quite unaware of it, until someone

breaks it. A favourite example is for a member of a family to behave at home as if he or she were in a restaurant or hotel — offer to pay for the meal, leave a tip under the plate, etc. Consternation is said to ensue. No accounts of rule-breaking studies of sexual behaviour appear to have been published; not surprising perhaps — it is a risky technique at the best of times and to add sex would be positively dangerous. (Plummer (1979) gives a brief account of the violence of public reaction in Britain against a pressure group seeking to lower the age of consent — which could be seen as an unintentional rule-breaking experiment.)

Cross-cultural comparisons are safer, although, as Rosenblatt and Anderson point out in their section, the information is not always entirely reliable. Ford and Beach (1952) document a number of restrictions on the form sexual invitations may take, some of them sufficiently widespread to form the basis of tentative generalizations.

One fairly general feature of human sexual encounters is that the most direct approaches tend to be forbidden. Most cultures require men to cover their genitals and virtually all require women to do so. Most cultures appear to forbid direct requests for sexual favours, although there are some exceptions listed by Ford and Beach; Balinese and Lepcha men can ask a girl if she is willing to have intercourse. Siriono men can ask but must whisper, while the men of Jaluit in the Marshall Islands ask for intercourse by pronouncing the name of the sexual organs. Women too are generally forbidden to ask outright; one exception is Bali again, while Lepcha women are said to break their culture's norm, and ask directly.

In most human cultures invitations are made in vague, symbolic or non-verbal, ways. A striking example of this is the custom of love magic described by Rosenblatt (1971). The man sets about attracting a woman by acts of magical significance performed in the girl's presence or to her knowledge, so that he communicates his interest indirectly. One could draw a parallel here with a man asking a woman to come to see a film with him, not because he especially wants to see it himself, or even because he thinks she wants to, but as a conventional form of invitation. It seems odd that humans — having the gift of language — should use vague, symbolic, easily misunderstood signals to attract each other. Animals have to rely on posture, vocalization, smell, etc., to attract mates, but at least have instinct to ensure that the signals are not misunderstood.

In fact the very feature of vagueness is a great advantage in courtship. The point about direct verbal invitations is that they tend to require

direct verbal answers, which either commit the speaker or offend the asker. Invitations given non-verbally or in symbolic form are not binding on either party and can be withdrawn or refused without causing affront or loss of self-esteem. Naturally this principle will only work if certain other rules are observed too. A person whose invitation, to come to see a film or whatever, is refused, should not press the point too far, for fear of making it clear that it is him or her that is unwelcome, not the film. (Yet just to make things difficult, some persistence after a first refusal is often culturally prescribed.) Another rule, first described by Goffman (1959), forbids one to comment on non-verbal behaviour in particular, or the progress of the encounter in general — the "taboo on second-order interaction". A piece of behaviour — a smile, or moving away — may often be just about as clear as the spoken word, but it is not done to say things like "why have you moved away, don't you like me?" or "why smile if you're not interested?" The taboo safeguards the essential feature of non-verbal behaviour — that it cannot "be taken down in writing and given in evidence". The same taboo also makes life difficult for people whose non-verbal behaviour creates the wrong impression; without "social skill training" (*v. infra*), they are unlikely to learn where they are going wrong.

　　Ford and Beach also report data on the distribution of initiative in sexual attraction — does the man or the woman make the first move? In most human societies custom seems to dictate that the man shall approach the woman, not vice versa. Ford and Beach list a few exceptions — the Maoris of New Zealand, the Kwoma of New Guinea, and some South Sea islands where both sexes can take the initiative. Sometimes the prohibition on female initiatives is taken literally — the Mbundu in Africa are reported to consider the slightest sign of interest in a woman to be shameful — but more usually the effect is to require women to express their interest indirectly. Changing ideas about sex roles in the West will presumably start to allow more women to take the initiative, but it is difficult to form any estimate yet of how far customs have changed. Davis (1978), studying British university students, found that males tended to be the "principal architects" of mixed sex encounters, dictating the pace at which intimacy of conversational topic developed.

　　There are also customs determining the sequence of events in courtship; these are more culturally variable. In the West there is a recognized scale of sexual intimacy, starting with kissing, and proceeding by touching breasts and genitals to sexual intercourse. There is no logical

necessity to this sequence, and other cultures do things in quite a different order. For example the Crow Indian male of North America is reported to seek a mate by crawling up to a tent at night, and trying to find a woman, whose genitals he then stimulates.

A conventional sequence of courtship approach often serves the twin purposes of allowing either party to back out without embarrassment if they change their mind, and of screening outsiders. Thus the Hottentot male is reported to court a female by first asking her parents for her hand, a request which is traditionally refused. He next watches her hut and learns where she sleeps, then slips in one night and lies down beside her, at which point she gets up and goes away. He returns the next night, and keeps returning each night, until she either decides against him by not being there when he comes, or accepts him, in which case she stays there all night and the marriage is consummated.

Deviant sexual groups are particularly likely to need a courtship sequence designed to avoid involving outsiders by mistake. Homosexuals often use private codes of language, constantly updated as they become public knowledge, meet in particular places, and follow particular dialogues. For example a male homosexual "pick-up" in London in the 1950s, described by Wildeblood (1956), started by asking for a light and giving a smile; continued with remarks about marriage and why the man was out at that time of night, and the offer of a drink; and ended by noting that the pub lacked a friendly atmosphere and naming one that did not — a known homosexual pub. A more recent account of male homosexual encounters in public toilets by Humphreys (1970) shows the same features: a reliance on custom, the use of symbolic acts, looks and gestures, rather than words, and a sequence that allows either man to back out without explanation or apology at any stage right up to the last minute.

Training

If attracting a sexual partner is a skill, like driving a car or playing tennis, then performance can be improved by training; the last 15 years or so has been a steadily increasing flow of research on social skill training (Hersen and Bellak, 1977). The early studies looked at general social unease and incompetence, often in psychiatric patients, but specialized lines of research soon took shape, including a series of studies of what has come to be called "heterosocial-sexual anxiety", now shortened to "heterosocial anxiety", and known more prosaically as "infrequent

dating". Most of the research seems to have been done with college students, and until recently most has been done on men, with the notable exception of Greenwald (1977). It is not surprising that student counsellors should start many of these programmes, since according to Shmurak (1973), 54% of college males' social anxieties centre around dating. (The figure for college women is a little lower — 42%.)

Curran (1977) provides a good critical review of the earlier research; he distinguishes between studies, like those of Martinson and Zerface (1970), which are based on the assumption that the shy male knows what to do but just needs practice, and the larger number of studies that assume his problem is that he does not know what to do. The former type of study — "response practice" — restricts itself to having the male practice asking for dates and talking to women, while the second — "response acquisition" — concentrates on extending the subject's deficient repertoire of responses by various packages of training. For example, McDonald *et al.* (1975), who give a slightly fuller account of their aims than many, set out to cover how and when to initiate conversation; how to communicate interest in another; how to judge a person's receptivity; where to go on dates; and when to initiate physical contact.

Various methods of training are used. Melnick (1973) used combinations of vicarious learning (watching others doing it properly), participant modelling (practising doing it oneself), self-observation (watching video-recordings of one's own efforts), and reinforcement (praise for doing the right things). The nine studies of this type reviewed by Curran all found some improvement, although as Curran notes, many were methodologically far from perfect, and results were often inconsistent and only marginally significant. Thus McDonald *et al.* (1975) found that "behaviour rehearsal" produced improvement in rated dating skill, with both of two therapists, but a lessening of rated anxiety with only one of the therapists; the same treatment programme, plus "extra assignments" in the student's own time, involving finding and talking to women, produced changes in skill and anxiety with only one therapist. To complicate matters further, both therapists managed an improvement in the subjects' mood, in an "attention–placebo" condition. All changes were significant only at the 5% level, and the one outcome unaffected by any combination of therapist and treatment was the number of dates the subjects managed to get during the follow-up period.

One or two general criticisms may be made of these studies — useful as they are. Many have fallen into the trap of employing complex designs

and small samples, so that results are often confused and of marginal significance. It is of course true that research in this area needs a minimum of three conditions — a waiting list control group, an attention–placebo group, and a social skill training group — but many studies are far more complex. Melnick (1973) divided his subjects into six treatment groups, each of ten subjects, then had to combine groups, to allow a rather weak test of his hypothesis using the chi-squared test.

A more substantial criticism of these studies, as of much social skill training in general, is that they rest on incomplete and shaky foundations of empirical knowledge about how sexual attraction and dating actually proceed in the real world. Most studies are prevented from giving much detail about what they actually teach their subjects to do, because of their journal article length, but the source of their insight into what advice to give must often be as obscure as the source of the computer dating agency's basis for matching clients. We do not at present have more than a fragmentary picture of how sexual attraction works in the real world.

Where one is dealing with a subculture, such as the American university campus, this lack may not be too serious since the main points are probably dictated by convention (although one would like to know what McDonald *et al.* (1975) tell their subjects about how to judge a person's receptivity). When one ventures off campus, one moves onto less certain ground. Crawford and Allen (1979) discovered this when attempting conventional social skill training with predominantly working-class male sex offenders, and say:

> For example, a widespread, and apparently socially acceptable technique for asking for a dance is almost the exact opposite of what we have been teaching our patients. You walk across, avoiding all eye contact, look as casual and disinterested as possible, do not smile, and, if you are one of the verbal ones, utter the single word "dance". Those with only average verbal skills simply tap the girl on the shoulder and jerk their head in the direction of the dance floor.

A different line of research denies that the shy male's problem is first and foremost that he does not know how to ask for dates or how to talk to women; his problem is more simple — he is afraid to. Hokanson (1971) approached the problem from this angle and employed systematic desensitization, in which the subject imagines himself in a series of progressively more threatening encounters with women, in one condition accompanying the imagined encounters with relaxation training, though not in the other. Both methods reduced the subject's reported anxiety, and increased his reported number of dates. A similar study by Rehm

and Marston (1968) also achieved some improvement, but mostly only on measures derived from the subject's self-reports; ratings and measures derived from a role-played date showed only one improvement. Most recently Glass *et al.* (1976) have used Meichenbaum's (1972) "cognitive" therapy, which operates on the assumption that the shy male's behaviour, when confronted by a female, is disrupted by negative thoughts, "self-verbalization" and "self-instructions", and that this can be prevented by teaching him to recognize these unhelpful thoughts and replace them by thoughts of himself performing competently — "coping imagery". A group of males trained in this method showed more effective behaviour on the Dating Behavior Assessment Test (DBAT), as did a group trained by conventional social skills training. However, only the "cognitively" trained group showed any generalization between the DBAT items they had trained on, and a fresh set of items they had not previously encountered. Once again, however, the result was significant only at the 5% level.

One perceives here the making of a classic pseudo-conflict, between social skill training and anxiety reduction approaches — a pseudo-dispute because it is surely obvious that both approaches have their contribution to make. Not knowing what to do makes people anxious, but a deficient repertoire of social openings surely is not the only source of heterosocial anxiety. One would like a lot more information about shy males; Wessberg *et al.* (1979) partly rule out one possible mediating factor, reporting that their infrequent daters were not significantly less good-looking than the frequent daters. Similar results were reported for females by Williams and Ciminero (1978). Greenwald (1977) on the other hand, also studying females, found large differences in rated attractiveness of frequent and infrequent daters.

One of the more interesting aspects of the studies of heterosocial anxiety has been the emergence of a number of broadly similar behavioural tests of dating skill. Arkowitz *et al.* (1975) employed a ten-item Taped Situation test, adapted from Rehm and Marston (1968), in which the subject hears a male voice set the scene — "At a party you go over to a girl and ask her for a dance" — then hears a female voice say "I'm not really much of a dancer", and then has to come up with an appropriate reply. Arkowitz *et al.* also videotaped their subjects talking to a female — a confederate whose behaviour was standardized — and analysed aspects of non-verbal behaviour such as smiling, looking, nodding, etc. Other researchers have used similar measures — the DBAT (Glass *et al.*, 1976) or the Role Played Dating Interactions (RPDI)

(McDonald *et al.*, 1975) — but have tended to use ratings of skill and anxiety rather than objective analyses of performance.

Of late these measures have come under scrutiny, as perhaps being artificial, and unlikely to show any transfer to real encounters outside the laboratory. This criticism is particularly relevant if one believes that anxiety matters more than skill; a shy male might be able to put on a very good performance in the security of the laboratory, only to fail badly in his first real encounter. Two recent studies (Bellack *et al.*, 1979; Wessberg *et al.*, 1979) have compared behaviour in a role playing test with behaviour while ostensibly waiting, with a person of the opposite sex, for the experiment to start. These two studies show that some transfer does occur, but it can be very limited. For example, eye-contact and smiling in the role played encounter correlated with eye contact and smiling "while waiting" are 0·49 and 0·44 respectively in male subjects, but only an insignificant 0·23 and 0·25 in females. Farrell *et al.* (1979) compared a variety of measures of dating skill — anxiety questionnaires, self ratings, ratings by confederates and by observers — and found some "generalizability" across measures, but only to a limited extent.

There is in fact no reason to suppose dating skill should prove to be monolithic; first, because few such hypothesized dispositions ever are (Mischel, 1968), and secondly because the thrust of the present account has been that social skills are complex, and consist of a minimum of four elements. A person may have trouble attracting a partner because he/she does not know the proper place to go or the proper things to do (Rules), because he/she fails to perceive interest or its absence (Perception), because he/she fails to say and do the right things (Response) or, because he/she uses the right approach on the wrong person (Translation). In turn each of these components can be broken down further; Cline (1964) suggested that perceiving others has a hierarchical structure, like that of intelligence, the two "group factors" being ability to perceive group opinions (stereotype accuracy), and the ability to perceive individual differences.

The way forward depends on one's aims. The student counsellor wants to solve his student's problems, so he probably needs techniques and outcome measures with high external validity. The social psychologist who wants to analyse a sequence of social behaviour faces more of a problem. He could, in theory, collect a vast amount of data on attraction, then factor analyse it — although Comrey (1978) suggests he would need a minimum of 2000 observations to achieve a definitive account. But would it be worth it? He is studying a culturally bound behaviour, so his account would not travel, nor would it remain true for very long.

5. References

Amis, K. *The green man.* London: Cape, 1969.
Arafat, I. and Yorburg, B. Drug use and the sexual behavior of college women. *Journal of Sex Research,* 1973, **9**, 21-29.
Argyle, M. *The psychology of interpersonal behaviour.* Harmondsworth: Penguin, 1967.
Argyle, M. *Social interaction.* London: Methuen, 1969.
Argyle, M. and Cook, M. *Gaze and mutual gaze.* Cambridge: Cambridge University Press, 1976.
Argyle, M. and Dean, J. Eye contact, distance and affiliation. *Sociometry,* 1965, **28**, 289-304.
Argyle, M. and Kendon, A. The experimental analysis of social performance. In Berkowitz, L. (Ed), *Advances in experimental social psychology.* Vol. 1. New York and London: Academic Press, 1965.
Argyle, M. and McHenry, R. Do spectacles really affect judgements of intelligence? *British Journal of Social and Clinical Psychology,* 1971, **10**, 27-29.
Argyle, M., Alkema, F. and Gilmour, R. The communication of friendly and hostile attitudes by verbal and non-verbal signals. *European Journal of Social Psychology,* 1971, **1**, 385-402.
Arkowitz, H., Lichtenstein, E., McGovern, K. and Hines, H. The behavioral assessment of social competence in males. *Behavior Therapy,* 1975, **6**, 3-13.
Aronson, E., Willerman, B. and Floyd, J. The effect of a pratfall on increasing interpersonal attractiveness. *Psychonomic Science,* 1966, **4**, 227-228.
Bakken, D. Regulation of intimacy in social encounters: the effects of sex of interactants and information about attitude similarity. In Cook, M. and Wilson, G. (Eds), *Love and attraction: an international conference.* Oxford: Pergamon, 1979.
Balswick, J. O. and Anderson, J. A. Role definition in the unarranged date. *Journal of Marriage and the Family,* 1968, **31**, 776-778.
Bauman, K. E. and Wilson, R. R. Sexual behavior of unmarried students in 1968 and 1972. *Journal of Sex Research,* 1974, **10**, 327-333.
Beattie, G. W. Floor apportionment and gaze in conversational dyads. *British Journal of Social and Clinical Psychology,* 1978, **17**, 7-15.
Bell, R. R. and Chaskes, J. B. Premarital sexual experience among coeds, 1958 and 1968. *Journal of Marriage and the Family,* 1970, **32**, 81-84.
Bellack, A. S., Hersen, M. and Lamparski, D. Role play tests for assessing social skills: are they valid? are they useful? *Journal of Consulting and Clinical Psychology,* 1979, **47**, 335-342.
Berscheid, E. and Walster, E. H. *Interpersonal attraction.* Reading, Mass.: Addison Wesley, 1969.
Brody, B. The sexual significance of the axillae. *Psychiatry,* 1975, **38**, 278-289.
Byrne, D. and Blaylock, B. Similarity and assumed similarity of attitudes between husbands and wives. *Journal of Abnormal Social Psychology,* 1963, **67**, 636-640.

Byrne, D., Ervin, C. R. and Lamberth, J. Continuity between the experimental study of attraction and real life computer dating. *Journal of Personality and Social Psychology*, 1970, **16**, 157-165.

Carns, D. E. Talking about sex: notes on first coitus and the double standard. *Journal of Marriage and the Family*, 1973, **35**, 677-688.

Casler, L. Marriage motives in two college populations. *Personality*, 1970, **1**, 221-229.

Clegg, F. Mammalian pheromones — sense or nonsense? In Cook, M. and Wilson, G. (Eds), *Love and attraction: an international conference*. Oxford: Pergamon, 1979.

Clements, W. H. Marital interaction and marital stability: a point of view and a descriptive comparison of stable and unstable marriages. *Journal of Marriage and the Family*, 1967, **29**, 697-702.

Cline, V. B. Interpersonal perception. In Maher, B. A. (Ed.), *Progress in experimental personality research*. Vol. 1. New York and London: Academic Press, 1964.

Cline, V. B. and Richards, J. M. Accuracy of person perception — a general trait? *Journal of Abnormal and Social Psychology*, 1960, **60**, 1-7.

Cohen, E. Arab boys and tourist girls in a mixed Jewish Arab community. *International Journal of Comparative Sociology*, 1971, **12**, 217-233.

Comfort, A. Likelihood of human pheromones. *Nature*, 1971, **230**, 432-433, 479.

Comrey, A. L. Common methodological problems in factor analytic studies. *Journal of Consulting and Clinical Psychology*, 1978, **46**, 648-659.

Cook, M. *Perceiving others: the psychology of interpersonal perception*. London: Methuen, 1979.

Cook, M. and Smith, J. M. C. The role of gaze in impression formation. *British Journal of Social and Clinical Psychology*, 1975, **14**, 19-25.

Corsini, R. J. Understanding and similarity in marriage. *Journal of Abnormal and Social Psychology*, 1956, **52**, 327-332.

Crawford, D. and Allen, J. V. A social skills training programme with sex offenders. In Cook, M. and Wilson, G. (Eds), *Love and attraction: an international conference*. Oxford: Pergamon, 1979.

Crow, W. J. and Hammond, K. R. The generality of accuracy and response sets in interpersonal perception. *Journal of Abnormal and Social Psychology*, 1957, **54**, 384-390.

Curran, J. P. Skills training as an approach to the treatment of heterosexual-social anxiety: a review. *Psychological Bulletin*, 1977, **85**, 140-157.

Dailey, C. A. *Assessment of lives*. San Francisco: Jossey Bass, 1971.

Davis, G. L. and Cross, H. J. Sexual stereotyping of black males in interracial sex. *Archives of Sexual Behavior*, 1979, **8**, 269-279.

Davis, J. D. When boy meets girl: sex roles and the negotiation of intimacy in an acquaintance exercise. *Journal of Personality and Social Psychology*, 1978, **36**, 684-692.

Duck, S. W. Personal similarity and friendship choice: similarity of what, when? *Journal of Personality*, 1973, **41**, 543-558.

Dymond, R. F. Interpersonal perception and marital happiness. *Canadian Journal of Psychology*, 1954, **8**, 164-171.

Eibl-Eibesfeldt, I. *Ethology: the science of behavior.* New York: Holt, 1975.

Ekman, P. and Friesen, W. V. Nonverbal leakage and clues to deception. *Psychiatry*, 1969, **32**, 88-105.

Exline, R. V. and Winters, L. C. Affective relations and mutual glances in dyads. In Tomkins, S. S. and Izard, C. (Eds), *Affect, cognition, and personality.* London: Tavistock, 1965.

Eysenck, H. J. Personality and sexual adjustment. *British Journal of Psychiatry*, 1971a, **118**, 593-608.

Eysenck, H. J. Hysterical personality and sexual adjustment, attitudes, and personality. *Journal of Sex Research*, 1971b, **7**, 274-281.

Eysenck, H. J. Sex, society and the individual. In Cook, M. and Wilson, G. (Eds), *Love and attraction: an international conference.* Oxford: Pergamon, 1979.

Farrell, A. D., Mariotto, M. J., Conger, A. J., Curran, J. P. and Wallander, J. L. Self ratings and judges' ratings of heterosexual social anxiety and skill: a generalizability study. *Journal of Consulting and Clinical Psychology*, 1979, **47**, 164-175.

Figley, C. R. Tactical self-presentation and interpersonal attraction. In Cook, M. and Wilson, G. (Eds), *Love and attraction: an international conference.* Oxford: Pergamon, 1979.

Ford, C. S. and Beach, F. A. *Patterns of sexual behaviour.* London: Methuen, 1952.

Garfinkel, H. *Studies in ethnomethodology.* Englewood Cliffs, N.J.: Prentice Hall, 1967.

Gibbins, K. Communication aspects of women's clothes and their relation to fashionability. *British Journal of Social and Clinical Psychology*, 1969, **8**, 301-312.

Giese, H. and Schmidt, S. A. *Studenten Sexualität: Verhalten und Einstellung.* Hamburg: Rowohlt, 1968.

Glass, C. R., Gottman, J. M. and Shmurak, S. H. Response acquisition and cognitive self-statement modification approaches to dating skill training. *Journal of Counseling Psychology*, 1976, **23**, 520-526.

Goffman, E. *The presentation of self in everyday life.* New York: Doubleday Anchor, 1959.

Goffman, E. *Behavior in public places.* Glencoe: Free Press, 1963.

Goffman, E. The arrangement between the sexes. *Theory and Society*, 1977, **4**, 301-333.

Greenwald, D. P. The behavioral assessment of differences in social skill and social anxiety in female college subjects. *Behavior Therapy*, 1977, **8**, 925-937.

Haggard, F. A. and Isaacs, K. S. Micromomentary facial expressions as indicators of ego mechanisms in psychotherapy. In Gottschalk, L. A. and Auerbach, A. H. (Eds), *Methods of research in psychotherapy.* New York: Appleton Century Crofts, 1966.

Hall, J. A. Gender effects in decoding nonverbal cues. *Psychological Bulletin,* 1978, **85**, 845-857.

Hersen, M. and Bellack, A. S. Assessment of social skills. In Ciminero, A. R., Calhoun, K. S. and Adams, H. E. (Eds), *Handbook for behavioral assessment.* New York: Wiley, 1977.

Hess, E. H. Attitude and pupil size. *Scientific American,* 1965, **212**, 46-54.

Hewitt, L. E. Student perceptions of traits desired in themselves as dating and marriage partners. *Marriage and Family Living,* 1958, **20**, 344-349.

Hoffman, M. L. Sex differences in empathy and related behaviors. *Psychological Bulletin,* 1977, **84**, 712-722.

Hokanson, D. Systematic desensitisation and positive cognitive rehearsal treatment of social anxiety. *Dissertation Abstracts International,* 1971, **32**, 6649B-6650B.

Humphreys, L. *Tearoom trade: a study of homosexual encounters in public places.* London: Duckworth, 1970.

Inbau, F. E. *Lie detection and criminal interrogation.* Baltimore: Williams Wilkins, 1942.

Jackson, E. D. and Potkay, C. R. Pre-college influence on sexual experience in co-eds. *Journal of Sex Research,* 1973, **9**, 143-149.

Jahoda, G. Refractive errors, intelligence and social mobility. *British Journal of Social and Clinical Psychology,* 1963, **1**, 96-106.

Jones, E. E. *Ingratiation.* New York: Appleton Century Crofts, 1964.

Kaats, G. R. and Davis, K. E. The dynamics of sexual behavior in college students. *Journal of Marriage and the Family,* 1970, **32**, 390-399.

Kanin, E. J. Selected dyadic aspects of male sex aggression. *Journal of Sex Research,* 1969, **5**, 12-28.

Kendon, A. Some functions of gaze directions in social interaction. *Acta Psychologica,* 1967, **26**, 22-63.

Kendon, A. and Farber, A. A description of some human greetings. In Michael, R. P. and Crook, J. H. (Eds), *Comparative ecology and behaviour of primates.* London and New York: Academic Press, 1973.

Kinsey, A. C., Pomeroy, W. B. and Martin, C. E. *Sexual behavior in the human male.* Philadelphia: Saunders, 1948.

Kinsey, A. C., Pomeroy, W. B., Martin, C. E. and Gebhard, P. H. *Sexual behavior in the human female.* Philadelphia: Saunders, 1953.

Kirkendall, L. A. *Premarital intercourse and interpersonal relationships.* New York: Julian Press, 1961.

Kirkpatrick, C. and Hobart, C. Disagreement, disagreement estimate and non-empathic imputation for intimacy groups varying from favourite date to married. *American Sociological Review,* 1954, **19**, 10-19.

Larsen, K. S. An investigation of sexual behavior among Norwegian college students: a motivation study. *Journal of Marriage and the Family,* 1971, **33**, 219-227.

Levitt, E. E. and Klassen, A. D. Public attitudes towards homosexuality: part of the 1970 national survey of the Institute of Sex Research. *Journal of Homosexuality,* 1974, **1**, 29-43.

Lewis, R. A. A developmental framework for the analysis of premarital dyadic formation. *Family Process*, 1972, **11**, 17-48.
Luckey, E. B. and Nass, G. D. A comparison of sexual attitudes and behavior in an international sample. *Journal of Marriage and the Family*, 1969, **31**, 364-379.
McDonald, A. P. and James, R. G. Some characteristics of those who hold positive and negative attitudes towards homosexuals. *Journal of Homosexuality*, 1974, **1**, 9-27.
McDonald, M. L., Lindquist, C. U., Kramer, J. A., McGrath, R. A. and Rhyne, L. D. Social skills training: behavior rehearsal in groups and dating skill. *Journal of Counseling Psychology*, 1975, **22**, 224-230.
McKeachie, W. Lipstick as a determiner of first impressions of personality: an experiment for the general psychology course. *Journal of Social Psychology*, 1952, **36**, 241-244.
Martinson, W. D. and Zerface, J. P. Comparison of individual counseling and a social program with nondaters. *Journal of Counseling Psychology*, 1970, **17**, 36-40.
Masters, W. D. and Johnson, J. P. *Human sexual response*. London: Churchill, 1966.
Mehrabian, A. Significance of posture and position in the communication of attitude and status relationships. *Psychological Bulletin*, 1969, **71**, 359-372.
Meichenbaum, D. Cognitive modification of test anxious college students. *Journal of Consulting and Clinical Psychology*, 1972, **39**, 370-380.
Melbin, M. *Alone and with others*. New York: Harper, 1972.
Melnick, J. A comparison of replication techniques in the modification of minimal dating behavior. *Journal of Abnormal Psychology*, 1973, **81**, 51-59.
Mercer, G. W. and Kohn, P. M. Gender differences in the integration of conservatism, sex urge, and sexual behaviors among college students. *Journal of Sex Research*, 1979, **15**, 129-142.
Mirande, A. M. Reference group theory and adolescent sexual behavior. *Journal of Marriage and the Family*, 1968, **30**, 572-577.
Mischel, W. *Personality and assessment*. New York: Wiley, 1968.
Murstein, B. I. Person perception and courtship progress among premarital couples. *Journal of Marriage and the Family*, 1972, **34**, 621-626.
Murstein, B. I. and Beck, G. D. Person perception, marriage adjustment and social desirability. *Journal of Consulting and Clinical Psychology*, 1972, **39**, 396-403.
Plummer, K. Images of pedophilia. In Cook, M. and Wilson, G. (Eds), *Love and attraction: an international conference*. Oxford: Pergamon, 1979.
Rapoport, R. The transition from engagement to marriage. *Acta Sociologica*, 1965, **8**, 3-55.
Rehm, L. P. and Marston, A. R. Reduction of social anxiety through modification of self-reinforcement: an instigation therapy technique. *Journal of Consulting and Clinical Psychology*, 1968, **32**, 565-574.
Reiss, I. L. Toward a sociology of the heterosexual love relationship. *Marriage and Family Living*, 1960, **22**, 139-145.

Reiss, I. L. *The social context of premarital permissiveness*. New York: Holt, 1967.
Rogel, M. J. A critical evaluation of the possibility of higher primate reproductive and sexual pheromones. *Psychological Bulletin*, 1978, **85**, 810-830.
Rosenblatt, P. C. Communication in the practice of love magic. *Social Forces*, 1971, **49**, 482-487.
Rosenthal, R. and DePaulo, B. M. Sex differences in eavesdropping on nonverbal cues. *Journal of Personality and Social Psychology*, 1979, **37**, 273-285.
Scheflen, A. Quasi courtship behavior in psychotherapy. *Psychiatry*, 1965, **28**, 245-257.
Schofield, M. *The sexual behaviour of young people*. London: Longmans, 1965.
Schutz, W. C. *FIRO: a three-dimensional theory of interpersonal behavior*. New York: Holt, 1958.
Shelley, D. S. A. and McKew, A. Pupillary dilation as a sexual signal and its links with adolescence. In Cook, M. and Wilson, G. (Eds), *Love and attraction: an international conference*. Oxford: Pergamon, 1979.
Skipper, J. K. and Nass, G. Dating behavior: a framework of analysis and an illustration. *Journal of Marriage and the Family*, 1966, **28**, 412-420.
Slater, E. and Woodside, M. *Patterns of marriage*. London: Cassell, 1951.
Steiner, I. D. Interpersonal behavior as influenced by accuracy of social perception. *Psychological Review*, 1955, **62**, 268-274.
Symonds, C. A vocabulary of sexual enticement. *Journal of Sex Research*, 1972, **8**, 136-139.
Tagiuri, R. Social preference and its perception. In Tagiuri, R. and Petrullo, L. (Eds), *Person perception and interpersonal behavior*. Stanford: Stanford University Press, 1958.
Tagiuri, R. Person perception. In Lindzey, G. and Aronson, E. (Eds), *Handbook of social psychology*. Vol. 3 (2nd edn). Reading, Mass: Addison Wesley, 1969.
Teevan, J. J. Reference groups and premarital sexual behavior. *Journal of Marriage and the Family*, 1972, **23**, 283-291.
Thornton, D. R. The effect of wearing glasses upon judgement of personality traits of persons seen briefly. *Journal of Applied Psychology*, 1944, **28**, 203-207.
Udry, J. R. Complementarity in mate selection: a perceptual approach. *Marriage and Family Living*, 1963, **25**, 281-289.
Vener, A. M., Stewart, C. S. and Hager, D. L. The sexual behavior of adolescents in Middle America: generational and American-British comparisons. *Journal of Marriage and the Family*, 1972, **34**, 696-705.
Walster, E. The effect of self-esteem on romantic liking. *Journal of Experimental Social Psychology*, 1965, **1**, 184-197.
Walster, E., Walster, G. W., Piliavin, J. and Schmidt, L. Playing hard to get: understanding an elusive phenomenon. *Journal of Personality and Social Psychology*, 1973, **26**, 113-121.

Weinstein, S. A. and Borok, K. The permissiveness of nurses' sexual attitudes: testing a stereotype. *Journal of Sex Research*, 1978, **14**, 54-58.

Wessberg, H. W., Mariotto, M. J., Conger, A. J., Farrell, A. D. and Conger, J. C. Ecological validity of role plays for assessing heterosexual anxiety and skill of male college students. *Journal of Consulting and Clinical Psychology*, 1979, **47**, 525-535.

Wildeblood, P. *A way of life*. London: Weidenfeld, 1956.

Williams, C. L. and Ciminero, A. R. Development and validation of a heterosocial skills inventory: the Survey of Heterosexual Interactions for Females. *Journal of Consulting and Clinical Psychology*, 1978, **46**, 1547-1548.

Zetterberg, H. L. The secret ranking. *Journal of Marriage and the Family*, 1971, **28**, 134-142.

Zuckerman, M. Physiological measures of sexual arousal in the human. *Psychological Bulletin*, 1971, **75**, 297-325.

6
Process, Filter and Stage Theories of Attraction

BERNARD I. MURSTEIN
*Department of Psychology, Connecticut College,
New London, Connecticut, USA*

If we disregard those quaint but scientifically wanting individuals who claim that the stars determine attraction, theorists of marital choice and interpersonal attraction may be classified into two camps which I will call "monolithic" and "complex". Monolithic theories are those in which a single principle predominates and seeks to explain all. The two most popular are "birds of a feather flock together" and "opposites attract", known better to students of marriage as similarity (homogamy) and complementarity. The fact that both theories used together can account for many relationships would be reassuring were it not for the fact that they contradict each other as all-embracing principles. The contradictions have been reconciled in other works (Murstein, 1971a, 1976). Our concern here is with the second class of theories, the complex ones, most of which can be classified as process theories.

Process theorists neither believe that there is a single explanation for attraction nor that attraction and relationships can be understood by measuring the traits of each individual in a dyad. They are concerned with *how* a relationship develops as much as, or more than, *what* traits or behaviours are involved. Process-filter theorists go a step further and posit that there are a series of "filters" operating so that those who fail the compatibility test at a point in time do not progress in their courtship to the next (deeper) stage of commitment. When these filters are viewed from a time framework, they may be called *stages*. In this chapter we shall describe briefly four process approaches which attempt conceptual clarification but have led to little if any research, and three theories which have been tested to some degree.

Theories that have not Generated Research

Bolton's Theory

Bolton was among the earliest of the process theorists; the flavour of his approach is captured by the following passage.

> the outcome (of courtship) is an end-product of a sequence of interactions characterized by advances and retreats along the paths of available alternatives, by definitions of the situation which crystallize tentative commitments and bar withdrawals from certain positions, by the sometimes tolerance and sometimes resolution of ambiguity, by reassessments of self and other, and by the tension between open-endedness and closure that characterize all human relations (Bolton, 1961, pp. 235-236).

Bolton goes on to describe different kinds of process patterns he calls *escalators* (situations with built-in momentum which, once started, convey the individual swiftly towards marriage). The *involvement* escalator results from interaction with the partner in so many varied and different ways (e.g. education, sex, recreational activities, daily schedule of coming and going, moral identity, and career plans), that the partner seems an intrinsic part of the individual's life almost without his volition. The *commitment* escalator can be interpersonal — going steady suggests love as the reason for the relationship, and love suggests engagement as the next step. Engagement adds public commitment to the interpersonal one and suggests early marriage. The *addiction* escalator might more properly be called "fear of isolation". The individual fears the withdrawal symptoms of exchanging "twoness" for isolation.

The *fantasy* escalator suggests that the individual compulsively adheres to the relationship as a symbol of a private fantasy or of the institutionally provided romantic one. The *idealization* escalator involves a worshipping of the other because an individual's self-esteem is united with the partner. Thus the more one can adore the fiancé and get others to do so, the greater the self-esteem. Finally, there is an *expediency* escalator (not formally listed by Bolton), which involves unexpected events, such as pregnancy, which speed up movement toward marriage.

Rapoport's Theory

Rapoport (1964) and Rapoport and Rapoport (1964, 1965, 1968) have described the courtship process as composed of nine tasks.
1. Establishing an identity as a couple.
2. Developing a mutually satisfactory sexual adjustment for the engagement period.

3. Developing a mutually satisfactory orientation to family planning.
4. Establishing a mutually satisfactory mode of communication.
5. Establishing satisfactory relations with others.
6. Developing a mutually satisfactory work pattern.
7. Developing a mutually satisfactory leisure pattern.
8. Developing a mutually satisfactory plan for the wedding and early marriage.
9. Establishing a mutually satisfactory decision-making pattern (Rapoport and Rapoport, 1965, p. 390).

No elaboration is given with respect to sequence, nor are there data bearing on the solution of these tasks to courtship progress.

Reiss' Theory

None of the aforementioned approaches is sufficiently structured to warrant being called a theory rather than an approach. Reiss (1960), however, has presented a scaffold of a theory which takes into account sequence as well as content. His wheel theory contains four spokes as shown in Fig. 1. The initial process is called *rapport*. When two people meet (the theory could apply to any kind of relationship, not only to marital choice), they quickly come to an assessment of the rapport that exists between them. They sense the degree to which they feel comfortable with, interested in, and understood by the other. To Reiss the degree of rapport is generally largely predictable, given knowledge of the social and cultural background of the two individuals.

If a feeling of mutual rapport exists, it leads to a feeling of relaxation, which encourages the onset of the second process, that of *self-revelation*. The individuals in this stage proceed to reveal intimate facts and feelings about themselves. Here, too, according to Reiss, the social and cultural factors point out the reason for differences. Some groups are socialized to talk readily on first dates, whereas others are taught to be more reserved. In Reiss' view, males are taught to reveal sexual intimacies to females earlier than females are generally ready to accept them, resulting often in the "battle of the sexes".

Self-revelation in turn leads to *mutual dependency*, or interdependent habit systems. Each member of the couple becomes conditioned to the other as a source of reward for many activities and behaviours: sexual partner, companion, and audience for the expression of feelings as well as for the recounting of personal triumphs and failures. These habits also are culturally determined according to Reiss.

The fourth and final stage, also culturally determined, is *personality*

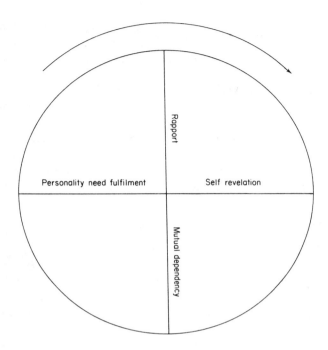

Fig. 1. *Graphic presentation of the wheel theory of the development of love (after Reiss, 1960, p. 143)*

need fulfilment, which includes the need to love, to confide in someone, and to stimulate one's ambition. The wheel may spiral several times, leading to increased rapport at each revolution, which leads to increased self-revelation, etc. It may also unwind in that an argument may lead to less rapport, which may discourage self-revelation, which may, in turn, detract from developing a continuing mutual dependency, which may inhibit personality need fulfilment, which may further destroy rapport, and so on. (The analogy is a little forced here. To unwind ought to signify going in an opposite or counterclockwise direction. But "unwinding" follows the same path as "winding".)

Reiss admits that much of the theory is tentative but claims that he has found some support for an aspect of the theory in a little survey that he conducted with 74 college students. These students received a sheet containing ten needs and were asked to list as many as they thought were important. Some needs showed little sex difference. For example, 60% of the boys listed needed someone to confide in, and 65% of the girls listed this need as important.

On the other hand, only 22% of the boys needed someone to look up to very much, whereas 70% of the girls scored this need as important. These findings are taken as supportive of the importance of cultural background in determining need fulfilment. Reiss further notes that Wheel Theory "seems to be capable of accounting for and interpreting much of the available field research on love relationships" (1960, p. 144).

I must confess, however, that I cannot see how Reiss' data and the Wheel Theory can account for any research evidence on love relationships. Though the sequence he postulates seems reasonable, the theory as stated is very vague and imprecise, and it lacks empirical data. That cultural factors influence the four stages will not be contested by very many, but this is hardly confirmation of the theory.

Huston (1974) independently has seemingly come to a similar conclusion about the theory. He has remarked that Reiss

> fails to adduce supporting evidence for the developmental sequence he describes or to link the stage of the relationship either theoretically or empirically to the strength and character of the love bond. Moreover, Reiss fails to consider factors which qualify or modify the supposed developmental process. It would be interesting to know, for example, the conditions under which self-revelation does and does not lead to the development of interdependent habits (p. 19).

Transitional Process Theory

Ryder *et al.* (1971) have proposed a *transitional process* model and have used it to characterize the ways in which people get married. According to Ryder *et al.*, the model may also be useful for describing other transitions such as divorce or having a child, but its principal function is to describe the social process by which people move from acquaintance-ship to marriage. There is an emphasis on third party influences, i.e. influence from individuals other than the two partners, such as friends or relatives. These third parties may exert a *joining* or a *separative* effect on the prospective couple. Stages in the transitional process are, in fact, defined by changes in the effects of these third party influences. The process begins with an *initiation* point, followed by stages of *latency*, *precommitment*, and *commitment*, which is then followed by the *transition point*, and the stage of *readjustment*.

Initiation is characterized by the joining effect of third parties. In short, friends or relatives tend to bring people together. While there are a number of examples in which this is obvious, even in those cases which seem to involve only the two partners, third parties turn out to have an

effect that may not be immediately apparent. For example, young people often go in groups to meet people at singles bars, or one individual might approach another after some urging from peers, or a peer might laud a potential partner's attractive features.

The subsequent stage of *latency* is also characterized by the *joining* effects of friends and relatives. Moreover, both initiation and latency seem to be characterized by a certain unexceptional quality, by an apparent lack of serious implications. Love at first sight is notable by its infrequent occurrence, and in the early development of a relationship, there seems to be little anticipation that the couple will really get married. According to Ryder *et al.* (1971), the apparently unexceptional nature of latency events is not just a coincidence, but may be an important facilitative feature of the transitional process. An apparent lack of serious implications may be one of the things that encourages the couple to interact and become more close, leading, paradoxically, to serious implications. Therefore the period of latency includes a feeling of relative freedom. Individuals seem to feel that the relationship can be ended at any time without serious consequences.

When it becomes apparent that the couple are likely to get married, the *precommitment* stage begins. This is the time in which there is a struggle over the relationship. It is the portion of the courtship that is usually characterized as romantic in the sense of lovers fighting to maintain their relationship in the face of external opposition. Assuming that the opposition is only external to the couple, it tends to come from friends and relatives. The same third parties who may have facilitated the relationship earlier, or at least not hindered it, may now be separative in their actions. Ryder *et al.* (1971) describe cases in which parents have introduced young people to each other only to oppose their relationship later when marriage became a possibility. Close friends and room-mates are likely to come forward during this time with negative information about a prospective partner's character or morality. Sometimes a room-mate will "protect" a young woman from having to talk to her partner, who may have come over to make up from an earlier argument. A message sent to one partner from the other by way of intermediaries is sometimes delivered in a distorted way, or not at all. Partners will be urged to wait until they have finished college, or got a job, or have had a chance to look around at other prospective partners. The closer a person is tied to some friend or relative, the more likely that friend or relative is to be opposed to the prospective transition.

Usually the precommitment stage ends in some kind of resolution.

Either the couple is separated, in which case the transitional process is over, or the opposition is given up, and it is agreed that the transition will take place, i.e. that the couple will get married. When such a resolution occurs, the stage of *commitment* has begun. During commitment, friends and relatives again change orientation and become joining in their effect. Concern shifts from *whether* or not there will be a transition to *how* the transition might best be arranged. There is no longer a feeling of freedom, a feeling that one can step out of the process if one wishes. Instead there tends to be a feeling that one is being swept along inexorably toward marriage. Confirming activities by friends and relatives are frequent, i.e. there are frequent instances of the two partners being treated as a single social unit. They are invited to places together, treated as a couple when present at social gatherings, and so on. Partners trying to move out of the process into other relationships may find themselves refused because they are "taken".

The importance of the *transition point* itself, the wedding ceremony and feast, tends to divert the couple from looking either backward or forward. Here, as in the commitment stage, parents are in effect trying to cut their losses, to incorporate the couple as best they can into the family.

After the wedding, there is the stage of *readjustment*. During readjustment, it is necessary to distinguish between individual and couple ties to third parties. Friendships and kin ties that are primarily to one spouse or the other tend to be separative and are reduced to some extent by almost all spouses. Ties that are primarily to the couple as a couple are *joining* and may be sought after by the couple almost as a felt obligation. Ties with parents during this period of time are somewhat more complicated, since they are sometimes overtly dyadic in nature, dealing with the couple as a couple, but covertly, or at a more subtle level, individual in nature. For example, a couple might socialize with the wife's parents, but conversation might develop in such a way that leaves the husband feeling left out, or that he or his parents have been slighted. Gift-giving from parents in the time shortly after marriage is described as substantial but is often *separative* in the sense that there is some felt competition as to whose parents have been the most generous. Almost invariably, couples claim to be independent in the sense that they do not feel the parents are doing anything exceptional in helping them, and they tend not to feel any obligation to their parents in return for their largesse.

Thus the Transitional Process Model presents courtship as a kind of struggle between *joining* and *separative* influences, largely coming from friends and relatives. Unlike most other views of this period of time, it

presents a social view, almost totally ignoring the internal psychology of prospective partners. It suggests, in effect, that new relationships tend to be disruptive of earlier relationships and, to some extent, opposed by those involved in these earlier relationships. Transitions, therefore, tend to get started almost in a subversive way, with serious consequences not clearly perceived by those who might otherwise oppose them. There is thus set up a kind of alternation effect such that third parties are joining in their influence when no transition is in prospect, *separative* when the transition is a possibility, and *joining* again when the transition is a perceived certainty, and they attempt to make the best arrangement possible with the forthcoming new relationship. This interesting model has not as yet been the focus of any research.

Kerckhoff and Davis' Theory

The first process theory to have garnered some empirical support was that of Kerckhoff and Davis (1962). They hypothesized a filter process in which, after an initial screening for homogamously cultural variables, a further selection of eligible spouses takes place on the basis of homogamy of values (value consensus) and complementarity. They collected a sample of 97 Duke University female college students, all of whom were engaged, "pinned", or "seriously attached". The woman received her test packet, filled it out, and her boyfriend was mailed the same questionnaire.The questionnaire data included Farber's "index of consensus", a task involving the ranking of ten standards of family success (Farber, 1957). By correlating the ranks of each member of the couple, a Spearman rank coefficient of correlation could be obtained for the couple. The more positive and higher the correlation, the greater the value consensus of the couple.

A second test germane to the present discussion was the Schutz FIRO-B test (1958). This test yielded a score called "reciprocal compatibility", defined as

$$|e_M - w_F| \quad + \quad |e_F - w_M|$$

where e stands for the behaviour that an individual wants to express *vis-à-vis* others, and w stands for the behaviour he wishes others to express toward him. The subscripts M and F stand for male and female. Perfect reciprocal compatibility occurs when the absolute difference of the behaviour the man wishes to express and the woman wants from him

equals zero, and the behaviour she wishes to express subtracted from that which he wants from her also equals zero.

About seven months after the initial testing, the subjects were mailed a brief questionnaire that in essence asked them how well their courtship had fared. They were given three choices. Those answering "We are nearer to being a permanent couple" (56 couples) were regarded as having made good courtship progress. Those who answered that their relationship was the same as seven months earlier or that they were further apart (38 couples) were regarded as not making courtship progress. Only 3 of the 97 couples for whom the original usable data had been collected were lost in the interim. Each of the variables, "value consensus" and three compatibility scores, "inclusion", "control", and "affection", were dichotomized as close to the median as possible.

Tests of significance were made by comparing the proportion of couples within each variable who were "high" and made courtship progress with those who were "low" and made progress.

For example, of those high in value consensus, about 73% made courtship progress, whereas of those low on value consensus, only about 46% did so. This difference was quite significant ($p < 0.01$). None of the three measures of compatibility was significant, although a trend was apparent in two of the three cases.

The most interesting finding occurred when couples were divided into those who had known each other for at least 18 months (long-term) and those who had gone together less than 18 months (short-term). Under these conditions, value consensus was associated with courtship progress for short-term relationships but not for long-term ones. For short-term relationships, high compatibility is not related to courtship progress in any of the three areas. However, for long-term relationships two of the three high compatibility scores are related to courtship progress.

It very much looks as if a filter effect was operating. For individuals in short-term relationships, value consensus seems to serve as a filter to screen out most couples whose members operate on a different set of values. By the time the courtship has persisted for some months, those couples who are going to split over differences in values generally will have done so. From then on (couples are now considered "long-term"), dissimilarity of values is no longer predictive of break-up. At this point, differentiation on the basis of psychological compatibility takes over, and those that have it are more likely to make better progress than those who do not.

The Kerckhoff and Davis (1962) results were rightly hailed as an

exciting advance in the study of marital choice. Although widely cited and reprinted, their work was not replicated for a considerable number of years. When the replication was done in two different places — the Universities of Massachusetts and Colorado (Levinger *et al.*, 1970) — high value consensus couples showed no greater courtship progress than low value consensus couples.

The heart of the matter lay in the differences between long- and short-term relationships. Kerckhoff and Davis found that for short-term relationships high value consensus was associated with courtship progress, with long-term relationships yielding a higher proportion of courtship progress for couples with high psychological compatibility. The Levinger *et al.* (1970) study did not support these findings.

In the Massachusetts sample, *long-term* (not short-term) relationships manifesting high value consensus showed more progress in courtship than did the low value consensus group — just the opposite of the findings with the Kerckhoff and Davis group. The Colorado sample showed even greater change. Here, as in Massachusetts, the long-term relationships showed significance instead of the short-term relationships, but the *low* value consensus group showed more progress than did the high value consensus group.

In the earlier study, in long-term relationships high compatibility couples showed a significantly greater percentage of courtship progress in two of the three areas studied. In the Levinger *et al.* (1970) study, the Colorado sample showed no significant findings for any of the three areas, whereas the Massachusetts sample showed significance in only one of the three areas.

Levinger *et al.* (1970) attribute the failure to replicate the earlier findings to the changing *mores* in the courtship culture in the approximately seven years intervening between the data collection of the two articles, the use of different samples, and the failure to employ couple-centred instead of individual-centred measures. However, they offer no evidence to buttress these speculations. Speculations aside, the fact remains that research on the Kerckhoff–Davis filter theory has yielded mixed results.

Lewis' Premarital Dyadic Formation Theory

Believing that a theory of marital choice is too difficult, Lewis limits himself to a theory of premarital dyadic formation. He posits six pair processes that "modal, middle-class, American couples progressively

experience through their dating and courtship careers" (Lewis, 1972, p. 22). These processes and their subdivisions are as follows:

A. The achievement by pairs of perceiving similarities in each other's
1. sociocultural background,
2. values,
3. interests,
4. personality.

B. The achievement of pair rapport, as evidenced in a pair's
1. ease of communication,
2. positive evaluations of the other,
3. satisfaction with pair relationships,
4. validation of self by the other.

C. The achievement of openness between partners through a mutual self-disclosure.

D. The achievement of role-taking accuracy.

E. The achievement of interpersonal role-fit, as evidenced by a pair's
1. observed similarity of personalities,
2. role complementarity,
3. need complementarity.

F. The achievement of dyadic crystallization, as evidenced by a pair's
1. progressive involvement,
2. functioning as a dyad,
3. boundary establishment,
4. commitment to each other,
5. identity as a couple.

(Lewis, 1972, p. 23).

A principal notion underlying Lewis' theory is that the success for a given process depends upon the successful fulfilment of the one immediately preceding it. Thus, those couples who have successfully achieved the first (A) (*similarity perception*) process, may be expected later on to achieve greater *pair rapport* (Process B) than those couples who have not successfully achieved Process A (they are low on similarity perception). All six processes may operate to some measure during the course of a successful relationship, but there is an optimal period of functioning for each variable.

Testing the Theory

Questionnaire data were collected at Time 1 from 173 dating couples, of whom at least one of each couple was a University of Minnesota student. Two years later (Time 2), attempts were made to reach the 346 students by telephone, and 314 were actually reached. Of the 173 couples, 58 had broken up; the mean number of months since break-up was 21. A 14-page questionnaire containing measures relating to the six processes described earlier was mailed to one partner; those who had broken up were told to reply to the question in terms of the month prior to the separation. On the return of the first questionnaire, an identical one was mailed to the partner. Subjects were asked not to collaborate on the answers, but no safeguards were instituted to prevent possible collusion.

A total of 91 complete couples' data was utilized in the analysis (53% of the original sample), of which some 30 couples had dissolved their relationships. This group was presumably fairly well through the early stages called for by the theory, in that 24% were formally engaged at the time of the first contact, and 60% had some commitment toward marriage. Somewhat rashly, Lewis states that the attrition rate failed to influence the longitudinal analyses. "For instance, differences in social and interpersonal characteristics, produced by respondent attrition, were negligible" (Lewis, 1973, p. 20). No documentation is made of this fact, however, and as Rubin and Levinger (1974) point out, since no data were collected from those bowing out prior to Time 2, it is impossible to check the validity of Lewis' claim.

The heart of the analysis involved testing the prediction that couples who had successfully moved through a task within Process A at Time 1 would also show high accomplishment for a task within Process B at Time 2. Couples who had not successfully resolved the given task at Process A, Time 1, should also be deficient in accomplishment for a task for Process B, Time 2.

I have used the language employed by Lewis to acquaint the reader with the path of his deductions. However, operationally speaking, what Lewis hypothesized was that, for example, if couples are trichotomized (both persons high, one person high, no persons high) for success for Process A, Time 1, the high group(s) should also be high for Process B, Time 2. Also, continuing couples, similarly, ought to score higher from Time 1 to Time 2 than dissolved couples.

Of a series of tests for differences in behaviour from Time 1 to Time 2, four out of 24 predictions were significant at the 0·05 level or better.

Differences between the continuing and dissolved groups were much more pronounced. Of 28 tests, 23 were significant. A further analysis showed that the Time 1 scores of continuing couples were significantly better than those of dissolved couples in eight out of ten tests computed.

The results lead Lewis to conclude that his data support the assumption "that a process which functions as a selection-rejection process at one stage of dyadic development may not be as salient at another stage" (1973, p. 24). A thorough analysis of the theory and data, however, indicates many problems.

Criticisms

Theory

Wolfe (1973) remarks that the theory is a checklist.

> After completing all six tasks, not only is the couple ready to get married, but it would seem that they never need return to these tasks again — that they become a permanent characteristic of the relationship. (If this were so, people would never get divorced) (p. 2).

Wolfe also noted that the theory does not explain the mechanisms by which the stages are achieved and is thus a process theory only in the sense "that the couple 'proceeds' from one item on the checklist to another" (p. 2).

Another difficulty is that the order of the sequence of six steps is not explained. Rubin and Levinger (1974) ask

> Why . . . should the achievement of pair rapport precede the development of role-taking accuracy, rather than vice versa? Or why should the perception of similarities come before rather than after the induction of mutual self-disclosure? (p. 229).

Yet another problem is that no information is given as to when one of the processes ends and the other begins. The failure of the theory to deal with a rationale for the sequence might be sidestepped somewhat by empirical support for the theory, but the data fail to do this. Why?

Research

The difficulty with Lewis' research may be illustrated by the reference to Table I which is a slightly modified version of Table 2 from Lewis (1973). The table indicates that couples who had scored better (higher) on Validation of Self (Process B) at Time 1 also scored better (lower) on

Table I
Mean scores for post-test achievement of openness* (stage C), grouped by validation of self by other (stage B-4) (after Lewis, 1973, p. 21)

	Both persons	High in Validation One person	Neither person
Post-test openness of continuing couples	15·0	20·7	21·7
Post-test openness of dissolved couples	16·2	23·0	23·6

*High scores indicate low degree of openness.

Openness (Process C) at Time 2. Lewis takes this finding as supportive of his theory, but a simpler explanation will account for his findings perfectly well. At the time of initial testing, many of the couples had been going together seriously for some time and were very close. Most of them would eventually become the "continuing" group. Let us suppose that other couples had been going together, but either intended no commitment toward marriage, or found their relationship to be in the doldrums — though still intact. These persons were destined to constitute the future "dissolved" group.

When the future continuing group was tested at Time 1, it scored higher on most of the tasks from Processes A through F than did the future dissolved group; sometimes a difference was significant, sometimes not, but a trend to do better on the tasks was generally noticeable. The subjects were retested at Time 2. Most of the subjects who had originally scored well at Time 1, were continuing their relationship (continuing group) and, *mirabile dictu*, they continued to score well at Time 2 for Processes A through F. Couples who had initially had a poor relationship generally would be expected to break up and become the dissolved group. Looking back at their relationship in the month preceding the break-up, it would be hardly surprising to assume that they perceived themselves as having done poorly in the various processes.

The simplest assumption therefore would be that the continuing group did better than the dissolved group on *all* of the processes. If this were true, then the Lewis theory would obviously be fulfilled but would have little significance. We would expect the continuing group to do better than the dissolved group not only on Process B at Time 1 and Process C at Time 2, but also on the converse, Process C at Time 1 and Process B at Time 2. The latter prediction would not be in accordance with Lewis'

theory, but would accord with the simpler explanation that continuing couples show consistency over two years' time. Had Lewis done such converse analyses, he might have strengthened the support for his theory. As it stands now, however, his analyses do not test the theory.

The same problem occurs with his report that continuing couples did better than dissolved couples on a number of tests at Time 1, when all couples were intact. By way of analogy, suppose we give a group of married couples a series of questionnaires about how well they relate. Two years later we find a number of them have divorced, while others have intact marriages. Going into the background of these subjects we find, not surprisingly, that at the original time of testing the subsequently divorced couples had been unhappy, quarrelled often, and evinced little empathy for their partners; those with intact marriages, in comparison, had been happier, had fewer quarrels, and showed more sensitivity to their partners. This finding would hardly qualify as supportive of any theory — it would simply be common sense.

The fact that some of the subjects were tested long after the relationship had broken up — conceivably as much as two years afterwards — presents a thorny problem with regard to the validity of responses. Remember that the dissolved couples were asked to describe the relationship in the month prior to the break-up. In addition to the fact that some details might merely be forgotten over a period of time, the more serious problem remains of individuals trying to justify a broken relationship. It would scarcely be surprising for them to lessen self-responsibility, to denigrate the partner somewhat, or simply to distort the ongoing process between the two, in order to make these details consistent with the *fait accompli* of dissolution.

Finally, the use of three-by-two analysis of variance as reproduced in Table I was technically ill-advised. A significant difference was reported between the validation groups, but these group differences could have been significant and yet the theory would neither be supported nor completely rejected. Suppose the mean for "both persons high in validation" were 20, for "one person high" 60, and for "neither person high" 20. This distribution would probably result in a significant F test, but would hardly support the theory. The reason is that the F test does not take into account the *order* of the means, but such consideration is necessary for Lewis' theory. It is not clear from Lewis' article (1973) whether the monotonicity of the groups' means (that "both members of a couple high" had to have the highest mean, "one member high" had to be second highest, and "no member high" had to be lowest)

was taken into account. If not, the F test was not testing the theory. In conclusion, Lewis' data do not adequately test his theory. This in no way invalidates it. However, theories that prove to be untestable or untested generally lose favour rapidly.

Stimulus–Value–Role Theory

This theory is a combination of a basic underlying factor accounting for the formation of relationships (exchange) and a parallel focus on the development of the relationship through three stages. Since it is impossible to describe the theory adequately by dealing with only its developmental aspects, it will be described in its entirety.

Stimulus–Value–Role (SVR) Theory is a general theory of the development of dyadic relationships. Designed initially to account for courtship, it has been extended with slight modification to account for friendship and husband–wife relationships as well (Murstein, 1971a, 1976).

It is an exchange theory, positing that when there is relative freedom of choice, attraction and interaction depend on the exchange value of the assets and liabilities that each of the parties brings to the encounter. The kinds of variables that influence the course of development of the relationship can be classified under three categories: stimulus, value comparison, and role. These variables operate during the entire course of courtship, but they are posited to be maximally influential at different stages of the courtship. Each of the three stages reflects, by its name, the kind of variables most influential during that period (e.g. stimulus variables are most influential in the stimulus stage).

The chief concern here will be the theory's ability to explain marital choice. However a theory of attraction to a dyadic relationship cannot aspire to perfect accuracy in predicting marital choice for a number of reasons. First, the search for a marital partner is often highly competitive. Individuals with a large number of interpersonal assets generally have many potentially marriageable partners. It is possible therefore that any given relationship in which they are involved may be highly successful, but their other relationships, not examined, may be even more successful. Focusing on a given relationship therefore, might distort the conclusions about the probability of the relationship terminating in marriage.

Secondly, individuals differ in their desire to marry. An individual who values marriage as a status very highly may be less stringent in his

requirements for dyadic compatibility than an individual who is not eager to rush into matrimony.

Although society has traditionally educated its youth to expect that close heterosexual dyadic relationships between unmarried youths will terminate in marriage, it is evident that more individuals than previously are courting longer and cohabiting without the benefit of matrimony. An increasing number (though still but a small fraction of the population) speak of having a close monogamous relationship without marriage. These factors, too, contribute to the imperfectness of dyadic closeness as a prognosticator of marriage.

Other factors influencing the incidence of marriage are timing, critical incidents, and the social network. "The right person at the wrong time" is a complaint often made by individuals who met highly compatible individuals at a time when they were not ready for marriage. Critical incidents such as a job transfer of one member of the couple to another city may precipitate marriage in some courtship couples but terminate it in others, depending on the developmental stage of the relationship. Finally, the social network: the relatives, friends, business associates of the couples may influence courtship by providing rewards or punishments which influence couple viability.

Courtship may be likened to a slowly accelerating conveyor belt whose destination is matrimony. An individual may jump off relatively easily in the early stages of courtship, but as the destination is approached it becomes rather hazardous, interpersonally speaking, to jump off — there would be a great deal of disappointment and embarrassment in explaining the circumstances to everybody. Depending on the pressure applied by the particular network and the courage of the individual, some individuals may be "conveyed" into marriage despite a late discovery of less than desirable compatibility. These various factors contribute to the conclusion that dyadic compatibility and marital choice are not synonymous. Nevertheless they are sufficiently correlated so that an understanding of heterosexual dyad formation can lead to an understanding of marital choice.

Exchange in Courtship

Essentially, an exchange approach maintains that each person tries to make social interaction as profitable as possible; *profit* being defined as the rewards he gains from the interaction minus the costs he must pay (Thibaut and Kelly, 1959). By *rewards* are meant the pleasures, benefits,

and gratifications an individual gains from a relationship. *Costs* are factors which inhibit or deter the performance of more preferred behaviours. A young man living in the Bronx, for example, might like a young lady from Brooklyn whom he met while both were at a resort. Back in the city, however, he may doubt that the rewards he might gain from the relationship would be worth the costs in time, and fatigue and danger of two-hour subway rides to Brooklyn.

Closely allied to rewards and costs are assets and liabilities. *Assets* are commodities (behaviours or qualities) that the individual possesses which are capable of rewarding the individual. *Liabilities* are behaviours or qualities associated with an individual which are costly to others.

A man who is physically unattractive (liability), for example, might desire a woman who has the asset of beauty. Assuming, however, that his non-physical qualities are no more rewarding than hers, she gains less profit than he does from the relationship, and thus his suit is likely to be rejected. Rejection is a cost to him because it may lower his self-esteem and increase his fear of failure in future encounters; hence he may decide to avoid attempting to court women whom he perceives as much above him in attractiveness.

Contrariwise he is likely to feel highly confident of success if he tries to date a woman even less attractive than himself where he risks little chance of rejection (low cost). However the reward value of such a conquest is quite low, so that the profitability of such a move is also low. As a consequence, an experienced individual is likely to express a maximum degree of effort and also obtain the greatest reward at the least cost when he directs his efforts at someone of approximately equal physical attractiveness, assuming all other variables are constant.

Couples need not be Matched on the Same Variable

It is not necessary, however, for equity of physical attractiveness to be present in order for a viable relationship to occur. Given that a man and woman are sufficiently acquainted with each others' respective assets and liabilities, it becomes possible for the less attractive member to compensate for his "weakness" in a number of ways. Suppose, for example, that the man is unattractive and the woman is attractive. He might render services to his partner far above what she gives him, waiting on her hand and foot. Consistent with this thesis is a study by Dermer (1973) which reports that the greater a woman's attractiveness, the longer the vacations she expects to take when married, and the fewer hours she expects to work to supplement her husband's income.

The attractive woman "pays" the man back through the status she confers on him by being with him, a cost (loss of status) she incurs in being seen with an unattractive man. Berscheid and Walster (1974), reviewing the literature, have indicated that individuals perceived to associate with physically attractive persons gain in the esteem in which they are held by others, whereas those persons consorting with unattractive partners lose status. The outsider looking only at the physical attractiveness of the couple may find them terribly unbalanced with regard to their exchange value and wonder what she possibly sees in him. The people who know the couple well, however, know that she exploits him miserably and wonder why he puts up with it. Yet the situation is balanced if all of the variables are taken into consideration.

No mention has been made thus far of the status accruing to an individual solely on the basis of his sex, but men in our society have traditionally enjoyed a greater social, economic, and political status than women (Murstein, 1974a). These advantages may be eroding, but they have not disappeared altogether. It follows therefore that men should be able to utilize this greater status to extract benefits prior to and during marriage. A physically unattractive man should find it somewhat easier to marry than a physically unattractive woman, and the United States statistics for 1969 indicated that for every 100 men and 100 women aged fifteen years and older, 31·4 men were married as compared to 28·9 women (Vital Health Statistics, 1972).

The complexities and limits of exchange theory have been discussed elsewhere in great detail (Murstein, 1980). Concern about equity of exchange is said to be a function of at least four important variables: (a) the exchange orientation of the individual, (b) the equality of the relationship, (c) the degree of intimacy involved, and (d) the perceived profitability of the intended behaviour. By and large, equity of exchange is held to be more influential in *attraction* of individuals to each other and in the *developmental* phases of a relationship than in *maintaining* an already established relationship. In the last named case, extradyadic and interpersonal factors may maintain a relationship in which equity of exchange has broken down. Thus exchange is more important in understanding why people marry than in why they stay married.

The Stimulus, Value and Role Stages

To understand the second basic concern of SVR theory, the development of the stages of courtship, a few words must be said about the locus in

which the relationship unfolds. This context may be categorized into "open" and "closed" fields.

An "open field" encounter is one in which the man and woman do not as yet know each other or have only a nodding acquaintance. Examples of such "open fields" are "mixers", a large school class at the beginning of the semester, and brief contacts in the office. (A "mixer" is an American social dance in which individuals or dormitory houses may participate. The participants do not come in couples, the idea being that one samples the field and changes partners frequently until a suitable partner is found; hence one "mixes" oneself among many possible partners.) The fact that the field is "open" indicates that either the man or the woman is free to start the relationship or abstain from initiating it, as they wish. The contrary concept is the "closed field" in which both the man and woman are forced to relate in some manner by reason of the roles assigned to them by the environmental setting in which they find themselves. Example of "closed fields" might be that of students in a small seminar in a college, members of a "Peace Corps" unit, and workers in a political campaign. This interaction generally enables the individual to become acquainted with the behaviour of the "other", which is then evaluated according to the individual's own system of values. This system is a compendium of values acquired in the process of acculturalization to the traditional or current tastes of society; values acquired from one's peers and parents; values derived from experience; and values resulting from genetically based predispositions, which may be labelled "temperament".

Individuals of course may be attracted to members of the opposite sex without necessarily contemplating marriage. The fact that almost all persons in the United States eventually marry, however, suggests that many of the heterosexual social encounters of young adults contain at least the possibility of eventual marriage; consequently, the general heterosexual encounter has been treated as the first step toward possible marriage.

Stimulus Stage

When two members of the opposite sex are in an open field (for example, a "mixer" dance) there generally has been a considerable amount of incidental screening which has eliminated many of the maritally non-eligible persons. If the "mixer" is held on a college campus, for example, attendance may be restricted to college students. Such students not only

reflect educational homogeneity, but they are apt to show greater than chance similarity on variables which are correlated with education: socio-economic status, age, intelligence, and, to some extent, values. There remains nevertheless sufficient variability with respect to some other variables for an active selective process. Variables such as physical attractiveness, temperament and sex-drive, have undergone very little selectivity through the factors which bring individuals to college, and so interpersonal encounters between the sexes may continue to result in widely varying responses from joy to repulsion.

There is ample evidence that initial impressions in dating depend largely on physical attractiveness (Berscheid and Walster, 1974). The importance of physical attractiveness resides in its being highly valued by society as a status-conferring asset, and in the fact that it is the only evidence of potential viability of the relationship prior to interaction. Moreover, all kinds of desirable personality and intellectual attributes are ascribed to the beautiful. They are viewed as "more sensitive, kind, interesting, strong, poised, modest, sociable, outgoing, and exciting . . . more sexual, warm, and responsive than unattractive persons" (Berscheid and Walster, 1972, pp. 46 and 74).

Initial impressions are not wholly dependent on the senses, however. An individual's stimulus value may also include information about his reputation or professional aspirations, which precede him into the initial contact. That Ronald Rabbitfoot is a star running back football player for Podunk University may compensate for his less than classic Greek profile.

In sum, initial judgements are formed on the basis of perceptions of the other and/or information about him. These may be obtained without any interpersonal contact whatsoever, or on the basis of brief introductions. It is questionable how much such initial impressions correlate with subsequent marital happiness. Nevertheless the stimulus stage is of crucial importance in the open field, for, if the other person does not possess sufficient stimulus impact to attract the individual, further contact is not sought. The "prospect" in question might make a potentially exemplary, compatible spouse, he might manifest value consensus and superb role compatibility with the perceiver, but the perceiver, foregoing opportunities for further contact, may never find this out. Consequently, persons with low stimulus attractiveness (especially those who are physically unattractive) are at a considerable handicap in an open field.

Because physical attractiveness is so highly valued, it would seem

logical that each individual would seek the most attractive partner available when information about the other characteristics is not available. Enjoyment of a date when interaction has been relatively brief also would probably be mainly contingent on the attractiveness of one's partner.

There is evidence that this is the case when either of two conditions exist: (a) the individuals have relatively little experience in dating and have not undergone the costs of rejection; and (b) an experimental paradigm is constructed in which the individual is more or less guaranteed a date (Berscheid and Walster, 1974; Huston, 1973). However, not everyone is physically attractive. If everyone could only be satisfied with a Venus or an Apollo most of us would be celibates. Obviously many of us choose someone less attractive than our ideal preference. This choice, it is postulated, follows the equity of exchange principle. Individuals of equal attractiveness possess equal rewarding power in the absence of other information, and would tend to be drawn to each other pending further information about the other.

Value Comparison Stage

If a couple approximates equality in their stimulus variables, that is if the weighted amalgam of each individual's perceived stimulus attributes (physical attractiveness, status, poise, voice, etc.) is approximately equal, they may progress to the second (value comparison) stage of courtship. It is impossible to fix a specific time limit for passage from one stage to another because the importance of each stage and kinds and rate of interaction between individuals will vary from couple to couple.

Figure 2, however, presents a series of theoretical average curves for the importance and duration of the three variables. The curves in Fig. 2, strictly speaking, apply separately to each member of the couple. It is possible for one member of the couple to be in the stimulus stage, whereas his partner is in the value comparison stage. For example he may be reacting primarily to her physical attractiveness, and she may have queried him on what he thought about women's liberation, equal careers, and childless marriage. He may not have found out much about her values, so that a disparity exists not only with regard to what each considers important in the relationship, but also with regard to the stage of courtship each is in. This disparity is not necessarily inimical to the relationship so long as each is highly rewarded by the relationship.

For many couples however the deepening of the relationship advances

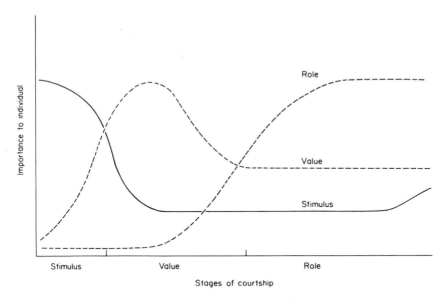

Fig. 2. *Stages of courtship in SVR Theory. (From Murstein, 1976, p. 123. Reproduced with the kind permission of Springer-Verlag.)*

in mutual fashion, and reciprocity in social penetration is typical. When she asks about his values, she may in turn supply her own views on the topic in question, or he may ask her about these views. Thus most couples should show some correspondence of movement through the various stages.

The termination of the stimulus stage may be defined as occurring at the point in the relationship when the stimulus variables, as a group, become less important to the relationship than the value comparison variables. Passage from the stimulus to the value comparison stage might occur in a matter of hours or it might take some weeks. It is also conceivable that such passage might not occur, but we shall deal with this eventuality when we have completed our description of the three stages of courtship.

The label "value comparison" has been used for want of a better name. I use the term value more as an inclusive rubric rather than in the narrow sense of the term. I infer under this term interests, attitudes, beliefs and even needs when they are seen as emanating from beliefs. The primary focus of the value comparison stage, in short, is the gathering of information by verbal interaction with the other.

Verbal interaction will surely be an important feature of the role stage,

which succeeds the value comparison stage. But in the role stage, the emphasis will be more on the dyadic relationship and will include commitment positions regarding depth of feeling for the other and desire for permanency, confirmation of the self-image, and accuracy in predicting the feelings and perceptions of the other.

The value comparison stage occurs when the couple has not as yet developed sufficient intimacy to learn and confess the innermost percepts, fears, aspirations, and concerns that each has. Nevertheless, there is much public and private information that each learns about the other in this period. Information is gleaned about religious orientation; political beliefs; attitudes towards people, parents, friends; interests in sports, the arts, dancing and the like.

The rate of progress through the value comparison stage depends on the rate of social penetration (Altman and Taylor, 1973). The couple exhibit increasingly larger areas of what they think and feel. They evaluate their comfortableness, the acceptance of what they reveal, and the effect of their disclosure on their partner's behaviour. In a successful relationship, the partner evinces acceptance of the values of the individual and discloses his own values. Self-disclosure among individuals promotes reciprocal self-disclosure, and the relationship may proceed to increasingly deeper levels of personality (Cozby, 1973).

In the most successful relationship, consensus on the important values intrinsic to the relationship is generally reached. Consensus is important for a variety of reasons. For one thing it reinforces our perception of the world as correct (Byrne and Clore, 1967). The satisfaction goes beyond simply being "right", because values are introjected into the self and help to define the self-image; hence she who rejects our self-image is often perceived as rejecting us. Moreover, persons with similar values are likely to engage in similar activities, thus further rewarding each other.

During the "value comparison" stage, though the stimulus and role variables are also operative, the importance of the stimulus variables has already waned somewhat. The majority of persons of disparate stimulus attractiveness who met, likely as not never developed a relationship. Many who started a relationship have broken up. The relatively few couples of disparate stimulus attractiveness who continue their relationship presumably have unusual compensating value consensus or role compatibility.

The testing of role compatibility is also underway, involving not only intimate verbal communication, but getting to know how to behave *vis-à-vis* the partner, as well as knowing what roles the partner can play in

satisfying one's own needs: friends, teacher, lover, critic. These roles not only involve the greatest intimacies, they also necessitate a great deal of time to master; hence the rate of growth of role compatibility is slower than that of value comparison, which involves only verbal interaction. There does come a time, however, when role compatibility supersedes value comparison in importance, marking the onset of the role stage, as shown in Fig. 2.

Role Stage

When a couple has survived the stimulus and value stages, they have established a reasonably good relationship. Some individuals may decide to marry at this point. However, for most persons, these are necessary but insufficient grounds for marriage. It is also important for the couples to be able to *function* in compatible roles.

Role is defined by English and English as "the behavior that is characteristic and expected of the occupant of a defined position in a group" (1958, p. 468). Sociologists tend to focus on the "defined position" with the understanding that the role is defined by an individual's culture, and that he adjusts himself into it as much as one does in purchasing a ready-made suit. My use of the term "role" however is much broader and individual-centred.

A wife's role as defined by her husband consists of *his* perception of the behaviour that is expected of a wife. His perception may be in part moulded by his culture, but part of it may stem from his own idio-syncrasies, which would not be found in his neighbour's definition of the role of a wife. In like vein, the wife's definition of the wifely role would consist of *her* perception of what the role should embody.

The role of a spouse may be subdivided into specialized functions which the individual is expected to execute in different situations. Thus, the husband's role may be subdivided into his role *vis-à-vis* his wife in private, in public, and in the family.

A primary feature of the role stage is the evaluation of the perceived functioning of oneself in a dyadic relationship in comparison with the role one envisages for oneself, and the perceived role functioning of the partner with respect to the roles one has envisaged for him. Personal, intimate behaviours are revealed much more slowly than are values, which can be expressed in more abstract, less intimate fashion. Also, many roles may be included within an overall evaluation of role

compatibility, which evaluation, therefore, may be difficult to make, whereas values are generally simpler to understand.

We can measure role compatibility by comparing expectation and perceptions of the fulfilment of expectation over a wide range of behaviours. Some culturally esteemed behaviours probably may not require measurement of expectations because they are almost universally perceived as rewarding. Individuals with both high social status and high nurturance needs, for example, are generally sought after because such individuals are easy to relate to, rarely self-centred, and sensitive and giving towards others. On the other hand, neurotics are high-cost persons who are difficult to relate to and often offer few rewards through interaction. Role compatibility is probably the most complex of all the stages and is probably never completely traversed, since individuals seem to be constantly adding new roles or modifying existing ones.

Types of Courtship and Cross-cultural Influences

Figure 2 describes what I conjecture to be the typical path of courtship for most middle class couples in the United States. Variations due to personality, economic, and cultural differences, however, would alter the graph somewhat. "Stimulus" types would hold stimulus variables to be most important over the course of the courtship. For such persons, marrying in the right class or profession would be paramount, and role interaction secondary. One thinks immediately of the exceedingly wealthy class in this regard. Here, values would be relatively unimportant in selection because class selectivity would be great and individual variability much smaller in comparison to class selectivity. In other words, if almost everyone within a class holds similar views, individual selectivity with respect to values does not seem to be a major issue.

The same would probably be true for other societies in which social change was relatively slight and class structure was stable. A Greek peasant might be most influenced by stimulus variables because almost everyone in the village held similar values. Role stratification also might be very rigid, a man's role and a woman's role being clearly defined and differentiated. In that case, the role stage along with the value stage might be of relatively small import.

In our own society, value consensus seems to be of greatest importance within professional and upper-middle class couples and of least importance in the lower class (Kerckhoff, 1972, 1974). In the lower class,

we may presume that the narrowed range of class variability for values and the structuring of roles makes individual selectivity with respect to these dimensions of lesser importance.

Since value comparison often serves as an introduction to role comparisons and role compatibility, it is easier to think of a "value-role" type than of either a separate "value" or a "role" type. This type would include individuals whose greatest rewards come from close inter-personal interaction with people. It would be of interest to determine whether "stimulus" types invariably married "stimulus" types or sometimes "intermarried" with "value-role" types.

Distinguishing Equity and Similarity

Similarity and equity are often bandied about as if they were equivalent terms. It is necessary however to distinguish between them because equity plays an important role in SVR theory, whereas similarity is of lesser importance. Similarity within the context of our discussion refers to the number of common components or the degree of similar structure two objects may have. If two individuals have similar values, it is meant that, if we ranked the values of each in order of preference, a high rank order correlation would result.

Equity, as used here, refers to equal rewarding power; hence two equitable persons might be totally dissimilar. The beautiful but poor woman who marries the ugly but wealthy bachelor represents an equitable balance of beauty and wealth.

The problem arises when members of a couple are equally represented on a variable so that they are both similar and equitable with respect to it. Generally, similarity functions as an antecedent variable. Individuals possessing similar values are drawn to each other because they receive consensual validation that their views are correct. In some cases, however, logic tells us that two people who share a socially undesirable characteristic may not necessarily be drawn to each other. They may in fact *settle* for each other because it is the best they can do. It is doubtful, for example, that two physically unattractive individuals are drawn to each other because they admire unattractiveness. Rather, they may have learned through experience that if they do not possess outstanding compensating attributes for their unattractiveness, they are apt to be rejected by more attractive persons whom they attempt to court. It is the presence of similars at the bottom of the totem pole which enables us to differentiate similarity as a socially desirable attracting agent from similarity as an equity or exchange factor.

Similarity can be non-rewarding even when the traits involved are socially desirable. Unless similarity leads to a rewarding experience, it may lead to competition and dissatisfaction. When both members of a couple possess strong needs to dominate each other, the couple may function less harmoniously than a tandem of a dominant and submissive member. The strongest interpersonal relationship, therefore, does not necessarily occur between the most similar types, but between those with equal rewarding power (equity), even where the variables contributing to these rewards are different for the partners.

Synopsis of Research on SVR Theory

In the more extensive treatment of SVR and other theories of marital choice (Murstein, 1976), 39 hypotheses relating to SVR theory were tested. Strong, moderate, and modest support was found for 33 of these hypotheses, with six being unsubstantiated, sometimes despite strong positive trends. Almost all of the research has tended to focus on the exchange portion of the theory, primarily because the financial resources were not available to study the developmental stages longitudinally. There is, however, some slight indirect support of these stages which in the interests of space cannot be discussed here. Instead, several of the more important hypotheses have been selected to give the reader the flavour of the research. First however a brief sketch of the subjects and the tests used.

Population and Tests

The subjects were tested in three samples in the late 1960s. They were predominantly college students from Connecticut universities and colleges from middle and upper class backgrounds. Couples generally knew each other fairly well (somewhat less than two years on the average) before volunteering for a study on "interpersonal relationships". The first group consisted of 99 couples who took the Minnesota Multiphasic Personality Inventory and the Revised Edwards Personal Preference Schedule among other tests. A year later, 19 new couples received more intensive testing including such "depth" measures as a lengthy interview, ink blot test, a thematic apperception test, and other tests. A year following, a third group consisting of 98 couples took another series of tests including the Marriage Expectation Test, specially designed to measure the physical, value, and role characteristics desired in a spouse.

This test was taken under eight different perceptual "sets" including such perceptions as boyfriend (girlfriend), self, ideal-self, ideal-spouse, and a prediction of how the partner perceived their partner, self, ideal-self, and ideal spouse. Six months after the initial testing, each subject received a follow-up questionnaire which asked how well the couple was currently doing together. Based on a rating sheet, the couple could be classified as having made good or poor courtship progress.

Research Findings

One of the most important assertions of SVR theory is that both the complementarity and homogamy theories are inadequate in accounting for marital choice because the individual seeking a marriage partner is concerned with neither similarity nor complementarity of needs. Rather, he seeks a partner who represents a fusion of his ideal-self and ideal-spouse, although, as we shall see shortly, he may be prepared to lower his aspirations somewhat if he perceives himself as not possessing high marital assets in his own right.

In general, however, when one is about to marry, he does tend to idealize his partner and to see him as close to his ideal-self and ideal-spouse concepts. This being the case, the tendency of an individual to marry someone he perceives as being similar or different depends largely on how closely his self-concept is to that trinity of desiderata, his ideal-spouse, his ideal-self, and his perceived partner (Fig. 3).

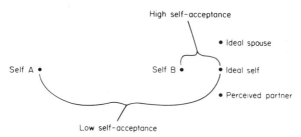

Fig. 3. *A, whose self and ideal-self concepts are far apart (low self-acceptance), will also see his partner as being unlike him, whereas B, whose self and ideal-self are close together (high self-acceptance), will also see his partner as being highly similar to the self. (From Murstein, 1976, p. 189. Reproduced with the kind permission of Springer-Verlag.)*

Figure 3 shows that individual B, who is highly self-accepting, is thus likely to perceive himself as very similar to his partner. Individual A, who is not highly self-accepting (i.e. there is a greater distance between

his self-concept and his ideal-self concept), tends to view himself as relatively dissimilar to his partner.

This model was validated in research by Murstein (1971b). The model also tends to explain the contradictory nature of earlier studies, which sometimes supported the "opposites attract" theory and sometimes the homogamy theory.

Another aspect of SVR theory is that men occupy a higher status than women in contemporary American society; consequently, the confirmation of the man's self- and ideal-self concepts by his partner should be more important to progress in courtship than is confirmation of the woman's concepts.

It was noted earlier that role compatibility in the *role* stage was essential for smooth courtship progress. Accordingly, it was predicted that couples *confirming* the self- and ideal-self percepts of their partners on the multi-itemed Marriage Expectation Test (perceiving their partners similar to the way their partners described themselves and their ideal-selves) would have made better courtship progress when checked six months later than couples who did not strongly confirm their partners' perceptions of themselves. It was likewise predicted that accuracy of predicting the partner's self- and ideal-self perceptions on the same test would likewise be associated with good courtship progress. Both hypotheses were significantly supported.

It was further argued that, in accordance with equity, individuals of lower status should have to render more services to individuals of higher status in order to attract and hold them. Women have historically occupied a lower status in society than men and even do so currently, though the gap in status appears to be narrowing (Murstein, 1974a). One way individuals of lower status can attract upper status individuals is by paying greater attention to them than vice-versa, and by confirming their images of themselves. Accordingly, it was predicted that women who made good courtship progress would have six months earlier been more likely to confirm their boyfriends' self- and ideal-self concepts and were also more likely to be able to have accurately predicted these concepts as compared to women who did not make good courtship progress. These predictions were also confirmed. It was further predicted that men's tendency to confirm and to accurately predict their partner's self- and ideal-self concepts would be less strongly associated with courtship progress, since the men would have less need to pay attention to, and confirm, their partners' self-perceptions if they, the men, possessed greater power in determining courtship progress. The data generally also supported this hypothesis.

In like vein it was predicted that the man's proneness to neuroticism would have poorer implications for advancement in courtship than the woman's neurotic tendencies, and this too was supported. Further, in accordance with equity, it was predicted that there would be a greater than chance similarity between members of couples for physical attractiveness, satisfaction with partner, neuroticism, and self-esteem. All of these hypotheses were supported.

The theory has also been extended to marriages, both intra-racial (Murstein and Beck, 1972) and inter-racial (Murstein, 1973), and to friendship (Murstein, 1971a, 1976) with results strongly supporting those found for premarital couples.

In sum, the data offer support to the exchange portion of the theory, but the sequential aspects have been tested only indirectly. Although these data support it, a crucial test would be a longitudinal study from the onset of the relationship to commitment or marriage. Such a study has not as yet been undertaken, a point noted by critics of the theory (Rubin and Levinger, 1974) and myself (Murstein, 1974b).

One difficulty is that the value stage must be tested early enough in the relationship before the value filtering has taken place. However, most couples volunteering for dyadic studies have known each other for many months and often years. Since value filtering may take place within hours or days of the onset of the relationship, an adequate test of value filtering has yet to be undertaken.

A second problem is that the value tests employed have been very brief, loaded with "social desirability" and probably inadequate measures of the value positions of the individuals. There is a clear need for a more comprehensive test of values. Thus at the present time the evidence that the value stage precedes the role stage is mixed, though the temporal primacy of the stimulus stage is soundly established.

Summary and Conclusions

Process theories are in many ways more appealing than monolithic theories. They mirror nicely the doubts, hesitancies, and complexities that surround the development of intimate relationships. They show also the multideterminism of factors making and breaking a relationship, including extradyadic as well as intradyadic factors. The price paid for this "realism" is a loss of theoretical elegance. These theories are difficult to test and sometimes to conceptualize. Yet they undoubtedly describe "real-life" relationships much better than the monolithic theories. It is likely, therefore, that future theories of interpersonal attraction will

concern themselves with selecting and weighing the influence of a considerable number of variables rather than searching for a single "alchemist's stone" which will magically explain all.

6. References

Altman, I. and Taylor, D. A. *Social penetration*. New York: Holt, 1973.

Berscheid, E. and Walster, E. H. Beauty and the beast. *Psychology Today*, 1972, **5**, 42.

Berscheid, E. and Walster, E. H. Physical attractiveness. In Berkowitz, L. (Ed.), *Advances in experimental social psychology*. Vol. 7. New York and London: Academic Press, 1974.

Bolton, C. D. Mate selection as the development of a relationship. *Marriage and Family Living*, 1961, **23**, 234-240.

Byrne, D. and Clore, G. L. Effectance arousal and attraction. *Journal of Personality and Social Psychology*, 1967, 6 (Monograph supplement (Whole no. 638)).

Cozby, I. Self-disclosure in human relationships. *Psychological Bulletin*, 1973, **79**, 73-91.

Dermer, M. When beauty foils. Unpublished doctoral dissertation, University of Minnesota, 1973.

English, H. B. and English, A. C. *A comprehensive dictionary of psychological and psychoanalytical terms*. New York: McKay, 1958.

Farber, B. An index of marital integration. *Sociometry*, 1957, **20**, 117-134.

Huston, T. L. Ambiguity of acceptance, social desirability, and dating choice. *Journal of Experimental Social Psychology*, 1973, **9**, 32-42.

Huston, T. L. *Foundations of interpersonal attraction*. New York and London: Academic Press, 1974.

Kerckhoff, A. C. Status-related value patterns among married couples. *Journal of Marriage and the Family*, 1972, **34**, 105-110.

Kerckhoff, A. C. The social context of interpersonal attraction. In Huston, T. L. (Ed.), *Foundations of interpersonal attraction*. New York and London: Academic Press, 1974.

Kerckhoff, A. C. and Davis, E. E. Value consensus and need complementarity in mate selection. *American Sociological Review*, 1962, **27**, 295-303.

Levinger, G., Senn, D. J. and Jorgensen, B. W. Progress toward permanence in courtship: a test of the Kerckhoff-Davis hypothesis. *Sociometry*, 1970, **33**, 427-443.

Lewis, R. A. A developmental framework for the analysis of premarital dyadic formation. *Family Process*, 1972, **11**, 17-48.

Lewis, R. A. A longitudinal test of a developmental framework for premarital dyadic formation. *Journal of Marriage and the Family*, 1973, **35**, 16-25.

Murstein, B. I. A theory of marital choice and its applicability to marriage adjustment and friendship. In Murstein, B. I. (Ed.), *Theories of love and attraction*. New York: Springer, 1971a.

Murstein, B. I. Self-ideal discrepancy and the choice of marital partner. *Journal of Consulting and Clinical Psychology*, 1971b, **37**, 47-52.

Murstein, B. I. A theory of marital choice applied to interracial marriage. In Abt, L. E. and Stuart, I. R. (Eds), *Interracial marriage: expectations and realities*. New York: Grossman, 1973.

Murstein, B. I. *Love, sex and marriage through the ages*. New York: Springer, 1974a.

Murstein, B. I. Clarification of obfuscation on conjugation: a reply to criticism of the SVR theory of marital choice. *Journal of Marriage and the Family*, 1974b, **36**, 231-234.

Murstein, B. I. *Who will marry whom? Theories and research in marital choice*. New York: Springer, 1976.

Murstein, B. I. Limits of exchange and equity theories. Unpublished paper, Connecticut College, 1980.

Murstein, B. I. and Beck, G. D. Person perception, marriage adjustment, and social desirability. *Journal of Consulting and Clinical Psychology*, 1972, **39**, 396-403.

Rapoport, R. The transition from engagement to marriage. *Acta Sociologica*, 1964, **8**, 36-55.

Rapoport, R. and Rapoport, R. N. New light on the honeymoon. *Human Relations*, 1964, **17**, 33-56.

Rapoport, R. and Rapoport, R. N. Work and family in contemporary society. *American Sociological Review*, 1965, **30**, 381-394.

Rapoport, R. and Rapoport, R. N. Family transitions in contemporary society. *Journal of Psychosomatic Research*, 1968, **12**, 29-38.

Reiss, I. L. Toward a sociology of the heterosexual love relationship. *Marriage and Family Living*, 1960, **22**, 139-145.

Rubin, Z. and Levinger, G. Theory and data badly mated: a critique of Murstein's SVR and Lewis's PDF theories of mate selection. *Journal of Marriage and the Family*, 1974, **36**, 226-231.

Ryder, R. G., Kafka, J. S. and Olson, D. H. Separating and joining influences in courtship and early marriage. *American Journal of Orthopsychiatry*, 1971, **4**, 450-464.

Schutz, W. C. *FIRO: a three dimensional theory of interpersonal behavior*. New York: Rinehart, 1958.

Thibaut, J. W. and Kelly, H. H. The social psychology of groups. New York: John Wiley, 1959.

Vital Statistics of the United States, 1969: Vol. 3, Marriage and Divorce. Rockville: U.S. Department of Health, Education and Welfare, 1972.

Winch, R. F. *Mate selection*. New York: Harper, 1958.

Wolfe, H. A theory of mate selection based on interaction. Unpublished paper, Pennsylvania State University, 1973.

Section C
THE WIDER CONTEXT

7
Human Sexuality in Cross-cultural Perspective

PAUL C. ROSENBLATT
and
ROXANNE M. ANDERSON
Family Social Science, University of Minnesota,
290 McNeal Hall, 1985 Buford Avenue, St. Paul,
Minnesota, USA

The fact that a chapter on the cross-cultural perspective is in a collection of chapters dealing with social relationships may be a sign that cross-cultural education in the area of social relations is still relatively unsuccessful. Ideally, relevant cross-cultural material would be assimilated to all theoretical perspectives and content foci (Rosenblatt, 1974a). Why has the ideal not yet been achieved? The answer to this question has two parts — one is the way in which people studying sexual attraction have typically used cross-cultural material, and the other is to do with the difficulties that arise in evaluating and using the cross-cultural material that has been available.

In the first two sections of this chapter we offer an extended discussion of the problems involved in looking at sexual attraction cross-culturally. These sections include criticism of the treatment of cross-cultural research in secondary works that deal with attraction. In examining the problems of looking at sexual attraction cross-culturally, we raise the issues of meaning and definition that would apply to any study of sexual attraction or to the analysis of any relationship in which sexual attraction is in some sense a possibility.

The Use of Cross-cultural Material in the Study of Sexual Attraction

People writing about sexual attraction, whose work has not been primarily cross-cultural, have generally used cross-cultural materials in three ways — if they have used it at all. First, cross-cultural material has been used to entertain the reader with the bizarre. In culture X, sexual advances are made in such-and-such a bizarre way; in culture Y, people find obese sexual partners most attractive. Such examples provide no illustration of theoretical concepts and no support for theory. In fact such examples may have adverse effects. They encourage readers to see specific cultures other than their own as homogeneous, which they are unlikely to be (Pelto and Pelto, 1975). To write as though the people of a given culture do any single, specific thing is to provide a misleading view of the complexity of the culture and the humanity of its bearers.

A second use of cross-cultural materials has been to document or illustrate generalizations about human nature. Although many scholars use the available documentation responsibly, some provide fantasy facts, making assertions that are not consistent with the cross-cultural literature. One may read, for example, that in most cultures it is taken for granted that sooner or later everyone falls in love. However, nobody has ever studied most cultures, and the relevant cross-cultural studies that deal with love (e.g. Coppinger and Rosenblatt, 1968; Rosenblatt, 1967; Rosenblatt and Cozby, 1972) suggest nothing about what people in other cultures take for granted. These studies do, however, indicate that there is considerable variability among cultures in how important love is as a basis of marriage; hence, it is wrong to write about people in "most cultures" having any specific practice or belief in the area of love.

A third use of cross-cultural materials has been to provide a frame of reference for evaluating Western culture. Do westerners tend to marry very young or very old in comparison with people in other societies? Are they unusually free, unusually restrictive, or about average in their regulation of premarital or extramarital relations? Here, too, one may read fantasy facts — for example, "most societies look at mate swapping more tolerantly than does American society". There is simply no information available that would warrant such an assertion.

Most salient when one uses cross-cultural material as a frame of reference for evaluating one's own society, but also at issue in any other use of cross-cultural material, is the validity of comparing cultures. Does it make sense, for example, to compare sexual attraction in one's own

culture with sexual attraction in other cultures when the meaning of "sexual attraction" as a concept varies greatly from language to language? In one language, lust may be a major component of the concept of sexual attraction; in another language idealization may be salient; in a third the concept of sexual attraction implies illicit, immoral attraction; and a fourth has no relevant concept. A scholar may choose to apply a single, uniform, operational definition across cultures, but whatever is found may be irrelevant to conceptualizations in many of the cultures studied and hence be out of touch with or even obscuring the understandings, expectations, and aspirations of people in those cultures. From a components of variance perspective, applying a uniform definition of sexual attraction across cultures may enable one to account for a small percentage of the variance, but one will have sacrificed the proportion of variance due to between and within culture variations in conceptualization. Even to speak about "sexual attraction" in the United States or England, without taking note of the rich and complex ways in which the concept is used from person to person and situation to situation, may cause one to overlook a considerable amount of what goes on. The dynamics of close relations in the west may arise to a substantial extent from individual differences in conceptualization and under-standing of sexual attraction.

The fact of variation across cultures in conceptualization points to the ethnocentrism of any topic of study, including sexual attraction. Sexual attraction as dealt with in this book is primarily a concept of western culture and languages, though even in the west there are wide historical (Gadlin, 1977), generational, subcultural and individual variations in the connotations of the concept. Sexual attraction as it is generally dealt with in this book has meaning within the context of the norms of western society for finding mates and sexual companions, and within the context of scripts in western society (Gagnon, 1973) for sexual encounters.

With an awareness of societal, historical, and individual differences in conceptualization of sexual attraction, one may hesitate to define sexual attraction. In a sense, *the* cross-cultural perspective on sexual attraction is one that points to definitional complexity. To develop that perspective, it seems preferable to start with a very simplistic working definition and then to elaborate upon it as required. The following, then, is a very basic definition that is the starting place for developing a sense of cross-cultural complexity. "Ego's" sexual attraction is defined by us as "interest in another person accompanied by a desire to have some sort of contact with that person that ego would define as sexual". This initial

definition excludes attraction that ego does not recognize as sexual even if another person can see sexual elements in the attraction. The definition omits attraction based on the other's entertainment value, intellectual stimulation, capacity to reward ego in verbal interaction, physical characteristics, and so on if the attraction stemming from these other characteristics is not defined by ego as sexual. There is no room in this definition for attraction blends; attraction that is, for example, both intellectual and sexual. By this initial definition, with which we will eventually disagree strongly, attraction is either self-defined as sexual (and therefore is sexual) or sexual attraction is absent. Moreover, the definition excludes many dynamics that might be important in drawing people together who might eventually become sexual partners or in holding together people who have become sexual partners.

To make more sense of the role of conceptualization of sexual attraction, it would be useful to have data on variations across cultures in sexual attraction concepts. Those societies in which concepts are very similar to those in the West might be most useful in future comparative studies of the dynamics of western-type attraction. Holding basic notions of sexual attraction constant, do relationships generally develop in the same way and have the same sorts of problems? By contrast, those societies in which the meaning of sexual attraction is quite different from western notions might only be useful in comparative studies of the societal basis of heterosexual relations, studies working at a sociological or culturological level rather than a social psychological one. What societal or ecological factors are associated with one conception of attraction versus another? One could also imagine a number of alternative books, rather than this one, that would arise from the salient concepts of other cultures and subcultures for understanding relationships — tolerance in relationships, finding peace despite being married, the control of disturbing impulses, approaches to the reduction of male oppression of females, verbal arguments in marriage, the maintenance of male dignity, the role of one's siblings in one's marriage, and so on.

Even if one studies societies with comparable, western-style conceptions of sexual attraction, the societies may differ substantially in how salient sexual attraction is as a basis of relationships. For example, in one society sexual attraction may be seen most often as something that develops after the onset of an arranged marriage; in another society it may be most often seen as a source of recreation for the upper class and of no consequence in the establishment of relationships for other people. If we can generalize from cognitive and labelling perspectives on sexual

arousal (e.g. Rook and Hammen, 1977), such differences may have implications for the dynamics and course of sexual arousal and a great variety of other sex-related phenomena. This perspective encourages greater relativism in discussions of the relationship between stimuli and arousal. Furthermore what would be labelled as sexual arousal in one culture might be labelled in a different way in another — consider, for example, cultures in which sexual intercourse is defined as depleting for men (Harper, 1969, writing about a gorup in South India), or as punishment for women, or cultures such as those in the New Guinea Highlands in which marriages are between members of enemy groups in which the conflicting loyalties could lead one spouse to try to harm the other in some way (Brown and Buchbinder, 1976; Ember, 1978). In such cultures, gut responses that could be labelled sexual arousal in the west might be labelled, or blended with, fear.

The difficulty in studying sexual attraction cross-culturally is further illustrated by consideration of sex differences. Cross-culturally the genders tend to differ, at any adult stage in the life cycle, in the resources to which they have access and in the means available to them to exploit these resources (Rosenblatt and Cunningham, 1976). The fact that such differences exist means that a sexual encounter between a woman and a man each of whom feel some sort of sexual attraction for the other may mean different things to the two of them. For each the encounter has the possibility of affecting access to the resources controlled by the other. Especially for the person who has fewer means of obtaining crucial resources, feelings during the sexual encounter may be complicated. The complications may include arousal stemming in part from desire for resources, simulation of interest in a sexual encounter when the real interest is in the resources to which it would give access, or attraction arising out of reactions to the other's resources. Rainwater (1971), for example, writes about the greater need for women than men in some cultures of poverty to use marriage as an escape from difficult premarital circumstances. Women in such circumstances may feel a hunger to escape their difficult home life that affects their feelings of sexual attraction with a desperation men would rarely feel. Watson (1973), to take another example, describes the involvement of Guajiro (Colombia) women in marital sexual relationships. From the very first ceremonial sexual encounter at the time of the wedding, a woman's response is typically tempered by her awareness of male control of property and male right to take an additional spouse. Watson further points out that the sexes among the Guajiro are constrained by norms of decorum for sexual

encounters that differ for women and men. One can speculate that norms of decorum in sexual encounters are related in all societies to other aspects of the social structure of gender relations and that the norms would affect to some extent both feelings of attraction and sexual response. For example, a Guajira who is aware that appearing too interested in sex could alarm her new husband may, in working at appearing decorous, modify her own feelings toward her husband and her own sexual response during intercourse with him.

Difficulties in Using Cross-cultural Material

As the preceding section of this chapter indicated, from a cross-cultural perspective one can question some of the uses of ethnographic accounts from other cultures in the study of sexual attraction, and one can question the very focus on sexual attraction. The former of these two problems stems in part from difficulties anyone would have in working with ethnographic accounts, and the latter may point to one reason those accounts have been difficult to use. The material will be difficult to use if one fails to realize how irrelevant the questions which may be important to westerners are in the lives of people in many other cultures. Beyond this, the problems in working with cross-cultural materials fall into two general categories, problems in use of reports of a single culture and problems in use of reports compiling material from a number of cultures.

Problems in Using Reports from a Single Culture

In working with material from a single culture, problems arise first of all from the concept of "Culture". A culture is a mental construction of observers. The construction includes a choice of spatial and temporal boundaries, but these boundaries often have no discontinuity with what is placed outside the boundaries. In addition a culture may often be depicted on the basis of a small and non-representative sample of individuals. Ethnographers doing the best they can, often give only their best guess about a great deal of culture content and even boundaries of culture. Ethnographers often have not been in a position to acquire information about tabooed behaviour or behaviour which, like sexual behaviour in most cultures, is usually performed in private. For several reasons they have often lacked comparable information from both sexes. Key informants tended to be of one sex (male) which makes any imputation of sex differences questionable. Or queries about sexual

feelings and relations risked difficulties between informant and ethnographer (cf. Gorer, 1967, p. 327; on the over-enthusiastic response of Sikkim Lepcha women to ethnographic inquiries) or were simply inappropriate. Ethnographers have often been more interested in other things than in heterosexual relations, and the reporting of sexual information has often failed to meet high standards of documentation in terms of counts, discussion of variability, discussion of situational factors, provision of direct quotations, citation of observed incidents, differentiation of rules from behaviour, and sensitivity to possible sources of invalidity of data.

Some ethnographies are insensitive as well to the difference between an outside observer's view of what goes on in the culture and an indigenous view. In the area of sexual attraction, it may too often have been only the outside observer's view that was reported. How indigenous people understood what was going on, how they categorized phenomena, what their theories of heterosexual relations were, and what their evaluations were of the ethnographer's questions and observations about sexuality generally went unreported. Even when the indigenous view was reported, it may often have been misunderstood. When ethnographers have asked informants about parent–child and sibling–sibling incest, the fact that informants in some cultures have responded with a look of puzzlement or with a response that has been reported as "incest is unthinkable" has at times been misinterpreted to mean that there is a taboo (a rule) against sex. One may quibble over whether a never-verbalized rule is a rule, but it is certainly possible that the reasons behind something never happening differ between a society in which there is a formal prohibition and one in which there is neither occurrence nor a conceptual system for thinking about its occurrence.

Cross-cultural Compilations

When it comes to the compilation of data from various cultures or the interpretation of compilations, the path has many hazards. For one thing, the question of the units being described is not a simple one. Cultures are not countries. Many national boundaries encompass an array of vastly different cultures. One example of the problems in using the country as a unit of analysis has to do with the use of national statistics. Although national statistics may never be very relevant to notions of sexual attraction, one may be tempted to use them. One of the most common errors in the use of national statistics is in the area of divorce. Divorce is

of course only indirectly relevant to sexual attraction. It can be seen as a jural act, an action altering obligations or kin group boundaries, or as many other things having nothing to do with sexuality. It also may arise out of sexual dysfunction or a loss of sexual interest in one's spouse or because one has found another partner who is more sexually interesting. To complicate matters one may cite sexual reasons for divorce when the sexual matters are actually relatively insignificant, and one may cite non-sexual reasons when sexuality is actually crucial. Thus divorce rates may, with appropriate caution, be seen by some as indicators of sexual attraction. In this regard, to assert that the United States has the highest divorce rate of any country is to lose track of much of the useful comparative data. Within any country there may be some cultures with very low divorce rates and others with very high ones. In the cross-cultural divorce literature there are a number of cultures with rates of break-up for cohabiting, child-producing, and heterosexual relationships far higher than that of the United States (e.g. Kanuri of Nigeria — Cohen, 1971; Central American Black Carib — Gonzalez, 1969; Kelantanese of Malaya — Raybeck, 1979; Turu of Tanzania — Schneider, 1971). Moreover, comparisons are complicated by the fact that cultures differ markedly in what is counted as married; a person may typically, in some cultures, go through many quasi-permanent, co-residential heterosexual relationships before entering the state defined as married.

The second hazard is the relevance of one's research question to the data available. It is possible to compile answers to a question that is not applicable to many of the cultures studied. The areas which people in virtually all cultures cope with are few, the major life cycle crises (death, birth and the onset of something like marriage), the tensions of living with others, issues in division of labour, and modes of satisfying basic needs for food, water, and protection from extremes of climate. Even in these areas, cultural understandings may vary to the extent that questions developed in one culture may be inappropriate to answer in most other cultures.

A third problem, related to the second, is the missing data problem. No matter what the issue, there will be missing data for some of the cultures in the ethnographic literature. If one is dealing with a relatively precise question, there will be quite a lot of missing data. At times the temptation may be to interpret the absence of data as having a meaning for a culture. For example, if incestuous relationships are not reported or are reported only in folktales, one might conclude that a culture lacks such

relationships. That, however, might be a grave error. The ethnographer and the ethnographer's informants may simply have been ignorant of relevant cases. Cases may have been hidden from view because their existence had been covered up by a move to another community, the development of a bogus genealogy, or even the normal ambiguity (to an outsider) of kinship terms from cultures with very different kin patterns. The ethnographer may not even have bothered to investigate the issue; or investigating it, the ethnographer may not have reported on the issue. Many ethnographers will not for example report activities that local police or courts would punish. Thus, to conclude that there is a universal incest taboo, one must make erroneous assumptions about ethnographic data.

Finally, any cross-cultural study deserves the challenge of alternative interpretations that would be given to any other study. In particular, one should be suspicious of cross-cultural literature, generated almost entirely by people well-imbued with western culture, consistent with western cultural biases — for example, that standards of physical attractiveness are more clearly defined in the evaluation of women than in the evaluation of men or that there is a double standard for premarital sex that gives men more freedom than women. With all these caveats, let us now move our consideration of attraction in cross-cultural perspective to an examination of questions of incest and exogamy.

Incest, Exogamy and Endogamy as Determinants of Sexual Attraction

People in all cultures seem generally to operate with some organization of sexual and marital choices. This organization of choices affects who one finds attractive and when it is legitimate to feel attraction. Of course as we discuss in the next section of this chapter, there are many places in the world where sexuality is so constrained or where marriage choices are so constrained by the actions of people who have authority over one, that the choices that are made can scarcely be said to be one's own. Nonetheless, in both the constrained situations and in the situations where choice is relatively free, choices seem to be made within a defined range. Some people are defined as too close to choose (rules of incest and exogamy) and some are too distant to choose (rules of endogamy). That is, in most cultures there seem to be limitations on who to have sex with and who to marry, such that close kin and members of outgroups are generally considered inappropriate sexual partners and even

inappropriate objects of sexual attraction. There is a fascinating literature on the application of these rules to specific cases and the treatment of ostensible deviations from the rules (see, for example, Boon, 1976; Huntsman and McLean, 1976). The rules may be unspoken and may be as much a matter of inference for people in the culture as they are for an outside observer. Patterns of incest rules vary somewhat from kinship system to kinship system — for example, there are societies in which uncle and niece or half-sister and half-brother would be considered in different kin groups, and therefore might legally copulate or marry, and in some instances do. Even where rules are explicitly stated, they may not be enforced. Deviant behaviour may not be punished in any clear way, and deviant feelings may generally be undetectable. And, of course, wherever there are sanctions against deviant behaviour the deviancy may occur in secret and go undetected.

There is an extensive literature on the social functions of rules of incest and endogamy (for recent reviews, see Ember, 1975; Parker, 1976). Although many people write as though acceptance of one functional explanation precludes acceptance of any other, to a large extent all explanations could be valid. There are biological–social explanations for incest and exogamy rules that hinge on the fact that inbreeding tends to produce higher rates of expression of deleterious recessive genes and hence higher rates of spontaneous abortion and of birth defect (Lindzey, 1967). Another common explanation of marriage rules, offered both by anthropological theorists and by indigenous informants, is that marriage choices in most cultures really pay off in terms of alliances; who one marries or who one's offspring marries affects the possibilities for making peace where there is internecine warfare, for trade relations, for assistance in times of trouble, for being put up for the night on a visit to another community, for allies in local disputes, for help in the arranging of other marriages, etc.

The two explanations of incest prohibitions that bear directly on sexual attraction are a role confusion explanation and a familiarity-breeds-contempt explanation. It is sometimes argued that incest would create serious role conflicts both within people and between people. If daughter marries father, for example, when should she respond to him as daughter and when as wife, and when should she respond to her mother as daughter and when as co-wife? There may be some validity to this explanation of incest prohibitions. For example, childhood association as "siblings" may create barriers to sexual attraction for a couple betrothed as children and reared together (Haas, 1969). Thus competing response

dispositions may be one explanation for the problems of Taiwanese minor marriages (see below). There are, however, several counter-arguments to the role confusion explanation of incest prohibitions. One counter-argument is that in many cultures in which kin marriage is common there are potentials for role confusion anyway. If I marry my classificatory sibling's offspring, I will then be both that person's uncle/aunt and that person's spouse. My sibling is then my sibling and my parent in-law. And my spouse is both my spouse and my niece or nephew. These problems exist in many cultures, and although we lack to date a generalizing research literature on how people resolve or head-off the confusions, the cultures seem to persist despite the potential for confusion. A second counter-argument against the role-confusion viewpoint is that in US families with incest, role conflict is often seemingly minimized through the tacit acceptance of the sexual relationship by other members of the family. For example if father and daughter are copulating, the wife/mother may simply act as though she does not know what is going on. Or in some cases she may actively encourage the relationship. If there is role confusion in such families, it does not seem to be so intense as to be disruptive of the incestuous liaison.

The other social function explanation offered for incest prohibitions that has direct relevance to sexual attraction processes is that incest rules prohibit disaster by preventing long-term relations between people whose too great familiarity would lead to revulsion, rather than to sexual attraction, and hence to marital instability. One could argue against this point of view that many societies function with high rates of marital instability, and that marriage is almost by definition a relationship leading to great familiarity.

Some people, however, find support for the argument that familiarity undermines relationships in data from Israeli kibbutzim (e.g. Talmon, 1964). On the typical Israeli kibbutz, people are raised from infancy in the closest proximity to their age peers. They sleep together, play together, shower together, are educated together throughout childhood, and remain in closest contact in their teens. Then when it comes to sexual choices or marital choices, these kibbutzniks look to another kibbutz for partners. This, it is argued, is proof of the unattractiveness of familiars. However, the kibbutz may yield greater familiarity than virtually any other situation in the world, so the kibbutz phenomenon may not be relevant to the understanding of other cultures. Even if the level of familiarity on the kibbutz is relevant to other cultures, it may be

that kibbutz ideology tends to reject internal competition, or that young male and female kibbutzniks who seem repelled by mutual familiarity tend, like young males and females elsewhere, to be at any age at different stages of physical and social development (Spiro, 1965, pp. 329–335). Thus the rarity of marriages within the kibbutz may be explained at least in part in terms of avoidance of internal competition and lack of attraction between people at different developmental stages.

The most compelling data on familiarity comes from the work of Wolf on minor marriages in Taiwan (Wolf, 1966, 1968, 1970). Wolf's work rests on the fact that in Taiwan some marriages were established when a girl was quite young. In such cases she would go to live in the household of her future parents-in-law and would grow up in close proximity to her husband-to-be. Wolf's data show that such marriages are much less stable and peaceful than marriages contracted between people who had not grown up in close proximity. Minor marriages, when they finally became official, had higher levels of marital strife, higher divorce rates, husbands more likely to use prostitutes, and lower levels of fecundity. Although it could be argued that the minor marriages founder on the rocks of familiarity, one of us previously argued that it is possible that the trouble with such marriages is that the minor bride grew up as a drudge in the house of her future parents-in-law (Rosenblatt, 1974a). Thus a minor bride might be seen as low status, dirty, and unattractive. Further it was argued that fertility might have been reduced as an artefact of venereal disease contracted through intercourse with prostitutes. Wolf has, however, brought new data and arguments to bear on the issue (Wolf, 1976). He has pointed out that marriages of a subgroup that included many former prostitutes were as fertile as other non-minor marriages, and the fertility of minor marriages did not drop over time, as one would expect if the onset of venereal disease had a cumulative affect on the population statistics. As for minor marriages being weaker because the wife had been a drudge or somehow of low status, Wolf pointed out that wives are drudges at the onset of the typical non-minor marriage, and that husbands in non-minor marriages that are uxorilocal marriages (marriage into wife's household) are low status. Yet these factors do not seem to have reduced the success of these non-minor marriages.

An interesting side-light on the familiarity argument comes from an ethnographic report on heterosexual relations among the Muria, a tribal people of India (Elwin, 1968). At least in the past, the Muria had a dormitory for unmarried youngsters, who were free to copulate and typically established long-term monogamous sexual relations. However,

marriage was rarely arranged between dormitory sexual partners. In the rare cases in which a formal marriage was contracted for a couple regularly copulating with each other, they were prohibited from further copulation until their marriage. Although there are alternative interpretations, one intriguing possibility is that the reluctance to arrange marriage for dormitory mates and the sexual prohibition during the betrothal period represent an awareness that sexual attraction is minimal when familiarity is too great. There is also evidence from Trobriand Islanders (Malinowski, 1929, p. 66) of the need for devices to make familiar people seem special in order to have strong sexual feelings develop among young people.

Arranged Marriage vs. Freedom of Choice of Spouse

Cross-culturally marriage, rather than sexual mating without marriage, is what seems important in people's lives. Although there are suggestions that people in some settings have done quite well without marrying and have preferred not to be married (e.g. rural Ireland — Messenger, 1971), and although there seems to be as yet no comprehensive research on those never married, marriage seems predominantly a life cycle stage across the species. There are of course enclaves throughout the world, particularly in the Caribbean and among poorer people in urban areas, where heterosexual matings that may or may not be called "marriages" are unstable, and there is little expectation that they will be stable, but it seems far more common than not in the world that people aspire to long-term heterosexual matings and that the societies in which they live value such long-term relationships (Murdock, 1949, Chapter 1). There are many societies in which non-marital sexuality is quite important, but sexuality still operates in the shadow of marriage. Hence it seems important to write about marital sexuality before entering a discussion of non-marital sexuality.

Marriages fall on a continuum from totally arranged (without any input from people to be married) to totally free (with family authorities having no formal right to influence a marital choice). Comparatively few marriages may have been established at either extreme. Even in the US, which is sometimes considered in other societies the paragon of societies with freedom of choice of spouse, the existence of homogamous mate choice suggests that family members have some influence on one's choice of mate. Although marriages are for many people in the world more nearly free than they were a generation ago (especially since the

government of the People's Republic of China has ordered that marriage arrangement end — Salaff, 1973), a very large number of extant marriages are based on relatively constrained choice. There tend to be class differences such that the wealthier and more powerful do more arranging (Goode, 1959; Rosenblatt, 1974a; Watson, 1973), but class difference aside one can find many arranged marriages in parts of the Muslim world, India, sub-Saharan Africa and in cultural enclaves throughout the remainder of the world.

What can be gained by arranging a marriage? As was argued above, marriages have the potential to grant families myriad benefits; especially where central governments provide little in the way of control of internecine warfare or compensation for flood and insect damage; where hotel, motel and restaurant facilities are unavailable to the typical traveller; where people's politics are influenced by kinship rather than ideology. In these cases, marriage arrangements can gain or lose a family much of value.

How does one engineer an arranged marriage for someone who has a normal biology, who is capable of lusting, who can see, hear, and smell the attributes of another? One part of the engineering is often the restriction of opportunity (Goode, 1959; Rosenblatt and Cozby, 1972). Where marriages are to be arranged, nubile individuals (particularly females) are sequestered and, if they travel, travel with chaperones. Contacts with opposite sex are held to a minimum. In addition, marriages are often established for a person while the person is still young, which minimizes the chances of lust leading to an uncontrolled, unarranged liaison. We calculate from Nag's (1968, pp. 193-195) data that the average age for first marriages of women in his non-random sample of 36 worldwide cultures is roughly 17 years of age. Such a low average implies that opportunities for free choice of spouse are, for the typical woman, somewhat constrained.

Attraction where Marriages are Arranged

Where marriages are arranged, couples who marry may typically have little contact before marriage. However, whatever contact they may have may be sufficient enough to allow for intense attraction. Sometimes, when marriages are arranged, the two potential spouses have some sort of meeting before the deal is closed. This may be quite formal and ceremonial or it may be set up to appear to be quite casual. The meeting allows them to make a cursory check of appearance and behaviour and allows them a chance to express opposition to a mating that seems

undesirable. Perhaps more importantly, it fuels a fantasy life and helps to develop strong commitment in the sense that it adds an element of personal volition to their marrying (see Rosenblatt, 1977, for a discussion of commitment theory). Of course arrangement may be between groups in close contact, not infrequently between groups already related by marriage. In some of those cases, the couple would have had quite a lot of casual contact.

The negotiations for marriage arrangement may involve agreements about property transfer and future obligations. Often the process of negotiation involves considerable expenditure itself, on gifts, feasting, ceremonies, oracles, marriage arrangers, and religious specialists. Where investments are high, people seem to work at protecting their investment by reducing the chances of the couple backing out of the arrangement. One mechanism that operates in this way is to restrict sexual contact once betrothal begins. Of course, in many societies where marriages are arranged, young people have no opportunity for sexual contact. But in some they do, and in these societies, if marriage has important wealth or alliance implications, sexual contact between betrothed persons is restricted more than it was before betrothal (Rosenblatt *et al.*, 1969). This is in contrast to what occurs in societies like the USA or Great Britain, where a commitment to marry tends to bring greater sexual contact in a couple. Apparently, where wealth and alliance factors are important, the risk of lovers' quarrels if a couple are intimate is great. People protect their investments and prospects by heading off such quarrels. In addition, the restriction on contact has some likelihood of fueling fantasy in the couple and of adding excitement to their initial marital contacts. In societies like the USA and Great Britain, kin groups lose relatively little if a lovers' quarrel breaks off an engagement. And since there are comparatively few pressures from family members to keep the couple on their path toward marriage, the couple may need to develop relatively strong commitment to each other. Establishing a sexual relationship is one means of doing that.

In lieu of sexual attraction, a second means of protecting commitments where marriages are arranged is to hold a big ceremony, or commonly a series of big ceremonies. The effort and publicity involved in such ceremonies tend to commit all participants (Rosenblatt and Unangst, 1974). To back out of an arrangement after considerable expenditure would be to invalidate investments and to waste resources that might be quite precious. And to back out after all the significant people in one's social world have seen one make a commitment would make such a move

very embarrassing. Ceremonies are present and more elaborate where marriage has important wealth and alliance implications (Rosenblatt and Unangst, 1974), presumably in part to protect investments. And the commitment involved is not only for the couple being married but also for the members of their kin group, who might have second thoughts about an alliance, trade commitments, and the like. A ceremony can also be seen as promoting attraction in two ways. The ceremony symbolizes and often makes quite explicit that now it is permissible to feel strong sexual attraction; constraints on having or expressing strong sexual feelings may now, in this particular relationship, be thrown aside. Beyond mere permission-giving, the ceremony often brings with it a strong sense that there *should* be sexual feelings. For example, off-colour jokes and stories about extraordinary levels of coital activity in the early days of marriage may be told. These may communicate to newly-weds that they should have strong sexual feelings for each other. The effect of such normative pressure may be debilitating for some people; but it may be that for many other people, the normative pressure to develop attraction helps to promote attraction. The sources of the strong attraction that fuel early sexual encounters in any culture in which there are strong normative pressures for attraction could include the excitement of doing what people value, of attaining a new status, and of engaging in an activity that people have been promising will be extraordinarily rewarding. These excitement sources might be absent where there is only a taken-for-granted quality to sex, without jokes, stories, ceremonial first intercourse and other normative pressures.

What happens when a couple who have had minimal contact with one another finds themselves married? Although they may have had rich fantasies about one another and have felt strong feelings of attraction, they would lack the broad base of attraction (shared experiences, history of rewarding each other, etc.) that might be present commonly where people freely choose mates. Occasionally a person in such a society resists marrying or copulating (e.g. Topley, 1975, for nineteenth century China; Cohen, 1969, summarizing data from a number of societies). For most, however, the expectation that they will get along, the barriers against escape from the relationship, the shared discomfort and stress, the pleasures associated with sexual contact, attainment of a higher status (marriage is often a source of status), satisfaction of curiosity about the opposite sex, and a number of other factors combine to help hold the newly married persons in the relationship and to bond them together. Of course the ideal marital relationship varies substantially from culture to

culture on such dimensions as self-disclosure, amount of talking expected, and even proximity of sleeping. So the pressure for compatibility may be less on couples with arranged marriages in many societies than on couples in western culture. In fact, it is commonly the case that where marriages are arranged, social relationships with people other than the spouse are more important than where marriages are not arranged. Married couples more often than not live with, or in close proximity to, the close kin of at least one of them. Frequently the in-marrier must work with and be supervised by a senior same-sex relative of the spouse. These relationships are often trying for the in-marrier. In many cultures, for example, there are tales and songs of the difficulties a new bride has with her mother-in-law. In such circumstances the relationship between the young spouses may provide a haven for the in-marrier. Whether it does or does not, the relationship of greatest anxiety and concern and the one in which compatability is more at issue may not be between spouses but between in-marrier and supervising in-law. If one asked people in such a culture to talk about attraction in relationships, sexual attraction might be subordinated to interest in attraction between in-marrier and in-laws. Or, sexual attraction between spouses may be responsive to resources made available by marriage and to relations with in-laws.

Attraction where there is Freedom of Choice of Spouse

What perspective can be acquired on relationships in western culture from looking at other cultures with freedom of choice of spouse? Perhaps the first place to look for perspective is the institutional supports for a freedom-of-choice system. Cultures with freedom of choice of spouse tend to have institutionalized means of promoting that freedom and hence of encouraging the development of feelings of sexual attraction (Rosenblatt and Cozby, 1972). First of all, they tend to have so-called opportunity situations — places and times for prospective mates to meet (Rosenblatt and Cozby, 1972). Cross-culturally, the most common opportunity situations seem to be markets, dances, and ceremonies marking religious, life cycle, and calendar events. In the USA and Great Britain, bars may serve as opportunity situations. Cross-culturally opportunity situations often include mechanisms for minimizing distress arising from shyness and from the anxiety involved in possible rejection. Many of the opportunity situations require ritualized contact, so that one will be able to show off one's appearance and some of one's behaviour

without the anxieties inherent in a free-floating interaction. Although opportunity situations may be relatively rare in cultures with freedom of choice but substantial restraint on non-marital sexual intercourse (e.g. Barbados — Stoffle, 1977), even in such cultures many relationships begin in the few opportunity situations that are available. Beyond the ritualized interaction in opportunity situations, many cultures with freedom of choice of spouse have mechanisms for communicating interest in another without having to face the risk of direct rejection (Rosenblatt, 1971). Love magic is one means of communicating interest in another; the use of go-betweens is another not uncommon way of communicating interest. Both these ways of communicating interest have a self-protective element; that, presumably, is one reason why love magic is more commonly present in societies in which people have anxieties about sexual relationships (Minturn *et al.*, 1969; Shirley and Romney, 1962). If the object of one's interest declines to express reciprocal interest, one can blame the quality of the magic or the quality of one's go-between. In the USA and Britain the consumption of alcohol or other drugs may serve to delimit anxieties dealt with by use of love magic and go-betweens in other cultures, and may also provide a partial excuse for rejection if rejection occurs.

Societies with freedom of choice of spouse often have mechanisms for facilitating a couple's building of ties in the absence of kin group involvement in the building and maintenance of ties. These mechanisms include components of sexual attraction. One mechanism, mentioned earlier in this chapter, is a reduction in restrictions on premarital sex. Another mechanism, one commonly associated with freedom of choice of spouse, is love.

Love does not seem to be a species-wide characteristic of heterosexual relationships. But in one form or another it is not uncommon. Societies differ markedly in how important love seems to be as a basis of marriage (Coppinger and Rosenblatt, 1968; Rosenblatt, 1967; Cozby and Rosenblatt, 1972). Those societies in which love tends to be important are typically societies with freedom of choice of spouse. Love involves, in varying amounts, sexual attraction, idealization of one's partner, expression of affection toward one's spouse to be, and impractical grounds of choice of spouse. Impractical grounds include things like physical attractiveness and quality of voice, as opposed to grounds like skill at subsistence activities and the alliances that would be created by mating. Love, at the level of the individual, can be conceptualized as building onto sexual attraction a broader range of intense feelings of

attraction and a set of beliefs that help to support the attraction. At the societal level, love can be conceptualized as a set of prescriptions for heterosexual relations and feelings and a set of practices for facilitating the development of the prescribed relations and feelings.

Although freedom of choice implies total freedom, matings in all societies with freedom of choice of spouse are free, in fact, only within rule systems. The rules indicate people who are undesirable to mate (people too close in kinship, people who are foreign or ethnically or religiously different, people who are much older or much younger than one, people who are much richer or much poorer than one, people whose kin live too far away or too close, people who are physically or socially handicapped, etc.). The rules vary from culture to culture in their coverage, in their degree of explicitness, and in the level of disapproval incurred by a rule violation. What is interesting from the point of view of the dynamics of attraction, and telling about human nature, is that most people seem to develop attractions only within the rules. There may be occasional attractions of rich with poor when that attraction violates rules, or of in-group member with out-group member, but generally people seem to be attracted to the people they should be attracted to.

One mechanism for attraction within the rules is aesthetics. Out-group members may be defined as unattractive in terms of physical appearance, garments, speech patterns, manners, etc; people of the wrong age may also be defined as unattractive. A well learned system of aesthetics is one device to maintain attraction within the rules. How such systems of aesthetics develop or change would be fascinating to study.

What factors operate to develop and to maintain an aesthetic system? When change occurs, how does it begin? Ford and Beach (1951, p. 86) report that there seem to be few cross-culturally general standards of physical attraction, with health and non-deformity having perhaps the clearest representation as factors affecting people in general. Beyond that there may be some preference for well-roundedness in females, though the meaning of that preference is unclear. In many places in the world, women who are well-rounded may come from wealthier families and may be healthier in the sense of being free from serious parasitic diseases and free from malnutrition. It is unfortunate that the Ford and Beach work and to some extent the ethnographic work on which it rested was so biased to looking at stereotypical western standards for initial attraction — i.e. at physical attractiveness. One could imagine that in any culture, including western culture, many other factors are involved in attraction — for example, seeing someone performing tasks relevant to gender role

or learning about what another person finds humorous. One might choose to define these other areas of attraction as outside of the area of sexual attraction, but that might be mistakenly prejudging the sexuality of many people. At any rate one can presume, though there has to our knowledge been no empirical study of development of aesthetic standards for attraction, that it is primarily societies with freedom of choice of spouse that can afford to have well articulated standards of attractiveness. It is these societies where people might be most often concerned about attraction (within the rules). So it is these societies that might most clearly have standards that separate out-group members from in-group members on the basis of attractiveness. Thus in cross-cultural perspective, it is as interesting to ask the question "Why are there standards of beauty, of sexiness, or of attractiveness?" as it is to ask "What are the standards?".

Another mechanism for attraction within the rules is the gating of entry to the "opportunity situations". Opportunity situations tend to pull together people who are in the right categories for mating. People very different in age may be excluded, as may married people. Foreigners are typically excluded. Therefore, one's opportunities tend to channel one's choices. In the west, where marriages are typically by free choice, it is easy to see how opportunities are channelled. Young people generally attend schools with the right kinds of people in them; there tend to be ethnic and religious ghettos; religious institutions tend to operate opportunity situations for the unmarried, and so on.

Cross-culturally, the issues of marriage between people who are socially unequal is a complicated one. There are societies where all people are more or less equal, but there are also plenty of societies in the world with some sort of stratification. From society to society and within societies people differ in their reactions to liaisons across strata. The aesthetic factors aside, one might consider an upward alliance very desirable because it brings access to many resources, or very undesirable because it dooms one to continual low status in crucial relationships or because one will never be able to reciprocate properly. A downward alliance may also be considered very desirable because one will be continually altercast as high in status or because one will not have to give much to maintain gift and help obligations, or it may be considered very undesirable because one's status will be lowered by the union or because one is acquiring dependents, or because one cannot expect much from one's relatives by marriage. The factors that are salient in these situations may be different for the young couple involved than for their kin. Thus

status differences may be fuelling sexual attraction for the young couple while putting off their kin, or interesting the kin while putting off the young couple. Attraction between status unequals may arise in part out of the inequality. A lower status person may be excited by contact with someone of higher status, by the excitement of exciting someone with more status, or by being dominated. A higher status person may be attracted to someone who can be dominated by the higher status, attracted by the prospects of elevating someone, or attracted by the greater freedom one might feel with a lower status person. There are no doubt many other factors that might operate, but it seems possible that in any relationship between status unequals, sexual attraction could be linked to status differences. It is also possible that from the point of view of people in a relationship there are always status differences. If so, the issue of marriage between status equals may not exist as a research category, and the only issues to be examined are the effects of variations in status inequality and of differences in perceptions of that inequality and the entanglement of status differences with feelings of sexual attraction.

Where there is freedom of choice of spouse, one might assume, particularly since love tends to be important where there is freedom of choice of spouse, that the ultimate goal of a heterosexual mating is something like intense love, including feelings of sexual attraction. Although love is more often important where there is freedom of choice, it often is not important. First of all, in all societies there is the risk of jealousy in one's kin group. Kin may be threatened if one is tied too strongly to one's mate. The protection against such jealousy may partly be public decorum, and it is quite common around the world that people express their affection and their lust in private rather than in public. In fact the importance of romantic love as a basis of marriage is associated with couple privacy in sleeping quarters (Cozby and Rosenblatt, 1971). It may also be that people mute their feelings or do not develop such strong feelings out of concern for, and out of involvement in, their relationships with their kin.

Even when there is some freedom to develop feelings of attraction, there may be factors working against the development, self-recognition, and/or expression of such feelings. Fear of over-population, of having too many mouths to feed, of injuring the life chances of offspring one already has — particularly in the absence of effective birth control technology — leads some people in some parts of the world (e.g. New Guinea Highlands) to be less involved sexually with their mates than they might

be (Lindenbaum, 1972). People may in such circumstances feel less sexual attraction to a mate. In addition, there are exotic sources of fear of one's partner — for example, fear of loss of strength if one becomes too intensely involved — and sources of reduction in attraction that are quite familiar to westerners — unresolved anger at one's partner, the entanglement of one's sexual relationship in a relationship power battle, and so on. People may also avoid developing feelings of sexual attraction because of previous painful experiences in sexual relationships, but this is a topic which has not received attention in systematic cross-cultural work.

An issue which the currently available cross-cultural literature does not help to resolve, but which is important to resolve, is the question of the relationship between feelings and the norms and agreements concerning what those feelings should be. Does labelling feelings of sexual attraction in a given relationship as inappropriate or sinful have an affect on those feelings? If one decides not to feel sexual attraction toward someone, does one actually do away with sexual attraction feelings, or might one simply move toward self-deception about those feelings? Related to this is a conceptual and methodological question that we can raise but are not prepared to answer — how much sexual attraction is enough to be counted as sexual attraction? If one feels fleeting attraction that one then decides to ignore and subsequently is unaware of should that be counted as attraction? Or is attraction a clear and persisting feeling? Perhaps the ultimate question that cannot be answered yet in this area by use of cross-cultural materials is whether one can feel what one decides to feel and do away with feelings or avoid feelings one decides not to have.

Beyond considerations of sexual attraction at the level of the dyad, in many cultures the crucial solidarities are not with one's partner but with one's work mates or with the larger group of people with whom one lives. It is comparatively rare around the world for one's close relationships over the adult lifespan to be primarily with a single person of the opposite sex with whom one lives to the exclusion of all other adults. Even in the west, such exclusivity may be more a thing of films and fiction than is generally realized. Certainly in the USA ties to children tend to mitigate involvement with one's spouse (Rosenblatt, 1974b; Ryder, 1973), though ties to children and the affect of such ties on heterosexual relationships may be stronger in some other cultures (e.g. Japan — Blood, 1967; Connor, 1976).

Transition from Arranged Marriage to Freedom of Spouse

There is a certain amount of flux at the level of the individual family or kin group and at the level of the society in how much marriages are arranged or free. Families and kin groups become more concerned with alliances and misalliances, for example, when they have more resources to lose in a misalliance. Although there are societal circumstances that tend to push toward societal wide increases in restriction of freedom of choice of spouse (the Islamic revolution of Iran in 1979 may be one example), in recent times most change at the societal level has been toward greater freedom of choice of spouse. Such freedom has been legislated in the People's Republic of China (Salaff, 1973), in Japan (Blood, 1967), and in some other societies, but in many other societies the freedom has developed out of other societal changes. These changes are quite diverse. They may include a reduction in the importance of alliances for peace making. They may include increases in education and wage labour which result in greater independence from influence of kin (see, for example, Strange, 1976, writing about a Malaysian community; and Blood, 1967, writing about Japan). Increased education and wage labour produce greater independence by allowing later age of marriage, increasing geographic mobility of young people, and by reducing dependence on the traditional economic system, which tied young people to family authorities.

Societies moving toward freedom of choice of spouse tend to build institutions for promoting freedom of choice. Blood (1967), for example, writes about the importance of contacts at work. And Salaff (1973) writes about the development of the Young Communist League and the Mao Tse-tung Thought study groups as opportunities for young people in the People's Republic of China to meet. She also points out that freedom of choice first affected people who were most free from filial pressures, people who were geographically mobile and whose status and rewards came most clearly from their adherence to the new order; that is, people in political leadership positions.

The movement to the new system is fraught with difficulties. People do not automatically jump at freedom. First of all, there is the complexity of relating to family elders who were reared under the old system, still retain a residual respect for it, and who may resent movement to the new

system because, among other reasons, it costs them the benefits they were implicitly promised when they as young people complied with the traditional system. That is, one can tolerate more easily the stresses of an arranged system if one realizes that eventually one will have the benefits of arranging marriages for one's own young people. When these benefits are lost, there are some people who feel resentment.

Perhaps the greatest tension in moving to a system based on freedom of choice is simply the lack of social skills and of attitudes necessary to cope with such a system. Blood (1967), Salaff (1973) and others have written about the uncertainties, insecurities, and bungling of young people, like young Japanese or Chinese, who have lacked models of how to behave, have been raised by kin who were reared under the arranged system, and who lacked confidence in their own criteria of choice. For some people the freedom creates a hunger for films, fiction, and gossip that provide an education in how to cope with freedom. For other people the demands of freedom seem too much, and they prefer to have a marriage arranged for them, perhaps with a clear-cut opportunity to veto the selected spouse. Thus one of the fascinating findings of studies of the newly created free marriage systems is the part some young people play in subverting their own freedom.

Outside the borders of the People's Republic, there has been movement toward greater freedom of choice in other Chinese populations. Salaff (1976a, 1976b, 1979) reports from Hong Kong on the effect of work experience on the movement toward freedom of choice of spouse. Young women who have been working outside the home (and given economic conditions there is not much freedom of choice in that) move toward freedom of choice of spouse in part because of the breadth of experience and influence in the family that comes with working, and partly because working delays when they will marry. It is even in the family's interests to delay marriage for a daughter, since that prolongs the time during which the daughter is bringing home a great deal of her pay to her family (Salaff, 1979; Salaff and Wong, 1977). However, in the long run, that may make for a daughter who tends to be too independent to have marriage arranged for her (Salaff, 1979), even if that is also in the interests of her family.

Love matches do not radically alter the characteristics of the partners that would have been expected had a marriage been arranged. This is partly because of who is available, partly because of the carry-over of old values, and partly because the movement toward love matches still leaves family elders with a substantial amount of influence. Thus, when Fox

(1975) compared homogamy in love matches and in arranged marriages in Ankara (Turkey) she found no difference.

Attraction Outside Heterosexual Marriage

Lusts Exist

As Ford and Beach (1951) have documented, there is certainly a great deal of evidence that at least some people in a large number of cultures experience lust outside of marriage. Indications of such lust include the large number of cultures that permit, tolerate, or at least do not often severely punish non-marital sexual relationships, and the scattered cultures with occasional orgies or with sexual hospitality for visitors. However, at least some non-marital sexual relations are fuelled by motives in addition to, or alternative to, lust — motives such as an interest in building or maintaining alliances. Quite often such non-marital sexuality operates in the shadow of marriage in that the norms of partner choice, of decorum and of ways of interacting, reflect norms for marital relations. Hence, it would be wrong, in cross-cultural perspective, to write of sexual attraction outside of marriage as though thoughts and norms dealing with current or prospective marriage were lacking or as though there were no norms governing non-marital sexual relations. Although systematic study is lacking and is sorely needed in this area, there are many case-study examples that provide suggestive support for the notion that attractions outside marriage operate in the shadow of marriage. The citing of specific cases is, of course, no substitute for formal study done with careful sampling. But in the absence of a set of comparative studies, we must either turn to anecdote or skip the topic of attraction outside marriage. It is hoped that in the future there will be a comparative literature to replace the case-study literature cited here.

For unmarried persons sexual dalliance may often lead to movement toward marriage, the movement may in some cases result from kin pressure. The young persons may prefer a more promiscuous life. Nonetheless, movement toward marriage commonly occurs. The classic case is the Trobriand Islanders, as described by Malinowski (1929). Unmarried people in the Trobriand Islands generally engaged intensively in sexual relationships, often without apparent thoughts of marriage. But as Malinowski described the situation, such relationships would often blend into what could be called premarital relationships in

the sense of developing commitment, intensity, and a high likelihood of marriage (Malinowski, 1929, p. 63). In other cultures too sexual relationships of unmarried persons may often, especially for more mature unmarried persons, develop into marital relationships (e.g. the Mangaians (Marshall, 1971) — a Polynesian society with comparatively great freedom of choice of spouse; one in which sexual encounters between unmarried persons serve as a principal means of screening potential spouses). In fact among the Mangaians sexual compatibility is established prior to a decision to develop a broad-based relationship. In some other cultures (e.g. the Gusii of Kenya (LeVine and LeVine, 1963, p. 61)) unmarried persons consciously avoid long sexual affairs in order to avoid escalating a relationship toward marriage. Thus sexual relationships among unmarried persons seem often to operate in the shadow of marriage.

The sexual relations between a married person and a person other than the spouse also seem quite often to operate in the shadow of marriage. It has often been noted in ethnographic accounts of extramarital sex that such relationships tend to be engaged in covertly, or at least not flagrantly, in order to avoid upsetting the marital relationships of the lovers (e.g. Berndt (1962) writing about the Eastern Highlands of New Guinea; Berndt and Berndt (1951, p. 26) writing about Australian aborigines; Elam (1973) writing about the Hima of Uganda; Colson (1958, p. 165) writing about the Tonga of Northern Rhodesia; Gregor (1974) writing about the Mehinacu of Brazil; Malinowski (1929, p. 69) writing about the Trobriand Islanders; and Nimmo (1970) writing about the Bajaw of the Philippines). Gregor (1974) puts it another way for the Mehinacu — that publicity of relationship is what distinguishes a marriage from an affair. Where affairs persist in being open, they tend to develop into new marriages (e.g. Benedict (1967) writing about the Seychelles Islanders; Bushnell and Bushnell (1971) writing about a Mexican village; and Gregor (1974) writing about the Mehinacu).

There appears to be a double standard in the regulation of non-marital sexuality (Ford and Beach, 1951, Chapter VI). Double standards, when present, generally allow males more freedom than females or punish males less for engaging in non-marital sexual relations. That information could be taken as evidence that male lusts are stronger than female lusts or are harder to control. However it may well be that the crucial sex difference is one of power to affect norms and regulations not one of sexuality.

Dynamics of Non-marital Sexual Attraction

Even where people do not seem to expect lusts to be expressed in marriage but tolerate or even encourage lusts outside of marriage, the lusts operate in the shadow of marriage in that they generally operate within marriage rules. That is, the permitted or attractive partners for non-marital affairs seem generally to be people with whom marriage would be or would have been legal. Whether sexual relationships in such cases are based on sexual attraction is not, however, always clear. There is suggestive evidence that people who are deprived of marital sexuality either are not always concerned about sexual attraction and are willing to engage whatever partner is available or, that for people who are deprived of marital sexuality a wide range of partners may be attractive. Malinowski (1929, p. 294) and Gorer (1967, p. 170), for example, both found that some dreadfully unattractive individuals were popular sexual partners under certain circumstances.

Deprivation of marital sexuality seems to be related also to the incidence of non-marital sexuality. For example, in cultures with polygyny (some men have more than one spouse) and with early marriage of females or late marriage of some males, there tends to be a high level of non-marital sexual intercourse (Wilson (1963, p. 161) writing about the Nyakyusa of Tanzania; and Paulme (1963) writing about tropical Africa in general) or a high level of extramarital sex of married women with unmarried males (Elam (1973, p. 190) writing about the Hima of Uganda). Among the Mangaians (Marshall, 1971), it is assumed that one will engage in extramarital liaisons during prolonged absences of one's spouse. LeVine (1959) has described a situation among the Gusii in which male deprivation of marital sexuality (due to late marriage of males, to very early marriage of females, and to comparatively severe restrictions on non-marital sexuality) has led to a very high rate of rape. However, definitional complexities exist, both for an outsider trying to determine a rape rate in the culture and for a person engaged in sexual encounters, since ordinary sex among the Gusii involves so much resistance on the part of the woman that it is difficult for one or both participants in a non-marital sexual encounter to decide whether what is going on is ordinary sex or rape. Despite evidence that deprivation is related to non-marital sexuality, it would be wrong to assume that the relationship is simple. Heider (1976) reports that among the Grand Valley Dani of New Guinea, where sexual intercourse is not defined as

important, people apparently sustain four to six years of sexual abstinence following birth of a child without signs of unhappiness and without non-marital sexual relations.

Materials are generally lacking for a comprehensive study of homosexual relationships. There are, for example, few studies that give, as Mead (1973) has for Samoa, quantitative data on homosexual experiences. Scattered accounts suggest that homosexual experiences tend to be primarily experiences of sexually deprived males (e.g. Davenport, 1965) or of adolescent exploration, as they were in Samoa. But until comprehensive research is carried out nothing can be said with any certainty.

Although there is no formal study of compensation patterns in non-marital sexual relationships, it is quite commonly reported that women in non-marital relationships are given gifts by their male partners (e.g. Berndt and Berndt (1951, p. 179) for Australian aborigines; Goody (1962) for the Gonja of Ghana; Colson (1958, p. 165) for the Plateau Tonga; Davenport (1965, p. 179) for a Pacific Island society; Elam (1972, p. 176) for the Hima of Uganda; Cohen (1971, pp. 106–107) for the Kanuri of Nigeria; Gorer (1967, p. 328) for the Lepcha of Sikkim; Gregor (1974) for the Mehinacu of Brazil; LeVine and LeVine (1975, p. 61) for the Gusii; Malinowski (1929, p. 269) for the Trobriand Islanders; Netting (1969) for the Kofyar of Nigeria; Nimmo (1970) for the Bajaw of the Philippines). The literature reports either no gift giving or, a lower likelihood of gift giving, by women to men for all of these cultures. Only the Kaska of Canada (Honigmann, 1954, p. 129) seem to have comparable gift giving levels for women and men. The role of gifts in sexual relationships may vary greatly from society to society, but the apparent commonness of such gifts is intriguing. The gifts may be a symbol of male power, a sign that it is common around the world to define male sexual need as somehow greater than female, or a symbol of relative control of goods cross-culturally (if males control more goods, they have more goods to give). Gifts may also indicate who is more actively involved in establishing a liaison (males may more often be actively involved, and the initiator of the relationship may feel the greater obligation to provide compensation). It should be added that males may also give compensation to the spouse or kin of an extramarital partner. In some societies they may ordinarily (or in some only if "caught") have to provide some compensation to a woman's husband or to some other male who somehow has authority over her (e.g. Mair (1965, p. 133) for the Ganda of Uganda; Colson (1958, p. 107) for the Tonga). Even where the

compensation is not given directly to people other than a partner, others may benefit from a gift to a lover — for example, others may eat the fish a Mehinacu lover gives to his extramarital partner (Gregor, 1974).

Non-marital sexual attractions also operate in the shadow of marriage in that they may be fuelled by the frustrations or boredoms of marital relations. A vivid example comes from Romonum, Truk, in the Pacific, where extramarital affairs seem to arise out of reactions to a marital system fraught with restraint and with a frustrating tangle of obligation and required respect (Swartz, 1958). Although the Trukese engage in casual extramarital relations, Swartz describes the high level of satisfaction they obtain from more intense liaisons in which constraints are minimal and opportunities for expressing otherwise pent up aggressive impulses are great.

One of the most intriguing suggestions to be found among ethnographic cases about the dynamics of sexual attraction comes from scattered assertions that first or early attractions tend to have a hold on people. In Tikopia, a Polynesian society, adulterous relationships tend to involve people who were lovers before marriage (Firth, 1957, p. 475). But these relationships sometimes operate with dynamics that go beyond mere persistence of attachment. The dynamics may hinge on the fact that one of the premarital lovers feels some rejection by the other (why did you not decide to elope with me?), and therefore the affair gives one a chance to make it vividly clear to one's former lover how much she or he lost, and in the process one can also take revenge on that person's spouse. However the literature suggests that elsewhere the attraction between people who had a relationship that preceded the marriage of one of them may be simply the retention of special feelings (e.g. Mangaians — Marshall, 1971; Trobriand Islanders — Malinowski, 1929, pp. 316–317). The Bemba seem to have recognized a related phenomenon. They have a theory that betrothed couples who have prepubertal intercourse and who subsequently marry each other have unusually stable marriages (Richards, 1968).

Another way in which non-marital sexual relations operate in the shadow of marriage cross-culturally is that there are scattered reports of cultures in which to have had a non-marital sexual relationship is to establish a set of ties and obligations with each other that go far beyond a simple, possibly short-term sexual relationship (e.g. among the Mehinacu — Gregor, 1974; and among the Rukuba of Nigeria — Muller, 1973). Finally, non-marital sexual affairs may even be defined as strengthening a marriage — for example, by providing a substitute

inseminator for an infertile husband; by providing an extra source of family income through the gifts and compensation paid by a woman's lover; by increasing appreciation of one's spouse (Berndt and Berndt, 1951, p. 50); or by increasing the value of a wife to a husband through his awareness of her desirability to others or through the alliances he builds with her lovers.

In extramarital sex, as in many areas of life, the forbidden and possibly dangerous is more attractive to some people. Although we can only provide scattered anecdotal support, it seems that in at least some cultures one element of sexual attraction is the excitement, intrigue, and risk involved e.g. Eastern Highlands of New Guinea (Berndt, 1962, Chapter 9). Berndt also writes about the need for variety and the rewards, in that culture area, of acting aggressively in one's own self-interest as fuel for extramarital affairs.

Maintaining and Restoring Lust

Sexual attraction, as defined at the beginning of this chapter, may to some extent be a temporary expedient. It may in many cultural settings operate to move a couple into or further into a relationship in which they become tied together by other bonds, particularly by bonds of mutual dependence and shared experience. From that perspective the decline of sexual attraction (as defined at the beginning of this chapter) may often be seen as of no particular consequence, and whether it is or is not present at the ending of a marital relationship may not be related to that ending. Heterosexual relationships that end may often end for reasons that have little or nothing to do with lust for one's spouse, and that lust may decline as a result of factors having nothing to do with the sexual aspects of a relationship. Reyna (1977), for example, writes about the rationality of divorce in a Chadian society, one in which childlessness has a marked effect on family food production and relatively often leads to divorce. In other societies too, childlessness may often be grounds for divorce (Rosenblatt et al., 1973). Westerners may also end heterosexual relationships for reasons far removed from the sexual aspects of a relationship, while experiencing the ending as resting on a decline in lust for the spouse. Heterosexual attraction may in such cases be a metaphor for other more practical processes, or decline as an artefact of the other processes. For example, a couple who cannot effectively make decisions together or who find that they have very different standards of household order might decide to end a relationship, but many may phrase their

description of what has happened in terms of a decline in sexual attraction. Sexual attraction (lust) may decline in some of those relationships, but only because the other factors are pushing the marriage toward a termination. This also suggests that when people in the west express a continuing sexual attraction, they may in some cases be experiencing some other sort of linkage (e.g. enjoyment of stability, feelings of loyalty). They may describe this linkage as sexual attraction (lust) because that is appropriate language to use. They may even experience the linkage as sexual attraction (lust) because that is the appropriate feeling to have.

Among the Mehinacu (Gregor, 1974) couples seem to restore attraction in their marriage by going on long trips together. The mechanisms operating are not obvious, though Gregor suggests that the absence may squelch competing affairs and it certainly gives others the sense of the couple as a couple. That sense of coupleness may help push the couple to be more tied together, both because others provide clearer expectations that they will be together and because the couple themselves perceive themselves that way. Couples can easily have too much contact (Rosenblatt *et al.*, 1979), but for those that can sustain substantial contact, the interactions during a long trip may help to tie them more closely together.

Concluding Statement

Beginning with a very basic definition of sexual attraction as feelings self-defined as lust, the chapter moves on to consider the cross-cultural variability in what elicits those feelings and how those feelings might be felt, when those feelings are experienced, when they are expressed, and how situations are established in which those feelings might be felt. Tentative generalizations are offered about sexual attraction in arranged and freedom of choice marriages, in parts of the world where marriage is changing from an arranged to a freedom of choice situation, and about the extent to which sexual attraction operates within the shadow of marriage around the world.

This chapter has argued that the western social psychological concept of sexual attraction is embedded in western culture and does not necessarily relate to the realities of many other people in the world. It has further argued that the ethnographic literature that seems to speak to the western concept of sexual attraction tends to be written from an outsider's perspective, and that it too often fails to represent the

understandings and feelings of the people within the cultures studied. Attraction for unmarried persons and for married persons seems channelled by, muted by, or encouraged by the connection the attraction has or would have with marriage. Marriages differ, however, in the involvement of kin in their establishment and continuation. So when and how sexual attraction generally develops varies as a function of kin involvement.

Many of the most basic questions remain to be answered. It is not even clear at this point whether it is meaningful to compare feelings of attraction cross-culturally. But it is hoped that this chapter will promote needed basic research and promote greater sophistication in the use of research.

7. References

Benedict, B. The equality of the sexes in the Seychelles. In Freedman, M. (Ed.), *Social Organisation: essays presented to Raymond Firth*. London: Cass, 1967.
Berndt, R. M. *Excess and restraint*. Chicago: University of Chicago Press, 1962.
Berndt, R. M. and Berndt, C. H. *Sexual behavior in western Arnhem Land*. New York: Viking Fund Publication in Anthropology No. 16, 1951.
Blood, R. O. Jr. *Love match and arranged marriage: a Tokyo-Detroit comparison*. New York: Free Press, 1967.
Boon, J. A. The Balinese marriage predicament: individual, strategical, and cultural. *American Ethnologist*, 1976, **3**, 191-214.
Brown, P. and Buchbinder, G. *Man and woman in the New Guinea Highlands*. Washington, D.C.: American Anthropological Association, 1976.
Bushnell, J. H. and Bushnell, D. D. Sociocultural and psychodynamic correlates of polygyny in a highland Mexican village. *Ethnology*, 1971, **10**, 44-55.
Cohen, R. *Dominance and defiance*. Washington, D.C.: American Anthropological Association, 1971.
Cohen, Y. Ends and means to political control: state organisation and the punishment of adultery, incest, and violation of celibacy. *American Anthropologist*, 1969, **71**, 658-687.
Colson, E. *Marriage and the family among the plateau Tonga of Northern Rhodesia*. Manchester: Manchester University Press, 1958.
Connor, J. W. Family bonds, maternal closeness and the suppression of sexuality in three generations of Japanese Americans. *Ethos*, 1976, **4**, 184-221.
Coppinger, R. M. and Rosenblatt, P. C. Romantic love and subsistence dependence of spouses. *Southwestern Journal of Anthropology*, 1968, **24**, 310-319.
Cozby, P. C. and Rosenblatt, P. C. Privacy, love and in-law avoidance.

Proceedings of the American Psychological Association, 1971, **6**, 277-278.

Davenport, W. Sexual patterns and their regulation in a society of the southwest Pacific. In Beach, F. (Ed.), *Sex and behavior.* New York: Wiley, 1965.

Elam, Y. *The social and sexual roles of Hima women.* Manchester: Manchester University Press, 1973.

Elwin, V. *The kingdom of the young.* New York and Oxford: Oxford University Press, 1968.

Ember, C. Men's fear of sex with women: a cross-cultural study. *Sex Roles,* 1978, **4**, 657-678.

Ember, M. On the origins and extension of the incest taboo. *Behavior Science Research,* 1975, **10**, 249-281.

Firth, R. *We, the Tikopia.* (2nd edn). Boston: Beacon, 1957.

Ford, C. S. and Beach, F. A. *Patterns of sexual behavior.* New York: Harper, 1951.

Fox, G. L. Love match and arranged marriage in a modernising nation: mate selection in Ankara, Turkey. *Journal of Marriage and the Family,* 1975, **31**, 180-193.

Gadlin, H. Private lives and public order: a critical view of the history of intimate relations in the United States. In Levinger, G. and Raush, H. L. (Eds), *Close relationships: perspectives on the meaning of intimacy.* Amherst: University of Massachusetts Press, 1977.

Gagnon, J. H. Scripts and the coordination of sexual conduct. In Cole, J. K. and Dienstbier, R. (Eds), *Nebraska Symposium on Motivation, 1973.* Lincoln: University of Nebraska Press, 1974.

Gonzalez, N. L. S. *Black Carib household structure.* Seattle: University of Washington Press, 1969.

Goode, W. J. The theoretical importance of love. *American Sociological Review,* 1959, **24**, 38-47.

Goody, E. N. Conjugal separation and divorce among the Gonja of northern Ghana. In Fortes, M. (Ed.), *Marriage in tribal societies.* Cambridge: Cambridge University Press, 1962.

Gorer, G. *Himalayan village.* (2nd edn). New York: Basic Books, 1967.

Gregor, T. Publicity, privacy, and Mehinacu marriage. *Ethnology,* 1974, **13**, 333-350.

Haas, M. R. Fear and the status of women. *Southwestern Journal of Anthropology,* 1969, **25**, 228-235.

Heider, K. G. Kani sexuality: a low energy system. *Man,* 1976, **11**, 188-201.

Honigmann, J. J. *The Kaska Indians: an ethnographic reconstruction.* New Haven: Yale University Publications in Anthropology No. 51, 1954.

Howard, A. and Howard, I. Pre-marital sex and social control among the Rotumans. *American Anthropologist,* 1964, **66**, 266-283.

Huntsman, J. and McLean, M. Incest prohibitions in Micronesia and Polynesia. *Journal of the Polynesian Society,* 1964, **85**, No. 2, 149-298.

248   *Paul C. Rosenblatt and Roxanne M. Anderson*

LeVine, R. A. Gusii sex offences: a study in social control. *American Anthropologist*, 1959, **61**, 965-990.
LeVine, R. A. and Levine, B. B. Nyansongo: a Gusii community in Kenya. In Whiting, B. B. (Ed.), *Six cultures*. New York: Wiley, 1963.
Lindebaum, S. Sorcerers, ghosts and polluting women: an analysis of religious belief and population control. *Ethnology*, 1972, **11**, 241-253.
Lindzey, G. Some remarks concerning incest, the incest taboo and psychoanalytic theory. *American Psychologist*, 1967, **22**, 1051-1059.
Mair, L. P. *An African people in the twentieth century*. London: Routledge, 1965.
Malinowski, B. *The sexual life of savages*. New York: Harcourt, 1929.
Marshall, D. S. Sexual life on Mangaia. In Marshall, D. S. and Suggs, R. C. (Eds), *Human sexual behavior*. New York, Basic Books, 1971.
Mead, M. *Coming of age in Samoa*. New York: Morrow, 1973.
Messenger, J. C. Sex and repression in an Irish folk community. In Marshall, D. S. and Suggs, R. C. (Eds), *Human sexual behavior*. New York: Basic Books, 1971.
Minturn, L., Grosse, M. and Haider, S. Cultural patterning of sexual beliefs and behavior. *Ethnology*, 1969, **8**, 301-318.
Muller, J. C. On preferential/prescriptive marriage and the function of kinship systems: the Rukuba case (Benue-Plateau State, Nigeria). *American Anthropologist*, 1973, **75**, 1563-1576.
Murdock, G. P. *Social structure*. New York: Macmillan, 1949.
Nag, M. *Factors affecting human fertility in non-industrial societies: a cross-cultural study*. New Haven: Yale University Publications in Anthropology No. 66, 1968.
Netting, R. McC. Women's weapons: the politics of domesticity among the Kofyar. *American Anthropologist*, 1969, **71**, 1037-1046.
Nimmo, H. A. Bajau sex and reproduction. *Ethnology*, 1970, **9**, 251-262.
Parker, S. The precultural basis of the incest taboo: toward a biosocial theory. *American Anthropologist*, 1976, **78**, 285-305.
Paulme, D. Introduction. In Paulme, D. (Ed.), *Women of tropical Africa*. Berkeley: University of California Press, 1963.
Pelto, P. J. and Pelto, G. H. Intra-cultural diversity: some theoretical issues. *American Ethnologist*, 1975, **2**, 1-18.
Rainwater, L. Marital sexuality in four "cultures of poverty". In Marshall, D. S. and Suggs, R. C. (Eds), *Human sexual behavior*. New York: Basic Books, 1971.
Reyna, S. P. The rationality of divorce: marital instability among the Barma of Chad. *Journal of Comparative Family Studies*, 1977, **8**, 269-288.
Richards, A. I. The Bemba of north-eastern Rhodesia. In Colson, E. and Gluckman, M. (Eds). *Seven tribes of central Africa*. Manchester: Manchester University Press, 1968.
Rook, K. S. and Hammen, C. L. A cognitive perspective on the experience of sexual arousal. *Journal of Social Issues*, 1977, **33**, No. 2, 7-29.
Rosenblatt, P. C. Marital residence and the functions of romantic love. *Ethnology*, 1967, **6**, 471-480.

Rosenblatt, P. C. Communication in the practice of love magic. *Social Forces*, 1971, **49**, 482–487.

Rosenblatt, P. C. Cross-cultural perspective on attraction. In Huston, T. L. (Ed.), *Foundations of interpersonal attraction*. New York and London: Academic Press, 1974a.

Rosenblatt, P. C. Behavior in public places: comparisons of couples accompanied and unaccompanied by children. *Journal of Marriage and the Family*, 1974b, **36**, 750–755.

Rosenblatt, P. C. Needed research on commitment in marriage. In Levinger, G. and Rausch, H. L. (Eds), *Close relationships: perspectives on the meaning of intimacy*. Amherst: University of Massachusetts Press, 1977.

Rosenblatt, P. C. and Cozby, P. C. Courtship patterns associated with freedom of choice of spouse. *Journal of Marriage and the Family*, 1972, **34**, 689–695.

Rosenblatt, P. C. and Cunningham, M. R. Sex differences in cross-cultural perspectives. In Lloyd, B. B. and Archer, J. (Eds), *Exploring sex differences*. London and New York: Academic Press, 1976.

Rosenblatt, P. C. and Hillabrant, W. J. Divorce for childlessness and the regulation of adultery. *Journal of Sex Research*, 1972, **8**, 117–127.

Rosenblatt, P. C. and Unangst, D. Marriage ceremonies: an exploratory cross-cultural study. *Journal of Comparative Family Studies*, 1974, **5**, 40–56.

Rosenblatt, P. C., Fugita, S. S. and McDowell, K. V. Wealth transfer and restrictions on sexual relations during betrothal. *Ethnology*, 1969, **8**, 319–328.

Rosenblatt, P. C., Peterson, P., Portner, J., Cleveland, M., Mykkanen, A., Foster, R., Holm, G., Joel, B., Reisch, H., Kreuscher, C. and Phillips, R. A cross-cultural study of responses to childlessness. *Behavior Science Notes*, 1973, **8**, 221–231.

Rosenblatt, P. C., Titus, S. L., Nevaldine, A. M. and Cunningham, M. R. Marital system differences and summer-long vacations: togetherness-apartness and tension. *American Journal of Family Therapy*, 1979, **7**, 77–84.

Ryder, R. G. Longitudinal data relating marriage satisfaction and having a child. *Journal of Marriage and the Family*, 1973, **35**, 604–606.

Salaff, J. W. The emerging conjugal relationship in the People's Republic of China. *Journal of Marriage and the Family*, 1973, **35**, 705–717.

Salaff, J. W. Working daughters in the Hong Kong Chinese family: female filial piety or a transformation in the family power structure? *Journal of Social History*, 1976a, **9**, 439–465.

Salaff, J. W. The status of unmarried Hong Kong women and the social factors contributing to their delayed marriage. *Population Studies*, 1976b, **30**, 391–412.

Salaff, J. W. Working daughters of Hong Kong: Modern times and the traditional family in colonized China. Unpublished manuscript, Department of Sociology, University of Toronto, 1979.

Salaff, J. W. and Wong, A. K. Chinese women at work: work commitment and fertility in the Asian setting. In Kupinsky, S. (Ed.), *The fertility of working women: a synthesis of international research*. New York: Praeger, 1977.

Schneider, H. K. Romantic love among the Turu. In Marshall, D. S. and Suggs,

R. C. (Eds) *Human sexual behavior*. New York: Basic Books, 1971.

Shirley, R. W. and Romney, A. K. Love magic and socialisation anxiety: a cross cultural study. *American Anthropologist*, 1962, **64**, 1028-1031.

Spiro, M. E. *Children of the kibbutz*. New York: Schocken, 1965.

Stoffle, R. W. Industrial impact on family formation in Barbados, West Indies. *Ethnology*, 1977, **16**, 253-268.

Strange, H. Continuity and change: patterns of mate selection and marriage ritual in a Malay village. *Journal of Marriage and the Family*, 1976, **38**, 561-571.

Swartz, M. Sexuality and aggression on Romonum, Truk. *American Anthropologist*, 1958, **60**, 467-486.

Talmon, Y. Mate selection in collective settlements. *American Sociological Review*, 1964, **29**, 491-508.

Topley, M. Marriage resistance in rural Kwangtung. In Wolf, M. and Witke, R. (Eds) *Women in Chinese society*. Stanford: Stanford University Press, 1975.

Watson, L. C. Sexual socialisation in Guajiro society. *Ethnology*, 1972, **11**, 150-156.

Watson, L. C. Marriage and sexual adjustment in Guajiro society. *Ethnology*, 1973, **12**, 153-162.

Wilson, M. *Good company*. Boston: Beacon, 1963.

Wolf, A. P. Childhood association, sexual attraction, and the incest taboo: a Chinese case. *American Anthropologist*, 1966, **68**, 883-898.

Wolf, A. P. Adopt a daughter-in-law, marry a sister: a Chinese solution to the problem of the incest taboo. *American Anthropologist*, 1968, **70**, 864-874.

Wolf, A. P. Childhood association and sexual attraction: a further test of the Westermarck hypothesis. *American Anthropologist*, 1970, **72**, 503-515.

Wolf, A. P. Childhood association, sexual attraction and fertility in Taiwan. In Zubrow, E. (Ed.), *Demographic anthropology*. Albuquerque: University of New Mexico Press, 1976.

8
The Dramaturgy of Sexual Relations

ROM HARRÉ

Sub-faculty of Philosophy, Oxford University,
10 Merton Street, Oxford, England

The Complexity of Social Psychology

Most branches of psychology are made difficult by the existence of two
extreme modes of production of discernible regularities in various
aspects of human action. At the one extreme are automatisms, modes of
functioning which seem to involve automatic mechanisms in which the
conscious attention and agentive control of the actor is not engaged.
These seem to be of two kinds — physiological automatisms such as
blinking reflexes; and habits, learned practices reduced to automatisms.
At the other extreme are autonomisms — modes of functioning which
involve consciously attended rules or exemplars by which action is
guided in effortful striving by the actor as agent. Again there seem to be
two kinds of autonomisms. There are those in which the actor follows
standardized rules or paradigms to realize conventionally prescribed
ends, and there are those where for his own personal projects an actor
makes his own plans and strives to carry them out.

The problems this dichotomy forces upon psychology are twofold. It is
clear that the methodology appropriate to the study of each extreme
mode of functioning must be radically different. Traditional types of
extensionally designed manipulative experiments could be appropriate to
the former, while the latter would require the kind of ethnographic
approach of cultural anthropology and of necessity must include
exploration of the actors' perception of events and attention to his
avowals of his plans. Psychology seems inevitably committed to two
distinctive and irreducible methodologies. But there is much in social life
that is not readily assimilated to either extreme. By what methods are we

to investigate the production of those action-sequences we colloquially call "chatting up", for instance? The problem field of sexual attraction and its transformation in social relations is shot through with phenomena in the intermediate realm. Traditional psychological method would approach the investigation of these phenomena with an extension of the method appropriate to automatisms. The ethogenic movement in psychology would tackle the study by an extension of the methods appropriate to autonomisms. In this chapter I shall be developing the latter tack.

To control our investigations I must begin by setting out some major distinctions to be confirmed or deleted as the investigation proceeds. My primary distinction is between process and presentation, or in other words, between dynamic performance and static appearance.

Dynamic Performances

We can distinguish, at least analytically, between sexual impulses and sexual rituals, that is the culturally specific practices through which sexual impulses are realized. I am inclined to think that ethologists have made out a convincing case for treating both impulses (including recognition capacities) and rituals *in the animal kingdom*, as genetically based. In some cases interaction rituals and recognition signals are linked; for example; Cullen (1972) has demonstrated the linkage for fireflies. No such case has been made out for human beings. We must begin by assuming that rituals and impulses are derived from different bases. But what about recognition? I shall be arguing that the recognition of another person as a sexual being is complicated for humans by reason of the ubiquity and preponderance of tertiary gender markers as elements in culturally specific sexual dramas. These markers, such as distinctive clothing for each sex, involve cultural conventions, not least as to which part of the body is sexually salient.

My first illustration, drawn from anthropological material, is directed to establish the distinction between impulse and ritual, the diverse components of sexual "attraction". It is not hard to find examples of two cultures enjoining and engendering "opposite" practices, that is practices centring on mutually contradictory ways of socially transforming and hence dealing with sexual impulses.

Static Appearances

The most important synchronic distinction needed for identifying the dramaturgical aspects of sexual relations separates sex as a criterion of human difference from gender. A sexual difference is biological and primarily anatomical. There may be differences other than anatomical at this level of analysis, but the empirical evidence is inconclusive (cf. Lloyd and Archer, 1976). Differentiation by gender is to be understood as marked in distinctive ways for public presentation of self as exemplifying a particular category of being.

Sexual relations and relationships are transformed into or represented by gender relations in social relationships. Mostly this involves symbolic transformation *within which self-presentation occurs*. To get a grasp even of the phenomena, let alone an understanding of the principles of their order, it seems obvious that we must begin with some kind of dramaturgical analysis, that is, by looking not so much at role but at conventions of role-representation. Parenthetically, it is worth expanding the difference between role and role-performance on the one hand, and conventions of role-representation on the other. Presumably one could give an account of role-performance entirely within a sociological framework of concepts and perhaps, even in terms of a general functionalism. The flight from and return to traditional gender roles in the Kibbutzim is vividly described by Tiger and Shepher (1975), but without any mention of the conventions by which the gender distinctions they are sociologically locating are actually realized, apart from the practical activities in which they occur. Tiger and Shepher do not tell us how they or the local inhabitants were able to tell whether they were encountering women or men. In this chapter I shall examine gender representation, the location of male and female humans in their expressive orders as men and women, girls and boys.

As a final note in this section, it is worth noticing the radical relation between sex and gender imposed on children in many societies, and most notably in the Victorian West. Since children were generally dressed in miniaturized versions of adult costume (children's clothing *per se* is an invention of the early twentieth century), there was as striking and vivid a public expressive display of gender distinction as one could imagine. Yet Victorian children were defined as "innocent", meaning non-sexual beings. Anatomical differences were transmuted directly into gender

differences without a reading as differences of sex. The Victorian child was strictly sex*less*.

Explaining Regularities: Rules

Those regularities in social life which are known or suspected to be autonomisms are characteristically explained by reference to rules, programmes, conventions, paradigms or exemplars, the following of which generates regularities observable to someone knowledgeable in the conventions of a society. Unlike the regularities produced by the natural mechanisms described in the laws of nature, social regularities exist against a background of possible (and sometimes threatened) violations. Rules can be broken, conventions flouted and exemplars ignored.

Clearly, what binds an agent's actions to a rule of conduct cannot be the natural necessity that binds a natural mechanism's to a law of nature. The most general answer to the question of the agent's relation to rule etc., is that the agent has some project. In this chapter I am concerned directly only with expressive projects. In a sexual encounter the agents may have the practical project of achieving sexual intercourse. I am interested only in the intermediate expressive projects of publicly presenting themselves as of a certain gender and within that gender as of worth.

Notice that just as in natural science the terms I am using to describe my interest and to introduce my explanatory framework are not intended literally. Terms like "rule" and "project" illuminate because they are under pressure from some small metaphorical transposition, just as are natural science terms like "natural selection", "force", and so on. Certain features of their literal use drop away. It would be as much a misunderstanding to try to find the conscious attention implied in the literal use of the terms "rule" and "project" as to look for the breeder in the process Darwin calls "natural selection".

Once we begin to introduce such metaphors as "projects" into our set of theoretical terms, we are permitted the contemplation of a new range of hypothetical entities and a new level of the analysis of action. Project talk involves the idea of means/end processes. So project talk with respect to the expressive order involves the idea of expressive ends and the means of their realization. Expressive performances offer themselves for further investigation. What ends do they bring about?

In general, we can distinguish social-functional ends (like establishing dominance over others) from presentational ends (such as being actually

thought of as a strong, reliable, potent male). It may be that the achievement of the latter is a way of achieving the former. But as ends, they are clearly analytically quite distinct. For instance, the presentational end may be achieved in a theatrical performance or in a work of fiction from which no socio-practical outcome could devolve.

The matter does not stop at this point. Anthropologists have pointed out how social practices can point beyond themselves to larger social matters. For instance creation myths employ commonsense understandings of the social dramaturgy of sexual relations to set forth the basis of social organization of the associations of men in a culture. These matters would repay close study by social psychologists of contemporary cultures, since they would reveal the variety of possible social psychologies of the sexual relations, the extent of the modes by which sex is transformed into gender for expressive purposes.

Just as in the natural sciences, neither the hypothetical productive process — rule-following — nor the relevant structure in the phenomenon — order at the level of social acts — the major elements of a scientific analysis of social phenomena, could be discerned by naive observation. Our study must begin by looking elsewhere than to the phenomena for rules and regularities which can be brought back to the phenomena to construct some data. I propose that we begin our search for the principles of order of the living out of conventional dramas of character, where the protagonists are seen by each other as sexual beings (displaying gender), by a reading of etiquette books (the social psychology of yesteryear) and of the problem pages of the press. The relation between etiquette and "character" is close. "The art of receiving guests is a very subtle one . . . but to be known as a perfect hostess is to possess a most enviable reputation and one to which all those who entertain should aspire" (Anon., 1940, p. 8). The scenario for a scene in the character drama unfolding at an evening party is described as follows:

> The hostess should receive her guests at the head of the staircase . . . as the names of the guests are announced she should shake hands with each, making some courteous observation, not with a view of inducing them to linger on the staircase, but rather of inviting them to enter the ball-room to make way for other guests (p. 82).

Gender performances are well defined: "it is invariably the place of the lady to take the initiative when meeting one of the opposite sex" (p. 21). A man "should always hastily remove the glove from the right hand offering it to the lady" (the hand rather than the glove one presumes) etc. Social psychology is in part a representation of the practices of our times

through which expressive presentations of self as of a certain kind of being is achieved. Current conceptions of etiquette should reflect the expressive system. The significance of that and similar systems for formulating a social psychology of performance is still I think unclear, but such studies are crucial to the competence aspect of that psychological field.

Kent (1979) has suggested that "aunties", a generic term for the authors of advice columns, be seen as "authoritative providers of moral permission". If this is so, their answers represent the tacit rule systems of the period for regulating certain relations between the sexes as represented to each other. One would expect to find comment both on what to do (and what not to do) and how to appear (and how not to appear).

I am going to assume that betrothal and marriage are the prime *social* transformations of sexual relations, potential and actual, into public social space. (Flirtation and teasing also deal with potential sexual relations, sharing something of the logical character of betrothal.) As such, betrothal and marriage deserve our attention, as indeed they do that of the readers of the problem pages and the aunties who write them.

(I note that marriage may be functioning as a metaphor for other relations, e.g. economic or religious — nuns marry Christ to enter fully into their Orders, though monks are not correspondingly bound by metaphor.)

Problems

With the help of the excellent study by Robin Kent (1979) we can follow the transformations of the rule system in England from the seventeenth century. First, the problems which have called forth from the auntie a display of the rules. At least in their formal structure the problems have remained the same:

(i) The assessment of risk, either in taking a step into a relationship, for instance marriage (a typical eighteenth century problem), or in breaking an existing relationship (a nineteenth century preoccupation), for instance by adultery, or even by spending too much time at the club.

(ii) How to deal with loneliness or despair. The problem page specializes in cases where (ii) is a consequence of misjudgement of (i).

(iii) Proposals to contract liaisons across social boundaries of class, race, religion, and nowadays of gender.

Rule Display as a Step toward Solutions

In response to the display of the problem by the correspondent, the auntie displays the rules of action and the expressive conventions of gender relative to situation and social role as it would be consequent on the realization of the relations. Aunties display consequences of the working of the rules and conventions to help in a rational assessment of risk. The principles governing the social transformation of sexual relations are strikingly and characteristically different in the three centuries covered in Kent's book. We do not know whether the difference is due to an increasingly wide readership, mapping existing rule-systems, or whether the rule-systems have changed.

(i) Eighteenth Century. In that century the expressive styles may have been related to economic categories such as money and property, at least among the kind of people for whom the newspapers were written, but it is very difficult to identify any connections. There are lots of examples of explicit formulation of the requirements of expressive style to express oneself as *man* or *woman*. In most of the examples I have studied, social relevant personal virtues *as publicly displayed*, dominate the catalogues, e.g. for expressing "femininity" — "complacent without meanness to her superiors, gentle and considerate to her inferiors . . . industrious according to her necessities, etc." (Kent, 1979, p. 50). There is no mention of a corresponding inner state relative to her inferiors, for instance that she should not despise them. The advice concerns only how she should appear. Similarly, "masculinity" is displayed in such public virtues as "slow of promise but sudden of performance, as apt to give as to take afront" (Kent, 1979, p. 37). And they are social virtues with respect to the living out of social events, at least to my ear, considered quite independently of the practical order of the management of the business of life.

(ii) Nineteenth Century. By the 1840s the expressive mode began to include domestic virtues drawn from the practical order of family life. Notice how similarly grounded are the expressive demands on the wives of 1852 and 1906.

A wife's duties. — A wife should endeavour to make her home as comfortable as possible, so that her husband may always look forward with pleasure to the time when he reaches home. Many husbands are driven from their homes to clubs and other places that they should shun, by the bad management of their wives or, what is worse, by their

want of discretion in exposing all their little faults to neighbours. That system of gossiping that some wives indulge in is frequently the cause of much misery; when a woman exposes her husband's failings, she breaks her marriage vow, and makes her home unbearable, perhaps forever. Whatever may be the private character of her husband, it should be defended rather than laid open to attack by the public. Your own good sense will guide you in the other domestic duties of a wife.

(The Family Friend, 1852)

Your husband may be irritating and exacting, but you should remember that he comes home weary and tired after his day's work. Naturally he expects to find a bright, smiling wife and a cosy meal waiting for him. You do very wrong to make a point of being out when he returns and leaving him to fend for himself. Mind, he does not spend his evenings away from home. Then, when it is too late, you may regret your present conduct. Take my advice and turn over a new leaf; be a true and loving wife, and I am sure you will not find your husband wanting in affection.

(The Cosy Corner, 2 June 1906)

(iii) Twentieth Century. Until well into the twentieth century purely sexual matters hardly appeared even in the most oblique reference. One must conclude that expressive presentation as man and woman occurred through tertiary differentia — clothes, social performances as part of a domestic team, and so on. But that somehow there was actually sexual intercourse at the back of it all could hardly have been deduced from the material by an astute but innocent Martian anthropologist. But there is a sharp presentational distinction in the way late twentieth-century males and females treat their own expressive presentations. Much more closely than at any other time they are related to the underlying organic distinction and associated performances. This appears in criticism of others as well as in the criticism of oneself (Kent, 1979, p. 259), that is as demanding or undemanding, competent or incompetent. One might hazard the guess that as public presentational styles become less differentiated, the requirement for expressive differentiation remaining stable, the organic aspects of male and female as biologically distinctive modes of being provide the only remaining material from which expressive presentations can be constructed.

Social Events as a Text in Need of Analysis

The specification of proper ways of acting and, linked with that, acceptable modes of being — that is, modes of self-presentation within

the expressive order — have so far appeared in this chapter as part of a rhetoric of the devices by which action and style, clothes and postures etc., are commented upon and criticized. To go from these items present in rather special kinds of events — those in which people and their performances come up for critical review by other people — to a classification of day-to-day activities as actions in presentations of self, requires a further step. Even if we see what people are doing as sequences of meaningful action, and their identity as expressive achievements, in that they seem to be perceiving each other as sexual beings, the perception may of course be asymmetrical — the nervous or neurotic woman perceiving mere amiability from a man presenting himself in a merely generalized social form, as sexual advances — there may still be many layers of significance to be penetrated in the interpretation of an action-sequence as accomplishing social acts. A social event could be seen as a "text" in need of interpretation.

The simplest hypothesis needed to get analysis under way, would be that the means for interpretation lies to hand in the concepts, principles and maxims in use by the folk in their critical, and interpretative, activities in commenting upon dramas of gender identity. But lacking an historical perspective, the folk may not be able to reveal all that a well-informed social scientist might. I illustrate this point from the changes that have happened in the way we perceive, and are allowed to perceive, other humans as social beings. To understand how perception of beings of distinctive gender can come about one must distinguish between presentation in image and representation in style. One must bear in mind Goffman's (1979) reminder that the expressive could be the only reality in which all such distinctions are actually created and made real. There might be no essences, no ultimate social natures associated with irreducable biological differences.

Representation in Image

One could start with catalogues of semantic appearances — clothes, sound of voice, smell, and so on. Consideration of the immense diversity of human dress and adornment practices should dispel any lingering assumptions of a natural catalogue. What is the "correct" smell or taste of a girl? Savoury or sweet? Or of a man for that matter?

Any catalogue of representations must take account of the philosophical distinction between social identity (qualitative identity) and personal identity (numerical identity). It seems that most people have

identity projects. Some people have the project of publicly representing and hopefully expressing, a social identity, managed by the sort of processes studied by Tajfel (1978). Others, secure in, or blind to social identity, have projects of publicly demonstrating personal identity, the kind of identity studied by DeWaele and Harré (1976).

Until very recently forms of gender identity presentation differed sharply between the sexes. Men subdued personal identity to a strong expressive social identity, in clothes, hairstyle etc. Women, within a framework of social identity pursued personal identity projects using all kinds of variations on basic motifs expressive of gender to represent themselves as unique beings. This is so striking a phenomenon, and so locally and historically bounded, that it deserves comment. Quentin Bell (1978) suggests that Veblen's (1899) explanation of this difference was due to the expresson of a ubiquitous commercial morality in the sobriety of men's clothes. Their uniformity left only the clothes and other tertiary accoutrements of the women as a point of conspicuous display, in which each man could illustrate his personal magnificence. To me, this is too bound by time and place to be wholly convincing but I cannot offer any alternative. The effect of military uniforms on male dress is unquestioned and there may be some explanation to be found there.

Gender representations seem to have degrees. Within gender there is a range of femininity and a range of masculinity within which there are, as it were, no questions asked. Neither dandies nor plain Janes call in question the gender expression, but there are expressive decrees which do call it in question, created quite simply by borrowing from the expressive repertoire of the opposite sex. Tweed suits, brogues, collar and tie, for women, are not just the get-up of feminine sportswomen; nor are handbags and chiffon scarves within the range seen fit for a dandy. They mark transgressions of gender identity boundaries. Unisex dress poses quite different expressive problems to which I shall turn below.

Those with secure, or highly specific social identities, have the complementary problem — how to create the impression of personal identity. All kinds of matters can be used in the realization of personal identity projects, including gender-markers. For instance, Miss Veronica Lake, *a* filmstar, developed a unique variant of feminine hairstyle, just as Mr Che Guavara, *a* revolutionary, developed a unique moustache. But these unique versions of gender-markers prompted a many-million-fold imitation, transforming Miss Lake and Mr Guavara into type-bearers, and their unique versions of gender-markers into symbols. A Veblen-like dynamics must be presumed to account for the rapidity of the

spread of these innovations and their debasement from expressive conventions to "mere" fashion.

Representation in Action-sequences

If we now turn to gender representation in action-sequences, traditional divisions of roles and the work associated with them could be used to found a presentational distinction based on what one should do. Effeminacy could be achieved presentationally by a man taking up women's work (knitting) and "machisma" by a woman taking men's jobs, e.g. mending cars (cf. the entertaining photographs on the cover of *Exploring sex differences* (Lloyd and Archer, 1976)). But a mere glance at anyone undertaking cross-gender activities reveals a second-order expressive device, the style or manner in which these jobs are done. There is no report in the literature, so far as I know, of a systematic empirical study on gender stylistics. For instance, the otherwise careful survey by Rosenblatt and Cunningham (1976) does not deal with stylistic expressions of difference at all. It would make a very interesting research project, since it could be extended both to the developmental dimension, how and why are gender-styles acquired; and historically and cross-culturally to how far presentational style is related to other culturally distinct gender appearances and practices, say in clothes or hairstyles. For instance, Japanese women's distinctive walking style may have descended from the style imposed physically through foot-binding.

The dramaturgical standpoint is, of course, the basis of an analytical model. It says nothing about how the activity under scrutiny is produced, except very generally requiring that that activity be the interactive product of personal projects generated within collectives. The discussion so far has been concerned largely with costume and some aspects of presentational style. Arguably the most important presentational quality of all is style of talk, both revelatory and creative of "character". Some preliminary studies of the stylistic features of male and female speech, within the expressive order, have recently appeared (Elyan *et al.*, 1978).

The rather preliminary character of the work so far undertaken appears in two ways: one methodological and the other theoretical.

(i) Methodological studies have largely used the matched-guise technique; that is, blind ratings in anomic environments of readings of standard passages by individuals deemed competent in two or more speech styles. Very clear differences of assumptions about character

relative to "voice" have emerged from this work. But at best this sort of study advances generalized competence only. It remains to be seen how this generalized competence or system of social knowledge and ability, interacts with the full "kit", so to speak, brought forth in expressive production itself. In the absence of all other presentational devices people can assign other people to social categories by "voice" alone.

(ii) Lacking an adequate sociology, and a clearly articulated sense of the expressive *order*, the theorizing that goes along with the studies so far reported has tended to be asocial, even individualistic. For instance, Trudgill (1974) uses a reward–approval explanatory scheme, which is necessarily individualistic. Giles (Elyan *et al.*, 1978) offers other individualistic, machiavellian frameworks of explanation in explaining the tendency among women to "upward accent convergence", though Trudgill, somewhat inconsistently, explains the tendency to "downward accent convergence" among men in a thoroughgoing social fashion, in terms of expressive projects to create a "tough" impression.

The preliminary work does suggest that there are expressive projects and that individuals as members of collectives know what is required of them in the social business of generating impressions through expressive presentations. The next step in this research ought to be much more concerned with dynamic and particularly *indexical* phenomena, so that the locations within the expressive order of appropriate occasions and socially proper others and the taxonomy of expressive projects legitimate within that order could be discovered. Then we might have the means to deal with the study of that aspect of the dramaturgical model one could call "part".

Cross-gender Expression

I have already touched briefly on cross-gender borrowings of symbolic accoutrements for expressive purposes. It is worth noticing how far this can go. There may be total transformation of gender accoutrements for expressive purposes among transvestites. Such a change is temporary and reversible since it involves no change of sex. The current possibility of physical sex change opens up a question of importance — namely how far the bodily sex differences are themselves regarded by people as

expressive representations of something deeper and abstract, the male form and organs expressively representing a person's machismo. Jan Morris (1974) in his/her autobiography, reveals a permanent inner conviction of femaleness as his/her essence long before the actual physical transformation. It seems clear from the way the matter is put that the outward male form was regarded as expressively inconsistent with the inner female essence. Clearly, the biological differentiation cannot reasonably be identified with the essence of sex-kind if the very biological organs are being conceived expressively. This raises some doubts as to the psychological correctness of the distinction between biological differentia and expressive differentia. We must allow for a relativization of the expressive element to the task in hand. This relativization would allow us to interpret a girl discarding her brassiere as a step towards using her more clearly revealed bosom as an expressive element in a presentation of an abstract femininity, transforming an organ into an accoutrement.

The Contribution of Anthropological Evidence

Given that gender-identity is recognizable through some expressive symbol system known in the culture, the next question concerns the dramaturgical conventions that govern the actual relations between members of expressively distinct groups. These can be illustrated from two different kinds of cases. There are some societies where there is a particular scenario for the carrying through of the social process of establishing relations, but in others the young persons who are forming the relationships are obliged to negotiate their own mutually agreeable sequence of events.

Most readers will be familiar, at least in principle, with Western Christian culture, in which sexual relations are taken to be a consequence of pre-established social relations. These predefined relations are a complex and historically changing mix of personal inclination and social and/or economic customs and practices. Anthropologists report that in a wide range of cultures this mode of organizing priorities is not followed. In many societies social relations between men and women, as for instance between husbands and wives, are consequent on pre-established sexual relations.

Among a wide variety of people, sexual relations are entered into independently of social order within which betrothal and marriage are formally brought into being. According to Evans Pritchard (1965),

among the Nuer, sexual relations are common place, unconcealed and do not, in general, have to be socially transformed into marriage. There is detailed documentation of this in Malinowski's (1929) *Sexual life of savages*. On entering upon adolescence "the boy develops a desire to retain the fidelity and exclusive affection of the loved one, at least for a time. But this tendency is not associated so far with any idea of settling down . . . nor do adolescents yet begin to think of marriage" (p. 54). Malinowski offers the psychological hypothesis that "the pre-matrimonial, lasting intrigue, is based upon and maintained by personal elements only. There is no legal obligation on either party" (p. 58). Marriage appears only as the ritual ratification, and so transformation, into a relation within the social order, of the last and most durable of what may have been a series of several sexual relationships entered into without ceremony. Some anthropologists have tended to root the distinction between societies in which marriage is a dramatization for social display and the ritual ratification of an existing relationship, and those in which it creates the relationship, transforming the people involved into beings of new categories, in an economic or production groundwork. Further psychological ramifications follow from this idea, but I cannot see how they could conveniently be explored, at least within current methodologies.

New Guinea

In exploring the way a society engenders social relations on the basis of an *independent* culture of sexual practices, it is instructive to go through the literature produced in the 1920s and 1930s about the customs and practices of the people of New Guinea. Cultural descriptions are largely the product of the observations of men who were primarily missionaries. Some were able to distance themselves sufficiently from their official commitments to contribute valuable anthropological descriptions. It seems that the practice of managing sexual relations and transforming them into social relations involved systematic sequences of gift-giving in various parts of New Guinea, though the details are widely different. Among the Ipe, for instance, as reported by Holmes (1924), boys carry through a fixed sequence of tests of affection with a possible mate. "On a favourable occasion he broke off part of his sago roll and gave it to her; if she ate it, he was encouraged to test her further. If she declined to, he knew he would have to seek elsewhere for a mate." The sago roll test is followed by the tobacco test, which is reported by other authors from

other parts of Papua, New Guinea. Holmes reports that the boys "had a final and supreme test . . . in the presence of the girl he bit a betel nut in half: one half he gave to her, the other he put in his mouth to chew; if she did likewise, so far as they were concerned the matter was settled: they were betrothed" (1924, p. 54). Holmes and other anthropologists of the time note that these sequences are preliminaries to betrothal or marriage and not to actual sexual relations. That is they conform with the thesis I am advancing in this chapter, that there are ritual practices for the social transformation of biological relationships. Another missionary anthropologist, Saville (1925), reports from another part of New Guinea on the customs of the Mailu people. They use a complex interplay between a public performance within a dramaturgy of the expression of love-sickness by a prospective bridegroom and a conventionally ordered sequence of food gifts from the boy's to the girl's family. The young man who is presenting himself as lovesick makes a great display of singing various mournful songs during the course of his daily life and equips himself with a companion, a confidante and go-between whose presence serves as an expressive mark of the state of the prospective bridegroom. When their joint performance has been sufficiently noticed, the boy's parents and paternal uncles begin to bombard the girl's family with a sequence of gifts, beginning with a small gift of cooked food. This is always accepted, to save face. But if the girl is uninterested in furthering the relationship, an identical gift is returned. Otherwise, the progression develops with more and more elaborate gifts, and more and more people involved in their reception, until finally an enormous donation of spears, mats and a pig seals the whole relationship. Among these people there is a well established and relatively strictly followed system for the social genesis of social relations.

The Engagement Game

Young people in Britain are not so fortunate as those of the same age and interests in New Guinea, since British families do not provide a standardized structure and system of support through which male/female relationships are to be expressively established and stabilized. From amongst the material collected by Rosser (1977) from conversations with young people, there emerged hints of a complex practice for bringing order into the relations between adolescents. The boys tended to change their partners fairly frequently but the girls wanted a steady relationship. Expressive goods seem to have been the basic issue, since a boy acquired

"character" by exhibiting a string of female conquests, while a girl achieved it by displaying a permanent relationship with a boy. Somewhere there has grown up a practice we would call the "engagement game". The girls control the boys by insisting on an "engagement" at the age of fifteen or sixteen years, and perhaps even younger. "Engagements" are publicly promulgated and serve as the basis for "complaints" from the jilted and for cooperation among the girls not to steal each other's boyfriends. Jilting does take place and boyfriends are stolen, but at least "the game" licences complaints and even sanctions. The structure of this practice is clearly a borrowing from older people. It may be elaborated to the point at which real engagement rings are demanded and displayed.

It can have tragic consequences, since the boundaries between fantasy and reality become blurred as the fantasy is in use as a real social practice involving real events. This blurring can lead to real sexual relations, and in some cases to real marriages with all the disastrous consequences for those too immature and inadequately equipped to cope with the real consequences of what is, in its original status, no more than a rhetoric and a kind of play-acting to achieve a modicum of social order. Rosser has noted that practices like the engagement game have appeared as the external parental regulation of adolescent relationships within the society — such as the control of acceptances of invitations, the hours at which one may be out, and so on — has now declined.

Polyandry in Southern India

The examples I have used to illustrate the practices by which the social transformation and control of sexual relations are achieved, are various. The anthropological literature shows an enormous variety of possible ways. One dimension which emerges very readily from the material is the sharp distinction between societies which distinguish between sexual intercourse and socially sanctioned sexual relations and those which do not. The anthropologists I have consulted are unanimous in agreeing that in New Guinea there is almost no relationship between sexual intercourse and socially expressed gender relationships, the former taking place quite independently of the latter. However, in the southern area of the Sahara the Muslim tribes who range those barren lands with their herds of camels seem to operate a system in which the two are rigidly related, so that the only way in which sexual relations can actually occur is in the course of the development of socially defined, publicly

promulgated relationships, and in particular the complex orderliness of the Muslim marriage ceremony, at least as far as sexual relations between the opposite sexes go. Now this throws in doubt any easy assumptions about universals, in particular universals which relate emotions to sexual relations and any assumption of a universal predilection to jealousy or exclusiveness of demand amongst men and women. We are accustomed in European contexts to the assumption that the traditionally defined "double standard" allowed a display of *machismo* by men in publicly exhibiting, even if only in ritualized form, a wide variety of conquests, while women were supposed to exemplify the domestic virtues of monogamy. A test for whether this system of practices and its associated emotions are universal could be devised by looking at a detailed study of polyandrous families in which one woman is married, differently in different societies, to a number of men. Fortunately, there is the superb study by Prince Peter of Greece (1963), made among the polyandrous peoples on the northern fringe of the Indian subcontinent. This work is of the highest quality, involving both external observation of the practices of people and systematic analysis of the accounts they give of the events and practices in which they play a part.

Prince Peter reports on a variety of forms of polyandry. For example, those involving fathers and sons, e.g. — "a father has invited his son to marry his step-mother" (1963, p. 563), or "a father makes himself a partner in the marital rights over his son's wife" (p. 563). According to Prince Peter, sons find great satisfaction in the first form and fathers in the second. So far, we seem to be in a world of emotions with which we are tolerably familiar. However, Prince Peter also notes that the reciprocal persons in these structures do not experience the kind of emotions which we might expect. Fathers do not seem to be put out by their sons sharing their step-mother, nor do sons seem to be put out by fathers sharing their wives. As Prince Peter notes, these relationships exhibit the extreme passivity of sons. The other pattern is of brothers sharing one wife, and this seems very widespread. The explanations appearing in the accounts illustrate different levels of analysis.

At a general level which one might call the anthropological, the practitioners of polyandry were agreed that the practice was sustained by a desire for offspring in both sexes, since they believed that the practice of polyandry was more likely to lead to children as experienced by people in the Himalayan foothills. Further, they were unanimous in asserting that the practice led to greater sexual satisfaction for the women.

A second level of analysis cited in accounts concerns the stability which

is to be found in polyandrous communities. This level we might call the social-psychological since it involves hypotheses or principles concerned with the propensities of people to quarrel. The Todas of Nilgiri in the mountains of southern India claim that they were polyandrous because fundamentally they did not want brothers to quarrel with each other, and the surest way to ensure family harmony was for the brothers to be married to only the one woman. In Ladak, on the other hand, the local people claimed that the stability of the polyandrous family and its desirability were based upon the avoidance of wives quarrelling and that peace and harmony were always present in the home where there was only one woman (Prince Peter of Greece, 1963, p. 563). In Ladak it seems that folk psychology expects the women of the household to quarrel, while in the Nilgiri hills it is the men who are prone to bad behaviour.

But there is a third level of analysis which we might call the affective or pure psychological. Tibetans claim that jealousy is a luxury which they cannot afford. People do feel it but it is never in evidence. According to Prince Peter's informants it sometimes leads to divisions in the household and to nervous symptoms. But he notes ironically that parental jealousy between sons and fathers, say, seems to be based more upon the problems of property and the likelihood of discrimination of inheritance than it has to do with the relationships between the wife and her many husbands. However, in somewhat contradictory vein Prince Peter mentions the frequency with which younger men prefer to be the sole husband and submit to polyandry only under family pressure. We have no means of knowing whether this sort of practice is a recent development as Tibet absorbs, however slowly and at whatever remove, something of the customs and ideas of the outer world, or whether it was a constant feature of Tibetan society and the emotional structure of those who lived in it. Whatever is our conclusion it seems clear that the relationship between a dramaturgy in which manly virtue is exhibited by the conquest of a large number of women forms no part of the polyandrous system of the peoples described in this classic monograph.

On the other hand, the degree to which a sense of individual worth and dignity is mixed up with family honour, which is itself defined in terms of the virtuousness of the women of the family, can be found in a number of Mediterranean or near-Mediterranean cultures. In the Sudan, for instance, there is a complicated set of concepts expressing personal honour and dignity which are conceptually related in the notions of people. Nordenstam (1968) has provided a detailed account of the

expressive order current among the southern Sudanese, in which the abstract moral quality of *sharaf* is defended through the moral defence of the family. *Sharaf* is something which everybody has by nature, devolving on a man from the honour or decency of his family. Its protection is essential, since once lost it can never be re-acquired. It is an abstract moral quality. Related to it, its expressive counterpart, so to speak, is *karama*. It could roughly be translated as personal dignity. Like *sharaf* it can be lost, and once lost is never recuperable. *Karama* is a property which is mediated by the attitudes of others to one's own actions, so that loss of *karama* can come about as much by one's own folly and bad behaviour as by the derogatory attitude of others. It is easy to see how *sharaf* and *karama* are related. No matter what a man may himself do, if his friends and neighbours pour scorn upon him because of the behaviour of one of his family, and in particular the alleged lack of virtue of one of the womenfolk of his family, no matter what he does, his *karama* is under threat. Such a system and the rigidity with which it is maintained seems to suggest a system of emotions and social practices which are very distinctly different from those reported amongst the polyandrous tribes of the Indian sub-continent. It seems, then, that it would be a mistake to assume a universal psychology with respect to the affective component sexual relations. These examples and the others alluded to in this chapter point to the over-arching role of the culture, particularly its dramaturgy, in displaying publicly and expressively what relations there are.

Historical Analysis

I have illustrated sufficiently, I hope, the disconnection between the dramaturgy of sexual relations and their biology, illustrating the cultural diversity of the former through anthropological examples. To clinch the matter it would be nice to be able to show how a structural analysis of literary texts can give us an insight into the historical transformations which have occurred in the dramaturgy of Western Europe, the means by which the biological and anatomical aspects of sex are transformed into forms of social being in expressive orders.

Why is historical analysis so important? When with the help of an analytical model, we seem to discern a regularity in human affairs, the scientific approach calls for an attempt to discover its source. Anthropological evidence and philosophical analysis suggest that our prime working hypothesis should be that the description of the regularity

is either a tautology, reflecting the structure of a conceptual system (cf. Louch, 1966; Gilbert, 1976; etc.) or a specification of a cultural convention, norm or practice. It would be naive to suppose that regularities in human affairs derive from universals of human nature (some sort of "laws") — though it would be foolish to so structure one's enquiries that this possibility was precluded.

Prime tests of social psychological hypotheses then should proceed by attempting to eliminate or substantiate two possibilities: either that the manifested regularity in conduct, speech, etc. is the empirical manifestation of a conceptual relation (cf. Gergen, 1979); or that it is a cultural artefact. The former requires detailed conceptual analysis of a working system of categories, such as are revealed in ordinary language (cf. Silver and Sabini (1978) for an excellent conceptual study of the social psychology of envy.) The latter requires a study of historical psychology. I turn now to some suggestions of research programmes to explore the latter.

If, as our French colleagues (Moscovici, 1976) maintain, *représentations sociales* embody folk psychologies, sociologies and even medical traditions, which, as exerting controlling influences on actual practices, serve to engender social forms, one obvious programme of research suggests itself immediately — an exploration of the implicit social psychologies of sexual relations to be found in plays and other literary works, that were very popular in their own times. Part of that popularity, it seems reasonable to suppose, derived from their "holding a mirror up to life". I have tried at least the beginnings of such a study of *Love's labours lost* (Harré, 1980) with some interesting results. The folk social psychology of Elizabethan times involves certain assumptions and practices that can be found still widely shared today. But there are other aspects of the theories controlling social life that are radically different. The very problem at the heart of the play, the exploration of the breaking point of male "will" to continence under the pressure of the presence of women, is not addressed as a *problem* (is its subject matter even a contemporary practice?) in *any* of the modern works I have consulted.

The dramaturgy of sex, the social form in which sexual relations could be expressively represented, underwent a radical transformation which is reflected in a great deal of the literature of the time, and in the appearance of that curious social phenomenon "the courts of love" (De Rougement, 1962). The courtly establishment of Eleanor of Aquitaine, uneasily married to Henry II, was a major centre for the development of the romantic ideal, around which the sexual psychology of that period

was modelled. A thorough comparative study of the range of possible social and expressive forms available for the transformation of sexual relations and impulses into social relations and practices, before and after this crucial period, would be of the greatest interest. Not least it would provide an opportunity to test the hypothesis of *réprésentations sociales*, that the practices of a society are a realization of the forms of life that that society holds to be possible. If there is a radical change in beliefs as to the range of the possible, there ought to be radical changes in self-presentational practices, expressive forms and modes of speech, and other devices by which public claims to legitimate modes of being are made.

Whenever a social phenomenon seems to be historically conditioned and culturally engendered and maintained, its existence as an adult practice demands a developmental account. A dramaturgy of sexual relations and a system of expressive conventions for the public representation of gender in non-primary terms are just such phenomena. Some studies of sex-role acquisition do exist (Ullian, 1976) but they are concerned with the static phenomenon of personality rather than the dynamic processes of expressive practices. Spence and Helmreich's (1978) survey is even more statically oriented than Ullian's. The only work I know which opens up the question of the "code", as it is called in ethnomethodology, that is the rules for "doing" masculinity and femininity as expressive presentations, is by Jeffrey Adams (1979). He has begun an exploration of the affective structural properties of fairy tales and of the codes of action associated with them. Affective structure and expressive code are very strongly manifested in that most sexual of fairy tales, Beauty and the Beast. A vigorous historical and cross-cultural research programme is clearly needed fully to exploit the analytical techniques made available by text analysts such as Barthes (1967). Long ago, Jacob Grimm proposed the study of the conventions embedded in fairy tales as a technique for investigating the historical social psychology of a tribe. Contrary to Freudian analysts who assume that the structure of a fairy tale is a manifestation of a hidden subjective dynamic of personal life, I believe the internal organizations of fairy tales exemplify the ancient conventions of self presentation in the public and collective life of a people.

Conclusion

In defining the range of social psychological problems and methods, I

suggested four modes of the production of action for the study of which distinctive empirical techniques are required. Physiological reflexes and ingrained habits are distinctive in their origins but alike in their normal immunity to artful manipulation in the effort to realize some project. But the realization in action of standard rules and conventions, and the improvisation of action for particular purposes are very much matters under an agent's control and utilized in the deliberate furtherance of projects.

I have tried to demonstrate that the distinction of, and relationships between, the sexes appear in the expressive order as gender presentations. To display oneself as a man or as a woman is a project best understood in dramaturgical terms as a staging of a character performance. This directs one's attention as a scientist to the study of psychological competence, that is, the knowledge of rules and rhetorical devices necessary for this performance to come off. Etiquette books and agony columns help to reveal the local rule systems, but more direct ethnographical work is required to identify such matters as symbolic costume, gender-expressive speech modes, etc., which make up the rhetorical resources for the social expression of gender.

Turning to relationships, even a brief examination of the anthropological literature and historical sources shows that they share the same features as personal presentations. Local conventions dominate the sexual emotions, such as jealousy and romantic love. Sexual relations as such are distinct from the social relations between people when they are presented as of distinct gender. The former are no doubt of biological origin. But examples show that the processes of the formation of the latter must be studied through the use of liturgical (ceremonial) and dramaturgical analytical models.

In this chapter I have tried to clarify the distinctions that must be drawn between the biological basis of sexual relations and the conditions for the dramatic presentation of corresponding expressive distinctions in social settings, the proper study of social psychology. In the latter field much remains to be done.

8. References

Adams, J. Conditions for the possibility of meaning in fairy stories. Unpublished paper, 1979.

Anon. *Manners and rules of good society.* London: Warne, 1940.

Barthes, R. *Elements of semiology.* London: Cape, 1967.

Bell, Q. *On human finery.* New York: Schocken Books, 1978.

Cullen, J. M. Some principles of animal communication. In Hinde, R. A. (Ed.), *Non verbal communication.* Cambridge: Cambridge University Press, 1972.

De Rougement, D. *Passion and society.* London: Faber and Faber, 1962.

DeWaele, J.-P. and Harré, R. The personality of individuals. In Harré, R. (Ed.), *Personality.* Oxford: Blackwell, 1976.

Elyan, O., Smith, P., Giles, H. and Bouris, R. RP-accented female speech: the voice of perceived androgyny. In Trudgill, P. (Ed.), *Sociolinguistic patterns in British English.* London: Arnold, 1978.

Evans-Pritchard, E. E. *The position of women in primitive societies.* New York: Free Press, 1965.

Gergen, K. J. Towards intellectual audacity in social psychology. In Gilmour, R. and Duck, S. (Eds), *The development of social psychology.* London and New York: Academic Press, 1979.

Gilbert, M. On being categorised in the speech of others. In Harré, R. (Ed.), *Life sentences.* London: Wiley, 1976.

Goffman, E. *Gender advertisements.* London: MacMillan, 1979.

Harré, R. Psychological variety. In Heelas, P. and Lock, A. (Eds), *Indigenous psychologies.* London and New York: Academic Press, 1981.

Holmes, J. H. *In primitive New Guinea.* London: Sealey Service, 1924.

Kent, R. *Aunt Agony advises.* London: W. H. Allen, 1979.

Lloyd, B. and Archer, J. *Exploring sex differences.* London and New York: Academic Press, 1976.

Louch, A. R. *Explanation and human action.* Oxford: Blackwell, 1966.

Malinowski, B. *The sexual life of savages.* London: Routledge, 1929.

Morris, J. *Conundrum.* London: Faber and Faber, 1974.

Moscovici, S. *Social influence and social change.* London and New York: Academic Press, 1976.

Nordenstam, T. *Sudanese ethics.* Uppsala: Scandinavian Institute of African Studies, 1968.

Prince Peter of Greece. *A study of polyandry.* The Hague: Mouton, 1963.

Rosenblatt, P. C. and Cunningham, M. R. Sex differences in cross-cultural perspective. In Lloyd, B. L. and Archer, J. (Eds), *Exploring sex differences.* London and New York: Academic Press, 1976.

Rosser, E. The engagement game. Unpublished paper, 1977.

Saville, W. J. V. *In unknown New Guinea.* London: Sealey Service, 1925.

Silver, M. and Sabini, J. The social construction of envy. *Journal for the Theory of Social Behaviour,* 1978, **8**, 313–332.

Spence, J. T. and Helmreich, R. L. *Masculinity and femininity.* Austin: University of Texas Press, 1978.

Tajfel, H. *Differentiation between social groups.* London and New York: Academic Press, 1978.

274   *Rom Harré*

Tiger, L. and Shepher, J. *Women in the kibbutz*. New York and London: Harcourt Brace Jovanovich, 1975.

Trudgill, P. *Sociolinguistics: an introduction*. Harmondsworth: Penguin, 1974.

Ullian, D. Z. The development of conceptions of masculinity and femininity. In Lloyd, B. and Archer, J. (Eds), *Exploring sex differences*. London and New York: Academic Press, 1976.

Veblen, T. *The theory of the leisure class*. New York: Macmillan, 1899.

9
Sexual Attraction in Animals

AUBREY MANNING
Department of Zoology, University of Edinburgh,
West Mains Road, Edinburgh, Scotland

The other contributors to this volume had a complex task. The sexual behaviour patterns of our species of which attraction is but one facet, have been shaped and distorted away from their simpler origins by millenia of cultural evolution. It is no longer easy to identify the selective forces which once formed them and it is hard to make many useful generalizations. Although the biologist is faced with a fascinating (if at times bewildering) range of variations in reproductive patterns, it is nearly always possible to relate their form to their function. Each animal's behaviour is adapted to leaving the maximum number of descendants. The constraints imposed upon animal multiplication are powerful; competition for food and shelter, the toll taken by predators and disease, all combine to maintain populations constant, taking decade with decade. It is rare that any large growth in numbers can take place. Human sexual behaviour must have evolved to fit us to contend with just such constraints; in some parts of the world now, as in the west until very recently, birth rates and death rates are still very high, just as they are in many animal species.

For a biologist, sexual attraction is but one, rather preliminary component of reproductive behaviour, but it offers some remarkable specializations of its own, a consideration of which will allow us to compare and contrast our own species with other animals. Discussion can be organized under two headings, namely synchronization in time and space and mate choice itself.

Synchronization in Time and Space

It might be argued that only the question of mate choice is relevant in this volume, but for most animals sexual attraction also means quite literally attracting the sexes together. The sexes have to be brought together and to be sexually motivated before choice can play any part. Human beings are almost unique in that both sexes are normally sexually active throughout the year. This factor has had a profound influence on the way human societies emerged and have developed since. Sexual behaviour can be seen as a major cohesive factor in human societies and we are certainly one of the "sexiest" species. Judges, bishops and others who have from time to time deplored some manifestation of human sexuality and spoken of "the animal side of our nature", should reflect that most animals are strictly celibate save during a brief breeding season.

Red deer, for example, show a six-week period of intense reproductive activity in the autumn rut, but once this ends the two sexes spend all the rest of the year in separate groups with virtually no contact (Lincoln, *et al.*, 1970). A number of our closest relatives, the primates, also have a limited breeding season (see Jolly (1972) for examples), with long periods when no females in the group come into oestrus and the males are sexually inactive. In rhesus macaques on Cayo Santiago off Puerto Rico, Conway and Sade (1965) showed that the testes of the males regress outside the breeding season, as does sexual motivation. Such observations must lead us to question whether primate societies are based upon constant sexual attraction as was often suggested in the early literature (e.g. Zuckerman, 1932).

Some tropical animals whose environment is relatively constant can afford to breed all the year round, but for most species conditions vary over the year. It is the crucial requirement to produce young at a favourable time of year which has determined breeding seasons. Sexual attraction and mating usually take their timing from birth or hatching. They occur one gestation or incubation period before the optimum time for production of young. For most ungulates in the northern hemisphere, for example, young must be born in spring and hence many, like sheep or red deer, mate in the autumn. Titmice and jackdaws rely heavily on various species of defoliating caterpillars to feed their nestlings. These are at their peak in early to mid-May so the birds mate and lay eggs three to four weeks previously and well before any caterpillars have appeared.

This anticipatory effect draws our attention to the importance of synchrony in sexual attraction. Both sexes must become sexually

motivated at the same season and this must be geared to the needs of the future offspring. It is nearly always the environment which provides the time cue. The precision of the cue is sometimes remarkable. The palolo worm of the Pacific reproduces on one night each year, swarming to the surface in their millions to shed eggs and sperm at dawn one week following the November full moon, presumably synchronized to a lunar and/or tidal rhythm. In vertebrates day-length is by far the commonest timer. It is, after all, the only really reliable cue in regions where the details of climate vary so much from year to year. Fifty years ago Rowan (1925) demonstrated the effects of day-length when he induced the finch *Junco hyemalis* to come into reproductive condition and begin singing in the depths of the Canadian winter at -45°C simply by providing electric light night and morning!

Ferrets and many other small carnivores are completely inactive sexually apart from a brief period in early spring, whose timing is controlled by the lengthening of the days. Sheep and deer mating in autumn because of their much longer gestation period, come into sexual condition with shortening day length.

A great deal is now known about the physiological and endocrinological events which underly the dramatic effects of changing day length (see Austin and Short (1972) for introductory reviews). The two sexes are brought into general synchrony by their common response to an external factor. Finer synchrony is provided by a series of secondary mechanisms which ensure fertile mating. As mentioned above, males and females are often dispersed or even segregated outside the breeding season so that some form of assembling signal is required. These are the most clear cut of sexual attraction mechanisms and there are many beautiful examples.

Male frogs and toads gather in the breeding ponds and call repeatedly to attract females. Male cicadas and crickets also use acoustic signals to assemble females and the territorial songs of birds act both to attract mates and keep rival males at a distance. Chemical signals are widespread amongst insects and mammals. They are perhaps most spectacular in moths, where the virgin females of many species "call" to males by releasing pheromones from their body surface. The males' antennae are no more than elaborate pheromone receptors (they respond to no other odours), and such is their sensitivity that with suitable wind conditions females can be detected from 4 or 5 km down wind.

The moths illustrate well one other aspect of sexual attraction which is of great importance in some animal groups. Human beings have few problems of species identification but a dozen or more species of moth

may be active simultaneously in the same area. If so we find that each species has a unique chemical attractant and that males are attracted only by their own species-specific pheromone. (Interestingly enough the range of suitable pheromone substances is not unlimited and some species share identical or almost identical chemicals but they are always species which are active at different times which minimizes the risk of confusion.) Thus the assembling signals are also a powerful mechanism for *sexual isolation* which prevents mating between members of different species. Such hybridization nearly always results in infertile or sub-fertile offspring, often no offspring at all. Since mating will always involve one or both sexes in some significant investment of time and resources, it is vitally important that individuals can identify mates with whom they can be fertile.

With mammals as with insects it is commonest to find that females signal their readiness to mate and males approach. As any owner of a bitch can testify, mammalian pheromones can operate over moderate distances. The pheromones are often derived chemically from breakdown products of oestrogens which are circulating at a high level just prior to ovulation. They are released in the urine and deliberate scent marking is often a part of oestrus behaviour in females. Ewes in oestrus will urinate when the ram approaches them and he investigates the scent. Thus the oestrus scent also operates as a close range signal and is probably also a stimulus to actual mating for males.

For social mammals, especially the primates where the sexes mostly live together permanently, primary sexual attraction only has to operate over close-range. Pheromone production at oestrus is a common attribute of female primates and vaginal secretions may also be involved in addition to urine, (see Michael and Keverne (1968) for a review). In a number of species the pheromonal signal is accompanied by conspicuous swelling of the whole perineal region, which also becomes brightly coloured. The function of the swelling is not at all obvious. It is difficult to argue that males require visual as well as olfactory stimuli to attract them, for primates usually live in closely knit societies in which there is ample opportunity for exploration of sexual status. Females show effective proceptive behaviour and approach males when they are in oestrus.

Goodall (1971) has some evidence that male chimpanzees are attracted to females in oestrus by sight of the huge, brightly coloured perineal swelling. She cites cases where males appear to have become excited and moved rapidly towards oestrus females (which she excruciatingly calls

"pink ladies") whose swellings have been glimpsed through the trees. Yet female gorillas show no visible signs of oestrus, although they live in denser habitat. Perhaps the closeness of their group structure removes the need, but we know other cases in monkeys where species with similar social structure and closely related taxonomically, differ markedly in the extent of their swellings (Clutton-Brock and Harvey, 1976).

This brief discussion of assembly mechanisms is sufficient to indicate that no hard and fast line can be drawn between distance and close-range attraction, or between mere assembling of the two sexes and mutual stimulation. The female's pheromones attract a male dog into her vicinity and also arouse him sexually. Assembly is followed rapidly by mating in many cases; certainly this is true for insects, amphibia and many mammals. There is no prolonged period of courtship before mating occurs and neither sex is attracted or attractive before each is fully fertile, so that synchrony presents few problems once the sexes come together.

In strong contrast to this pattern of sexual behaviour is that found in many birds, where assembly is followed by a period of courtship and pair formation which may extend for weeks before actual mating takes place. Such behaviour is characteristic of monogamous birds and it is usually the males which come into reproductive condition first. They set up territories, which are carved out during aggressive disputes with other males, and begin singing or other types of display which attracts females.

The details of pair formation vary greatly between species, but we know that in some cases females are not reproductively mature when they first join males on their territories. It takes time for their ovaries to become fully active after the winter's quiescence, for their oviducts to grow and eggs to form. The stimulation — probably mostly visual — provided by courtship is an important factor in causing such growth. This phenomenon, which involves the active participation of the female in courtship, has been particularly well studied in the laboratory ring dove (*Streptopelia risoria*) by Lehrman and his group (Lehrman, 1964). With monogamous birds of this type actual mating is delayed until a nest is built and ready to receive the fertilized eggs. Courtship and pair formation provide the finer degree of synchrony required for successful mating.

Mate Choice

Thus far our review of sexual attraction in other animals has provided

little possible grounds for comparison with our own species. Assembly and sexual isolation are not problems that arise with us and even if human pair formation and courtship sometimes bears a superficial resemblance to that just outlined for monogamous birds, it clearly does not serve the same function in physiological terms. However when we turn to examine the choice of sexual partner from those available, then perhaps some more reasonable comparisons can be drawn. Certainly one of the factors which leads to the evolution of a mating system in which courtship occurs may be the opportunity such courtship provides for choosing between mates.

The biologist's approach to mate choice in animals has been to relate it to "fitness". Fitness is used in its Darwinian sense to mean the ability to compete and survive to reproduce and leave the maximum number of descendants. Any genetically based changes to behaviour which increase fitness will be passed to more descendants and hence through natural selection, fitness will be maximized. Of course mate choice is only one component of fitness but in sexually reproducing animals it will always be an important one.

It is likely to be even more important for females than for males. The reason for this lies in the basic inequality of the size of sperm and eggs. Females will always have to invest more energy in producing their eggs and commonly have to invest even more energy later in order to raise the young — mammals are an especially powerful example of this disparity. Once a female has mated she is likely to be committed to a series of related reproductive and parental activities and if her mate was less than maximally fertile she will pay a relatively heavy penalty in evolutionary terms. Females of some short-lived animals, such as many insects, may mate only once in their whole lives; small mammals such as shrews and voles have only one reproductive season, they do not survive a second winter. It is thus a matter of great consequence for females to select a good mate, one of the correct species and fully fit.

The position for males in monogamous species is essentially the same as for females, but in the great majority of animals males are, at least potentially, polygynous, i.e. they can mate with several females. Their best reproductive strategy is then to mate as often as possible, since the cost of sperm is low and they can be replaced rapidly. It will not usually pay to be too discriminating; better to risk a few less than maximally fertile matings than to lose any opportunity to mate.

We must now look at the criteria which animals can use to choose to mate; what features can serve as cues to high fitness? It is these cues

which natural selection will render sexually attractive. Their nature will depend on the social organization and, in particular, the mating system of the species concerned and this in turn, will be influenced by its food supply and other aspects of its ecology. Some general rules can be extracted from the wealth of natural variation; Emlen and Oring (1977) provide a full review.

Monogamy is the simplest system in many ways. As mentioned previously, it is rare except amongst birds where many species are insectivorous; it has often proved impossible for one parent to collect enough food for a brood of young. It is also common to find that the male feeds the female ("courtship feeding") during the period when she is forming the eggs — a time of maximum demand on her food reserves. Carnivorous birds such as owls, hawks and eagles, where live prey must be hunted down also require both parents to be active in rearing the young. Significantly the few mammals which are monogamous include a high proportion of carnivorous and insectivorous species (Kleiman, 1977). Again it is presumably impossible for one parent to catch enough prey and the female will need help with food during lactation — the time of maximum demand on a female mammal.

Because there is roughly equal parental investment in monogamous species, mate choice will also be fairly symmetrical; males and females both have to choose good mates who will be good parents as well as sexual partners. In line with these requirements it is characteristic of monogamous species that males and females are similar in size and appearance. There may be some sexual dimorphism, but there are none of the extravagances of plumage, manes, antlers or large size which are often found in males of polygynous species.

Most monogamous species are territorial and males sing or perform other conspicuous displays which advertise their occupation. It is reasonable to suppose that not only are these displays in themselves attractive to females, but so also is a good territory, i.e. one which will provide a breeding site and a good food supply. There is good evidence that some female birds do choose mates according to the quality of the territory they are holding. In areas where the habitat is especially favourable with a good food supply, bobolinks and red-winged blackbirds are polygynous and males have more than one female in their territory. This means that each female has to rear the young more or less on her own, but the abundant food supply allows this. In areas of poorer habitat each territory has only a single pair — presumably the full-time attention of the male is now essential. Males will compete for territories in the best

areas, so a female who throws in her lot with a male in the best areas is likely to have picked one who is strong and fit.

It is not at all clear how males in monogamous, territorial species can choose females and few authors have even commented on this problem. Yet for the majority of such males the choice of a mate is crucial to breeding success. It is common among territorial birds to find that a male's first response to the arrival of a female is aggressive. This reaction has sometimes been regarded as an inevitable result of the male's high level of aggression early in the breeding season. He needs to repel all intruders vigorously and, it has been argued, the female is a conspecific who may anyway look very similar to a rival male. This argument is not as unrealistic as it may seem from a human point of view. We know that there is a good deal of overt aggression in the courtship of many animals. The female's response to attack can distinguish her from a rival male for whereas the latter will flee or fight back, females may flee but they may stay put and take up a submissive posture. It could be that a female's willingness to remain and withstand the male's hostility is a measure of her breeding condition and general fitness. If so then the male's initial aggression may have some significance for mate choice also — an attractive female is one who stays in his territory despite his attacks.

The situation is totally different in polygynous species of which the most familiar examples are birds such as pheasants, sage grouse, black grouse, birds of paradise and bower birds, and the majority of mammals, especially many ungulates, seals and primates. The common characteristic of all these animals is that the female provides the major part of care and sustenance for the young. In extreme cases the male plays no part at all beyond mating, as in all the birds mentioned above and the seals. In some ungulates such as the zebra the stallion moves in company with four or five mares and their young offspring and he offers considerable protection against predators. The same is true of primates, where the adult males are important for defence of the group as a whole.

The onus of choice in polygynous species is almost entirely with females. Because of the ecology and life history of the species concerned, the male offers her little more than his genes and she must choose a male of proven fitness. Conversely we find much less discrimination amongst males who will mate with as many females as they can.

Since one male can mate with many females there is always competition between males for the attention of females. This intra-sexual competition is one component of sexual selection, the nature of which was first described by Darwin. Brown (1975) provides a good modern

account of sexual selection and mating systems, with many examples. Darwin recognized that "adornments" which serve only to attract mates could evolve under the influence of competition between males. Certainly it is the rule for sexual dimorphism to be at its maximum in polygynous species.

Sometimes the main aspect of such dimorphism is size. Males of polygynous primates are larger and more powerful than females. This is particularly marked in baboons and gorillas although clear enough in macaques, vervets, langurs and chimpanzees. (This is in marked contrast to the similarity size in the males and females of several monogamous primates, e.g. marmosets and gibbons.) Size differences reach a peak in the seals. Male elephant seals and fur seals can be three to four times as heavy as females. There are violent battles between males on the mating beaches where they struggle to set up territories. The largest males gather large harems (15-20 females is common) on their territories which they defend against all others. Females are attacked if they try to leave and enter another male's territory. Although it may appear that the males are dictating events, there can be little doubt that the females are seeking out the most dominant males. The reproductive rewards of such dominance are enormous. Le Boeuf and Peterson (1969) found that in one colony of elephant seals 6% of the males inseminated 88% of the females. There is high mortality amongst males, and females who mate with those few most dominant males are certain to maximize the fitness of their offspring.

The situation is somewhat similar in polygynous primates. Females tend to approach and stay with the dominant male or males when they come into oestrus and these males certainly father most of the young. However, although younger males are largely excluded from mating, inter-male competition is less intense than in the seals and probably most males father some offspring at some stage of their life since dominance changes hands as individuals grow older.

We do not know for certain what aspect of the dominant males is attractive to females in these cases. Size alone may be sufficient in the seals — it is likely to be directly related to fitness — but the situation must be more complex in primates. It is clear from laboratory studies that primates of both sexes can develop preferences for particular mates and evidence is now accumulating from wild chimpanzees of similar preferences (see Tutin, 1975). Although the preferred males are always competent adults it is certainly not always the largest and most powerful males who are the object of such preferences. We must suppose that other features and prior experience are the basis for attraction.

There are some examples where size alone is known to determine sexual attraction. These concern some cold blooded vertebrates which continue to grow throughout life, e.g. frogs and toads and some fish. Size is thus a reasonable measure of age (itself quite a good indication of fitness in the struggle to survive) and is also related to reproductive potential — the larger the animal the more eggs or sperm it can produce. In toads, Davis and Halliday (1977) have shown that when the sexes assemble in the breeding ponds females seek out the largest males, probably identifying them by the tone of their calls. Males similarly try to mount and clasp large females. In fish, female guppies are larger than males and bear live young. Choice tests have shown that males always direct most of their courtship and copulation attempts towards the larger of two females.

But size is by no means the most conspicuous sexually dimorphic character in polygynous species. The extraordinary plumage of male peacocks, lyre birds and birds of paradise are also the result of sexual selection. Sometimes males gather communally to display — the display grounds or leks of blackgrouse and ruffs are an example — and females visit the male group. Some male ungulates also set up display grounds of this type (e.g. the Uganda Kob — Leuthold, 1966). In other cases each male has a territory on which he displays to all females who come near; lyre birds and birds of paradise behave in this way. In the bower birds the extravagances of display are not in the male's plumage but in the remarkable decorated bower which he constructs and leads females to.

With lek species it is relatively easy to identify which males are particularly attractive to females. (A lek is a display ground divided into a cluster of territories held purely for mating.) It is always those whose display areas are at the centre of the lek. Here the territories, if we should call them that, are small, the males are densely packed and there is a good deal of inter-male aggression as well as sexual display. Work with the blackcock has shown that it is the older males who occupy the central areas, there are young males holding the much larger territories at the periphery of the lek. Each season males return to the same lek and there is a turnover of males in the central area. In general, the choice as it presents itself to females is not unlike that in seals or red deer — they approach and mate with the central males who have proved their fitness by their ability to hold a territory there against all rivals.

The basis for choice in the non-lek species is not so well understood. To human eyes one male bird of paradise or one satin bower bird's bower

tends to look very like another. Doubtless if we studied and compared more closely, differences would come to light and perhaps we could relate them to mating success. Certainly we would not expect the evolution of such extravaganza of displays and plumage unless there were intense competition between males to attract mates. We are hampered in our analysis because we have little idea which particular aspects of the displays are attractive to females. The displays of a bird of paradise are amazing and arresting to us, females of these species mostly stay close to the males when they are displaying and also appear to watch them. Presumably they are responding in some way which allows them to compare one male with another.

We would also expect that the differences between males bear some relation to fitness. Darwin realized that if some adornment of plumage were attractive to females it could evolve in a population, even if it had no other function. Selection will favour females whose sons are more attractive to females and so on. It is possible that once such an adornment and the response of females to it has begun to evolve, then sexual selection by females will lead to its further elaboration, even to a point at which it is disadvantageous to the males which carry it in all respects other than mating success. Darwin speculated about the extraordinary wing feathers of argus pheasants and the tail of peacocks. It seems not improbable that they are a handicap to escaping from predators, for example. But the argus pheasant which attracts six females and then falls prey to a carnivore would leave more descendants than a dowdier male who lived on but failed to attract any mates. Of course this is to take the arguments to extremes, and presumably there must come a point of optimum adaptiveness at which sexual selection and selection for mobility, feeding ability, etc. are in balance. We know very little about the relationship between a male's adornments and his more general fitness. Zahavi (1975) has suggested that it is precisely by the fact that he can survive whilst carrying the handicap of extravagant plumage, that a male proves his fitness to a female. Other biologists do not agree and the matter is well discussed by Halliday (1978).

As we have just seen, the proximate factors which influence female choice are not always known. We assume that she must be able to choose fit males because females which did so in the past will have left more descendants to spread through the population. For many animals we also assume that learning or experience is not involved in choice. Insect females, for example, commonly mate only once in their lives and for many other species also the opportunity to benefit by experience in mate

choice is effectively absent. There must be some inborn mechanisms which guide them towards appropriate mates. The widespread occurrence of "female coyness" as it has been called, with the male playing the role of the active suitor, gives females time to identify a male as of the correct species and probably gives some information on his fitness also.

For comparison with the human situation those species where experience is known to play a role are the most relevant. Relatively few monogamous species mate for life and most choose a new mate each season. We do not know if their successive choices are effected by experience. In long-term monogamists information is also scarce because we rarely have adequate long-term studies, but Coulson's (1972) work on the kittiwake has shown experience at work in mate choice. Kittiwakes usually keep the same mate from year to year and are more successful if they do so. A male and female who have bred together before settle down more quickly than new pairs to the essential shared rhythm of incubating the eggs. Most of the incubation is by the female but the male relieves her at the nest each day so that she can go to feed. If he does not do so, or does so irregularly, the pair are less successful. After such an unsuccessful season, divorce is common and the female takes a new mate in the next spring. Similarly Lorenz (1979) has found that divorce, which is virtually unknown in his greylag goose colony, does occur if a young pair have failed to breed successfully.

It is most likely that experience plays some role in the choice of mates in primates. The social organization does not allow for maximum flexibility and the dominant male of the moment in polygynous groups remains the choice of the great majority of females. However, as mentioned previously, chimpanzees show marked individual preferences which may be based on experience. As yet our evidence is largely anecdotal but none the less important. Females, as well as males, appear to vary in attractiveness. Goodall (1971) noted that one female — the famous Flo — was particularly avidly courted by males each time that she came into oestrus. We do not know whether any such preferences are related to biological fitness, but it seems unlikely because of the difficulty of animals being able to measure the quality of their mates unless obvious cooperation is involved, as in the kittiwakes. Le Boeuf (1967) found that individual preferences shown by bitches for particular dogs, developed before they had bred for the first time.

The remarkable phenomenon of sexual imprinting is an example of experience affecting sexual choice in a most dramatic way, although the

criteria for choice are totally unrelated to fitness as we have been considering it. The behavioural development of many birds and mammals, where attention has been primarily concentrated, incorporates a period during which they learn the characteristics of the parent or parents. They subsequently direct their sexual behaviour towards the parental type. The classical observations and experiments by Lorenz and his group on geese and ducks are now famous. We must distinguish between "filial imprinting", where young birds come to follow the first moving object they see after hatching, and sexual imprinting itself. The latter usually occurs rather later in development and develops over a longer period.

In some cases there appears to be virtually no limit to the objects which can serve for sexual imprinting. Mallards have been imprinted on cockerels, domestic chickens on cardboard boxes and giant pandas on human beings. Sexual imprinting has commonly been said to be irreversible and in extreme cases may be so, but the strength of such attraction and its modifiability can be affected by changing the length of and age at exposure to the parent figure. Sluckin's (1972) book discusses imprinting in relation to early learning, whilst Immelmann (1975) and Bateson (1979) direct attention to the adaptive nature of the process. Bateson suggests that learning in detailed characteristics of the parents and of brood or litter mates (for they also influence the process) is a means whereby an animal can acquire the correct species identification but also avoid too great a level of inbreeding. All animals vary sufficiently in plumage pattern, coat colour, smell, etc. to allow for detailed discrimination. Bateson (1978) found, for example, that a Japanese quail prefers to mate with birds which are similar but not identical to the birds with which it was raised. There is an "optimal discrepancy" which should mean that incestuous pairing can be avoided. Gilder and Slater (1978) found that female mice spend more time exploring the smell of male mice of the same strain as themselves — but not their brothers — than they do exploring the scent of their brothers or males from another strain. We should note that the majority of studies have concentrated on imprinting in males because it is easier to score choice in the actively courting sex, but there can be no doubt that females imprint also and selectively approach males according to their early experience as in the case just described.

Sexual imprinting can be seen as a way of optimally matching an animal's sexual choice but it is not an option available to all species. It can operate only if there is some parental care or at least close contact

between siblings. It is impossible for brood parasites such as the European cuckoo, which specifically must *not* imprint on its foster parents as a sexual model, though young cuckoos may well learn such characteristics for future reference as a host for their eggs.

Human Comparisons

It would be evasive not to attempt some comparisons between our own and other species. Yet for all the reasons mentioned at the very outset of this review comparisons are difficult. There is, in phylogenetic terms, an artificially large gap between ourselves and our nearest living relatives. In geological time intermediates existed until very recently, and *Homo sapiens* is a relatively young species. Nevertheless, the absolute pervasiveness of cultural evolution has blurred so many of the effects which natural selection may have had upon our behaviour.

Short (1979) suggests that the degree of physical sexual dimorphism in our species suggests a moderate degree of polygyny in our recent ancestors. Certainly polygyny is not uncommon in human cultures although its present day occurrence is more determined by social than biological factors. The search for a biological basis for human behaviour continues to exert its fascination. Perhaps it appeals to a deeply ingrained fatalism for, in the absence of any hard evidence, it is often assumed that genetically controlled traits are more difficult to change than cultural ones. The recent "sociobiology" movement is the latest manifestation of this theme. Much the most thorough and balanced modern account of this whole controversial area is that of Ruse (1979). Some of the extreme sociobiological disciples have little hesitation in explaining even the finer points of human sexual behaviour as a direct result of natural selection (e.g. Wilson, 1979). The drawback to this approach is that the extravagant diversity of human social mores means that with sufficient selectivity, one is always able to cite a sexual custom upon which to base a biological theory. It is only amongst the real universals of human cultures that we can hope to detect the imprint of natural selection and these are not likely to involve detail but only generalities.

Thus we may consider the possibility that there is an "optimal discrepancy" in the choice of a human mate, as we have just been discussing for animals. There is a good deal of evidence that, where free choice is allowed by the culture, men and women tend to choose mates who resemble themselves both physically and intellectually, but on the other hand, incest avoidance is almost universal. We can only speculate

about such inherited tendencies as may be manifested here but the evidence from cultures in which children are reared together outside normal family units must be relevant. Shepher (1971) and others have pointed out that the genetically unrelated groups of children in the old style Israeli *kibbutzim* never intermarry within the group. This strongly suggests that the experience of being reared together as young children precludes full sexual bonding. Bateson (1979) discusses further evidence from Taiwanese culture where in arranged marriages, the future bride was adopted into the groom's family as a child and subsequent sexual bonding was inadequate. Whether all sexual attraction is absent is another matter — certainly it is not always absent within normal families — but it remains a possibility that the processes of human sexual development and choice run parallel to that of animals which show sexual imprinting.

The other aspect of sexual attraction where parallels could be drawn concerns the choice of a mate in relation to fitness. Clearly what constitutes fitness has evolved culturally far beyond the biological considerations, yet it would be foolish to suggest that human beings ignore such factors, and standards of physical beauty have often reflected strength and fertility. Social status and the control over resources represented by wealth have often replaced them as attractions for marriage, but marriage is sometimes unrelated to sexual attraction itself which probably remains more firmly linked to physical appearance, although not dominated by it.

It is easy enough to construct all kinds of analogies between the preliminaries to human marriage and the strategies of mate choice in animals. After all, most women still have to choose a mate with care and an eye to the resources he can provide, and in this way the outcome they seek does resemble that sought by many female birds. So long as we recognize the relative superficiality of the analogy, no harm is done. This conclusion is less than startling but it is the safest one. All animal species have much that is unique about them and if animals can teach us anything, it is that similar ends can be achieved by very different means.

9. References

Austin, C. R. and Short, R. V. (Eds). *Reproduction in mammals.* Vols 3 and 4. Cambridge: Cambridge University Press, 1972.

Bateson, P. Sexual imprinting and optimal outbreeding. *Nature*, 1978, **273**, 659-660.
Bateson, P. How do sensitive periods arise and what are they for? *Animal Behaviour*, 1979, **27**, 470-486.
Brown, J. L. *The evolution of behavior*. New York: Norton, 1975.
Clutton-Brock, T. H. and Harvey, P. H. Evolutionary rules and primate societies. In Bateson, P. and Hinde, R. A. (Eds), *Growing points in ethology*. Cambridge: Cambridge University Press, 1976.
Conway, C. H. and Sade, D. S. The seasonal spermatogenic cycle in free ranging rhesus monkeys. *Folia Primatologica*, 1965, **3**, 1-12.
Coulson, J. C. The significance of the pair bond in the kittiwake. *Proceedings of the Fifteenth Ornithological Conference*. Leiden: Brill, 1972.
Davis, N. B. and Halliday, T. R. Optimal mate selection in the toad *Bufo bufo*. *Nature*, 1977, **269**, 56-68.
Emlen, S. T. and Oring, L. W. Ecology, sexual selection and the evolution of mating systems. *Science*, 1977, **197**, 215-224.
Gilder, P. M. and Slater, P. J. B. Interest of mice in conspecific male odours is influenced by degree of kinship. *Nature*, 1978, **274**, 364-365.
Goodall, J. *In the shadow of man*. London: Collins, 1971.
Halliday, T. R. Sexual selection and mate choice. In Krebs, J. R. and Davis, N. B. (Eds), *Behavioural ecology: an evolutionary approach*. Oxford: Blackwell, 1978.
Immelmann, K. The evolutionary significance of imprinting. In Baerends, G. P., Beer, C. and Manning, A. (Eds), *Function and evolution in behaviour: essays in honour of Professor Niko Tinbergen FRS*. Oxford: Clarendon Press, 1975.
Jolly, A. *The evolution of primate behavior*. New York: Macmillan, 1972.
Kleiman, D. G. Monogamy in animals. *Quarterly Review of Biology*, 1977, **52**, 39-69.
LeBoeuf, B. J. Interindividual associations in dogs. *Behaviour*, 1967, **29**, 268-295.
LeBoeuf, B. J. and Peterson, R. S. Social status and mating activity in elephant seals. *Science*, 1969, **163**, 91-93.
Lehrman, D. S. The reproductive behaviour of ring doves. *Scientific American*, 1964, **211**, 48-54.
Leuthold, W. Variations in territorial behaviour of Uganda kob *Adenota kob thomasi* (Neumann 1896). *Behaviour*, 1966, **27**, 215-258.
Lincoln, G. A., Youngson, R. W. and Short, R. V. The social and sexual behaviour of the red deer stag. *Journal of Reproduction and Fertility Supplement*, 1970, **11**, 71-103.
Lorenz, K. *The year of the greylag goose*. London: Methuen, 1979.
Michael, R. P. and Keverne, E. B. Pheromones in the communication of sexual status in primates. *Nature*, 1968, **218**, 746-749.

Rowan, W. Relation of light to bird migration and developmental changes. *Nature*, 1925, **115**, 494-495.

Ruse, M. *Sociobiology: sense or nonsense.* London: Reidel, 1979.

Shepher, J. Mate selection among second generation kibbutz adolescents and adults: incest avoidance and negative imprinting. *Archives of Sexual Behavior*, 1971, **1**, 293-307.

Short, R. V. Sexual selection and its component parts, somatic and genital selection, as illustrated by man and the great apes. *Advances in the Study of Behavior*, 1979, **9**, 131-158.

Sluckin, W. *Imprinting and early learning.* (2nd edn). London: Methuen, 1972.

Tutin, C. E. G. Exceptions to promiscuity in a feral chimpanzee community. In Kondo, S., Kawai, M. and Ehara, A. (Eds), *Contemporary primatology (Proceedings of the fifth international congress on primatology).* Basel: Karger, 1975.

Wilson, G. D. The sociobiology of sex differences. *Bulletin of the British Psychological Society*, 1979, **32**, 350-353.

Zahavi, A. Mate selection — a selection for a handicap. *Journal of Theoretical Biology*, 1975, **53**, 205-214.

Zuckerman, S. *The social life of monkeys and apes.* London: Paul, Trench and Trubner, 1932.

Subject Index

Marital intercourse, 33, 43
Marshall Islands, 164
Masochism, 69, 78
Masturbation, 24, 26-28, 33-35, 37, 39, 40, 43, 45, 51-53
Mate choice, 194, 195, 279-288
Mbundu, 165
Medieval criteria, 15
Mehinacu, 240, 242, 245
Memory, 94, 115, 127
Methodology, 25, 70, 118, 121, 148, 158, 167, 190, 191-193, 220-223, 251, 261, 264
Mexico, 240
Mice, 287
Micromomentary facial expressions, 162
Minor marriages, 226, 289
Misattribution, 131-132
"Mixers", 198
MMPI, 206
Mobility, 237
Monogamy, 279-282, 286
Mother-in-law, 231
Moths, 277
Muria, 226

NATIONAL DIFFERENCES, 152, 153
Natural selection, 254, 288
Need for predictability, 99, 100
Neurosis, 70, 204, 259
Neuroticism, 68, 72, 74, 85, 86, 153, 209
New Guinea, 165, 219, 235, 240, 241, 244, 264-265
New Zealand, 165
Nigeria, 222, 242, 243
Nocturnal emission, 29, 35
Non-verbal behaviour, 150, 156, 157, 160, 165, 169
Non-verbal leakage, 157, 162
Norway, 152
Nyakyusa, 241

OAKLAND GROWTH STUDY, 17

Occupation, 19, 27, 31, 71
Open field, 198
Opportunity, 231, 232, 234
Optimal discrepancy, 287, 288
Oral sex, 29, 30, 45, 86, 152
Orgasm, 37, 40, 41, 43, 69, 77, 87
Orgasmic responses, 26
Orgies, 239
Owls, 281

PACIFIC ISLANDS, 242, 243
Pair formation, 279
Palm presentation, 162
Palolo worms, 277
Parents, 81
Path analysis, 118
Peacock, 284, 285
Pedophilia, 66, 74
Permissiveness, 27, 35, 39, 43, 44, 53, 83, 87, 151
Person perception, 93-138, 146, 149, 203, 207, 259
Personality, 6, 10, 68, 73, 79, 86, 105, 122, 124, 145, 150-153, 158, 181, 199
Petting, 29, 33, 34, 36, 41, 43
Pheasants, 282, 285
Pheromones, 162, 277, 278
Physical attractiveness, 3-20, 25, 74, 96, 96, 116, 122, 124, 127, 127, 138, 150, 151, 153, 169, 196, 197, 199, 200, 223, 232, 233, 241, 289
Physiological aspects, 25, 51, 251, 276
Piaget, 95
"Playing hard to get", 25, 163
Plumage, 284, 285
Polygyny, 241, 280-283, 286, 288
Popularity, 3, 11
Polarization, 103-105, 107, 112, 117, 119
Polyandry, 266
Polynesia, 243
Pornography, 25, 46, 78, 84
Posture, 161
Pre-commitment phase, 184

27159529R00060

Printed in Poland
by Amazon Fulfillment
Poland Sp. z o.o., Wrocław